This book is a bold attempt to start mapping out how to transform the destructive potential of social conflict into something more constructive, both imaginatively and practically. I would encourage anyone seeking creative solutions to intractable conflicts to read this path-breaking work by Dr. Arai.
(Kevin P. Clements, Director of the National Center for Peace and Conflict Studies at the University of Otago, New Zealand)

Tatsushi Arai conceptualizes the creative process of conflict resolution that is required when conventional, institutionalized mechanisms for handling conflict fail. He persuasively demonstrates how conflict parties and intermediaries can generate creative – nonconventional, yet workable – solutions with a comparative analysis of diverse cases of conflict resolution.
(Herbert Kelman, Richard Clarke Cabot Professor of Social Ethics, Emeritus, Harvard University)

The power of creativity is a mystery. This book helps the reader to systematically unlock this mystery and assist scholars and practitioners of peace and conflict resolution in envisioning how to become more creative in resolving conflicts.
(Mohammed Abu-Nimer, Professor of International Peace and Conflict Resolution, American University)

Creativity and Conflict Resolution

This book explores how creative ways of resolving social conflicts emerge, evolve, and subsequently come to be accepted or rejected in inter-group relations.

Creativity and Conflict Resolution explores a subject with which political communities involved in social conflict have always grappled: creative ways of imagining and actualizing visions of conflict resolution. This is an ambitious question, which concerns human communities at many different levels, from families, regional-independence movements, and national governments, to interstate alliances. The author argues that unconventional viability lies at the heart of creativity for transcending seemingly intractable inter-communal conflicts. More specifically, conflict resolution creativity is a social and epistemological process, whereby actors involved in a given social conflict learn to formulate an unconventional resolution option or procedure.

Demystifying the origin of unthinkable breakthroughs for conflict resolution and illuminating theories of creativity based on seventeen international case studies, this book will be of much interest to students of conflict resolution, peace and conflict studies, human security, public policy, and IR.

Tatsushi Arai is an Assistant Professor of Conflict Transformation at the SIT Graduate Institute in Vermont, USA. He has a PhD in Conflict Resolution from George Mason University in Virginia, and extensive international experience as a trainer, mediator, and dialogue facilitator.

Routledge studies in peace and conflict resolution
Series editors: Tom Woodhouse and Oliver Ramsbotham
University of Bradford

Peace and Security in the Postmodern World
The OSCE and conflict resolution
Dennis J.D. Sandole

Truth Recovery and Justice after Conflict
Managing violent pasts
Marie Breen Smyth

Peace in International Relations
Oliver P. Richmond

Social Capital and Peace-building
Creating and resolving conflict with trust and social networks
Edited by Michaelene Cox

Business, Conflict Resolution and Peacebuilding
Contributions from the private sector to address violent conflict
Derek Sweetman

Creativity and Conflict Resolution
Alternative pathways to peace
Tatsushi Arai

Creativity and Conflict Resolution

Alternative pathways to peace

Tatsushi Arai

LONDON AND NEW YORK

First published 2009
by Routledge
2 Park Square, Milton Park, Abingdon, Oxon OX14 4RN

Simultaneously published in the USA and Canada
by Routledge
270 Madison Ave, New York, NY 10016

Routledge is an imprint of the Taylor & Francis Group, an informa business

© 2009 Tatsushi Arai

Typeset in Times New Roman by Wearset Ltd, Boldon, Tyne and Wear

All rights reserved. No part of this book may be reprinted or reproduced or utilized in any form or by any electronic, mechanical, or other means, now known or hereafter invented, including photocopying and recording, or in any information storage or retrieval system, without permission in writing from the publishers.

British Library Cataloguing in Publication Data
A catalogue record for this book is available from the British Library

Library of Congress Cataloging in Publication Data
A catalog record for this book has been requested

ISBN10: 0-415-47276-8 (hbk)
ISBN10: 0-203-87318-1 (ebk)

ISBN13: 978-0-415-47276-0 (hbk)
ISBN13: 978-0-203-87318-2 (ebk)

To my dear son Justice and to the future world that his generation will inherit from his father's

Contents

	List of illustrations	viii
	Foreword	ix
	Preface: a word to the reader	xi
	Acknowledgments	xiv
	List of episodes of creativity	xvi
1	Introduction: in search of points of departure and stepping stones	1
2	Exploration: sixteen episodes of creativity	18
3	Theory-building: a comparative case analysis for identifying emerging themes and building on enduring concepts	96
4	Illustration: a case study of the first satyagraha campaign in South Africa from 1906 to 1914	138
5	Conclusion: implications for research, practice, and pedagogy	198
	Appendix: questionnaire for researcher-practitioner interviews	212
	Notes	216
	Bibliography	230
	Index	236

Illustrations

Figures

1.1	The working definition of creativity for conflict resolution	2
1.2	The five-phase model of conflict resolution creativity	10
2.1	Peace diagram for transcendence	78
3.1	The longitudinal nature of creativity: a revised working model	105
3.2	A Type B phenomenon contributing to an alternative pathway	110
3.3	A Type C phenomenon contributing to an alternative pathway	110
3.4	Four levels of analysis and three types of system–element link	116
4.1	Map of South Africa before 1914	143
4.2	Application form for registration of an Asiatic adult	157

Tables

2.1	Summary of the five episodes of conflict parties' creativity	25
2.2	Summary of the nine episodes of intermediaries' creativity	44–45
2.3	Summary of the two episodes of creativity demonstrated by actors playing a dual function	88
3.1	Comparison between a Kuhnian paradigm and a conflict paradigm	126
3.2	Conflict paradigms, alternative realities, and heuristic pointers: five selected cases	129
4.1	Means and ends in Gandhian religiosity	168

Foreword

Tatsushi Arai's book, *Creativity and Conflict Resolution*, is itself a piece of creativity, with its seventeen compelling cases of conflict resolution, and eleven theories of creativity. Maybe not all of the seventeen cases are equally compelling, but something creative introduced some kind of discontinuity, there was a new element, at least new to those concerned. However, the proof of the pudding is said to be in the eating, let us say in the consumption, and the proof of conflict resolution is in its sustainability. Some of them do not quite pass that test. But the creative element may nevertheless be valuable, and worth knowing for anyone involved in conflict.

And that makes Arai's book a goldmine of creative thinking about creativity. Being a firm believer in that C-word as a major missing element in so many processes, far above that other C-word for good chemistry between parties – with a recent book of mine addressing exactly that (*50 Years: 100 Peace & Conflict Perspectives*, Transcend University Press, 2008, www.transcend.org/tup), some reflections on the obstacles to creativity might perhaps be in order. I do not say limits, the sky is the limit. If something creative – in inside or outside parties, in process or outcome – does not work, I would dogmatically stand for meta-creativity, for more searching for a compelling image of a new reality to which the parties nod and say, "Yes, I could live in that one." Nonviolence and empathy are conditions. But conflict is incompatibility, and resolution spells compatibility, so the road from one to the other must transcend the already existing. Creativity, hence, is not a sufficient condition but usually a necessary one.

What, then, stands in the way? In one sentence: actors deeply engaged not in solving but in winning, victory, the V-word. To conflict parties committed to the goal of winning, Other is the problem, not the relation to Other. Bring Other to heal, and the world is right. Other is Evil, up against our good Self, there can be no compromise, no creative "transcendence," only victory for the Good over the Evil. Moreover, Other should not only be deterred from exercising his evil craft, but be crushed never to rise again. This discourse has a firm grip on many minds.

Is there any creative approach to that one? Maybe. I try alternative history of the future. "OK, imagine you crush Other, there is capitulation. Then, in your view, what will happen?"

We are in a guessing game. The answer, "Other will give in and correct his wrongs" can be met with the question, "Would you have done that in his situation?" The answer is by no means given in advance, but the process is important. The lawyer is about to win a divorce case; is it obvious that winning is the answer? Is "I was right, s/he was not" really the highest good in the world? Could repairing the relationship be better?

Not always. Autocracy, slavery, colonialism, and imperialism are not on the sick row for repair. They are rather on the death row for the abolition of the underlying social relations that sustain them, but not of the dictators, slave-owners, colonialists, and imperialists. These forms of structural violence represent social relations that should not be creatively saved. They have lived their unfortunate lives and some euthanasia may be beneficial. And the magic of creativity lies in a compelling image of the alternative, so compelling to all involved, so respectful of their legitimate aspirations, that it becomes a *causa finalis*, a force of pull, not of push.

Read Arai and learn more about creativity than you thought there was to learn. And be wiser in the process.

Johan Galtung
Founder of TRANSCEND: A Peace and Development Network
Manassas, Virginia
October 2008

Preface
A word to the reader

Dear reader,

Welcome to the journey of creativity! I am truly grateful that this book, a product of my long-term commitment and intensive inquiry, has found its way into your hands, as an invitation to imaginative thinking, critical reflections, and interactive dialogue with me, the author. Writing this preface gives me a unique opportunity to share with you at least a small part of the personal journey that has culminated in this book. I sincerely hope that my personal reflections will contextualize the unique focus of my inquiry and enrich your experience of reading this book.

As a practitioner, educator, and researcher in the field of conflict resolution and peace-building, I have worked over the years with a wide range of people grappling with social conflicts in different parts of the world – from refugees returning to post-genocide Rwanda, to Palestinian teenagers suffering from bullying at school in their countries of refuge, to Iraqi government and civil society leaders driven out of their motherland after receiving death threats, to Japanese truck drivers arguing with their station managers. Throughout these and other encounters, I have always come across people searching for creative solutions to seemingly intractable conflicts that they had been tackling. And indeed I myself, having been introduced to them as an "expert" in conflict resolution, have also emphasized the importance of creativity to them. However, every time the need for creativity was mentioned in these dialogues, workshops, and training sessions, an inner voice was calling from within me and confronting me with unsettling questions: "So what does it mean to be creative in this particular context of tension and frustration? And, by the way, do *I* really know how to become creative in problem-solving and at the same time politically relevant to the actual stakeholders on the ground?" My responses to these questions have been highly tentative and intuitive until I decided to look into the question of creativity more seriously and systematically.

Although it is commonplace to argue that creativity is essential for conflict resolution, there has been little systematic knowledge generated and articulated about what we really mean by creativity in resolving social conflict. A partial and superficial understanding of creativity tends to mystify what it takes to activate the creative potential inherent in individuals and communities, resulting in remarks like "I am not creative enough to solve such a difficult problem!" Remarks like these have been overheard frequently in classrooms, in corridor conversations after heated staff meetings, and during coffee breaks in conflict resolution workshops and donor conferences. In many ways, these voices have resonated with my inner voice, seeking an answer.

This book has taken these challenges seriously and attempts to demystify the structure, processes, and dynamics of creativity. It has emerged from my desire to articulate learnable and teachable elements of creativity and make them accessible to conflict parties, policymakers, civil society leaders, students, and indeed anybody else seeking ways to activate and rediscover the creative potential inherent in human relations.

At the heart of my inquiry into creativity is a search for common threads and patterns across a wide range of "breakthrough solutions" to inter-communal conflicts. These threads and patterns may not achieve the status of a social scientific law, or invariance, in the strictest sense of scientific causality. I would like to make this reservation explicit because I am aware that conditions under which social conflicts and their solutions emerge are so fundamentally diverse and unique from context to context that any attempt to find generalizable principles across contexts and levels of analysis – from family to nation – appears unpromising. As this book will demonstrate, however, there *are* nevertheless some evocative patterns across diverse contexts of creative social change that leading scholar-practitioners working with social conflict have found rather consistently. In the pages that follow, I have articulated some of the most intriguing patterns of constructive social change that deserve the serious attention of policymakers, practitioners, researchers, and students in search of solutions "out of the box."

These evocative patterns, it seems, converge on two central themes, which may be formulated in two complementary questions. First, how do conflict parties and intermediaries come to discover fresh principles of conflict analysis and communicate among themselves and their constituents what is at the heart of their conflict from such fresh perspectives? Second, how can they gradually de-entrench their entrenched perspectives on the conflict at hand and progressively work toward reorganizing their patterns of conflict-prone behavior and relationships into a more constructive form of functional coexistence, with the best chance of acceptability and sustainability? In short, this study is a search for patterns of thinking and social action that seek to break patterns of conflict-prone relationships, with the view toward reshaping them into more promising, constructive patterns.

As the author who has thought through the structure and flow of the entire argument with utmost care, I earnestly wish the reader could sit with the book in a quiet place for an uninterrupted period of time and pay undivided attention and read it from cover to cover. Yet, as a reader myself whose reading time is always interrupted by multiple tasks competing for urgent attention, I am well aware that such a wish may not be so easily fulfilled. In fact, the more successful I am to draw attention from the kind of readers willing and able to make serious, tangible impact on social conflict as policymakers, practitioners, scholars, and students, the more likely it is that reading this book is in competition with other time-sensitive tasks at hand.

Anticipating this possibility as inevitable, I have concluded each chapter with a detailed analytical summary, often in simple bullet-point format, especially in Chapters 2 to 4. In addition, Chapter 5, the concluding section, contains a detailed summary of the entire book. It is hoped that this arrangement will give the reader an option to go through particular sections of interest first and still get a sense of what the larger picture of my argument is, with the help of the section summaries. These arrangements are also intended to enable the reader to come in and out of the thought process of grasping my argument without losing a sense of continuity of various ideas interwoven throughout the book.

Finally, a word of caution is in order. This book was written primarily for the audience already familiar with some basic concepts of peace and conflict studies, either through prior academic training or through practical experience in handling conflicts. As such, it might pose a unique challenge to those who have just started exploring the subject. Having said this, I would also like to note that I have given careful consideration to the way I communicate my thoughts throughout the book, in order to make it as accessible as possible to the widest range of readers.

I would like to cordially invite you, the reader, on this unique journey of inquiry, which I firmly believe is breaking new ground in the scholarship and practice of conflict resolution and peace-building.

Sincerely,
Tatsushi Arai

Acknowledgments

Knowledge emerges like a new wave in the ocean. When it takes shape, it amasses parts of adjacent waves surrounding it. One can hardly discern which parts of the ocean's water have formed the particular wave, for each wave is a microcosm of the ocean itself. This study, like a wave, has emerged as a confluence of numerous inspirations derived from the ocean of human relationships, in which I have been immersed during the past several years of inquiry, and possibly since long before. In view of the entire ocean, my attempt to acknowledge particular individuals is helplessly limited to those whose contributions will be found most conspicuous on the pages that follow. Yet my heartfelt appreciation is extended to the entire ocean of relationships from which this study has emerged.

I am particularly indebted to the researcher-practitioners of diverse backgrounds who dedicated their precious time to answering my interview questions and generously granted permission to reproduce their real-world experiences in this book. Those whose interviews appear in the text include (with the organizational affiliations they held at the time of the interviews in 2003–5): Professor Linda Johnston at George Mason University (GMU); Dr. Hazel Henderson; Dr. Mubarak Awad at Nonviolence International and the National Youth Advocate; Professor Richard Falk at Princeton University; Dr. Ron Pundak at the Peres Center for Peace; Professor Majid Terhanian at the University of Hawaii at Manoa and the Toda Institute for Global Peace and Policy Research; Dr. John Burton; Somali Ambassador Abdullahi Said Osman; Professor Herbert Kelman at Harvard University; Professor Vamik Volkan at the University of Virginia; Finnish Ambassador Klaus Törnudd; Professor Johan Galtung at Transcend; Professor Emerita Elise Boulding at Dartmouth College; Dr. Louise Diamond at The Peace Company; and Dr. Harold Saunders at Kettering Foundation and the International Institute for Sustained Dialogue.

The interviewees whose insights do not appear explicitly in the text but who have contributed substantially to conceptualizing various aspects of the study include, but are not limited to: Professor Roger Fisher at Harvard University; Ambassador John McDonald at the Institute for Multi-Track Diplomacy; Professor Michelle LeBaron at the University of British Columbia; Professor Mohammed Abu-Nimer at the American University; Dr. Mary Clark; Professor

Manulani Aluli Meyer at the University of Hawaii at Hilo; Dr. Sheila Ramsey at Crestone Institute; and Professor Wallace Warfield at GMU. In addition, I have benefited significantly from my interviews with GMU-based internationally renowned artists, including Professor Y. David Chung (visual art); Professor Paul D'Andrea (theater); and Professor Susan Shields (dance and choreography).

I would also like to express my heartfelt appreciation to GMU Professors Kevin Avruch, Christopher Mitchell, Evans Mandes, and Richard Rubenstein, who guided and inspired me at all stages of my doctoral dissertation research, which became the basis of this book. Their contributions are illustrative of the time and efforts dedicated generously by many other faculty members and colleagues at GMU's Institute for Conflict Analysis and Resolution (ICAR). I am also indebted to the intellectual inspirations and warm collegial support I have received since 2006 at the SIT Graduate Institute, especially from Professors John Ungerleider and Paula Green in the conflict transformation program. Many thanks to all.

Finally, I am deeply grateful for my wife Yuchun, who has dedicated her entire being to supporting me day and night throughout the prolonged project period. She literally took her behind-the-scenes effort as her own peace work, and through it, constantly reminded me of the significance of my work. No less important than her contribution is the example of peace work set by my mentor in life, Dr. Daisaku Ikeda, a Japanese pioneer in the global dialogue of civilizations, who has been a constant source of encouragement not only for this project, but also for my vision to practice lessons learned from this inquiry in the turbulence of social conflict, with sustained commitment, courage, and hope.

Episodes of creativity

Names in the parentheses refer to the scholar-practitioners who served as primary informants for the respective case studies.

Conflict parties' creativity   24

"Accidental teenage pregnancies": the need for giving up (Linda Johnston)   26
Environmentalists for Full Employment: connecting dots in a new way (Hazel Henderson)   28
Palestinian nonviolence: sharp resistance through empowerment (Mubarak Awad)   30
The US–Vietnam War: adjusting power asymmetry through deep listening (Richard Falk)   32
The Oslo peace process: stretching the envelope to its utmost (Ron Pundak)   34

Intermediaries' creativity   43

A racial conflict in Tajikistan: appealing to the parties' inner resources (Majid Tehranian)   43
An American Labor dispute: throwing the mediator rulebook out of the window (John Smith – Pseudonym)   47
The civil war in Sierra Leone: joint appeals through local communication channels (Abdullahi Said Osman)   53
The Indonesia–Malaysia–Singapore conflict: philosophical creativity (John Burton)   54
An Israeli–Palestinian problem-solving workshop: expecting unexpected discoveries (Herbert Kelman)   58
Estonian–Russian psychoanalytic dialogue: activating symbols constructively (Vamik Volkan)   62
The Cyprus conflict: sustained commitment to bicommunal peace (Louise Diamond)   66

The Helsinki process: tapping the potential of a small neutral state
  (Klaus Törnudd) 71
The Peru–Ecuador border dispute: transcendence with a quantum
  jump (Johan Galtung) 76

Creativity demonstrated by actors playing a dual function 88

Children–parents dialogue: transferring the Quaker method from a
  community to a family (Elise Boulding) 88
Kissinger's shuttle diplomacy in the Arab–Israeli conflict: principled
  flexibility for a "peace process" (Harold Saunders) 92

1 Introduction

In search of points of departure and stepping stones

The research question and the purpose of the inquiry

This study explores creativity for conflict resolution. It aims to generate useful hypotheses and models of practice and policymaking informed by empirical findings. The key question is: how do creative approaches to conflict resolution first appear, evolve over time, and subsequently come to be accepted or rejected in a given social and epistemological context of inter-group conflict? In this inquiry, creativity is defined as *unconventional viability*. More specifically, it refers to a social and epistemological process where an actor or actors involved in the conflict learn to formulate an unconventional resolution option and/or procedure for resolution, and a growing number of others come to perceive it as a viable way of coping with the underlying problems from their collective and subjective point of view.

The two interrelated elements of conflict resolution creativity, unconventionality and viability, are both multifaceted concepts. They have emerged through trial and error from years of exploratory inquiry that has culminated into this book.[1] On one level, unconventionality entails altering or even breaking through a conventional reality of conflict. Much of the inquiry conducted in social science in general and conflict analysis in particular is designed to account for the nature of given conventional realities. Explaining and understanding conventional realities requires data, analysis (causal, correlational, or otherwise), evaluation, description, and diagnosis. It focuses on the past, or otherwise on plausible links between the past and the present. It is a realm of empirical reality, or *what is*. In contrast, envisioning unconventionality in a given social and epistemological context requires entering into the realm of potential realities, or *what can be*. It is often inseparable from normative visions, or *what ought to be*. Exploration of potential realities activates such belief systems as worldview, value, culture, cosmology, ideology, and religiosity. It directs one's attention to such modes of thinking and action as prognosis, prediction, therapy, resolution, and "practice" in general. In short, unconventionality in conflict work is derived from conscious efforts to shape the future, or more precisely the present–future link, beyond conventional realities of conflict.

On another level, unconventionality entails reshaping what is considered a conventional reality in a given local context of collective subjectivity. In this

2 Introduction

respect, unconventionality has the spatial and relational dimensions, in addition to the temporal dimension discussed already. Because a conflict remains intact as long as parties with different aspirations are unable to interrupt their confrontational patterns of interaction, breaking the patterns, which come to form what the parties might consider a conventional reality, inevitably invites resistance. Therefore, taking unconventional action for conflict resolution requires mobilizing the cognitive and emotive resources of the parties and other attentive stakeholders in such a way as to break the conventional patterns that have sustained their conflict.

To be *useful* for conflict resolution, unconventional visions and actions must be viable. The essential core of viability is the practical effectiveness for resolving conflicts at hand. This quality inherent in creativity for conflict resolution distinguishes itself from utopian thinking of impractical types. The requirement of effectiveness also implies that viable action must be informed by empirical conflict analysis that illuminates underlying roots of the problematic reality in question. Part and parcel of effectiveness is ethicality, the concept rephrased variously by such terms as morality, legitimacy, and justice. Although the multifaceted nature of ethicality in conflict resolution may not be fully explored within the scope of this inquiry, it is suggested, at least in theoretical terms, that any attempt to advance direct and structural violence consciously and conspicuously,[2] however unconventional it may seem, fails to meet the mandatory standard of ethicality. Therefore, for example, the arguably unconventional behavior of the kamikaze hijackers on September 11, 2001 in the US is outside the scope of this inquiry. In short, viability is a confluence of effectiveness and ethicality, or according to Lederach (1999), "justpeace." Integrating the twin components of unconventionality and viability, the working definition of creativity for conflict resolution may be presented in a simplified form as in Figure 1.1.

The scope of the inquiry

To clarify the scope and nature of the inquiry further, five points deserve mention. First, the study aims to generate hypotheses and models of creativity that are practically useful and empirically supported. It is not, however, intended

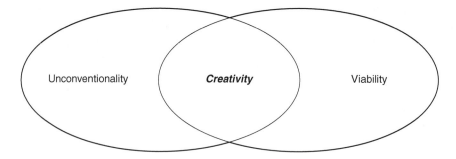

Figure 1.1 The working definition of creativity for conflict resolution.

to formulate a general theory of creativity suited to causal explanation. Nor is it assumed that the infinitely complex phenomena of individual and collective creativity can be reduced to a formula. What is both useful and achievable is a systematic exploration of roadmaps to creative social changes that have taken place in specific local, empirical contexts, carrying heuristic values suggestive for other temporal, spatial, and relational contexts. In short, designing working frameworks for generating locally specific roadmaps to creative solutions is the goal of this inquiry.

Second, creativity will be explored in the context of conflict resolution, but not in such other contexts as science and art. For the purpose of this inquiry, conflict is defined as a difference or a set of differences that affect the identities and meaning-making processes of two or more actors, individual or collective, involved in interdependent relationships, desirable or not. Thus conflict may be constructive or destructive, or both at the same time. Conflict resolution is a social process through which root causes and contexts of a given conflict are systematically assessed and effective nonviolent means explored to eradicate destructive effects of the underlying problems. Therefore, the act of creation intended to resolve conflict is a unique social phenomenon, one that is highly subjective, controversial, and contextualized in human relationships and meaning-making patterns. It is in this specialized domain of human activities that creativity is explored.[3]

In addition, the term "conflict resolution" is used in its broadest sense in this study, encompassing a range of practice types used to cope with conflict. These types include, but are not limited to, conflict prevention, mitigation, institutionalization, reconstruction, and reconciliation. The broad conceptualization is necessary because the study of creativity for conflict resolution is still at a very early stage. Excluding potentially relevant phenomena related to conflict resolution from the scope of empirical inquiry would not be promising for this exploratory project.

Mention must be made on how this highly specialized type of creativity compares to artistic and scientific creativity, two of the popular domains of contemporary creativity research spearheaded by Western-trained psychologists and interested others. From a bird's eye view of human activities, it is observed that artistic creativity primarily concerns product development, whether in tangible or intangible form, while scientific creativity aims at theory development, often stimulated by practical application. Impressionistically, one might suggest that conflict resolution creativity requires both theory and product development, for envisioning potential realities is theoretical in nature yet translating the abstract visions into concrete action and social change entails elements of product development.

Another angle of comparison is how creative change is evaluated as such in a given social and epistemological context. As suggested in Thomas Kuhn's (1996) study on scientific communities, scientific creativity tends to be accepted or rejected by appeal to standards set by exemplars of "successful" breakthroughs and by influential community leaders within a given discipline of inquiry. On the contrary, standards for evaluating artistic creativity are significantly more elusive and less disciplined, reflecting the less structured nature of epistemic communities that accept or reject artistic innovations. As will be elaborated later, the discussion on evaluative standards and epistemic communities is hardly applicable to conflict resolution creativity in a given local context of practice, except in a highly metaphoric and analogical sense.[4] This is because the nature of creativity under study is context-specific, and creativity is perceived as such by particular conflict parties and stakeholders involved in a given temporal, spatial, and relational context of conflict. Therefore, the study will *not* focus primarily on creativity that makes sense only to trained researchers and practitioners in the emerging field of conflict resolution, broadly defined.[5] Where professional practitioners' creativity interacts with context-specific, local creativity and the two types are inseparable (for example, in cases where Western-trained researcher-practitioners are themselves parties to particular local conflicts under study), locals' creativity is considered the foreground and primary in focus and professionals' creativity its background.

Third, the unit of analysis for the study is a social process of creation. It is distinguished from many studies of artistic, scientific, and other types of creativity that focus primarily, if not exclusively, on creative individuals, their personality types, and their intra-personal processes and dynamics. The suggested theoretical and methodological focus is justified because conflict resolution is quintessentially relational and social in nature, to the extent that the conventional focus on individuality in contemporary creativity research is deemed inadequate for the present purpose. It is emphasized, however, that this study will look into intra-personal processes and dynamics of individual "creators"; yet it will do so guardedly for the ultimate purpose of understanding creative *social* processes, of which individual creativity is part.

Fourth, the study explores inter-group conflicts but excludes conflicts in which an interpersonal relationship is central. Intrapersonal and interpersonal relations will be discussed to the extent necessary for providing sufficient background of inter-group conflicts under study. Conflict settings of interest range from families to local communities, to nations, to international entities. Yet they share such organizational and systemic features as iterative activities, consciousness of kind, role expectations, and norms (Hechter *et al.* 1990; Hechter 1990; Vaughan 1992).

Fifth and final, the primary focus of this inquiry is on the conscious realm of human activities, individual and collective, where ideas may be verbalized at will. This study will treat as secondary the subconscious, where ideas are available only on recall, and the unconscious, where ideas are not available even on recall but occasionally emerge in dreams and other spontaneous inner processes when unconstrained by conscious control. However, the kind of conscious processes under study is expected to stimulate, guide, and interact with the subconscious and unconscious processes that take place inevitably and simultaneously.[6] Therefore, working hypotheses and models of creative practice will suggest how to activate conscious processes conducive to creativity while remaining mindful of subconscious and unconscious processes as a companion of the conscious.

The significance of the inquiry

This study is part of the author's long-term commitment toward narrowing the gap between the theory of conflict analysis and the practice of conflict resolution. Reflecting on the field of conflict research, one realizes that many theories focus on the sources, processes, and dynamics of conflict. However, theories useful for resolving conflict are not only fewer in number, but also underresearched. The dearth of theoretical insights useful for resolution is partly responsible for frequently observed situations in which practitioners, policymakers, and conflict parties in inter-communal tension fail to come up with solutions despite their detailed analyses of the conflicts at hand. At the heart of this problem lies the lack of adequate awareness of the fact that the ways of making sense of reality for conflict analysis are related to, but are in fact qualitatively different from, the ways of mobilizing the body, mind, and spirit for envisioning and actualizing conflict resolution, both individually and collectively. Although both logic and evidence appear to support the widely-accepted link between conflict analysis and resolution of one type or another, a crucial question for better utilizing the link is still to be answered: how should conflict parties and intermediaries sensitize themselves to envision and actualize workable solutions that go beyond their habits, experiences, intuitions, and ideological commitments while using their conflict assessments effectively? The study of creativity is a first step toward answering this question.

Envisioning what can be and what ought to be, beyond what was and what is, requires value judgments. They are shaped and reshaped not only through cognitive and emotive processes at the conscious level, but also through meaning-making processes that take place beneath the conscious, namely, the preconscious. Because a value judgment implicit in a given attempt at envisioning and actualizing a potential reality is derived from sustained developmental processes starting in childhood, it is inferred that every act of creation, at least in a psychoanalytic sense, has been prepared, perhaps for years, up to the point of creation.[7]

This conjecture opens up unfamiliar ways of conceptualizing the analysis–resolution link. For example, the nature of the link explored so far presupposes the conscious as a primary realm of creative activities. The method of principled, interest-based negotiation developed and popularized by Fisher *et al.* (1991) follows this line of reasoning to a significant extent, consistent with the prevailing tenet of Western-trained professionals in conflict resolution. What appears to remain unquestioned – and perhaps unquestionable for its axiomatic status – is the assumption that conflict analysis necessarily *precedes* resolution in sequence. However, insights into the developmental process of the preconscious and value judgments which it shapes suggest that at least part of the images of resolution options remain submerged in the human mind until appropriate contexts of conflict emerge as an opportunity for their application.[8] In other words, at the preconscious level images of potential resolution options are in search of conflicts. From these two positions emerges a third one, analogous to a Hegelian synthesis: attempts to analyze and resolve conflicts may co-arise in a dialectical relationship over time, shaping and reshaping one another like a door and doorframe readjusted to each other repeatedly until they fit together. More specifically, the third position illustrates the possibility that images of preferred action, whether verbalized consciously as value judgments or not, build up over time since childhood, while unfolding social and epistemological contexts of conflicts continuously reshape these evolving images in the human mind.

Reflecting on these three possibilities, one realizes that the analysis–resolution link, which practitioners often take for granted as a sequential flow, is far more complex and multifaceted than is commonly understood. These possibilities suggest that creation of resolution options is an intricate endeavor that requires well-reasoned yet flexible attempts to explore human consciousness and its longitudinal, developmental processes. Such attempts become further complicated when interacting with the collective conscious and preconscious, shaping and reshaping inter-group conflicts. The present study, which focuses primarily on the conscious as its foreground, falls far short of realizing the grand vision of inquiry into the analysis–resolution link outlined here. However, it is important to state explicitly that this study aspires to be at least a preliminary attempt at articulating what is knowable in what appears to be a vast realm of human and social creativity for conflict resolution, much of which remains unknown and unheeded.

Finally, the relevance of this inquiry is gauged in relation to recent literature in creativity research and conflict resolution. Some have already begun exploring the role of creativity in conflict resolution. Many of their works have focused specifically on individual psychology (Coleman and Deutsch 2000; Gruber 2000). Experimental studies have identified conditions conducive to creative problem-solving, such as analogizing (Spector 1995) and cooperative exchange of information (Gruber 2000). Yet these studies were conducted under tight experimental control; their applicability is too limited in the context of far more complex realities of inter-group conflicts, particularly ones involving violence. Other researchers highlight techniques of reasoning, such as integrative agreements (Pruitt 1987), lateral thinking (De Bono 1985), and strategic sequencing of negotiation issues (Hare and Haveh 1985). However useful these studies of skillful reasoning may be, they fail to pay sufficient attention to the social and epistemological contexts that frame individual reasoning. Yet others attempt to capture both individual thinking and its socio-political context, but their views are limited to their own anecdotal episodes and ideographic reflections (Cohen 1993; Fogg 1985; Gerardi 2001) rather than systematic, empirical analysis. Given this background, the present empirical study aims to supplement the micro focus of the existing literature with more social, epistemological, and historical aspects of creativity, particularly in the context of inter-group conflict.

Empirical and theoretical background

In search of promising starting points and useful stepping stones, three strands of preparatory activities were conducted concurrently in order to conceptualize the framework of inquiry: (1) a review of selected contemporary literature on creativity research and other related subjects; (2) exploratory interviews; and (3) preliminary case studies.[9] Because of the study's unique focus on creative social processes of inter-group conflict resolution, instead of more conventional units of analysis (such as creative personalities), much of the theoretical knowledge accumulated through contemporary creativity research, however useful as general background knowledge, played only a supplementary role in shaping the research design, working assumptions, and other essential elements of this inquiry. Therefore, although insights derived from literature are interwoven throughout this and following chapters whenever necessary, an independent section or chapter on a literature review, typical of extensive studies of this magnitude, does not find a specifically designated place in what follows.

The other two types of activities, the exploratory interviews and preliminary case studies, were designed to start discovering what appeared to be knowable and learnable from readily accessible and concrete empirical examples of creativity for conflict resolution, or at least some suggestive elements thereof. They generated critical working assumptions and useful empirical examples that shaped the research design. For this reason, each of these two strands of activity deserves brief mention in this section, while the insights generated through these activities will be summarized in the next section in the form of working assumptions and frameworks of analysis.

At the earliest phase of the inquiry, a series of thirty-one interviews were conducted with conflict researchers and practitioners of diverse regional, disciplinary, and professional backgrounds in the US and abroad. The criteria for selecting the interviewees include familiarity with conflict resolution practice, as well as accessibility in the Washington DC area or alternatively by phone or email. The central questions that guided these preparatory interviews include: (1) What is your definition of creativity in the context of inter-group conflict resolution?; and (2) What is the most creative resolution outcome and/or procedure by which to resolve an inter-group conflict you have either created, implemented, or otherwise observed closely in your career? At later stages of this preparatory interview project, several natural scientists and artists with distinguished backgrounds in creativity were also consulted in order to compare scientific and artistic creativity with conflict resolution creativity, with the view toward conceptualizing the latter.[10]

Another strand of preparatory activities was a study of twenty cases recognized as creative for a variety of reasons, suggested by either the interviewees or by relevant literature. The cases were characterized as either "successful" or "failed" attempts in the actual implementation of resolution options in complex inter-group relations. Of interest in reviewing these cases was how the resolution outcomes and/or procedures in question first emerged with sufficient clarity for practical application, as well as what kinds of thinking and social interactions appeared to have enabled, or inhibited, those social processes to emerge and evolve over time. The reviewed cases include, but are not limited to:

- The first nonviolent civil disobedience movement, known as satyagraha, in 1906–14, organized by M. K. Gandhi and other Indian community leaders in South Africa, as well as the subsequent development of this method in India.
- The Helsinki process of 1973–5 for multilateral relationship-building in Europe during the Cold War.
- The Oslo peace process in the early-to-mid-1990s on the Israeli–Palestinian relations.
- The first informal problem-solving, or Second-Track, dialogues organized to resolve the Indonesia–Malaysia–Singapore conflict in 1965–6.
- The 1998 settlement of the Peru–Ecuador border dispute.
- The political process that led to the 1978 peace agreement between Egypt and Israel, known as Camp David I.
- The common security policy in the international context of *perestroika* under the leadership of Mikhail Gorbachev in the mid-to-late 1980s.
- The settlement of the identity-related conflict between half-indigenous Métis people and the Canadian government, with emphasis on the 1980s and 1990s.
- Recent "peace business" initiatives in Kashmir, Caucasus, and Cyprus.[11]
- Diverse approaches to conceptualize the territorial and political status of the Kurile Islands, Northern Ireland, Jerusalem, and the Falkland Islands.
- A range of shared sovereignty arrangements, such as Andorra, the Åland archipelago between Finland and Sweden, and the Cameroons as ruled by the French and British colonial administrations.

These two types of preparatory activities generated useful findings, some of which contributed to formulating working assumptions and frameworks of analysis, a questionnaire for researcher-practitioner interviews, and promising cases for in-depth inquiry. Each of these subjects will be elaborated shortly.

Working assumptions and frameworks of analysis

Based on the preliminary findings, a creative social process of inter-group conflict resolution is hypothesized in terms of five phases, analogous to manifestations of conflict dynamics such as latency, emergence, escalation, and termination. The phased approach to conceptualizing creativity is suggested because conflict episodes collected from the thirty-one exploratory interviews indicate *longitudinal* transitions perceived by conflict parties about how creative resolution options and procedures first appeared and later evolved. Moreover, contemporary creativity researchers have developed a number of phased approaches to conceptualizing creative processes. One of the most popularized classical approaches is the four-stage model developed by Wallas (1926). The four stages are: information (a creator gains familiarity with the subject area); incubation (the creator reflects on the subject through trial and error); illumination (the creator comes up with a solution, sometimes subconsciously); and verification (the creator tests the applicability of the solution). Conceptual models of this kind have heuristic value for the present inquiry. However, this study needs to go beyond the conventional micro focus on intra-personal psychological processes through which new ideas are generated and innovative products invented. Therefore, an alternative framework of analysis is necessary to capture the social, epistemological, and longitudinal nature of creativity for inter-group conflict resolution.

The suggested framework was used for the methodological purpose of establishing theoretical comparability across a wide range of inter-group conflicts under study, thereby standardizing procedures of data collection and analysis. Each of the five phases is defined as follows.

Incipience: a social process through which at least some kernel elements of the creative resolution outcome and/or procedure in question have already appeared. At this stage, however, these elements are still ill-defined. They are far from integrated or framed in a coherent, actionable manner. Their applicability remains unexplored and unclear.

Origination: a social process through which kernel elements of the creative outcome and/or procedure come to be defined, framed, and integrated for application and shared by at least some primary stakeholders in the conflict.

Evolution: a social process through which kernel elements of the creative outcome and/or procedure are shaped and reshaped through sustained social interactions among the primary stakeholders and others involved in the conflict. Throughout this process, the applicability of the creative approach is continuously challenged as its influence grows or declines, expands or contracts.

Acceptance: a social process where proponents of the creative approach, as well as bystanders attentive to it, come to share or at least acquiesce in the reality in which the proposed approach has already gained such social significance that it can no longer be excluded from serious public discussion. Acceptance is both an extension and subtype of evolution in its unique form. In reality, acceptance may or may not occur in every social context of conflict resolution, at least in a clearly definable and observable way. The concept should therefore be viewed as an ideal category of creative phenomena, actual or potential.

Sustenance: a social process through which the momentum of the creative outcome and/or procedure is anchored in the given local context as legitimate. Like acceptance, sustenance is also both an extension and subtype of evolution because a given creative approach continuously shapes and reshapes its form and influence even after acceptance. A creative approach reaching the sustenance phase develops new patterns of thinking and social interactions and routinizes them. Over time, such sustained momentum to further the social change makes the creative approach no longer creative, ending the hypothesized life cycle of creativity and possibly preparing ground for yet another creative change of an analogous type or of a qualitatively different type to appear.

These five phases are summarized in Figure 1.2. As the subsequent findings will make clear, these longitudinal phases are conceptual categories recognizable only by analysts looking at the given social and epistemological context of conflict from outside. For example, at incipience and even at later phases, conflict

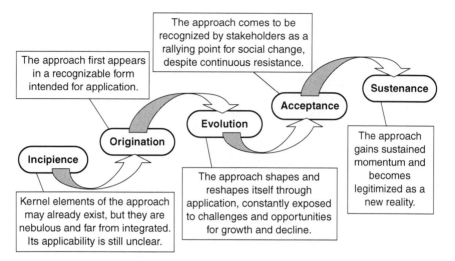

Figure 1.2 The five-phase model of conflict resolution creativity.

Note
This working model is designed to provide a graphic overview of the incipience, origination, evolution, acceptance, and sustenance phases of a given social and epistemological process of conflict resolution creativity. The model summarizes how different social movements and events, illustrated in arrows, converge and diverge, shaping and reshaping the longitudinal process of creation. The five phases, by no means linear in progression, are defined in the boxes.

parties are not always conscious of what outsiders may view as a conflict – even a violent one – in which the parties have been interlocked. Likewise, conflict parties tend to be unaware of what could be considered kernel elements of creative approaches unless they consciously reflect on their experiences in retrospect or informed outsiders deliberately elicit their reflections. Yet this heuristic and analytical value of the model is precisely the reason why an instrument of this kind is devised, even at the obvious risk of oversimplifying complexities of conflict, in order to elicit self-reflective insights through in-depth interviews and other means of data collection. To counter the risk of molding complex realities into formalistic rationality and linearity, conscious efforts were made throughout data collection and analysis to search for pathways that appear to be outside the five-phase model, with the possibility in mind to revise it at a later stage of inquiry.[12]

However, describing all five phases comprehensively in each of the social and epistemological contexts of creation under study is exceedingly complex and clearly goes beyond a manageable scope of inquiry. Besides, research on conflict resolution creativity is still at an early stage, and what is feasible as a first step is to explore processes, dynamics, and contexts of *origination* in some depth. The other four phases will be discussed as the background of origination whenever necessary to illuminate possible precursors and consequences of origination.

It is worth explaining why the entire life cycle of creativity has to be conceptualized despite the fact that the study looks primarily at origination. The exploratory interviews and the preliminary case studies suggested that most stakeholders in conflict recognize a creative change only in retrospect, as already mentioned. Admittedly, creators with foresight are sometimes convinced that their initiatives are creative even at the point of origination, if not incipience. However, immediate followers of the initiators come to acknowledge the given change as creative sometime after its origination and most likely during its evolution. An important question is raised: why do some creative changes come to be accepted after their first appearance, but other changes come to be rejected? One promising way of answering this question is to examine what has actually occurred at origination in a given case and then to look at the entire life cycle of the attempted change longitudinally, both forward into possible evolution, acceptance, and sustenance and backward into incipience. This reasoning process by no means seeks to explain whether and how causal links may be established between consecutive phases, but it contributes toward enhancing reflexivity in conflict resolution practice. In order to prepare for a more comprehensive longitudinal study, this project has first hypothesized the entire life cycle of the creative process and then empirically explored origination as a starting point for future inquiry.

In addition to hypothesizing creativity longitudinally, the study has also identified a range of working assumptions and typologies of conflict resolution creativity, inspired by the exploratory interviews and preparatory case studies. The following three concepts are found particularly useful as a heuristic basis for understanding empirical data and theorizing creativity:[13]

1. Outcome (or substantive) creativity and process (or procedural) creativity.
2. Creativity shaped at the system level and the element (or agency) level, or more generally, creativity emerging at different levels of analysis.
3. Paradigm-accepting creativity and paradigm-breaking creativity, or more generally, plausible relationships between creativity and paradigm shifts.

These typological concepts refer to ideal types of social phenomena which are rarely found in their exact forms in reality.[14] They are intended to offer points of departure and stepping stones when exploring ways to make sense of complex realities of inter-group conflict. They also serve as conceptual tools to help articulate what ways of thinking and social interaction exist, how they are similar and different, and what other types have to be devised to understand forms of thinking and interaction that do not fit into any of the suggested typologies. Methodologically, the three working concepts helped to design interview questions and facilitate exploratory data analysis. Because these concepts have played an essential role throughout the study, they need to be defined with concrete examples, in anticipation of a fuller exploration of each concept later, in Chapter 3.

First, outcome (or substantive) creativity and process (or procedural) creativity are distinguished. Outcome creativity refers to unconventional viability illustrated by a substantive resolution outcome itself. The "shared sovereignty" solution to the territorial dispute over the Åland Islands between Finland and

Sweden in the early 1920s exemplifies this type. On the other hand, process creativity is defined as unconventional viability exercised in the procedural means by which to resolve conflict. The first satyagraha, or nonviolent civil disobedience, campaign in 1906–14 led by M. K. Gandhi and other South African Indian community leaders exemplifies this type. Because these two cases, identified in the course of the preparatory case studies, are found particularly useful to illustrate the outcome–process typology, as well as the other working concepts, each of the cases deserves a brief description.

In the Åland Islands question, the two primary conflict parties were the Swedish and Finnish governments, each vying for exclusive sovereignty over the heavily fortified archipelago of Åland, inhabited by the ethnic Swedish majority and the Finnish minority and located in the strategic maritime routes between the two countries.[15] Although the "shared sovereignty" solution presented by the arbitrators of the League of Nations in 1921 appeared to have settled the dispute diplomatically and illustrates the acceptance phase, the decision did not emerge on a clean slate. It drew from decades of bilateral and multilateral negotiations between Åland islanders' delegations, Great Britain, Germany, France, the US, Sweden, and Russia, with the last being the sovereign ruler of Finland until 1917. Historical evidence shows that these many years of diplomatic negotiations had presupposed exclusive sovereignty as an unquestioned premise until November 1918, when Finnish General Carl Gustaf Mannerheim began exploring the applicability of condominium, or shared sovereignty, in his personal conversation with British diplomat Robert Civile in London (the origination phase). The proposed scheme reflected an unconventional way of thinking because the British, French, Swedish, and other stakeholders continued to propose territorial exchange, division, Swedish exclusive ownership, and other measures that presupposed zero-sum thinking until, and even after, the 1921 settlement (the evolution phase). To the extent that this settlement for political coexistence survived the coming years of tension between Finland and Sweden and the turbulence of World War II and the Cold War in Europe, the case illustrates elements of viability as well. In terms of the outcome–process typology, the shared sovereignty arrangement of Åland was substantively creative because it emerged and evolved successfully against the norm of exclusive national sovereignty pervasive in the Westphalian tradition of Europe.

On the other hand, the first satyagraha campaign of 1906–14 exemplifies process creativity. The major conflict parties involved in this social process included the South African governments, both provincial and national, and Indian communities of Hindu, Muslim, and other socio-cultural backgrounds based primarily in the Transvaal and Natal.[16] Other non-European immigrant communities, European stakeholders, and native South Africans either opposed or supported the movement, or otherwise remained indifferent. The campaign was officially launched in a mass meeting held in Johannesburg in September 1906 and attended by some 3,000 Indians. Its primary purpose was to protest against the Asiatic Law Amendment Ordinance that the government intended to introduce, requiring all Indians in the Transvaal, including women and children, to offer finger and thumb impressions at the specially created Asiatic Department and receive compulsory certificates of registration. Under the leadership of Mohandas K. Gandhi and other organizers, active members of the South African Indian community pledged not to submit to the law, willingly suffer consequences including imprisonment, and use nonviolent means of civil resistance to repeal the law (the origination phase). The campaign grew and declined over the years. It was shaped and reshaped continuously by the internal dynamics of the South African Indian community and the government, as well as by the on-going negotiations between them (the evolution phase). The acceptance phase of the satyagraha campaign ensued gradually in the course of evolution, as both the government authority and a growing number of sensitized Indians came to actively support or oppose the movement.

This campaign illustrated an unconventional pattern of social change, partly because the South African Indian community had taken many similar pledges before but had never done so explicitly and solemnly under the name of God. Unconventionality was also evident in the actual implementation of the pledge, as well as in the campaigners' firm commitment to defying the conventional patterns of violent resistance exercised by some sections of native South Africans and organized European laborers under similar circumstances at the time.[17] On the other hand, signs of viability were most visible when the government introduced a new law in 1914 to work more conciliatorily with the South African Indian communities, at least for a brief period of time. Finally, in terms of the outcome–process typology, the first satyagraha campaign was procedurally creative because the social process of nonviolent civil disobedience made strides toward transcending the prevailing norm of violent resistance, the latter being a conventional means by which to achieve political ends from the bottom up in the particular historical and geographic context of the movement.

Despite the suggested distinction between process and outcome creativity, the two concepts are interdependent in reality because process inevitably shapes outcome. Moreover, for those whose immediate substantive goal is to devise a procedure, coming up with a creative process represents an act of outcome creativity, at least from their subjective perspective. For these reasons, any episode of unconventional viability entails both procedurally and substantively creative qualities in varying degrees. A similar way of synthetic thinking and interaction applies to the definitions of the two other working assumptions. Theoretically, exploring the outcome–process link is important because it has been a focal point of discussion in social science in general and peace and conflict research in particular.

Second, creativity generated at the system level and the element (or agency) level of analysis is distinguished. As will be elaborated later, a system refers to a network of actors involved in a conflict while elements correspond to actors, or agents, whose interactions constitute a system. For the purpose of the in-depth interviews conducted for data collection, the term "agency-led creativity" was used to describe a social process through which prominent actors, or agents, spearhead unconventional yet viable changes for conflict resolution. Many aspects of the first satyagraha campaign, led by Gandhi and others, illustrate this type.

In addition, the preparatory studies also suggested another, perhaps less familiar, way of conceptualizing the origin of creative change: unconventional viability may emerge interactively and organically as a function of the whole system from which it arises. This possibility was termed "systemically induced creativity" for the purpose of the in-depth interviews, and defined as a social process through which creative change evolves from institutionalized process and structure. More specifically, systemically-induced creativity develops from combined effects of institutionalized interactions, communication patterns, decision-making rules, leader–follower relations, organizational norms, and group consciousness, despite the lack of sustained presence of one or more prominent leaders. Theoretically, systemically induced creativity, unlike agency-led creativity, presupposes interchangeability of agents. The shared sovereignty solution to the Åland Islands question appears to be of this type because it evolved despite the fact that the leading negotiators changed frequently. The system–element typology is significant for social science theory, for it sheds light on the on-going debate on the relationship between system and element.

Finally, paradigm-breaking and paradigm-accepting creativity is considered. Of interest is whether and how the concept of paradigm shift developed by Thomas Kuhn (1996), a leading philosopher of scientific history, is applicable to creativity in inter-group conflict resolution. In the natural sciences and other well-structured domains of inquiry, a paradigm is referred to as an organization of community practices within a given discipline (Nickles 1999). To be useful as a framework of data collection, the idea has to be conceptualized in a less discipline-specific manner. It is thus defined more flexibly for this study as an exemplary mode of thinking and action recognized as such in a given social and epistemological context.

Given this revised definition, paradigm-breaking creativity, or a paradigm shift, is understood as a process of breaking recognized modes of problem identification and resolution, with the possible effect of creating new modes. In the Åland case, some elements of paradigm-breaking creativity were evident because the substance of autonomous rights, including socio-cultural and linguistic provisions for Finnish–Swedish coexistence, marked a distinct departure from the rigid application of the Westphalian mode of exclusive internal sovereignty. To the extent that the monolithic, all-or-nothing notion of national sovereignty – the mode of European inter-state relations predominant during World War I and beyond – was sharply contrasted by the multi-functional view of cultural, administrative, diplomatic, and military sovereignty, the Åland solution was a paradigm shift.

However, it is significant to keep in mind that a paradigm shift is but one possible type of unconventional yet viable social change. In theory, varying degrees and kinds of unconventional viability which emerge within a given recognized mode of thinking and action and which fall short of a paradigm shift to transform the mode are regarded as paradigm-accepting creativity. In other words, paradigm-accepting creativity is a default category definable in relation to paradigm-breaking creativity. Yet in reality, paradigm-breaking and paradigm-accepting creativity is hardly distinguishable from an empirical standpoint because of the multifaceted nature of any inter-group conflict. For example, the Åland solution entailed not only paradigm-breaking but also paradigm-accepting elements, and these two types of phenomena co-arose in an indistinguishable manner. The paradigm-accepting elements were particularly salient when the arbitration decision of 1921 granted Finland diplomatic and political sovereignty, if not socio-cultural and linguistic one, following the Westphalian mode of external sovereignty and independent statehood. As illustrated by this example, the suggested typology of paradigms is used in this study not as a framework of dichotomous reasoning, but as a heuristic stepping board to explore what kinds of creativity may be definable in both empirical and potential realities and how different kinds relate to one another.

To further this line of reasoning, Kuhn's thesis on the possible relationships between paradigm-breaking and paradigm-accepting creativity is suggestive. According to Kuhn (1996), it takes a sustained commitment to paradigm-accepting activities, unconventional or not, to arrive eventually at paradigm-breaking discoveries in the natural sciences. In his view, this inference is justified because in the natural sciences, discovering the inability of existing paradigms to resolve "anomalous" problems through detail-oriented, paradigm-accepting exercises, known as puzzle-solving, help revolutionary path-breakers eventually come up with a categorically different mode of thinking, paving the way toward a paradigm shift. Does this epistemological pathway in the Kuhnian worldview apply to creativity in inter-group conflict resolution? If not, what other pathways might be suggested to account for unconventional yet viable shifts to emerge? Understanding the proposed typology from an empirical perspective is an important first step toward answering these questions.

The research design

Two cumulative steps were taken for data collection and analysis: (1) a comparative analysis of sixteen cases; and (2) an in-depth single-case study. The first step started with a series of sixteen interviews with researcher-practitioners, who described their hands-on experiences in creating conflict resolution processes. Chapter 2 will present these sixteen episodes of conflict resolution creativity and explore theoretical implications of each. The sixteen cases were then compared qualitatively, with the view toward discovering what common threads might emerge across these distinctly different contexts of creation, by paying due attention to the diverse ways of thinking and social interaction involved. The comparative analysis also explored how the three working typologies introduced earlier could be applied cross-contextually and how, if necessary, they could be reformulated for theory-building. Chapter 3 will describe findings in this theory-building exercise.

The first phase of the inquiry, which will be discussed in Chapters 2 and 3, addresses the primary goal of this study. However, to refine some of the major themes and hypotheses generated at the first phase, a supplementary second phase is introduced. The second phase aims to illustrate how the themes and hypotheses, discovered as discrete concepts through the first phase, interact with one another, synergistically or otherwise, within the historical and geographic context of the first satyagraha campaign of 1906–14 in South Africa. As will be explained in Chapter 4, the first satyagraha campaign was selected for an in-depth case analysis because, despite the passage of time and its unique qualities as a social change process, it cogently illustrates some of the core findings of the first phase. Careful reflections on this event also help contemporary conflict workers vicariously experience how to weave the various discoveries in this study together in an organic whole of at least one historical episode of epoch-making creativity. For data collection, the case study of satyagraha's origination drew on archival sources and selected literature. Steps taken for data analysis were exploratory and qualitative in nature, as in the first phase.

Based on these two phases, Chapter 5 will summarize key findings and their implications for practice, research, and pedagogy. This concluding chapter will also propose a new method of conflict resolution dialogue termed "cross-contextual case studies" that seeks to integrate the essential findings for conflict work.

The rationale for the research design outlined above and its essential features requires explanation, with emphasis on the following four considerations. First, the two-phase approach to case studies was adopted for generating and exploring a wide range of working hypotheses. Because the existing theoretical knowledge of creative social processes for conflict resolution is still limited in depth and breadth, the primary objective of the study is defined as discovering useful typologies. Conceptually, typological knowledge is the most elementary level of analytical category, falling far short of causality but preparing an indispensable first step toward theorizing correlations between different types of social phenomena related to conflict resolution creativity. Given this exploratory, discovery-oriented nature of the inquiry, qualitative case analysis is preferred to other established methods presupposing well-refined working theories, such as the experimental method and large-N case analysis.[18] Likewise, the survey method is precluded from consideration, for it also presupposes a well-defined theoretical basis for sampling representative respondents in an effort to elicit descriptive knowledge on conflict resolution creativity.

Second, the two phases of case analysis were introduced to explore creative social processes in actual historical, geographic, and relational contexts, rather than in simulated ones. While many contemporary studies in creativity research spearheaded by Western-trained psychologists view creative individuals as a unit of analysis, this study looks into social processes through incipience, origination, evolution, and beyond as its primary analytical focus. This difference in conceptual focus is reflected in the methodological choice of case-based inquiry into actual social contexts and processes, instead of simulating them for the purpose of observing individuals' thinking and interaction patterns under artificially controlled conditions. The fact that the essential participants in the social processes under study and their inner reflections were available and accessible by way of in-depth interviews for the first phase and archival sources, such as Gandhi's memoirs and his own journal articles, for the second phase made this methodological choice viable and effective.

Third, the selected multi-method approach offers an analytical framework within which the sixteen-case comparison is effectively complemented by the single-case analysis that follows. Because of the inherently inductive nature of comparative analysis, abstract themes emerging from the sixteen concrete contexts have to be formulated for clarity as if they were discrete conceptual items de-contextualized from the specific temporal, spatial, and relational settings.[19] Epistemologically, this tendency of "unitizing" is unavoidable as a step toward theory-building of any kind. However, since this study seeks to generate theoretical and methodological insights useful for practical conflict work, the single-case analysis was designed as a complementary second phase in order to illustrate at least one way of re-contextualizing the emerging themes and working typologies within the integrated whole of Gandhi's and other leaders' reflective practice. The single-case study at the second stage seeks to neither confirm nor infirm the working hypotheses. Its purpose is to cogently illustrate how they work together in the given context, in an effort to refine and elaborate them for clarity and practical use.[20]

Fourth and final, due to the unique, exploratory nature of the design, the level of validity expected from the study is necessarily limited. Conceptually, the first phase compares the sixteen cases of diverse historical and regional backgrounds, from meso to macro to mega, and it thus contributes, at least in a preliminary manner, toward constructing hypotheses with significant external validity. However, the unique nature of the discovery-oriented, qualitative process for the first phase, let alone the second, generates only a limited level of internal validity that accounts for hypothesized relationships between creativity and possible enabling factors to be explored. This assessment becomes particularly evident when one compares the selected design with more explanation-oriented, confirmatory methods unsuited for this inquiry. While accepting this assessment as an inevitable given, the study nonetheless seeks to minimize anticipated threats to validity of both types, by way of making the processes of data collection and analysis as reliable and accountable as practically possible. Concrete measures to counter validity threats will be discussed in Chapter 2.

2 Exploration

Sixteen episodes of creativity

Overview and methodology

The researcher-practitioner interviews were conducted to discover and articulate a range of working propositions on creativity for conflict resolution. Consistent with the overall purpose of this study, the analysis of interview results focuses primarily on: (1) definitions and hallmarks of creativity and (2) its origination phase, highlighting ways in which creative resolution outcomes and/or procedures first appeared. Discussion on incipience, evolution, acceptance, and sustenance is secondary and supplementary. These four phases are explored when they help to illuminate the two primary subjects in focus. The analysis of the interviews will generate a broad range of empirical discoveries and theoretical insights across the collected episodes of creativity.

The present chapter first outlines the methodology used for analyzing the sixteen episodes and then describes some of the essential findings. The next chapter will draw on these findings and build a range of working theories of conflict resolution creativity, with implications summarized to suggest an analytical framework for the in-depth case study of satyagraha in Chapter 4. Because the present chapter and the next one are guided by one coherent set of methodological considerations for the comparative case analysis, which is distinguished from the single-case analysis in Chapter 4, the discussion that follows will outline all the steps of inquiry taken for both Chapters 2 and 3 in an integrated manner. These methodological issues under consideration are: the unit of analysis, data collection, operationalization and analysis, and reliability and validity. Moreover, the present chapter will discuss three types of findings: creativity demonstrated by (1) conflict parties; (2) intermediaries; and (3) actors fulfilling both functions at the same time. Building on these empirical findings, the next chapter will discover and generate working theories of conflict resolution creativity, by utilizing such heuristic tools and typologies as the five-phase model (or the longitudinal nature of creativity), process–outcome, system–element (or levels of analysis), and paradigms.

Reflecting on the quantity of data collected from the thirty-one preparatory interviews as a guide, it was determined that 15–20 in-depth interviews would be adequate to achieve the stated objectives and to build a solid basis for the in-depth case study to follow. Sixteen interviews were actually conducted and analyzed. Because of the exploratory and complex nature of the study, the conventional logic of sampling was neither useful nor applicable to select the interviewees, but it offered an analogical basis for systematic selection. The criteria for selection included the following four considerations:

1 At least ten years of hands-on experience in resolving or otherwise coping with inter-group, socio-political conflicts, including inter-communal, intra-national, international, and global ones. It was noted that years of professional experience per se would not automatically generate creative insights. Yet the preparatory interviews led to the working assumption that experienced practitioners would be more likely to have used or at least observed a rich menu of approaches, some of which might have involved creativity, either paradigm-driven or paradigm-breaking.
2 Diverse representation of roles, including conflict party, policy advocate, negotiator, facilitator, consultant, mediator, arbitrator, trainer, and university-based researcher. An attempt was made to ensure that at least one-third of the interviewees would be conflict parties and the rest would be third parties. The criterion for distinguishing between the two types was the interviewees' self-reported roles in the particular conflict episodes that they chose to discuss in their interviews. The need to categorize the interviewees was informed by the preliminary finding that this difference was likely to affect perceptions about which resolution options would be considered creative and which ones would not.
3 Diverse representation of organizational affiliations, including research institution, NGO, government, and international organization.
4 Diverse representation of geographic contexts of conflict work, such as the Middle East, North America, and West Africa.

The underlying rationale for selecting these criteria was: the more diverse the types of experience are, the broader range of sensitization processes one can identify, consistent with the exploratory purpose of the study. However, because the population of potential interviewees was excessively large and globally spread and the resulting arbitrariness in interviewee selection had to be controlled, an important fifth criterion was introduced: first-hand experience in having actually created, and preferably implemented, creative procedures and/or resolution outcomes in inter-group conflicts. For the purpose of interviewee selection, creative cases were defined as ones that were first nominated in the thirty-one preparatory interviews or otherwise suggested in relevant literature, and then carefully studied and evaluated by the author as consistent with the working definition of creativity. Inclusion of this fifth criterion led to the selection of such cases (and corresponding interviewees) as the Helsinki process in the mid-1970s (former senior Finnish diplomat Klaus Törnudd), the 1998 settlement of the Peru–Ecuador dispute (TRANSCEND Director Johan Galtung), and the Oslo peace process of 1993 (Israeli negotiator Ron Pundak). While the proposed fifth criterion guided interviewee selection, it was considered a preference, not a mandatory requisite, because many of the most ideal interviewees were inaccessible and the available resources for the project were limited.

An overview of the sixteen completed interviews indicates that overall, the five criteria for interviewee selection were well utilized and applied. Consequently, the sixteen episodes represent a wide range of perspectives on creativity useful for the exploratory purpose of this inquiry. For example, all sixteen interviewees have over ten years of relevant experience, meeting the first criterion for selection. With respect to the roles they played in the episodes that they chose to discuss, five of them were conflict parties in such capacities as an advocate, negotiator, and consultant, nine were intermediaries in such functions as a mediator, facilitator, and university-based researcher, and the remaining two played both types of roles. As for organizational affiliations, six of them worked as either private citizens or NGO representatives, four held the status of academics and/or educators, and six acted on behalf of governments or inter-governmental organizations. In terms of the geographic locations of the conflicts, four of them took place in North America, three in Asia,[1] three in Europe,[2] four in the Middle East, one in Africa, and one in South America. Finally, regarding the levels of analysis on which the interviewees' efforts focused most intensively, ten episodes addressed the macro- to mega-level, where nations, states, and/or transnational collectivities were in conflict, and six were at the micro- to meso-level, where conflicts occurred between small groups of individuals and/or between small intra-national groups. In short, the sixteen episodes cover a broad spectrum of conflict-related phenomena useful for exploratory theory-building.[3]

An overview of the sixteen episodes also reveals that they vary not only in terms of the five criteria, but also with respect to the degrees of "success" and "failure" in actualizing creative visions. Some of the episodes illustrate pathways that failed to transition from the origination phase onward; others illustrate creative processes tailing out in the course of evolution; yet others illustrate what the interviewees consider a successful transition through acceptance and sustenance. As will be demonstrated later, the range of cases illustrating varying degrees of "success" and "failure" will help to explore the longitudinal nature of creativity systematically and inspire future research and practice.

The interview questions, attached at the end of the book as an appendix, reflect the objectives of the study. The questions were formulated based on the preparatory studies that suggested such starting points of inquiry as the five-phase model, enabling and limiting factors for each phase, and other working models and typologies of creativity. Before the actual interviews for data collection, several test interviews were conducted to examine the content of the questionnaire, revise the sequence of the questions, and refine the precise wording of each. The test interviews demonstrated that the questions were both clear and open-ended enough to elicit a range of views necessary to meet the exploratory purpose of the inquiry. For data collection, the interviews were tape-recorded with permission, transcribed, and edited according to the standardized format of presentation. The transcriptions, omitted for brevity in what follows, were used as a basis for data analysis.

The unit of analysis is an episode of conflict resolution chosen and described by each of the interviewees. An episode, for the present purpose, is described as a bounded system of temporal–spatial context in which events and interactions unfold among actors seeking to realize their aspirations.[4] It is emphasized that in this study, the interviewees are considered *informants* of the social and epistemological processes, which they helped to "create" as leaders at best and observed as participants at least. But they, as individuals, are not regarded as units of analysis. Although the informants' intra-personal dynamics, personalities, styles of reasoning, roles in conflict, and numerous other attributes shaped the nature of their episodes and their interpretations of them, their inner processes were but a portion of the relational and social changes under study. Therefore, efforts were made not only to explore how the interviewees thought and acted as individuals, but also how their relational and social contexts of conflict changed as a whole, using the former as a window of opportunity to explore the latter. This conceptual distinction is important not only to make the inquiry useful for the inherently social practice of inter-group conflict resolution, but also to distinguish itself from a range of psychological studies already conducted that focus primarily, if not exclusively, on creative personalities and intra-personal processes.

To operationalize interview results into data sets for comparative analysis, an interpretive framework was devised and applied to summarize essential findings from each interview.[5] The framework is comprised of five elements:

- profile of the interviewee, including his or her role(s) and organizational affiliation(s);
- definition of creativity suggested by the interviewee;
- description of the conflict, including the time period and geographic context, the primary parties involved, and their aspirations and/or issues as perceived by the interviewee;[6]
- description of the creative action taken, followed by preliminary indications as to what happened as a result of the action, if known;
- general lessons on creativity drawn from the episode and formulated as working propositions, with emphasis on its essential hallmarks and its origination phase.

Using this framework, each of the interviews was first operationalized as a discrete episode. The sixteen episodes were then compared systematically for theory-building.

To generate useful lessons from each episode with methodological consistency, two rules were followed:

1 Identify enabling factors *described by the interviewee* as essential for the origination phase.
2 Identify enabling factors *interpreted by the author* as both corresponding to the interviewee's central themes on creativity and relevant to the overall research questions.

The first rule is self-explanatory. The second is harder to operationalize with consistency and precision, but it is necessary and justifiable. In the course of the interviews, it became clear that creative discoveries of resolution options tend to be highly intuitive in nature. Consequently, when asked to articulate how the interviewees, on their own or together with others, came up with what they considered creative options, many of them started their answers with, "I don't know." Follow-up questions and subsequent inquiry revealed that psychologically, many of their activities for creation had taken place at the subconscious level. In addition, it was also observed that many of them had never thought of conflict resolution creativity consciously until they were asked to verbalize their thoughts on the subject for this study. As a result, they tended to explore ways to articulate their inner thoughts, sometimes without a clear flow or organization of ideas. For these reasons, it became necessary for the author to interpret and articulate essential factors derived from the respective episodes. However, in order to control arbitrariness and standardize interpretation, the relevant publications that have been produced, and preferably also recommended, by the interviewees were consulted extensively to corroborate the accuracy of the author's interpretations. In addition, the interviewees' feedback was sought on draft interpretations in writing as much as possible. To aid in the exercise of interpretation and articulation, the working models and typologies of creativity introduced earlier, such as process–outcome and system–element, were used consistently as a point of reference.[7]

Challenges to the reliability and validity of the interview results are acknowledged. First, each episode was told by only one person involved in the conflict. It is likely that his or her evaluation of the conflict resolution activities is not shared by other major stakeholders involved in the same conflict. Different interpretations are attributed in part to different interpretive lenses worn by different stakeholders, as well as by the nature of experiences that they had, according to their roles in the conflict. Second, human memories of past events, especially ones that occurred decades ago, are elusive, selective, and even manipulative. In the process of telling and retelling the episodes and with the passage of time, the interviewees' recollections of their experiences may have been shaped and reshaped repeatedly. Third, there are risks of demand characteristics, defined as subjective motives held by the interviewees who consciously or subconsciously attempt to fulfill the role which they think they are expected to fulfill as informants. In the present study, demand characteristics were likely to manifest in the form of expert urge, or the desire to demonstrate presumed expertise and retell "war stories."

None of these and other equally serious threats to reliability and validity are perfectly controllable given the methodological choices made by this study. For this reason, one may expect only a modest extent to which the findings reflect conflict resolution creativity in empirical terms. However, to counter the first and second threats, relevant supplementary sources, including the interviewees' own writings, were consulted to triangulate their self-reported episodes whenever necessary and possible. To control the third threat concerning the expert urge, a supplementary interview question was inserted in the questionnaire, asking the interviewees to explain why they selected the particular episodes to illustrate creativity.[8]

The next step in data analysis, the results of which will be discussed in the next chapter, was a systematic comparison between the sixteen cases. Its purpose was to generate typological knowledge useful for theory-building. From the sixteen cases, fifty-nine propositions on creativity were drawn. On compiling the list of these propositions, differences and similarities were explored between them. Some interviewees reported, for example, that they were inspired by other practitioners' conflict resolution activities or historical cases observed elsewhere in order to come up with their own breakthrough solutions. Propositions illustrating this type of thinking were categorized as "analogizing." Similarly, five other categories such as "value commitment" and "combining known elements in a new way" were derived from comparison and exploration, and will be explained in Chapter 3.

As a general rule, a new conceptual category was developed when three or more cases shared a distinctly analogous feature. Beyond this rule, it was considered neither feasible nor appropriate to predetermine the exact scheme of categorization due to the highly abstract nature of the operationalization procedure. However, to ensure procedural consistency and accountability, each of the emerging categories of proposition was defined as articulately as possible and illustrated by the propositions that have generated the conceptual category.[9] No attempt was made to fit all sixteen episodes or fifty-nine propositions into defined categories. The propositions illustrating unique qualities of thinking and action were treated as self-standing and kept discrete.

Although the episodes were collected from diverse experiential backgrounds, no claim is made that the common features that emerged from the comparative case analysis are representative in a statistical – or any other – sense. Nor is it assumed that they are more significant than the discrete propositions that fail to cluster together to form conceptual categories. This is because no sampling technique was used in the present study for data collection, for its sole purpose was to generate typological knowledge with accountability. Having recognized this limitation, however, it is also inferred that the emergent categories offer promising typological knowledge for future research and practice because they typify creative changes observed across a number of *distinctly different* contexts. In short, the generalizability of the final results is necessarily limited, but they provide useful points of departure for rigorous inquiry and application.

In addition to the findings on the defining features of creativity and its origination phase, empirical discoveries and theoretical insights will be discussed in Chapter 3 regarding the longitudinal nature of creativity (the five-phase model), the outcome–process link, the system–element link (or the levels-of-analysis question), and the relevance of paradigms. While the search for commonalities between the sixteen episodes is empirical, data-driven, and inductive, discussions on these working assumptions will go beyond this frame of reasoning. They will not only summarize relevant empirical findings, but also suggest useful hypotheses on conflict resolution, using the findings as a point of departure to explore how to envision and actualize potential realities beyond conflict.

For clarity of presentation, the sixteen episodes are divided into three categories according to the roles played by the interviewees: (1) conflict parties (five episodes); (2) intermediaries between conflict parties (nine); and (3) actors playing both roles at the same time (two).[10] Conflict parties are defined as primary stakeholders working to attain their aspirations, even at the cost of obstructing others involved in the confrontational relationships from fulfilling their needs. Intermediaries refer to the parties working to mediate conflict parties or otherwise help them cope with their conflicts constructively from what they claim to be an impartial standpoint. Although impartiality is hardly verifiable in any conflict situation, the working definition is considered sufficient for the methodological purpose of categorizing episodes. Finally, stakeholders playing both roles pursue these two functions at the same time, often claiming the role of intermediaries, but in fact pursuing their own vested interests.

In principle, the episodes were categorized according to the roles reported by the interviewees themselves. However, where the interviewees' roles were multifaceted, complex, and/or ambiguous, an independent judgment was exercised by the author to place the corresponding episodes in appropriate conceptual categories. When such a judgment was exercised, its rationale was articulated to ensure accountability. Each of the three categories corresponds to an independent section, comprised of a brief introduction, an analysis of the creative episodes that belong to the category, and an interlude that summarizes findings in the section.

Conflict parties' creativity

Overview

The five episodes that illustrate conflict parties' creativity are summarized in Table 2.1 for an overview. The table shows (a) the interviewees' names; (b) the geographic contexts and time periods of the conflict episodes; (c) the roles played by the interviewees in the conflicts; (d) the primary conflict parties, their aspirations and/or issues, and the creative actions taken; and (e) the definitions of conflict resolution creativity offered by the interviewees. The episodes are listed in the order of appearance in this section.

The five interviewees are categorized as conflict parties, but their roles and approaches to conflict are significantly different. An impressionistic overview of the five cases indicates that Awad and Falk took a clear advocacy stand, consciously trying to change the behavior and mindset of their opponents,[11] Johnston and Pundak aimed at bringing the two sides together despite their being on one side of the conflict, and Henderson attempted both. Although these three orientations differ, the five practitioners approached their conflicts as parties pitted against their adversaries. For this reason, they are clustered in the same category for the purpose of analysis.

Table 2.1 Summary of the five episodes of conflict parties' creativity

Interviewee	Region and time	Role	Episode	Definition
Linda Johnston	US, mid-1990s	Health clinic supervisor and conflict party	To transform a value conflict between the health clinic staff and teenagers over "accidental pregnancies," the clinic hired the teens to work with the staff to educate peer teens on pregnancy issues	Giving up a formal procedure, realizing the inadequacy of working assumptions
Hazel Henderson	US, 1970s–1990s	NGO-based advocate and consultant	Spread the NGO network Environmentalists for Full Employment to transform the tension between those seeking more employment and others advocating environmental sustainability. Creating an ethical capitalist economy in the US and elsewhere	Connecting dots in a new way, reframing conflict in a broader context
Mubarak Awad	Israel–Palestine, 1985	NGO-based educator, advisor, and advocate	Helped 500 Palestinian villagers unite and work nonviolently to remove fences built by Israelis, with unprecedented firmness to face risks. The Israelis retreated	Organizing sharp directed resistance through public empowerment
Richard Falk	US–Vietnam, 1968	University professor, lawyer, and advocate	The US intervention in support of South Vietnam against socialist North Vietnam as background. Risked meeting North Vietnamese leaders and bringing a peace proposal to Washington, only to be rejected. (A failed attempt to create a desired change)	Listening to weaker parties deeply and correcting power asymmetry by appeal to law
Ron Pundak	Israel–Palestine, 1992–3	NGO-based unofficial negotiator and conflict party	The Oslo peace process. Envisioned a "big picture" solution first and then designed specific steps backward. Applied innovative principles such as draft zero, deniability, and Gaza First	Thinking outside the box but working within the system and on its edge

26   *Exploration*

Depending on which of the three perspectives one adopts for analysis in this and the other two sections that follow, one may come up with a completely different judgment as to which episodes should be considered creative and which ones not. In fact, because all sixteen interviewees defined conflict resolution creativity differently, it is likely that there would be little or no consensus among them as to what creativity means and which episodes genuinely illustrate creativity of one type or another. However, the purpose of the present study is not to settle this debate. The thesis under consideration is that each of the episodes told by the selected informants contains at least some elements of creativity, either paradigm-accepting or paradigm-breaking. Therefore, the central question is *not* whether the episodes are creative, but *which aspects* of the episodes contribute to building general knowledge of conflict resolution creativity and in what way.

Episodes of conflict parties' creativity

"Accidental teenage pregnancies": the need for giving up (Linda Johnston)

Linda Johnston is a Visiting Professor of Conflict Resolution at George Mason University in Virginia.[12] She views creativity as a process of giving up a formal routine procedure out of a realization that it will not work in the given context of conflict. Before she started her career as a university-based educator and researcher-practitioner in the 1990s, she spent twenty years as an administrator and supervisor at public health clinics in the US, managing and resolving conflicts that involved patients, physicians, fellow administrators, and other stakeholders. Johnston illustrated creativity through her attempt, in the mid-1990s, to resolve a conflict between pregnant teens and her staff over their value difference at one of the teen pregnancy clinics that she was supervising.

For years, the issue of teenage pregnancies had been a serious concern for Johnston's clinic, as well as for the local community at large. Some teens had 3–5 pregnancies before they turned eighteen. They kept coming back to the clinic every year. To reduce accidental teen pregnancies, Johnston's clinic received funding and launched a special project. As part of the project, the clinic invited teens with a record of pregnancy and asked their views about the issue. To the astonishment of the staff, the teens indicated that their pregnancies were not accidental but intentional. From the clinic's point of view, the pregnancies must have been accidental because the teens were not supposed to be pregnant in the first place. Some staff maintained that the teens should change their value. They even suggested refusing to serve the teens if they remained irresponsible in their behavior and repeatedly became pregnant. Underlying the staff's position was their commitment to their identity need. Highly educated and esteemed, the professional medical staff could hardly entertain the thought that their assessment of the problem could have been wrong. From the teens' perspective, however, the tax-funded public clinic must serve the public by all means. Whether the teens should or should not become pregnant was the question that the teens should answer themselves, it was not a question for the clinic staff. Some teens were even ready to take the issue to court if the clinic refused to treat them because of the value difference. As the supervisor, Johnston was a member of the clinic staff. But philosophically and emotionally, she was caught in the middle. Trying to find a way out, she reminded herself that the overarching mission of public health clinics was to serve the public where they were, not where the clinics wanted the public to be.

After days of heated debates between Johnston and her staff, the clinic decided to hire teens to offer pregnancy and sex education for pregnant teenagers. This new policy required the staff to give up part of their strongly held value and identity as medical professionals. It also meant turning part of the process over to the teens, instead of dictating to them what the outcome of the project should be from the staff's point of view. Over the years, the shared ownership of the project came to be institutionalized through various organizational procedures of the clinic. For example, the clinic asked some of the teens to sit on the committee together with the staff to review the teen pregnancy project. Johnston also hired qualified teens at other clinics that she was supervising in order to offer peer education in breastfeeding and childbearing.

Among a number of theoretical implications drawn by Johnston, three of them help explain the origination phase of creativity. First, what shook the staff's value and identity was the shock value of the teens' remark that their pregnancies weren't accidental." The shock forced the staff to start thinking that their understanding of the reality was not absolute. This forced Johnston and some like-minded staff to start exploring solutions outside the conventionally accepted approach that centered on giving teens adequate sex education and tools for birth control. Second, what enabled the staff to refocus their assessment and solution was the self-reflective capacity, tolerance of ambiguity, and humility to transform part of their identity and value in order to work with the unexpected reality. In other words, the ability to change oneself was a key to origination. Third, and seemingly contradictory to the second point, a certain type of identity and value commitment helped to enable the staff to envision and accept creative change. Johnston observes that medical professionals at public health clinics tend to value service for the poor, disenfranchised, and marginalized in society instead of valuing their personal ideological commitment and material gains. Despite their sustained resistance to the clinic's new policy due in part to their expert identity, many of the staff eventually came on board because of the organizational commitment to serving the needs of the public. On the one hand, their identity as medical experts prevented them from accepting the creative shift. On the other, their identity as part of the public service organization encouraged them to work with it. Finally, one of the precursors of the origination phase was the staff's frustration that resulted from years of efforts already invested in the prevention of accidental teen pregnancies. The urgency for changing the status quo psychologically prepared the staff to explore workable solutions, creative or not. Another important psychological and social precursor was the exploratory atmosphere created by the special project. Johnston reflects that the project enabled the staff to get out of the conventional mode of daily service and think about the subject more expansively and freely than usual.

Environmentalists for Full Employment: connecting dots in a new way
(Hazel Henderson)

Hazel Henderson is an internationally recognized independent futurist and alternative economist based in the US. She is one of the leading architects of the Calvert–Henderson Quality-of-Life Indicators, which she launched in 1996 as an alternative to gross national product (GNP) and as part of her long-term campaign to establish cross-generational sustainability as a core principle of economics. Henderson defines creativity as an intuitive and holistic process of connecting dots in a new way. To illustrate her understanding of creativity, Henderson described her experience as a grassroots advocate in the 1970s in establishing a nationwide network of NGOs, Environmentalists for Full-Employment.

In the 1970s, Henderson tackled a question: can we achieve a higher level of employment without harming our natural environment excessively? The underlying conflict involved job seekers, workers, and trade unions striving for full-employment, on the one hand, and concerned citizens demanding the preservation of the environment, on the other. In general terms, the assumption of the environmentalists was that economic growth was increasing opportunities for employment, but it was also encouraging a greater exploitation of the environment as a resource base. Henderson reframed this conflict in a broader social context and proposed sustainability as a new basis for economic activities. Her vision was to create an economy with less capital input and more labor. As part of her efforts to put this vision into practice in the late 1970s, Henderson wrote her manifesto for sustainability at her kitchen table. She then mailed it to over 300 environmental NGOs throughout the US and sensitized them through speeches and dialogues. Henderson argued that environmentalists should join with labor unions to strive for full-employment and invite them to work together for sustainability.

She recognized that the existing economic model, NAIRU, or non-accelerating inflation rate of unemployment, was not only inadequate but also unethical. The model presupposes an unemployment rate of 5.5 percent as a natural condition necessary for keeping inflation under control. This implies that it is inevitable for millions of job seekers to be unemployed as a price for a non-inflationary economy. The idea offended her sense of social justice. She decided to demonstrate that the NAIRU model was incorrect and that it would be possible to run an economy with a much lower rate of unemployment. This conviction was supported by her observation that the high level of inflation that the US economy was facing during those years was attributed chiefly to the soaring prices of natural resources, including oil from the Organization of Petroleum Exporting Countries (OPEC).

To propagate this principle, she relied solely on the effective use of information, applying her model of social change in practice. She avoided forming an organization of her own. Instead she encouraged each of the local environmental NGOs to incorporate her manifesto as part of the organization's mandate and to start a local advocacy group on its own called Environmentalists for Full-Employment. In the course of campaigning for this goal, Henderson actively traveled around the US and offered speeches and dialogues with environmentalist organizations and networks. She faced criticism from some elite environmentalists who argued that Henderson was propagating a socialist ideology. Despite the obstacles she encountered, the movement for establishing local Environmentalists for Full-Employment organizations expanded rapidly throughout the US. Momentum grew for an alliance of environmentalists and labor unions to work together toward the common goal of full-employment and sustainability.

Lessons learned from this episode include the insights into how a deep value commitment shapes a creative social change. Henderson's experience in the 1970s echoes another episode that she described in the interview. The experience involved developing a new economic indicator as an alternative to the widely accepted GNP model and producing an alternative financial news series based on the new principle. The two episodes share a pattern of thinking: from *what is* to *what ought to be*. In the episode of the 1970s, Henderson's act of creation started by identifying the problems such as the popular acceptance of high rates of unemployment. The process of problem identification grew in tandem with her deep criticism of the prevailing trends of thinking, including NAIRU. Her critical reflections opened the way toward envisioning and crystallizing an alternative to the status quo in the form of an NGO network for sustainability. Her vision guided her action to locate potential partners and sensitize them toward working together. In this respect, Henderson's act of creation emerged and evolved out of her value commitment to *what ought to be* transcending *what is*. With her value commitment, she was clearly seeing and naming prevailing paradigms of thinking that she wanted to challenge and transform, even from the very early stages of her advocacy activities.

Strongly linked to her style of value commitment is the way she resolves social conflict: reframing it in a broader context. In an attempt to overcome the tension between pro-job and pro-environment advocates, Henderson brought labor unions and environmental NGOs together, toward the shared goal of economic and social sustainability. Her act of reframing required uniting, bridging, and integrating actors and goals, instead of dividing, separating, and dissecting them. It was also intended to expand the time horizon from the present to the future, taking into account "the needs of our grandchildren," to quote Henderson. While reframing is a widely used technique for conflict resolution in general, Henderson's approach is more specifically geared toward a possible paradigm change by way of tackling a social conflict creatively. Her episode illustrates how the combined effect of reframing and integrating previously unconnected actors and goals can help create a new paradigm of social interaction. In short, hers is an approach to reframing across paradigms.

Finally, Henderson's experience exemplifies how to connect dots in a new way. To envision an act of creation, she starts with the working assumption that ingredients of social change already exist somewhere in society. In her view, what is important is not only the intellectual task of conceptualizing how to connect them, but also the actual work of going out in society and finding institutional allies for realizing the vision. Henderson has observed that potential allies often remain unaware of the presence of one another until somebody shows them how they can work together. In the present example, labor unions and environmental NGOs had not foreseen the possibility of partnership until Henderson and her allies began creating the Environmentalists for Full-Employment network to sensitize them. What enabled the partnership to emerge was the common goal of sustainability and the campaigners' hard work that weaved together the previously unconnected actors and goals in a new way.

Palestinian nonviolence: sharp resistance through empowerment
(Mubarak Awad)

Based on his background in the practice of active nonviolence, Mubarak Awad describes creativity as the capacity for organizing sharp, well-directed resistance to injustice by empowering large masses of people for social change. As president of the international NGO, Nonviolence International, he has educated Palestinians and helped them organize numerous nonviolence campaigns to resist Israeli military operations and occupation.

In 1985, Israeli troops seized a portion of the land in a Palestinian village near Bethlehem. About 500 people lived in the village, which was as small as three acres in size. Some people of the village came to Awad, who was working as an NGO-based activist and educator promoting grassroots nonviolence activities. They desperately wanted their land back from Israelis and sought Awad's help. After some discussion with the villagers, Awad told them,

> OK. You can go and take the land. Start taking out the fences built by Israelis on condition that you promise not to throw stones, you are all ready to be killed, nobody will run away, and nobody will even have vulgar language against the Israelis. Go and bring all the men, all the women, and everything. Let's do it.

While Awad told this to them, he somehow wished that they would never come back to him because the thought of taking such action scared him. But in three days, a fellow from the village came back and informed Awad that the whole village was ready to take action. They started removing the fences in front of Israeli soldiers and tanks. The Israelis soon started shooting. The villagers knew that it was their last day and they were all going to die. Despite the danger, the villagers persisted with their claim, took the fences down, and nobody ran away. Eventually an Israeli military commander came to the villagers and said, "Sorry. This land is yours. We apologize…" The Israelis then went to take land elsewhere. Awad claims that this episode illustrates the power of active nonviolence.

The nonviolent action described here clearly went against the norm of ordinary Palestinians in the region as of the mid-1980s. In Awad's observation, Palestinians usually remained quiet in the face of Israelis taking their land. They were afraid of Israeli guns. They did not want to fight for their land. Awad helped the people who were willing to fight nonviolently. But he saw many others who were unwilling to fight and lost their land. Despite the success of nonviolent action in the 1985 incident and months of celebration that followed in the village, Awad finds no evidence to suggest that nonviolence has gained sustained momentum in the village and that it has been continuously practiced since then.

Among many insights drawn from this episode, four points deserve attention for theory-building. First, the origination phase of the nonviolent action was inspired by exemplary successes experienced elsewhere. Before the 1985 incident, Awad frequently visited Palestinian villages and discussed nonviolence with villagers. He explained to them how Gandhi drove the British out of India. He also shared stories about nonviolence movements of women, students, and labor unions in other parts of the world. Some Palestinians later visited Awad to discuss their own problems, such as their trees being removed and their houses being demolished by Israelis. It is inferred that models of action taken by people in similar settings enabled the Palestinian villagers to choose the unconventional act of nonviolent resistance, instead of the conventional mode of resignation and obedience.

Second, Awad observes that despite the sustained efforts in public education for nonviolence, many Palestinians lacked sophistication to organize effective action. They did not know how to call journalists, human rights groups, governments, and other members of the international community to publicize their nonviolent action. Considering this challenge, Awad worked to empower Palestinians so that they could organize their campaign more effectively and create a political mechanism in which the public could learn about the deaths of nonviolent activists. In the 1985 incident and other cases, Awad observed that empowerment of ordinary people was the key to origination, and the absence of empowered masses limited the potential for initiating nonviolent social change.

Third, the villagers' commitment to risk-taking was essential for the origination of nonviolent action. Reflecting on this and other similar experiences, Awad observes that people take nonviolent action when they are deeply committed to their cause. He also stresses that people's commitment comes not only from altruism, but also from selfish motives. For example, some villagers who have taken decisive action for their self-interest remain silent about the lands confiscated in other villages. Some are unwilling to help fellow Palestinians in other villages plant trees to reciprocate the help they have previously received. Regardless of the exact nature of the villagers' motives, the firmness of their commitment distinguished their success in 1985 from their previous unsuccessful experiences under similar circumstances.

Finally, closely related to the firmness of their commitment was their sense of collective identity and leadership in the village. Reflecting on this and other episodes, Awad believes that pride and prestige play a crucial role in initiating nonviolent action in many Palestinian villages. Village leaders feel that they would lose face if their land were to be taken. When village leaders are willing to die for saving face, they tend to encourage fellow villagers to work together for their cause. The effectiveness of village leadership is inseparable from the sense of togetherness upheld by fellow villagers. Faced with common problems, some leaders and fellow villagers come to sense that they have to work together for the same cause, good or bad. When such a sense of togetherness grows, village leaders often demonstrate their willingness to take full responsibility for the consequences of their planned action, including the possible deaths of fellow villagers. In the 1985 incident, the villagers' pride, strengthened by their collective identity and their leaders' commitment, was essential to explain why they risked their lives to retake such a tiny piece of land. This observation is consistent with the fact that they celebrated their success for months after their small but significant victory.

The US–Vietnam War: adjusting power asymmetry through deep listening (Richard Falk)

Richard Falk is a Professor Emeritus of International Law at Princeton University. Based on his extensive experience in international law and politics, Falk argues that creativity is derived from listening to weaker parties deeply and correcting power asymmetry between conflict parties through law. He illustrates his understanding of creativity by referring to his 1968 visit to North Vietnam as a university professor and American peace activist working against the US military involvement in the region. The civil war between US-supported South Vietnam and socialist North Vietnam lasted from 1959 to 1975. The US intervened directly from 1965 to 1973. Salient issues included the North Vietnamese need for freedom from foreign oppression and socio-economic justice through a socialist reform, the South Vietnamese desire to deter invasions by North Vietnam by relying on Western support, and the US fear of communist expansion in Southeast Asia supported by the Soviet Union and China.

Before Falk left for the North Vietnamese capital, Hanoi, in June 1968 as a legal specialist and representative of American peace movements, the US State and Defense Secretaries asked him to deliver a letter to North Vietnamese leaders whom he was due to meet. The letter was to be given to Falk on condition that he would promise not to speak publicly against the war any more as a peace activist. Falk declined to deliver the letter because he felt obliged to maintain his integrity as an advocate for peace movements. To date, he does not know what message the letter contained.

When Falk went to North Vietnam, he was aware that he was the first American who could maintain contact with both American and North Vietnamese high-ranking officials as a peace activist and as an established university professor. Falk held several meetings with the North Vietnamese Prime Minister, Pham Van Dong, who outlined an acceptable framework for ending the war with the US. On returning to the US, Falk was interviewed by the *New York Times*, CBS

News, and other media organizations, gaining significant publicity. The *New York Times* covered Falk's visit to North Vietnam on the front page for a few days.

According to a *New York Times* report on July 12, 1968, messages brought back by Falk from the North Vietnamese leaders included their willingness to help form a coalition government with the Saigon-based regime in South Vietnam.[13] In late April 1968, influential urban intellectuals and professionals of neutralist and pacifist backgrounds formed an opposition political party, the Alliance of Nationalist, Democratic and Peace Forces, in South Vietnam. The North Vietnamese government supported the Alliance as a third force to help break the stalled talk about forming a coalition government by the North and South Vietnamese leadership. The top leaders of the Alliance included only one self-declared communist, Dr. Duong Quynh Hoa, who had been a member of the French Communist Party and was appointed Deputy-Secretary General of the party. In their conversations with Falk, Prime Minister Pham Van Dong and other senior officials expressed their commitment to supporting a proposed coalition of the Alliance and the existing Saigon-based regime to work together in South Vietnam. The South leadership reportedly dismissed the party formation as a ploy of North Vietnamese communists, and the proposed coalition government was never formed.

In Falk's opinion, this proposal of 1968 was more favorable to the US position than what National Security Adviser Henry Kissinger would later negotiate to achieve in 1972. The secret agreement reached in Paris by Kissinger and his North Vietnamese counterpart Le Duc Tho was that the US would accept North Vietnamese troops to stay in South Vietnam in exchange for the North Vietnamese acceptance of the US-supported Saigon regime to remain in power even after the withdrawal of the US troops.[14] It later became evident, however, that this arrangement did little to mitigate the conflict after the US withdrawal in 1973. Instead the arrangement paved the way for the North Vietnamese to take over Saigon in 1975 and establish a unified socialist country. Falk observes that as of 1968, the US government was not willing to consider what could have been a far better outcome that could have saved half the lives lost in the war. Because the proposal brought back by Falk was not accepted by the US, he sees his efforts only as a hypothetical success that failed to be realized.

While the episode falls short of depicting a holistic picture of creativity from a longitudinal perspective, it does illustrate how an unconventional approach could emerge and begin to take shape in defiance of a predominant discourse of war. Focusing mainly on the unconventionality component of creativity, three lessons are learned. First, the role and social status held by the interviewee became an indispensable condition for the unconventional and risky action to take place. As pointed out by Falk himself, the Logan Act in the US prohibited private citizens from engaging in diplomacy with foreign governments. Going to Vietnam in 1968 was potentially illegal. However, the fact that Falk held a professorship at a prestigious university and had testified on the Vietnam War in the US Senate hearings under the auspices of Senator Fulbright helped legitimize his trip. In addition, he discussed the reason for his trip before his departure in his meetings with his friends who held senior positions in the US government, including the Assistant Secretary of Defense and the Deputy Assistant Secretary of Defense. These personal relationships coupled with Falk's advantageous status helped him carry out his visit. Moreover, from his fellow peace activists' point of view, Falk made an ideal representative for these reasons. A proposition derived from this episode is that the social role and status held by the creator and the implementer go a long way toward either legitimizing or de-legitimizing creative action, and these factors may even serve as an indispensable prerequisite for origination.

Second, this episode, like many others collected in this study, epitomizes risk-taking as an enabling factor for creative action. Falk could have been arrested in the US or captured in North Vietnam at any moment in the summer of 1968 if it had not been for necessary conditions for his successful departure and return being met. In this sense, it is inferred that the stronger the structural inertia of the status quo, the more risks the creator has to face.

Third, this episode, unlike many others under study, illustrates at least one possible scenario where the potential of creative change emerged but later *failed* to evolve. In historical hindsight, one is tempted to ask: why did it fail? Empirically this question is not answerable because numerous factors came into play. However, reflections on this question offered by Falk himself suggest a useful starting point for exploring possible answers. He notes, for example, that he was too easily discouraged by the unwillingness of the US leadership to listen to him. He treated the US leadership as deaf and unable to listen. He was also too willing to accept the failure of his mission. In retrospect, however, he feels that he could have made more effort than he did. For example, he believes that he could have more effectively used his affiliation with Princeton University as well as the high-level contacts he had in the US State Department and Congress. He also believes that he could have done more public writing and speaking on the subject. Overall, he reflects that if he had been "less realistic and more dedicated," he could have created a more tangible impact. A lesson learned is that persistent engagement in the process and tenacious persuasion of those with the capacity to reshape the conflict is essential for initiating a transition from origination to evolution.

The Oslo peace process: stretching the envelope to its utmost
(Ron Pundak)

Ron Pundak was one of the Israeli intellectual architects and negotiators in the 1993 Oslo peace process that aimed to pave the way toward resolving the Israeli–Palestinian conflict. He reflects that creative negotiators think outside the conservative box, "but not necessarily in an avant-garde manner outside the body politic." To Pundak, the challenge in Oslo concerned how to work within the national consensus while "pushing the envelope to its utmost." The interview focused primarily on the events that had occurred in 1992 and 1993. Salient issues concerning the two nations include, but are not limited to, refugee repatriation, the status of Jerusalem, delineation of borders, and diverse arrangements to fulfill self-determination.

Working in Oslo as an unofficial arm of the Israeli deputy foreign minister Yossi Beilin and foreign minister Shimon Peres, Pundak and his senior colleague Yair Hirschfeld were able to introduce an innovative procedure of negotiation, which has been shaping the framework of Israeli–Palestinian negotiations continuously since Oslo. The procedure involves looking at a large picture of perceived outcomes, instead of delving into details first. It calls for looking at a possible future first, and then working backward to design immediate steps.

Pundak reflects that much creativity was demonstrated in the way draft documents were written. For example, when the representatives came to the second meeting in Oslo, they brought a unique agenda called "draft zero." In conventional Israeli–Palestinian negotiations, both parties brought their first drafts to the table. In those conventional negotiations, Israelis presented one draft and Palestinians another, and then they bargained to convince each other. But the draft zero was meant to be a draft *before* the first one. It included the ideas that the two Israeli negotiators heard from Palestinians in the preparatory meetings before Oslo, in the first Oslo meeting, and in the parallel local dialogues in Gaza and the West Bank. It also included what the two Israelis knew about the policy of Israel, areas of maneuvering on both sides, and some additional unexplored areas open to maneuverability. The draft zero encouraged the parties to refrain from extreme starting positions and hard bargaining. The negotiators attempted to jump beyond the conventional mode of unproductive haggling. Every time they sat for dialogue, they tried to bring fresh ideas in order to get closer to a possible endgame and move away from the beginning.

Another sign of creativity was the invention of the "I & P approach," or the Israel and Palestine approach, which came out of the first Oslo meeting. The idea was that whenever there was an agreement on particular sentences drawn from draft zero, the negotiators made it a rule to incorporate them into their "draft one." But whenever there was a need expressed for more deliberation on certain points, they either continued the discussion to solve the problems or juxtaposed dual positions, the Palestinian position marked as "P" and the Israeli position as "I." When dual positions were noted, the two sides bypassed those difficult parts for the time being and moved on to other issues. Despite these flexible steps taken, disagreements persisted over certain issues, leading the negotiations to bog down occasionally.

Creativity was also demonstrated in the principle of deniability. Because the dialogue participants were unofficial representatives, they enjoyed the flexibility of tentatively agreeing on certain issues, reflecting on them later, and coming back to say, "Sorry, we thought they would work but they actually won't." Moreover, the Oslo negotiators had less fear of possible leakage than official negotiators elsewhere because the unofficial parties could always deny and do away with whatever tentative agreements were under consideration.

In May 1993, five months after its beginning, the status of the Oslo negotiation was upgraded from informal to formal. Still the participants could continue to discuss openly and flexibly among themselves because their process remained as a back channel in Norway and it was away from public attention at home. Pundak reflects that the whole process continued to be filled with creativity, despite the transition from informal to formal status. At early stages of interactions, the two sides adopted a future-oriented win–win mode instead of a zero-sum game trapped in the past. The Norwegian setting offered a constructive atmosphere in which the participants could intensively work in a manner unbounded by conventional diplomatic codes of conduct. The absence of any third parties such as American observers was in favor of the process.

After the secret negotiations were revealed to the public in August 1993, the initiative was transferred from Oslo to Washington DC, where a formal Declaration of Principles was signed on September 13, 1993. Pundak observes that the outcome of the Oslo negotiations was no less creative than the process. Two examples illustrate outcome creativity. One is the "Gaza–Jericho first" approach. It was decided in the accord that Israelis were to retreat from Gaza and Jericho within three months of the signing of the agreement so as to enable the PLO to set up a self-governing authority, which would gradually lead Palestinians in East Jerusalem and other territories toward full autonomy.[15] Similar ideas about the status of Gaza and Jericho had been known for some time before Oslo, but the way they were translated into action was unprecedented. The second example of outcome creativity is what was stated in Annexes III and IV of the accord. These documents laid out the details of Israeli–Palestinian economic cooperation in a manner never attempted before.[16] For example, Annex III, Protocol of Israeli–Palestinian Cooperation in Economic and Development Programs, lays out joint development programs of cooperation in such fields as water, electricity, energy, finance, transport and communications, trade, industry, labor relations, social welfare, environment, and the media. More specifically, creativity was demonstrated on a number of fronts, such as the decision to conduct a feasibility study to create free trade zones in Gaza and Israel. Annex IV, Protocol on Israeli–Palestinian Cooperation Concerning Regional Development Programs, offers a blueprint of economic development programs not only in the West Bank and Gaza, but also in a broader Middle East context of the conflict, in anticipation of international financial support. Proposed regional projects include the establishment of a Middle East Development Bank and a joint Israeli–Palestinian–Jordanian plan to better utilize the Dead Sea area.

Pundak's reflections on the Oslo process suggest several propositions on the nature of creativity for resolving inter-group conflict and on the way creative action originates. First, a balance has to be struck between working within the existing framework of political consensus and stretching its boundaries to the utmost.[17] Theoretically, this balance requires assuring convergent thinking while exploring possibilities of acceptable divergence, or out-of-the-box thinking. One reason for seeking the balance between convergence and divergence is the dual need for political viability in the eyes of the constituencies, on the one hand, and unconventionality to get out of the long-standing impasse, on the other. In the case of Oslo, the commitment to the political consensus and convergent thinking was illustrated by the supervision of the entire process by high-ranking foreign ministry officials and the controlled exchange of views at the elite level. Pursuit of political consensus and legitimate representation was sought by establishing a direct link between the PLO and the Israeli government. Although the effort was distinctly different, and thus divergent in nature, from the parallel official talks in Washington DC, which excluded the PLO, it was convergent from the viewpoint of the Oslo negotiators who accepted the PLO as a legitimate negotiation partner. On the other hand, the desire for divergent, out-of-the-box thinking was illustrated in the form of secret unofficial negotiations away from public scrutiny at home. In addition, elements of what Pundak considered process and outcome creativity, such as draft zero, I & P, deniability, and Gaza–Jerico first, marked a departure from conventional modes of Israeli–Palestinian negotiations. In Pundak's view, despite these efforts to "stretch the envelope to its utmost," they stayed within the confines of broad political consensus, at least from the viewpoint of those who supported the Oslo accord.

Second, creative attributes of the negotiation process and outcome emerged from years of similar experiences and academic training on the part of the participants. According to Pundak, precursors of the various defining elements of the Oslo process had evolved gradually. Simply put, creativity had evolved from continuity. For example, a range of creative measures – such as the I & P approach and the deniability principle – emerged gradually and naturally from years of experience that the two Israeli negotiators, Yair Hirschfeld and Ron Pundak, had accumulated through their academic training in Middle East politics as well as in local unofficial dialogues with Palestinians. In 1989, for instance, Hirschfeld participated in "proximity talks" with Palestinian representatives in the Netherlands, through the mediation of the Dutch government. Because it was illegal to have direct Israeli–Palestinian contact at that time, the Israelis stayed at one hotel, the Palestinians at another hotel, and they exchanged ideas through the shuttle diplomacy of Dutch mediators. Pundak also practiced diplomacy and dialogue extensively for the Israeli government before Oslo. He reflects that the techniques and models of negotiation adopted in Oslo had evolved from the combined effect of knowledge, experience, and instinct stimulated by the participants' practical and academic background. Their prior experience in unconventional activities helped them think creatively about how to design the Oslo process out of the box. In this sense, the creative change did not emerge from scratch. Its precursors evolved from sustained engagements in similar efforts attempted elsewhere.

Third, the reasoning process used in Oslo, as well as in the subsequent bilateral negotiations in which Pundak participated, enabled the negotiators to envision long-term best-case scenarios first and then to think backward to decide immediate steps. It was a "future–present approach" in terms of the temporal sequence considered. Pundak contrasts this sequence with the "present–future approach" used in the failed talks at Camp David in 2000 between the Israeli and Palestinian delegations headed by Prime Minister Ehud Barak and PLO Chairman Yasir Arafat, respectively. In Pundak's view, the Camp David summit was doomed to collapse because the negotiators tried to build up agreements step-by-step from the present to a possible future, instead of envisioning possible end results first. Although the perceived link between the future–present approach and the effectiveness of negotiation is still to be examined empirically, its plausibility suggested by Pundak is noteworthy given the historical breakthrough made in Oslo.

Fourth, the social climate of the venue helped the negotiators explore unconventional ideas in a significant manner. The setting prepared in Oslo invited openness, flexibility, and joint exploration unconstrained by public attention and directive third-party intervention. Pundak's observation on this point is consistent with the literature in psychology that suggests positive correlation between an open, informal climate and creative thinking.

Fifth, creating such a confidential congenial climate of communication required risk-taking on the part of the participants whose constituencies remained hostile to one another. As Pundak mentioned, the Israeli and Palestinian negotiators in Oslo constantly felt fear of possible leakage, which would have jeopardized months of their efforts at any moment. Because creating ways to change the momentum of conflict necessarily defies those wanting the conflict to continue, risk-taking is considered an essential element of creativity.

Sixth, beyond the immediate environment, or the micro climate, of the talks, the macro socio-political context of parallel negotiations played a significant role in defining the value of the Oslo process as a creative alternative to failed talks elsewhere. From October to December 1991, about a year before the preparatory meeting for Oslo was held in December 1992, multi-party Arab–Israel negotiations were held in Madrid under the leadership of US State Secretary James Baker. Subsequent meetings continued at the US State Department in Washington DC until June 1993. Observing these official talks at that time, Pundak was certain that they were bound to fail because they did not include PLO representatives. He also recalls that the talks in Washington DC stalled with the political crisis triggered by the Israeli deportation of Hamas and Islamic Jihad members. Seeing the failure of the official negotiations, the representatives in Oslo came to realize that theirs was the only channel making progress. The relative value of the unofficial Oslo talks increased as the official Washington talks failed. In hindsight, important questions surface: What if the official talks in Washington DC produced significant outcomes? Would Oslo have mattered as much as it actually did? No definitive answers are forthcoming to these counterfactual questions. Yet one can reasonably infer that Oslo would have been less significant and less dramatic if it had not been for the failure of the alternative official channels. By the time the Oslo talks were revealed in public in August 1993, some two months after the Washington talks came to an end, public readiness for a surprise effect peaked against the backdrop of pervasive hopelessness. The interdependence between the failures in Washington DC and the relative success in Oslo offered a unique historical context in which the creative qualities of the process and outcome of Oslo were readily appreciated by many. In short, the macro socio-political context mattered as a prerequisite for creative acts in Oslo to be appreciated as such.[18]

Finally, to appraise the creative process in Oslo comprehensively, one cannot avoid asking the important question: Why did it fail in the end? Clearly the question exceeds the scope of this inquiry, partly because numerous factors beyond the Oslo negotiators' control came into play between the 1993 accord and its demise in the following years. However, related and more focused questions can be asked for creativity research: Were there any enabling factors of creativity in the Oslo accord that inhibited its implementation? Or more broadly, is there any correlation between the perceived "success" in its origination phase and the apparent failure in the acceptance and sustenance? To answer these questions, consideration of the post-1993 political situation in Palestine and Israel is essential. The demise of the Oslo process was crystallized by the Palestinian Intifada, or uprising, that was triggered by Israeli General Ariel Sharon's public visit to the Muslim shrines atop the Temple Mount on September 28, 2000. Yet clearly, the momentum for an all-out military confrontation had been building for years before 2000. Milestone events that had built the destabilizing momentum included the assassination of Israeli Prime Minister Yitzhak Rabin in November 1995 by a religiously motivated Jewish nationalist; the victory in Israeli elections of the right-wing Likud led by Benjamin Netanyahu, replacing the pro-Oslo Labor Party in May 1996; and numerous acts of terror carried out throughout the 1990s by Palestinian militants of Hamas and other Islamist groups opposing the Oslo accord.

Analyses abound by conflict researchers and historians about why Oslo eventually failed. For example, the Middle East history specialist Arthur Goldschmidt (2002) observes that the combined effect of Palestinian extremists' acts and the shifts in Israeli domestic politics accounts for the demise of Oslo. On the other hand, Johan Galtung, a Norwegian peace researcher familiar with the host country, points out twelve reasons for Oslo's failure, including the following:

> Extremists, meaning Hamas and Likud/Orthodox, were excluded. The agreement was between PLO and Labor/Secular-Modern; probably related to the Norwegian social democrat idea that "reason is in the middle." This works in moderate Norway, but not when more than 50% may feel excluded. They also have peace concepts. When excluded they will announce themselves (like killing Rabin, like suicide bombing).
> (Galtung 2004: 108)

The observations of Goldschmidt, Galtung, and many others evaluating the Oslo process make it harder to reject the inference that there *was* a problem built into the origination phase which, combined with other factors, let the acceptance and sustenance phases fail. According to this line of reasoning, it appears that enabling factors of Oslo's origination such as confidentiality, informality, flexibility, and non-extremists' representation ran counter to the plausible conditions for successful acceptance and sustenance. These conditions included public legitimization of agreements and broad-based consensus-building for the kind of policy that could have incorporated non-mainstream positions. This inference on the tension between the micro context of decision-making and the macro context of policy implementation has been popularized by such conflict researchers as Herbert Kelman (1993), who refers to the former as change and the latter as transfer.

For the purpose of creativity research, this proposition has to be carried a step further. As far as the Oslo process is concerned, it is plausible that the enabling factors for its *unconventionality*, which facilitated the origination phase, became limiting factors for its *viability*, particularly in the acceptance and sustenance phases. For example, the secret informal dialogue between the Labor-supported Israelis and PLO representatives was conducive to "pushing the envelope to its utmost," to use Pundak's terms. But the very same condition that assured out-of-the-box thinking made it inevitable to preclude the perspectives of Hamas, Likud, and others, who later rendered the Oslo framework unworkable by channeling their dissent through coercive means. In short, one may argue that there was indeed a correlation between the origination and the acceptance/sustenance. It is also plausible that the factors facilitating these phases were contradictory to one another, at least within the unique context of the Oslo process. Whether this proposition has a wider appeal beyond this particular case is still to be explored in comparison with other cases.

Interlude (1): reflections on conflict parties' creativity

Analysis of the five episodes has generated a range of working propositions on the nature, origination, and other aspects of conflict resolution creativity. This interlude recapitulates them succinctly in preparation for an integrative theory-building exercise that will be conducted in Chapter 3. Due to the very nature of abstraction and theorization being undertaken, each of the working propositions represents nothing more than a partial, fragmentary element of the given organic context – historical, geographic, and relational – from which the particular element is extrapolated and de-contextualized. Inherent danger lies in the inductive reasoning of this kind: these working propositions have to be formulated devoid of *contingency*, a quintessential condition for building social theory and applying it to reality. This means that induction of abstract attributes from concrete cases, if performed without caution, obscures or even ignores a set of empirical conditions under which the theoretical propositions are held tenable.

Given this theoretical background, it is emphasized that the working propositions listed in this interlude do not represent well-refined theories with contingencies spelled out and built into them. Instead, they merely reflect "pre-theoretical" ingredients and building blocks, some of which will be integrated later in Chapter 3 for the purpose of more systematic theory-building. Consequently, each of the working propositions under consideration may appear tenable in the specific episode from which it is drawn, but the same proposition may appear completely untenable or even antithetical to conflict resolution creativity in a distinctly different context under study. To compile the following list of preliminary findings, therefore, all the context-specific attributes, which may or may not be generalizable across contexts, are kept intact, in anticipation of a systematic, comparative analysis for theory-building in Chapter 3.

Exploration 41

"Accidental teenage pregnancies" – Linda Johnston:

1. Frustration from previously unsuccessful attempts and the unconventional mode of exploration became a precursor in this particular context.
2. Unexpected encounters with shocking revelations may open one's mind to a new mode of thinking.
3. Self-reflective capacity and humility to reshape one's identity and value facilitates creativity.
4. Reaffirming one's value commitment and identity orientation helps to persevere in realizing creative shifts despite obstacles.

Environmentalists for Full Employment – Hazel Henderson:

1. A forward-looking value commitment to a future vision (that is, sustainability in this case) helps to identify problems, criticize reality, and create alternatives.
2. Reframing issues within a broader context stimulates creativity, even across paradigms.
3. A creative social change requires defining and bridging actors and goals in a new way.

Palestinian nonviolence – Mubarak Awad:

1. Exemplary images of Gandhi and other models of active nonviolence inspired the unconventional action.
2. Empowerment of activists is essential for the origination of nonviolent action.
3. People's deep commitment to their cause convinces them to take risks necessary for creativity.
4. Community leaders' commitment and their members' collective identity strengthened their resolve in this incident.

The US–Vietnam War – Richard Falk:

1. Influential social status and personal relationships made the unconventional action possible.
2. Risk-taking in the face of social resistance was essential for creative action to emerge.
3. The process failed to evolve after origination partly because of the lack of tenacious persuasion.

The Oslo peace process – Ron Pundak:

1. A balance was struck between working within the existing framework of political consensus and stretching its boundaries.
2. Precursors of the process emerged from extensive practical and academic experiences of analogous types.

3   The negotiators explored long-term best-case scenarios first and immediate steps second.
4   The open, flexible, and exploratory climate free from public scrutiny stimulated creative ideas.
5   The negotiators took risks to be creative in Oslo while their constituencies back home remained hostile to one another.
6   The macro social context, including the failure of parallel official negotiations, enhanced the relative value of agreements produced by the informal Oslo process.
7   The unconventional nature of the problem-solving process, though conducive to origination, limited the effectiveness and ethicality of acceptance.

The approaches taken by Awad, Falk, and Pundak were concerned primarily with conflict resolution *processes*, namely, ways of dealing with the conflicts rather than devising the actual substance of possible resolution *outcomes*. The actions taken by Johnston and Henderson had both substantive and procedural elements. Despite these and other differences, there were important similarities with respect to the origination phase. In all five cases, there was the awareness of conventional reality shaping and sustaining the conflict. Conflict resolution creativity, at least in the self-reported terms of the interviewees, emerged in such a way as to reshape and restructure how the conflict ought to be understood. In the case of the teenage pregnancies episode presented by Johnston, for example, the unquestioned assumption of the clinic staff was that the pregnancies had been accidental. Johnston's act of creativity emerged as a result of challenging that common sense and reshaping the value conflict into a collaborative working relationship with teens. Similarly, the Oslo peace process materialized when the long-standing denial of the PLO's representative capacity was reversed through an unofficial and unconventional mode of direct bilateral talks. In all five cases, the initiatives for breaking the conventional boundaries required significant risk-taking on the part of the initiators. Risk-taking was made possible by their commitment to certain ideologies, needs, values, and worldviews. In the case of Johnston, for example, the commitment was made to the need for community service. For Pundak and his Israeli colleagues, it was the practical necessity of dealing with the PLO as a Palestinian counterpart in direct bilateral talks.

As will be discussed later, these features of conflict parties' creativity are not categorically different from those of intermediaries' creativity as far as the origination phase is concerned. However, the two types of episodes differ appreciably with respect to how creative processes and outcomes come to be accepted or rejected. Among the key factors distinguishing between the two types is the role of *constituents* represented by the perceived creators, that is, the leaders spearheading social change. This subject will be revisited in the next interlude and discussed more fully after intermediaries' creativity is illustrated for comparison.

Intermediaries' creativity

Overview

The nine episodes that illustrate intermediaries' creativity are summarized in Table 2.2 for an overview. The episodes are listed in the order of appearance in this section.

The nine approaches are considered relatively impartial despite the different roles played by the interviewees. For example, Burton, Kelman, and Volkan played the role of academic consultants and facilitators in problem-solving workshops, or Track-Two dialogues, in which their impartiality was an essential requirement for staying engaged. Diamond's bicommunal activities in Cyprus also illustrate Track-Two peace-building facilitated by an impartial third party, but her emphasis was more on training and support for the actual implementation of locally initiated projects, beyond academic consultancy.

On the other hand, Smith (pseudonym) worked for an American state agency as a mediator, Osman represented the Organization of African Unity (OAU), and Törnudd served the Finnish government that sought to maintain neutral status between the US and Soviet camps. These three processes of third-party intervention were all bound by institutional frameworks and mandates to refrain from being overtly partial to one side or the other. Finally, Tehranian and Galtung intervened in more informal capacities, the former as a private citizen and the latter as an NGO-based peace worker, without vested interests in the resolution outcomes apart from the overarching goal of making peace.[19]

Episodes of intermediaries' creativity

A racial conflict in Tajikistan: appealing to the parties' inner resources (Majid Tehranian)

As an Iranian scholar-practitioner trained in political economy at Harvard, Majid Tehranian views creativity as a historical process of "getting out of the box" while staying fully conscious of historical memories that constrain people within the box. He identifies leadership as a particularly important factor to let people out of the box. Having taught at Harvard, Oxford, Tufts, Tehran, and elsewhere, Tehranian currently holds a visiting faculty position at the Soka University of America in California. He was the first director of the Toda Institute for Global Peace and Policy Research from 1996 to 2008 and continues to serve the Institute as a senior advisor. The Toda Institute is a multidisciplinary network of over 600 peace scholars across the five continents working collaboratively on such issues as human security, global governance, social justice, and global economy. As a practitioner, he facilitates dialogues among academicians and influential opinion leaders across cultures and civilizations. In the conflict episode on Tajikistan discussed in the interview, Tehranian played the role of an impartial intermediary outside his professional capacity.

The episode concerns a small-scale conflict against the historical and political background of racism, ethnic tension, and post-socialist industrialization. In

Table 2.2 Summary of the nine episodes of intermediaries' creativity

Interviewee	Region and time	Role	Episode	Definition
Majid Tehranian	Tajikistan, 1992	Informal mediator	Mediated a conflict between a Nigerian passenger and Tajik and Russian airport staff over prohibited carry-on baggage. Appealed to the parties' religious and cultural values to help them reconcile with one another	Getting out of the box while staying fully conscious of historical memories that constrain people within the box
John Smith (pseudonym)*	US, mid-1990s	Government mediator	Labor mediation between teachers' union and management. Stepped out of neutrality, proposed a substantive settlement, and took no follow-up questions. Prevented a possible public crisis by breaking accepted rules of labor mediation	Inventing new options and helping parties invent ones. Persuasion different from inventiveness
Abdullahi Said Osman	Sierra Leone, 1994	International organization representative, conciliator, and mediator	Civil war in Sierra Leone. The opposition hiding in the bush, inaccessible. As OAU representative, formed a joint committee with the UN and the Commonwealth. Successfully communicated with the opposition through the Pope's local representative as a go-between	Building a new basis for working together and going beyond conventional means of mediation
John Burton	Southeast Asia, 1960s	University-based scholar, facilitator, and consultant	Convened informal confidential meetings to resolve the conflict between Indonesia, Malaysia, and Singapore; pioneered Track-Two problem-solving workshops; demonstrated conflict resolution as an alternative to power politics	Discovering common needs and new possibilities through in-depth conflict analysis, outside the paradigm of power politics
Herbert Kelman	Israel–Palestine, 1970s	University-based dialogue facilitator	The conflict between the Israeli and Palestinian national movements as background. His first Israeli–Palestinian workshop invited a PLO representative, enabling him to discover legitimate representation and mutual recognition as a key to resolution	Thinking outside traditional frameworks, across disciplines, but contextualizing ideas for applicability

Name	Location, Date	Role	Activity	Approach
Vamik Volkan	Estonia, mid-1990s	University-based psychoanalyst and dialogue facilitator	Co-facilitated psychoanalytic dialogue between Estonians and Russians. Held a community party for local politicians near a former Soviet military site that Estonians took over for dangerous live target practice. Helped them realize their chosen traumas from Soviet rule and urged them to stop the exercise	Playing with symbols in such a way as to make destructive potential of conflicts less destructive
Louise Diamond	Cyprus, 1990s	NGO-based trainer and advocate	Helped Greek and Turkish Cypriots organize bi-communal activities despite the inter-communal conflict, with the commitment to grassroots-based conflict transformation and reconciliation	Activating different modes of thinking outside daily routines
Klaus Törnudd	Europe and North America, early-to-mid-1970s	Diplomat, negotiator, and moderator	The Helsinki process. Multilateral talks convened by Finland to improve communication between the US and Soviet camps. Sustained dialogue with no vetoes, equal status of all, comprehensive agenda-setting with three "baskets," and confidence-building measures. Successful evolution into CSCE/OSCE	Coming up with new formulas and expressions which help to persuade negotiating parties
Johan Galtung	Peru–Ecuador, mid-1990s.	NGO-based consultant and mediator	Created a binational ecological zone in the disputed border area, transcending the parties' long-standing commitment to drawing a border line	Transcending incompatible goals through Hegelian synthesis; quantum jump

NOTE

* The interviewee, a professional American mediator with decades of distinguished experience in dispute resolution in the United States, is bound by a confidentiality agreement with conflict parties and wishes to refrain from using his real name. His pseudonym, John Smith, was adopted by the author and will be used throughout this book.

1992, Tehranian was traveling in Tajikistan. The time period coincided with the second year of the civil war triggered by the fighting between former communists in power and opposition groups seeking more equitable political representation in the newly independent nation. When he was about to leave the country and was waiting for his flight at the airport, he saw an African man being attacked and overwhelmed by two white men. The outraged African man was cursing the other two.

Tehranian approached the African man and asked, "What happened? Brother, what can I do to help you?" After some conversation, Tehranian learned that the man was from the Ibos of Nigeria. Tehranian told him, "I know the Ibos are wise people," and inquired more about why he had come to be involved in the trouble. The man told Tehranian that he was a university student in Moscow and was visiting Tajikistan. When this incident happened, he was on his way back to Nigeria. The student bought a bulky air conditioner in Tajikistan and wanted to carry it on the plane and bring it back to Nigeria. He paid the airport staff $100 to check it in. However, the two men, one being a Tajik policeman and the other being the Russian husband of the Tajik airport employee who handled his check-in procedure, stopped him. The student was told that it was illegal to take anything of industrial value out of Tajikistan. The law was meant to protect the still unstable economy in the newly independent country from being exposed to unrestricted commercial competition. When the Nigerian student asked the staff to get his $100 back, they replied defiantly, "Which $100?" The reply further infuriated the student. He protested to the airport staff but he was beaten up. The student told Tehranian that he was determined to shoot the staff to take revenge on their racist action. Tehranian also learned that the student's rage grew even further because of the racial tension he sensed between Russians and Africans in Moscow. The student pointed out a recent incident in which a few African students were killed in Moscow, presumably because they went out with Russian women.

After hearing the student's complaints, Tehranian asked him, "What's your religion?" The student replied, "I'm a Christian." Tehranian asked him further, "Do you remember the scene of Christ being crucified?" invoking the sense of Christian forgiveness in the student's mind. The student burst into tears. Tehranian told him that it would not be worth taking revenge. He also suggested the student to forget about the $100 and return the air conditioner to the shop in order to get his money back. However, the student complained, "They took not only my money but also my passport! I can't travel without my passport." Hearing this, Tehranian suggested, "OK. What if I talk to them and get your passport back? Can you forget about the $100?" The student accepted Tehranian's suggestion.

Tehranian walked over to the Tajik airport employee at the receptionist desk. She was the person with whom the student had argued earlier about his air conditioner. Seeing the persistent protest of the African man, the Tajik woman called her Russian husband, who came and, together with the Tajik policeman, beat up the student. As a native speaker of Persian, Tehranian spoke to the woman in Tajik, a Persian dialect. Hearing Tehranian's suggestion, she said, "OK. We can get the passport back to him.... But we have already initiated a police report on this incident. So in fact, it may be difficult to get the passport back." In the meantime, the Nigerian student reaffirmed his willingness not to pursue his $100 anymore. Tehranian told the attendant, "You Tajik are very hospitable people. You are generous to people from foreign countries. The African gentleman is a foreigner visiting your country for a short period of time. After some reflections, he now promises to be more reasonable." Eventually the airport employee agreed to give the passport back. Because Tehranian's departure time was fast approaching, he had to leave the site without seeing what was to follow from his mediation effort. The episode was a small incident that lasted for a brief period of time. But it contained many important historical and socio-political factors in the background.

At the heart of Tehranian's approach to mediation was his conscious appeal to the *higher ideas* that mattered to the parties. For the Nigerian student, Tehranian appealed to the image of Jesus and the meaning of Christian forgiveness. The man appeared to be suddenly awakened to his inner voice, imploring "Lord Jesus! Please forgive me." For the Tajik woman, he appealed to the Tajik culture of hospitality. Both parties accepted Tehranian's appeals and began working toward resolving the conflict. Yet why did they accept his appeals? One possible interpretation of the parties' inner shifts is that having activated their cultural and religious values, they began reflecting critically on their frames of mind that generated the conflict. It appeared that their inner shifts allowed their position-taking attitudes to subside and let more empathetic feelings to come out. Tehranian's act of creation, motivated by his own value commitment to anti-racism, encouraged the parties to make their own value commitments. This process of inner change entailed not only creativity but also other qualities of conflict resolution, such as empathy and humanization. Tehranian's practice of moral creativity is similar to that of several other interviewees who pointed out value commitment as an enabling factor for creative social change. On the other hand, Tehranian's method is distinctly different from many others' approaches because his appeal to higher ideas is intended to help the conflict parties invoke their morality and their creativity from within, instead of introducing intermediaries' creativity to the parties.

An American labor dispute: throwing the mediator rulebook out of the window (John Smith – pseudonym)

As a leading practitioner of dispute settlement in the US, John Smith (pseudonym) describes the creativity of third-party neutrals as the ability to come up with new ideas and help conflict parties come up with new ideas themselves. He stresses that creativity must be distinguished from other qualities necessary for mediation, such as the ability to persuade parties to accept creative options. Since the 1970s, Smith has served in over 2,000 cases of dispute in the US, involving such issues as labor, business, environment, and government. He has worked as a mediator, arbitrator, administrative law judge, and in other neutral capacities. Currently Smith directs a self-initiated project aimed at integrating separate strands of conflict resolution into a whole that justifies being called a field. Before establishing the current project, Smith was director of another self-initiated multi-year project that intended to build mutually beneficial relationships between conflict resolution researchers and practitioners. The episode that he chose to illustrate his understanding of creativity is a labor dispute that he mediated in the early-to-mid-1990s in a rural town of the US.

To introduce the subject of third-party creativity at the most elementary level, Smith uses a hypothetical labor dispute in which a union demands a 3 percent wage increase and the management sticks to the initial offer of 2.5 percent. In this scenario, one of the typical solutions that come to mind is to introduce a flexible understanding of *time*: the management offers 2.5 percent for the initial few months and asks the union to wait until the new annual budget allows the management to provide a 3 percent increase *later* in the year. For experienced labor mediators, this thought process is hardly creative. But for novice mediators, inventing options of this kind requires creativity. Smith believes that the basic pattern of thinking remains generally applicable to those who seek to be creative as intermediaries. In his view, the process of third parties' creation requires listening carefully to what the parties say they need, understanding what they really need, and seeing what they are not seeing that more or less answers their expressed needs.

The conflict episode that Smith described to illustrate his understanding of creativity concerns a union comprised of about 200 teachers and based in a rural town. One of the salient issues involved in the case was the political tension that surfaced between them when their contract expired. American unions generally work under contracts with employers. When their contracts expire, their conflicts surface. When a contract becomes due for renewal, all the politics in public–employer relations come to bear on the employers' side and all the internal politics in the union come to bear on the union side. A range of difficult issues surface. In this particular instance, the teachers' union and the employers tried to resolve many of the difficult issues on their own, but they failed. They did not hire outside facilitators to help them resolve their dispute, unlike many similar cases. The result was that the stakeholders on both sides became extremely frustrated and outraged. Finally they filed a request for mediation with the state agency where Smith was working. The agency assigned him to mediate the case because of his familiarity with disputes of this nature.

After some assessment, Smith realized that the parties were barely keeping their temper under control. The political relations were deteriorating rapidly between the two parties, and within each party. He could not even bring them together in the same room. In the lengthy conversations with Smith, neither side made a proposal because any offer made by anybody could have been seen as inflammatory. Outside the meeting rooms, both sides were making emotional statements in the media and rallying public support for their positions. Political tension was peaking. The union expressed their readiness to go on strike. It was clear that a crisis was looming, with the possibility of far-reaching consequences. Despite these negative signs, Smith began to see a possible way of settlement after numerous hours of conversation with each side.

The nature of creativity that Smith exercised had two interrelated aspects: substance (outcome) and procedure (process). On the substantive level, Smith could envision a complete package of settlement which would allow each party to barely live with the result. Twenty or so elements in the package included such conventional issues as wage and health insurance. He was able to envision how to write various pieces of contractual language in such a way that both sides could live with the outcome. He balanced a number of elements of the monetary offer by the employer to the union. The offer included mathematically complicated wage proposals. The teacher wage structure was designed in the form of an extremely complicated chart. The chart was so structured that if a 3 percent increase was to be made for a certain category of employees, it would make a substantial difference in the whole chart and the total budget for wages. Smith came up with a chart that would allow each side to barely secure a majority vote to adopt it. In addition, he came to see where the alliances stood on each side that would allow various compromises to be made and others not to be made. He also sensed who cared, and how much, about what composition of issues among all the people on both sides.

On the procedural level, creativity was demonstrated by the highly unconventional process through which Smith proposed the package and a follow-up process. He noticed that the most serious problem was the fact that the emotionally charged parties could not afford to put a proposal together by themselves, although its content was becoming increasingly clear to him. Because they were deeply aggrieved, neither side could formulate an offer without insulting the other side. Considering the extremely inflammatory relationships between the parties, Smith could not let anybody make an offer. Making an offer would have been taken as "bad news" and even as a betrayal to those committed to their stated positions. Therefore, despite being in the position of a neutral third party, Smith decided to make an offer himself. Unlike international mediators, labor mediators do not usually make an offer because they are expected to remain impartial. In this instance, Smith went beyond the conventional mode of labor mediation.

He set specific rules for the parties, the kind of which he had never set and which he hopes he never has to set again. Because of the high tension, he could not afford to let the parties discuss various elements of his proposal, nor could he afford to let the parties work together to build a mutually satisfactory deal. Therefore he decided to present a one-time comprehensive package deal that would leave no room for questioning by the parties. His decision was justified in his mind because if he were to answer their questions, he would have been asked to discuss what he had learned about the sensitive politics of each side, which the parties themselves could not share without inflaming their relationships further.

Smith structured his discussion with the parties carefully. First, he took the chief negotiator of each side out in the hall, following a common procedure of labor mediation. He told the chief negotiators that he had an unconventional idea in mind and that it would be the only way that might keep the situation from getting worse. In his mind, the idea had a good chance of succeeding. He shared a rough outline of his offer with both representatives in confidence so that it could be kept from the rest of the group members. After Smith explained the outline to the chief representatives, he told them that he was ready to present it to other people but he would not take any questions about it. He then asked the chief negotiators if the proposal might fly. The two looked at each other nervously and told him that it might. Smith sought the chief negotiators' permission to make the offer to other group members. The two agreed. He then described what steps he would take to make the offer. The representatives again agreed.

With their agreement, Smith met with each group separately. He told each party that he was ready to make a proposal to each side if agreeable to them. But he also told them that he was going to set rules under which he would present the proposal. The rules were spelled out as follows:

- The two sides come into the same room.
- The mediator explains *exactly* what the parties need to do to settle the case.
- No questions may be asked.
- The meeting is over as soon as the proposal is explained.
- The mediator will never see the parties again.

In addition, Smith told each party the following:

> This is the last thing I can do for you. This is the best I can do for you. There is a lot of trade-off involved in it. There is a lot of unhappiness involved in it. But if you don't do this, all of you are going to be extremely unhappy. Things can get much worse or a little better. A little better is what I can offer, and I have a way that is expected to work for you. But there is only one way I can do this: my way or not at all. I would like you to give me permission to present my offer to you. But when I do so, my mediation is over.

Each side agreed on Smith's procedure. He then brought the two groups together. To prepare for this joint session, he had spent half an hour writing down the exact details of his offer and checking them first by himself and then with the chief negotiator of each side before presenting it to the two parties. He told the parties that the offer was meant to be their settlement. The meeting was called off as soon as the offer was explained.

For a follow-up procedure, Smith suggested that the two parties should meet again separately in two different locations one week later. In the follow-up meetings, the chief negotiators and their constituents were asked to discuss whether they could live with the offer. In addition, the chief negotiators were asked to inform Smith about the result of their meetings. Smith was told that a week later, both sides adopted the deal. In fact, it was Smith who had to call the parties two weeks later to learn that they had adopted it. His follow-up phone calls were necessary because the mediator became extremely unimportant to the parties as soon as the dispute was settled.

Smith reflects that his procedural creativity was demonstrated when he threw the mediation rulebook out of the window. He believes that it was an act of creativity because it violated all the rules of mediation. His justification for this exceptional action is that anything else would not have worked in that context. When Smith started his career as a mediator, he was told that mediation was the only field in which there were no tools or no rules. In this instance, he violated all the conventional rules. He abided by the rule of no rules.

In his judgment, the case was exceptional and called for an exceptional approach. His approach was a directive way of telling the parties to take his offer as a final settlement or otherwise have no offer at all. Usually, labor mediators do not risk making such a take-it-or-leave-it offer because if the offer is rejected, they cease to be useful to conflict parties. Only when mediators can continue to influence parties' decisions can they be effective and useful. In this case, Smith judged that his job was already over at the point of making his offer. He sensed that the action he chose to take should be taken regardless of whether the parties ended up with accepting or rejecting his offer. In his mind, the content of the risky one-time offer needed to be absolutely right and appealing because there was no second chance. Yet Smith knew that he would have nothing to lose because he could see only one possible settlement that might fly. In addition, time was running out as he anticipated the possibility of crisis emerging any moment.

Smith's episode and reflections offer a unique window of opportunity to understand the nature of creativity exercised within a well-institutionalized context of mediation practice, particularly in the US. To start with, it must be noted that his creativity emerged when he threw the mediation rulebook out of the window. His action contradicted accepted rules partly because there were well established rules of American labor mediation and Smith was intimately familiar with them. As in many other "conventional" forms of dispute-handling procedure – ranging from Western litigation to the Hawaiian *ho'oponopono* method of community-based reconciliation – practitioners following established norms and rules are expected to operate within them. As an experienced labor mediator, Smith was well versed in conventional procedural rules, parties' and other stakeholders' expectations, the roles of chief negotiators and their constituents, their career perspectives at stake, flows of time, momentum of bargaining, institutional structures of the union and management, boundaries between tolerable and intolerable negotiation behavior, the nature of issues, typical contractual language, and numerous other factors that shaped his practice. Because these factors had been routinized, institutionalized, and embedded deeply in the stakeholders' mindset, it was easy for Smith to imagine how to break the conventional framework of practice, while it was extremely difficult and risky for him to actually break it.[20] Although it remains unclear whether the parties themselves perceived conventionality and unconventionality the same way the mediator did, it is evident that Smith's act of creativity came into fruition partly because of the well-established conventions that defined unconventionality, at least from the mediator's perspective.

Smith's experience illustrates an epistemological process where the thorough knowledge of what is expected to work conventionally helps people anticipate what is not likely to work and go on to envision what might work outside accepted boundaries. The episode illustrates the dynamic tension between conventionality and unconventionality, where out-of-the-box thinking was born out of the urgency to remedy perceived deficiencies of conventional practice. In other words, the mastery of conventionality gave birth to the need and capacity for unconventionality.

This observation directs one's attention to the relationship between paradigm-breaking and paradigm-accepting creativity. As discussed earlier, paradigm-breaking creativity involves divergence from the accepted paradigm of practice, in line with Thomas Kuhn's main thesis in his classic *The Structure of Scientific Revolutions*. On the other hand, paradigm-accepting creativity refers to unconventional viability sought within the accepted paradigm of practice. Reflecting on Smith's episode, one realizes that his pathway to the out-of-the-box solution illustrates part of Kuhn's thesis. Kuhn argues that sustained thorough-going pursuits in paradigm-accepting practice, known as puzzle-solving, may lead to a discovery of its limitations, direct one's attention to the need to overcome the paradigm, and eventually open a path to create a new paradigm that transcends the limitations. Because Smith had thoroughly mastered the paradigm-accepting practice of dispute resolution after handling some 2,000 cases, it is plausible that he had already walked through nearly all known pathways of conventional puzzle-solving before he encountered this exceptional case. When he chose to take the unconventional path, he knew, at least in his own subjective judgment, that all known alternative pathways were closed, mainly because of the highly volatile political circumstances. Although caution must be exercised in any inference that draws on limited factual information, Smith's episode appears to illustrate at least one plausible pathway from paradigm-accepting, puzzle-solving practice to paradigm-breaking creativity in Kuhnian terms.

Another lesson learned from Smith's reflections is that his act of creativity was contingency-based,[21] consistent with the experiences of many other interviewees. He chose the unconventional course of action because he was conscious that many of the presumed factors for successful mediation were readily available. His risk-taking behavior was contingent on those factors. Particularly essential among them were the chief negotiators' ability to maintain confidentiality during the one-week cooling-off period, their capacity to fully explain Smith's proposal to their constituents, and the timing of the pre-crisis situation in which public actions with devastating consequences were coming any moment. In the interview, Smith reflected that had it not been for the sense of extreme urgency, he would not have performed the act of creativity that he dared to undertake. His reflections indicate that his decision for risk-taking was contingent on the rational thinking of causality, prognosis, and prevention supplemented by intuition and experiential knowledge. Therefore, the episode illustrates a contingency-based process of creation where the practitioner's conscious appeal to his conflict theory determined whether, when, and how to break boundaries of conventionality.

The civil war in Sierra Leone: joint appeals through local communication channels (Abdullahi Said Osman)

According to Abdullahi Said Osman, creativity consists of devising an innovative approach, setting new processes in search of peace and stability, generating new visions, and establishing a new basis from which actors can work together to resolve conflict. He emphasizes that going beyond conventional modes of conciliation and mediation is often required to highlight human elements inherent in complex African conflicts. As Assistant Secretary General of the OAU in the 1990s, he played a pivotal role as a conciliator and mediator in the civil war in Sierra Leone, which he described to illustrate his understanding of creativity.

Osman views the civil war in Sierra Leone as a struggle for power and resources between the military regime ruling the country through corrupt technocrats, on the one hand, and the opposition group, Revolutionary United Front (RUF), led by Foday Sankoh spreading the sense of terror, on the other. The RUF started its insurgency campaign in the east and south of the country in March 1991. Internal roots of the war include decades of domination by military regimes in Freetown and the desire of Sankoh and sympathetic clan leaders based in the countryside to topple the central authority for adjusting socio-economic inequity. External roots of the war include Liberian President Charles Taylor's collusion with Sankoh for destabilizing Sierra Leone and benefiting from diamond revenues generated in the mineral-rich areas seized by the RUF.

It is against this backdrop that the OAU Secretary General sent Osman to Sierra Leone in February 1995. The OAU, UN, and Commonwealth representatives formed a joint committee and sent a joint appeal to conflict parties, believing that one organization alone would not be as effective as all three working together. In retrospect, Osman observes that the sense of unity and joint action stimulated creativity and became a major breakthrough. Because the opposition leaders were hiding in the bush, the alliance of the three delegations asked for the good offices of the Pope's representative in Freetown to relay the joint appeal to the RUF leaders. The representative sent a joint appeal to the RUF via its radio transmission facility in Freetown. The idea of asking the Pope's representative to become a go-between originated in the delegates' conversations with locals in Freetown, who told them that the RUF leaders would listen to nobody but the Pope's representative. To supplement this line of communication, Osman and his colleagues also employed the behind-the-scenes channel of the British radio transmission. Moreover, they widely disseminated their joint appeal through the local radio, TV, and newspapers. They even appeared on the TV to campaign for their joint appeal.

As a result of several weeks of these and other concerted efforts, an opportunity for dialogue was finally created between the RUF and the government, with the essential intermediary role provided by International Alert and other NGOs. On the international level, joint appeals for mobilization culminated in the establishment of peace-keeping operations in Sierra Leone. Despite signs of partial success, however, it turned out that Sierra Leone had to go through several more years of continuous violence after the completion of Osman's mission.

Two lessons are learned from this episode. First, Osman reflects that the formation of the joint committee comprised of the three international organizations illustrates creativity. Although the extent of creativity demonstrated by this action remains to be evaluated more rigorously with empirical evidence, the episode illustrates that the commitment to guiding principles, such as unity and joint action, became a source of inspiration for a new mode of thinking and action.

Second, the interveners learned from locals' knowledge about the existing channel of communication between the Pope's representative and the opposition leaders, and applied the local knowledge to initiate an act of procedural creativity. It is conceivable that the outside interveners alone would have been unable to come up with this initiative without the local knowledge. Conversely, it would have been difficult or perhaps impossible for the Sierra Leonean government and other local actors to open communication with the RUF on their own initiative, even if they had known of this existing channel of communication. The creative act emerged partly from the conventional local knowledge and partly from the unconventional application of the existing local knowledge by the resourceful outsiders. Thus the potential for change emanated from continuity, and the continuity became a stepping stone for change; the relationship between conventionality and unconventionality, between creative change and continuity was dialectical and interdependent in nature.

The Indonesia–Malaysia–Singapore conflict: philosophical creativity (John Burton)

A pioneering scholar-practitioner in conflict resolution, John Burton views creativity as a process of discovering conflict parties' common needs and new possibilities that open up as a result of in-depth analysis.[22] He argues that conflict analysis has to be carried out outside the conventional framework of power politics and deterrence in order to generate creative resolution options. Prior to his academic life, Burton had played such important roles in diplomatic service as being a member of the Australian delegation to the San Francisco Conference to set up the UN in 1944–5 and Permanent Head of the Australian Diplomatic Service in 1945–50. Challenging the prevailing paradigm of power politics that he experienced firsthand as a senior diplomat, Burton has dedicated the remaining years of his career to establishing the academic field and practice of conflict resolution in Australia, the UK, the US, and elsewhere. To illustrate his understanding of creativity in conflict resolution, Burton discussed his attempts to resolve the conflict between Indonesia, Malaysia, and Singapore through a series of six informal, confidential problem-solving workshops in London from December 1965 to June 1966 for unofficial representatives nominated by the respective heads of state.

The conflict became manifest on the international scene in June 1961,[23] when Prime Minister Tunku Abdul Rahman of the Malayan Federation publicly expressed his willingness to incorporate the northern Borneo territories of

Sarawak and Sabah, located in the southwest of the Philippines, and Singapore, both as part of the Federation which was due to become independent from British colonial rule. Incorporation of Singapore was particularly important for the Malayan government to secure a strategic seaport. The British government welcomed Rahman's suggestion as a viable way of decolonizing its territories in Singapore, Sarawak, and Sabah while maintaining its influence over the region. To this end, the British government was willing to retain its base in Singapore and conclude a defense agreement with Malaysia. On the other hand, Indonesia – under the leadership of President Sukarno – strongly opposed the Malayan enlargement plan and the sustained British political–military presence as being imperialist. Sukarno insisted that northern Borneo, known as Northern Kalimantan, be an integral part of Indonesia. With the official declaration of independence by the enlarged Federation of Malaysia in September 1963, anti-British and anti-Malaysian riots and violent attacks by Indonesian "volunteers," many of whom were trained by the Indonesian army, escalated dramatically in northern Borneo and Jakarta. The conflict grew even more complex when Singapore gained independence from Malaysia in August 1965 and became an autonomous conflict party as a sovereign state.

Burton and his colleagues held the first informal, confidential workshop with unofficial representatives from the three countries in London in mid-December 1965. Burton reflected on this week-long discussion and wrote an essay, "A case study in the application of international theory: Indonesia–Malaysia–Singapore" in January 1966 to be presented at an academic conference in London. In it, he characterized the essence of the trilateral relations as fear-based. According to Burton, the Indonesians felt encircled by and isolated from the neighboring states that accommodated continuous British military presence and harbored rebels who were threatening Indonesia's stability. The Malaysians' fear was generated by internal and external Chinese influence, which Malays interpreted as a communist threat to their British-supported fragile stability. The Singaporean government remained fearful of the sustained tension between the Western-styled English-speaking leaders and their Chinese-speaking electorate because of its implications for their internal stability. The Singaporean leaders were also concerned about the vulnerable geographic location, surrounded by Malaysia and Indonesia. In Burton's analysis, the fear of the three parties was mirrored by their struggle for both controlling and participating in the decision-making processes that could shape the regional political environment. Burton also argued that the perceived fear was attributed in part to the disruption of communication between the parties, who were scapegoating one another instead of facing the serious *internal* problems that had surfaced after attaining independence from colonial rule. Those problems included fragile national unity, minority–majority tension, separatist movements, and illicit economic activities that hampered development.

One of Burton's objectives in the informal meetings was to help the parties re-establish tripartite communication. His working assumption was that once the parties could re-establish direct communication, they should be able to depict more objective perceptions about one another and discover common ground in such areas as their urgent need for national unity and socio-economic development.

Because of their unprecedented nature in the field of international peacemaking, the workshops illustrated process creativity. By the fall of 1965, it had become apparent that a range of official diplomatic efforts for conciliation and mediation by the Philippine, Thai, Japanese, American, and British governments, as well as the UN, were deadlocked. It was around this period that Burton and his colleagues proposed British Prime Minister Harold Wilson to help them launch an unofficial channel of communication between the three conflict parties. With Wilson's backing, an invitation was sent to the three heads of state, asking them to nominate a few close friends for informal discussion. The request was answered favorably, due in part to Burton's personal connection with the respective governments' senior leaders, with whom he had built working relationships in the late 1940s as Permanent Head of the Australian Diplomatic Service. Each government sent one to two participants to the discussion sessions. To facilitate their first week-long meeting, held in London in mid-December 1965, a multidisciplinary panel of eleven scholars, mostly Australian and British, was formed. Their areas of specialization included political science, social psychology, sociology, and Southeast Asian studies. The discussion was intended to be confidential, informal, and exploratory, with no rigid agenda imposed by the panelists. No records of the discussion were kept, except each participant's personal notes that might be used to report back to his government. Although no set protocol was followed, it turned out that the first meeting started with a description of the conflict from each party's point of view and proceeded to exchange opinions and feelings on various issues between the participants. The panelists occasionally injected theoretical and analytical questions into the discussion in order to help the participants probe more deeply into the roots of the conflict and explore future possibilities.

In the author's interview, Burton stressed the nature of outcome creativity that emerged from the series of workshops. He recalls that a creative exploration became possible when the parties began thinking about why they were fighting in the first place. The facilitators asked them to consider, for example, whether they were fighting for the territory under dispute, for the right to control the population, and/or for other perceived needs. Discussions revealed that their real issues included their fear of outside intervention and their concern over Chinese influence, both domestic and external, the latter being a subject that invited particularly strong emotional reactions from the Malaysian and Indonesian participants. In Burton's recollection, these realizations of the participants enabled them to gradually shift their attention to the possibility of sharing resources in northern Borneo, instead of each claiming its exclusive control over the territory.

In his reflective paper presented at an academic conference on June 3, 1966, three days before the sixth and final workshop was held, Fred Emery, another leading member of the facilitators' team, described this shift from a unique angle. In Emery's view, the shift illustrated a process of "re-centering," in which the parties restructured their way of defining their conflict in a manner more conducive to resolution based on a broader and deeper understanding of its roots. Emery noted:

> [S]ome of the social scientists attempted to tackle directly the key conflict area of Sabah and Sarawak. As could be expected, that evoked strong attempts to justify the public positions taken by each nation. Progress was made only when the focus of discussion was shifted to the problems concerned with the presence of the British Strategic Reserve based on Singapore and Malaya. This effectively re-centered the problem and led quickly to a resolution of the conflict.
>
> (Emery 1966: 5)

Viewed in the overall context of the conflict resolution process, Emery's observation appears to reflect a shift in the participants' focus from the desire for exclusive territorial control to an attempt to satisfy their deep-rooted security needs. Despite the different ways of interpretation held by Burton and Emery, the two seem to complement one another in support of Burton's thesis that in-depth analysis opens up new possibilities for resolving a seemingly intractable conflict.[24]

Two general lessons about the nature and origination of creativity may be drawn from this episode. First, Burton has inferred from this and other activities that the deeper the conflict analysis is, the more creative possibilities open up for conflict resolution. His rationale is that in-depth analysis reveals less visible yet more fundamental aspects of the conflict at hand and contributes to the process of searching for resolution options that have not been considered before. In the conflict between Indonesia, Malaysia, and Singapore, for example, the informal discussion enabled the participants to probe into the deep roots of their fear in such areas as outside intervention and minority–majority tension, so that they could finally start thinking about how to go beyond their initial mental frame of exclusive territorial control. Burton's assertion on the analysis–resolution link stands in sharp contrast to some other researcher-practitioners, who claim that in-depth analysis is hardly relevant or even antithetical to creativity.[25] This important debate will be revisited later.

Second, in Burton's mind, the workshops of 1965–6 were intended to tackle not only the conflict between the three countries, but also a larger metaphysical conflict – one that had been evolving between those advocating power politics, on the one hand, and others, like Burton, struggling to establish conflict resolution as an alternative philosophy, on the other. According to Burton, power politics attributes "the right of power elites in the family, at the work place, in society or in the international system to determine the behaviors of others."[26] On the other hand, conflict resolution, in his view, acknowledges the human being as an autonomous individual and seeks to find ways to satisfy deeply ingrained human needs at all levels of society without the use of coercive means.[27]

On the incipience and origination of the pioneering problem-solving workshops, Burton recalls that he had been searching for an opportunity to "test" and demonstrate the validity of his conflict resolution approach in practice as of the mid-1960s. Soon after he left diplomatic service, he started teaching International Relations at University College in London. By the time of this first teaching assignment, Burton had written *Peace Theory: Preconditions of Disarmament*. Yet during the first year of his teaching, he was asked to use Georg Schwarzenberger's *Power Politics* as his main textbook. It was apparent that Schwarzenberger's thesis was in sharp contrast to Burton's. Therefore, from the second year onwards, Burton used his own approach to teach International Relations. This caused significant opposition from his colleagues, who criticized Burton's peace theory approach as too unrealistic and naïve. It was during this period that the conflict between Indonesia, Malaysia, and Singapore was growing in scope while conventional diplomatic efforts were deadlocked. Considering Burton's personal connection with the senior leaders of the three countries, he sensed a real chance of generating a positive impact on the conflict.

Burton saw that bargaining in conventional diplomacy tended to reinforce power politics because it typically favored "high-power" parties over "low-power" parties. He also believed that the parties' commitment to bargaining and power politics tended to render intermediaries' role marginal because they would find little room for open communication and constructive relationship-building. To "test" his conflict resolution approach, Burton proposed informal, confidential meetings free from the counterproductive influences of diplomatic bargaining and power politics. In this respect, the pioneering workshops of 1965–6 illustrated creativity inspired by the value commitment to the emerging paradigm of conflict resolution and to the active resistance to the pervasive paradigm of power politics. In short, they exemplified *philosophical creativity*.

An Israeli–Palestinian problem-solving workshop: expecting unexpected discoveries (Herbert Kelman)

Herbert Kelman is a social psychologist by training and a pioneering researcher-practitioner in conflict resolution at Harvard University. He has contributed extensively to the application and elaboration of John Burton's problem-solving workshop method[28] in the Israeli–Palestinian conflict since the late 1960s. Reflecting on a quarter-century of his practice inspired by Burton's methodology, Kelman observes that creativity requires getting out of widely accepted, customary ways of formulating conflicts and looking at them from different perspectives. In his view, a creative approach is stimulated by considering different levels of analysis, actors, contexts, and roles. He also suggests drawing insights and experiences from different domains of inquiry and applying them in a way congruent with the particular context of conflict that needs resolution. Having described the key ingredients of creativity, however, Kelman stresses that creative work is an emergent outcome of "sweat" or hard work, not something one can seek in a well-planned, predictable manner.

To illustrate his understanding of creativity, Kelman described his first experience in organizing an Israeli–Palestinian workshop in 1971 for a Harvard graduate seminar. In this and numerous other workshops, he served as a facilitator and consultant for dialogue participants. Despite his Jewish origin and childhood experience under Nazi rule, he has aspired to serve as an impartial, even-handed third party for Israelis and Palestinians in dialogue.

In Kelman's view, at the heart of the Israeli–Palestinian conflict in the early 1970s was the tension between the two national movements, each claiming its exclusive national identity linked to the land which they both demanded, while denying the right of the other side. It is in this political climate that Kelman and his colleague, Stephen Cohen, organized their first problem-solving workshop on the Israeli–Palestinian conflict. To select workshop participants, Kelman and Cohen sought to find advanced doctoral students of Israeli and Palestinian backgrounds in the Boston area. At that point, they did not intend to invite high-ranking political influentials. Although they could easily find Israeli participants, they found it much harder to locate Palestinians willing to join the exercise.

Although the workshop was a pilot session for the modest purpose of academic learning and it was to be held away from the Middle East geographically, the reluctance of Palestinians was anticipated. As of 1971, the PLO was still emerging on the international scene as a political movement.[29] Yasir Arafat was elected PLO chairman in 1969 as a new political figure whose credentials were still contested internationally. In those days, the PLO was widely regarded in the West as a guerrilla organization committed to armed struggle. Recognizing it as a political entity was a taboo in many quarters. Kelman, too, was still undecided about how to understand the PLO's status.

Because of the volatile political climate, sitting with Israelis was unacceptable to many Palestinians. For them, having dialogues with Israelis meant legitimizing Israel. Despite these difficulties, Kelman managed to find a Palestinian doctoral student from Jordan. The student was hesitant to join the exercise because he did not want to be perceived by others as legitimizing Israel. However, he indicated that if Kelman could bring somebody from the PLO, then he would have no problem with participation. He recommended Kelman his Palestinian friend from Israel who was working in the PLO office in New York. Kelman took a bus ride to his residence in Newark, New Jersey and persuaded him to join the workshop.

Kelman reflects that the suggestion of the Palestinian student had far-reaching implications for his future work. For Palestinians, meeting with Israelis meant legitimizing Israelis and recognizing them as a party. The same applied to Israelis meeting with the PLO. Although the fellow from the PLO office came informally as an unofficial individual and not as an official representative, these observations still applied. From the Palestinian student's point of view, the fact that the PLO staff was coming to the workshop meant that it was acceptable for other Palestinians to participate in it. For them, the presence of the PLO official, despite being in his unofficial capacity, prevented them from being misunderstood as alternative representatives to the PLO.

Their concern was well grounded. Over the years, Israelis had been trying to approach Palestinians in the West Bank in search of alternative (non-PLO) interlocutors in political negotiations. Although the Israelis tried dialogues with Palestinians in the West Bank, they failed, partly because many mainstream leaders in Palestinian society, inside and outside the occupied territories, had come to accept the PLO as the only legitimate Palestinian representative. Knowing this political context, Palestinians from the West Bank did not want to be seen as an alternative to the PLO, even in academic workshops away from home. Because of this background, the fact that the PLO official was due to participate in Kelman's workshop gave other Palestinians a tacit permission to participate without causing intracommunal tension.

Before 1971, Kelman had not critically asked himself what kind of participants he needed for workshops. Through this experience, he learned the importance of *legitimate* participants in order to make the workshops politically relevant. In the Israeli–Palestinian context, political legitimacy in the eyes of many Palestinians rested in the PLO. In retrospect, Kelman observes that he could have realized this point through his academic experience. But in reality, he learned it through the practical experience of selecting workshop participants. He ran into the problem and came across a solution experientially and unexpectedly. As years went by, the need for legitimate representation became increasingly obvious in his practice of conflict resolution.

In one of the dialogue sessions that Kelman facilitated, Israeli participants told their Palestinian counterparts, "If only we could negotiate with reasonable people like you, instead of people from the PLO!" The Palestinians replied, "We *are* the PLO." Later, in the same workshop, the Palestinians told their Israeli counterparts, "If only we could negotiate with people like you instead of Zionists!" prompting the Israelis to say in response, "We *are* committed Zionists!" On this and other occasions, both sides needed to learn that if they wanted relevant political negotiating partners, they had to turn to legitimate, mainstream representatives – and that such partners were readily available. This realization touches the very substance of the Israeli–Palestinian conflict, namely, the non-recognition of each other's national identity.

Kelman had gradually learned through this 1971 episode and other experiences that the Israeli–Palestinian conflict was between the two national groups denying the national identity, existence, and authenticity of each other. This understanding of the conflict made it possible to appreciate that mutual recognition was essential for resolving it. In the Israeli–Palestinian conflict, mutual recognition meant the need for accepting each other's national leadership and self-identification before moving forward in any negotiation. Kelman believes that the 1993 Oslo accord, which in his view marked a historical turning point in the Israeli–Palestinian relations, became a reality due in large part to the emergence of mutual recognition.

Kelman's experience was a process of *discovery* as much as creation. His discovery was primarily about how to design a conflict resolution process. Three salient features characterize the discovery process that led to what he considered creative revelations. First, it was highly intuitive. Asked to describe in the interview how his insights into the meaning of legitimate representation first appeared, Kelman immediately responded, "The idea didn't even emerge. It just came out of the practical considerations and the necessity of putting a team of participants together." The discovery was unplanned and unpredictable. His self-reflection echoes those of many other interviewees who struggled to articulate what they viewed as their moments of creation.

Second, it was emergent through hands-on experience. Because of his academic work that had preceded the 1971 episode, he had long held a clear intellectual understanding of kernel ideas that had come to shape his discovery. The ideas included the importance of legitimate representation, national identity, and mutual recognition in conflict resolution. Yet these concepts were crystallized and integrated coherently only through the actual interactions with others surrounding him. For example, Kelman distinctly remembers that while taking a bus ride from New York to Newark to meet the PLO representative at his residence, he was constantly questioning himself, "What am I doing? Why am I going to the home of a PLO official I don't even know?" In the course of taking this and many other steps, he was not sure of their significance. Yet the meaning of each step he took was revealed to him only *after* he had experienced it. In this respect, experiential learning was essential for his discovery and creation.

Third, the discovery process was contingency-based. It was a series of small interrelated revelations that guided him step by step and gradually built up to the larger discovery of the meaning of legitimate representation. For example, the first trigger of action that led Kelman toward the discovery was the suggestion by the Palestinian student to invite the PLO official. By following his suggestion without understanding its political implications fully, Kelman came to grasp the nuance of intra-communal tension among Palestinians as well as the relationships between them and the PLO. Each step he took was contingent on the one before. Each of the preceding steps helped shape the steps that followed and consequently led to what he thought was the whole picture of discovery. Metaphorically, it resembled a choreographer visualizing movements of dancers on the stage, with each movement crystallized in his or her mind step by step, gradually opening up a range of possible movements to unfold.[30]

It is also observed that the intuitive, emergent, and contingency-based process of discovery was made possible by a combination of chance and purpose. Chance was welcomed and seized within the methodological framework of problem-solving workshops. For example, contingent actions taken every step of the way, starting with the invitation of the PLO official, were unplanned. But they were within the wide range of possible actions that felt consistent with the broader purpose of making the workshop a success. As Kelman mentioned in the interview, the commitment that he and his colleague shared to the exploratory mode of thinking and action made it possible to remain open-minded and to risk defying the perceived taboo of accepting the PLO as a legitimate partner in dialogue. It was within this bounded flexibility that unexpected twists and turns evolved and were seized as relevant, instead of being discarded offhand as irrelevant. As a result, the accumulation of small revelations and surprises was translated into a larger picture of discovery.

Finally, the whole picture of the discovery and creation has become clear in Kelman's mind *only in retrospect*. Despite the theoretical precursors in his mind, the meaning of legitimate representation was far from clear in the early stages of his activities, such as the convening of the 1971 graduate seminar and the bus trip to the PLO official's residence. Reflecting on this episode today, Kelman senses that he would not be able to discuss it as an isolated event. It makes sense to him in retrospect because it fits into his overall experience, including his academic work prior to 1971, his encounter with John Burton in 1966, and the wealth of experience that he has accumulated since 1971. A range of theoretical issues considered during those years include legitimacy, national identity, nationalism, and conflicts between national movements. To him, the content of his discovery and creation has come to bear a coherent meaning only in the overall context of his personal history. The discovery was a foreground and the historical context a background: without the context as a background, the foreground would not have been found to exist in the first place.

Estonian–Russian psychoanalytic dialogue: activating symbols constructively (Vamik Volkan)

To Vamik Volkan, creativity means symbolizing. More precisely, it means playing with symbols in such a way as to make the destructive potential of conflict less destructive. As founder of the Center for the Study of Mind and Human Interaction (CSMHI) in the School of Medicine at the University of Virginia in Charlottesville, and a former member of the Carter Center's International Negotiation Network in Atlanta, Georgia, Volkan is internationally recognized as a pioneering researcher-practitioner in the psychology of large groups in ethnic tension, terrorism, societal trauma, and national and international conflict. In the multi-year Estonian project launched jointly by CSMHI and the Carter Center in 1994, he played a central role as an analyst, consultant, and facilitator for a series of psychoanalytic dialogues with the conflict parties, mostly high-ranking political leaders of Russian and Estonian origins.

CSMHI and the Carter Center began their psychoanalytic research and dialogues with influential Estonians and Russians in April 1994, about three years after Estonia gained independence from the Soviet Union in September 1991.[31] Estonia is a small Baltic country of about 1.5 million people. Of this, 62 percent is Estonian, 30 percent Russian, and the rest from miscellaneous minority backgrounds. From the Middle Ages till 1920, when Estonians won the war of independence, Estonians had been ruled by foreign occupiers such as Vikings, Germanic knights, Danes, Swedes, Russians, and Germans. One of the most traumatic periods in recent Estonian history started in 1940, when the Soviet Union militarily seized the country. In 1941, Estonia became a battleground between Nazi and Soviet armies, and 60,000 Estonians, about 6 percent of the nation's population, were either deported, sent to prison camps, or drafted into the Soviet military. By 1949, only two-thirds of the pre-war population of Estonian nationals remained in the country. Although the end of the Soviet rule in

1991 brought Estonians freedom from foreign occupation at last, it also opened up a whole range of social problems. For example, thousands of former Soviet troops and hundreds of Soviet military facilities remained in the Estonian territory even after independence. Disputes over how to demarcate a new border with Russia surfaced. Criteria for granting Estonian citizenship became a focus of controversy, particularly for citizens of Russian heritage who migrated to Estonia generations ago as well as those who came during the Soviet era.

It is against this historical background that the multidisciplinary team from CSMHI and the Carter Center invited influential representatives from Russia, Estonia, and the Russian speakers' communities in Estonia, and held small-group dialogues three times a year for three consecutive years, starting in 1994. One of the important activities organized by the team was to visit "host spots" – such as military facilities, national cemeteries, and monuments – together with the dialogue participants. The aim of the tours was to help the participants express suppressed emotions hidden at the subconscious level so as to stimulate authentic interactions among them.

Volkan's approach to conflict is distinctly different from most of the other interviewees' under study because he focuses explicitly on psychodynamics, including the unconscious. However, like some other interviewees, Volkan limits his primary role to the *analysis* of conflicts while refraining from designing or implementing concrete resolution options. He believes that his creativity is demonstrated in his effort to generate a safe, reassuring context in which conflict parties can come to terms with fantasized images of themselves, their adversaries, and their conflict, in order to adjust their future expectations more realistically. Examples of his creative practice are to be evaluated within this highly specialized framework of inquiry.

Volkan observes that at the simplest level, conflict parties' creativity is demonstrated when they play with symbols, such as metaphoric expressions, to discuss their conflict. For example, some dialogue participants in the Estonian project referred to Russia as an elephant and Estonia as a rabbit, and went on to discuss possible ways in which the relationship between Russians and Estonians might be played out. Use of the metaphors helped the participants express their deep feelings, such as the fear of the Estonian rabbit being stepped on by the Russian elephant if the rabbit were to befriend the elephant carelessly. In Volkan's view, the participants could hear and acknowledge deep emotions of the other side through playful exchanges of metaphoric expressions, which then contributed to humanizing mutual images within a reassuring context of dialogue.

Another level of creativity is demonstrated by the dialogue facilitators. Volkan described the CSMHI-sponsored community mobilization activities in the Estonian village of Klooga as an example of the facilitators' creativity. The episode is described by Volkan as follows:

> The newly established Estonian military was using a field adjacent to Klooga for live target practice, which greatly concerned Klooga's inhabitants, both Estonians and Russians, because it posed a real danger to them

and to their children. The Soviet Army had used this range for military practice, and now the Estonians were repeating the same behavior. The "hidden transcript" went something like this: "We Estonians can now identify with our aggressors. Intellectually, we know that today Klooga houses Estonian citizens and Estonian children too, but in our minds we continue to see this place as a Soviet military base. Thus we bomb it, repeatedly."

The almost daily "bombing" of Klooga truly was dangerous. We were afraid that children playing nearby could be injured or killed. When the CSMHI team tried to talk to county officials and parliamentarians (some of them participants from the original dialogue series), we found great resistance to stopping the "bombing" of Klooga. As one parliamentarian put it: "This place now belongs to us. We can do whatever we want there. The Estonian Army is our pride and joy."

(Volkan 1999: 191–2)

Volkan reflects that part of his creativity was in his capacity to read the "hidden script" of the bombing, recognize it as a manifestation of the Estonians' collective trauma, and translate the script in terms accessible to the local officials. On recognizing that the officials failed to heed the warnings, the facilitator team took a next step with creativity, as described in Volkan's recent writing:

On July 4, 1997, CSMHI threw a big community-wide party in Klooga. We also invited several of the Estonian and Russian-speaking participants from the national level dialogues to come with their families. Most of them lived in Tallinn [the capital of Estonia] and had never been to Klooga. After the party, we invited our guests for a walk around the town in hopes that the "bombing" practice would resume so that they could see what it was like. Sure enough, the deafening explosions began. The military exercises were impossible to ignore and provided unmistakable evidence of what Klooga's inhabitants lived with every day. In spite of seeing for themselves the dangers of this practice, however, our guests from the Parliament still could not bring themselves to do something about it. It appeared that to do so would be politically incorrect.

In the end, it was the Klooga residents themselves who got results. CSMHI helped bring to their consciousness these "hidden transcripts" and, with Endel Talvik [an Estonian psychologist trained by CSMHI], increased their political consciousness and organizing skills. Then, on their own, the townspeople drew up a petition calling for a halt to the military exercises. They got hundreds of signatures and sent it to the President of Estonia. Eventually, the bombing stopped.

(Volkan 1999: 192)

An enabling factor for the origination of the facilitators' creative act was their unique psychoanalytic lenses through which to interpret what the "bombing" symbolized. An equally important factor was their ability to create an informal, open, and inviting context in which influential officials could see and hear symptoms of Estonians' collective trauma. Because the analysis and the follow-up action focused on the collective *unconscious*, it was certain that CSMHI's intervention was to be viewed as unconventional – whether creative or not – from the viewpoint of the Estonians' *consciousness*. It is inferred that delving into the parties' unconscious for analysis and follow-up action touched their unquestioned axioms of faith in social life, generating a sense of both unconventionality and resistance.

In the interview, Volkan shared a glimpse of his understanding of the unconscious in relation to creativity. He outlined the formative process of children's creativity based on Donald W. Winnicott's theory of transitional experience. Because the theory is essential for Volkan's understanding of symbols, it deserves elaboration.[32]

According to Winnicott, a new-born baby creates and maintains an illusionary sense that he is the all-powerful center of all being because whenever he expresses his desires, his mother tries to satisfy them unconditionally. In his subjective world, for example, he "creates" his mother's breast to feed himself. Winnicott calls this illusionary sense "subjective omnipotence." The illusionary world looks real to the child, especially when the mother's dedication to caretaking is unconditional and selfless immediately after the child's birth. However, as the urgency of intensive caretaking appears to decline over time in the mother's mind, she gradually shifts part of her attention back to her own needs and away from her selfless dedication to her child. This transition on the part of the mother makes the child realize that he can no longer enjoy subjective omnipotence. He gradually learns that he must consider his mother's needs and subjectivity in addition to his own. Thus the child comes to terms with the *objective reality* of interdependence between him and his caretakers. Winnicott calls this shift from subjective omnipotence to objective reality "transitional experience."

Transitional objects such as a teddy bear and other types of toys help the child cushion the fall from the world of illusionary self-centeredness to the world of mutual accommodation and interdependence. Transitional objects supplement good mothering; they help to create a protected environment in which the child feels safe to explore these two modes of relationship between self and others despite the ambiguity of sense-making during the transition. The awareness of protection and reassurance offered to the child enables him to play freely with the tension between self-centeredness and interdependence, between illusion and reality. It is this healthy playfulness during the transition that fosters the child's creativity in art and culture. Moreover, a nurturing transitional experience shapes a basic psychological template of personhood. It has far-reaching implications for adult life, in which a healthy balance between the sense of reality and imagination remains essential for meaning-making.

Drawing on Winnicott's theory, Volkan elaborates his understanding of creativity in conflict work. In his view, individuals in conflict have the choice of channeling their frustration into creative meaning-making. In early childhood, a person struggles to get his needs satisfied, especially when he is hungry, sleepy, and wet. He tries to satisfy his needs by attracting his mother's attention. That is the first battle he wages. If he cannot satisfy his desires because of his mother's inattention, she becomes his "enemy" in the struggle. On the other hand, if the mother feeds him and satisfies his needs, she is his ally. As he grows up, he can better balance realistic desires with unrealistic ones. Consequently he comes to form a more realistic view about his mother: "My mother is a nice person but sometimes not so nice."

When large groups and their representatives are traumatized and regressed, they make fantasized enemies. Their fantasized images represent reality or unreality, or an intricate mix of both at the same time. However, by understanding, verbalizing, and playing with metaphors that represent the adversaries' images and by invoking creativity and empathy in that process, conflict parties may foster a more realistic relationship with the other side. Such an adjustment in mental images becomes possible because of the psychological capacity cultivated in early childhood to balance reality with illusion. However, it is inferred from Winnicott's theory and Volkan's elaboration that in severely regressed societies, both children and caretakers fail to enjoy nurturing transitional experiences. Consequently, the whole generation of societal members may grow up without a reasonable balance between reality and illusion. A critical question is raised: Can people in such severely regressed societies develop the essential psychological capacity to play with metaphors and symbols in order to adjust their worldviews creatively and constructively? An attempt to answer this question is likely to contribute to the understanding of an important relationship between creativity and the collective unconscious in inter-group conflict.

Volkan's discussion on transitional experience stimulates a number of fundamental questions about creativity, the unconscious, and human nature that go beyond the scope of the present inquiry.[33] Most fundamentally, his psychoanalytic discussion directs one's attention to the essential role of the unconscious in creativity. It further suggests the need for conceptualizing incipience as well as part of origination on a more expansive time horizon than one might conventionally think. This is because precursors of an act of creativity may remain "hidden" underneath the conscious for an extended period of time before they are crystallized at the conscious level. The unconscious origin of creative ideas and behavior makes one infer that some of the precursors of creativity date back to the creators' early childhood. Therefore, in psychoanalytic terms, images of creative resolutions are in store even *before* one identifies and analyzes a conflict at hand.

The Cyprus conflict: sustained commitment to bicommunal peace
(Louise Diamond)

As a pioneering practitioner in grassroots-based conflict transformation and reconciliation, Louise Diamond observes that creativity involves activating different modes of thinking that do not usually operate in daily life and opening the mind to different ways of being in the world. With the former US diplomat John McDonald, Diamond founded the Institute for Multi-Track Diplomacy (IMTD) in Washington DC in 1992. At IMTD, Diamond and McDonald advanced the practice of multi-track peace-making, which coordinates governments, NGOs, businesses, private citizens, research/training/education, activism, religion, funding, and the media as an organic whole. In the conflict between Turkish and Greek Cypriots in the early-to-late 1990s that she chose to discuss in the interview, Diamond played the role of a trainer, consultant, and peace advocate for bicommunal conflict transformation and reconciliation activities.

The background of the Cyprus conflict is summarized based on Diamond and Fisher (1995). In 1960, the bicommunal Republic of Cyprus won independence from Britain, despite the long-standing guerilla campaign of Greek Cypriots against their colonial master in pursuit of their self-determination and union with Greece. The bicommunal power-sharing arrangement in the republic between majority Greek Cypriots and minority Turkish Cypriots proved short-lived as their political maneuvering plunged into widespread violence in 1963. As Turkish Cypriots' desire for survival was voiced strongly, the two communities were increasingly segregated. The conflict escalated dramatically in 1974, when an Athens-inspired coup was staged against the government of bicommunal power-sharing. In the meantime, Turkey militarily intervened for the stated purpose of protecting Turkish Cypriots and restoring the power-sharing arrangement. During the 1974 fighting, the two communities were segregated almost completely. While the Greek Cypriot population was concentrated in the south of the island and maintained international legitimacy, Turkish Cypriots under President Rauf Denktash declared an independent Turkish Republic of Northern Cyprus in 1983, which was recognized only by Turkey.

Reflecting on her peace-building practice in Cyprus and other parts of the world, Diamond observes that there are at least three different ways in which creativity plays a role. Those are: a creative method of practice; creativity as a way of thinking to resolve conflict; and the effective use of creative arts. A creative method refers to an approach to practice that has not been tried before and that breaks new ground. Creativity as a way of thinking refers to a basic principle necessary for "getting out of the box" within which the problem was created. This corresponds to the thinking of Einstein, who observed that one would not be able to resolve a problem with the same mindset that had created it. Finally, creative arts refer to music, drama, theater, rituals, and other activities that are outside the mainstream toolbox of diplomats and peace-builders. Diamond observes that the peace-building activities she started in Cyprus in 1991 illustrate all three types.

The creative method of practice launched in Cyprus was a series of grassroots-based *bicommunal* activities for reconciliation and conflict transformation. When Diamond first landed in Cyprus as a consultant hired by an American association of applied behavioral scientists, there were virtually no joint peace-building activities across the line of the communal division. After some assessment, she learned about the local needs for training in conflict resolution. Together with her local hosts, she crafted a menu of conflict resolution training based on their skill level and their needs. For the initial two years, Diamond offered training for Turkish and Greek Cypriots separately. According to Diamond and Fisher (1995), her project offered about 250 hours of training for approximately 200 individuals between October 1991 and April 1994. After this initial stage of intensive training, Diamond shifted her attention to the next stage, where she formed a core group of local leaders in each of the two communities. The core groups were comprised of the individuals who stood out during the initial few years of her project and who were personally excited about conflict work. The core groups from both sides gathered to organize a Bicommunal Steering Committee (BSC) at the end of 1992 to work together for peace-building across the line of inter-communal tension.

The significance of the BSC has to be understood in the historical context of the conflict. At the time of Diamond's intervention in the Cyprus conflict, there existed few bicommunal activities and groups. There were problem-solving dialogues between the two communities organized by Christopher Mitchell, John Burton, Herbert Kelman, Ron Fisher, and other scholar-practitioners starting in the 1960s. Yet even those activities, except for Ron Fisher's, were mostly discontinued by the time Diamond started her work. Therefore the establishment of the BSC was unconventional. The ownership of the BSC was built from the ground-up instead of the top-down. The committee members decided what activities to organize, how to organize them, and who should be involved. It took Diamond and others three years of intensive preparatory work to reach the point where substantive bicommunal activities became possible. These activities illustrate the first type of creativity, namely, a creative method of practice.

The second type of creativity concerning the principle of thinking for conflict resolution was emphasized throughout the training sessions. The training was designed to help participants access and activate their own creativity for problem-solving and generating workable options "out of the box." To apply the third type of creativity through the use of art, the training incorporated mini-dramas, sculpting, and drawing. In addition, Diamond introduced Joseph Montville's "walk through history" concept to help the training participants learn alternative images of conflict history. They placed a long piece of paper in the middle of the floor to illustrate a timeline of history. Each side was then asked to take sheets of paper, write down on each sheet what each group perceived as a defining moment in the history of the conflict, and attach all the sheets at the appropriate year on either the left or right side of the timeline. As a result, two maps of conflict history were created on the floor, one illustrating a Greek Cypriot perspective and the other a Turkish Cypriot perspective. The participants from both communities walked along the timeline, looking to the right and looking to the left. They witnessed two completely different versions of history. Diamond sensed that the method was extremely powerful. The exercise demonstrated the use of creative art that enabled the participants to understand the history of their conflict more interactively and holistically than a conventional mode of analytical discussion. As an applied social scientist, Diamond knew that people had the capacity to learn from kinesthetic experience and mental stimuli. She believes that if people move their bodies and walk through the timeline kinesthetically, their experience creates a distinctly different effect than sitting on chairs and analyzing their history intellectually.

The evolution, acceptance, and sustenance phases of the bicommunal social change were no less significant than its origination. Although Diamond is modest in her view about the extent to which her project has influenced Cypriot society at large, her reflections illustrate signs of social change that have come out of the sustained bicommunal activities. The bicommunal movement evolved and interacted with a range of socio-political forces that had been shaping and reshaping the Cyprus conflict during the 1990s. For example, the government of Turkish Cypriots became so concerned about the growing trends of the bicommunal activities that it made them illegal in 1997. Diamond held a conversation with Turkish Cypriot President Rauf Denktash over his concerns. Soon thereafter, however, the Turkish Cypriot government had to abandon its ban on bicommunal activities. The government was forced to legalize unhindered interaction between the two communities because it could no longer cope with the increasing public demand for the bicommunal movement. Another sign of acceptance of the bicommunal activities was that the UN Security Council and the US State Department both incorporated the bicommunal principle as their official policies in Cyprus. The movement also attracted the attention of European financial sponsors because the negotiations over the accession of Cyprus to the European Union increased the publicity of the conflict as well as of the peace-building approach that looked promising for additional funding.

Diamond also observes signs of sustenance that have been generated by the bicommunal activities. At the grassroots level, participants in the training created a bicommunal choir and folk dance group, despite serious political risks and resistances. Another trainee organized a historical reunion of elderly villagers who had been separated for decades because of the inter-communal division. At the government level, many of the ideas that had evolved from the dialogues between Diamond and local project participants were incorporated into the official peace negotiations facilitated by UN Secretary General Kofi Annan in the early 2000s. Several of the central figures in the formal negotiation process, as well as in the two governments, have at one time or another participated in the training programs that Diamond and her colleagues offered.

Parenthetically, it deserves mention that despite a number of bicommunal activities initiated by Diamond and others over the years, their impact on the substantive resolution of the political stalemate is still to be seen. The UN-sponsored "Annan Plan," which proposed a bicommunal, bizonal federation comprised of two equal constituent states with a single international identity, was put forward in April 2004 for separate referendums by the two communities. While 67 percent of Turkish Cypriots supported the proposal, 76 percent of Greek Cypriots voted against it for fear that the plan would fail to address Turkish military threats and the prospect of eventual secession of the North. Despite the political deadlock in 2004 and yet another failure of UN-mediated talks in 2006, the negotiations resumed in September 2008 between the newly elected Greek Cypriot president Demetris Christofias and his Turkish Cypriot counterpart, Mehmet Ali Talat. This fresh round of talks arguably represents the best chance that the island has seen to date, given the two new leaders' willingness to go beyond their predecessors' uncompromising approaches to negotiation.

Years after Diamond's involvement in bicommunal peace-building, the two sides remain sharply divided. Despite the turbulence of on-going negotiations and political uncertainties, however, several lessons on creativity may be learned from Diamond's initiatives in the 1990s. Theoretical implications of this episode are significant, not so much for their novelty as for their relevance to what is already well known and theorized in the study of social change.

Considering the way the bicommunal movement first appeared in the early 1990s, it is inferred that Diamond's act of creation was one of tenacious value commitment. Her paradigm of practice, seeking grassroots-based transformation and reconciliation in non-secretive public spaces, was distinctly different from the prevailing professional paradigm of confidential, elite-based transactional negotiation. As of the early 1990s, her approach was bound to be perceived as unconventional, not only by the Cypriot political leaders who opposed everything bicommunal, but also by mainstream practitioners of conflict resolution at that time. In this sense, the episode illustrates creativity generated by the value commitment to grassroots advocacy and what Diamond refers to as social peace.

The episode also illustrates the functional linkage between the origination and the subsequent phases of creativity. The signs of acceptance and sustenance observed in the late 1990s and the early 2000s demonstrate how the seeds of capacity-building planted by Diamond's training and other grassroots initiatives in the early 1990s began to generate visible results several years later. From the viewpoint of attentive stakeholders such as the US State Department, the UN, and European financial sponsors in the late 1990s, the viability of the bicommunal approach became visible *only after* it had demonstrated signs of tangible impact in Cypriot society. Metaphorically, the seeds of creativity came to be known as having existed only after the fruits, which had come out of the seeds planted earlier, were discovered. What enabled the program implementers and participants to let their stakeholders make that "discovery" was not so much of their intellectual innovation as their persistent efforts. This incremental process of communal acknowledgment evolved from their tenacity, as well as from various socio-political factors at work that provided the background of their tenacious efforts. One indication of their tenacity was the fact that Diamond's trainees actively disseminated their leanings about conflict transformation in their local communities through dozens of public events such as panel discussions, lectures, press reports, radio broadcasts, and television interviews.[34] Another indication of tenacity was Diamond's consistent efforts to inform local influentials and international officials about the bicommunal activities. In the origination phase in the early 1990s, Diamond and other program implementers began their work with the firm commitment to the unconventional bicommunal approach. With this value commitment, they persisted and took risks for a sustained period of time. The persistence and risk-taking began to bear fruits in the form of evolution, acceptance, and sustenance, years later. In other words, the effectiveness of the evolution, acceptance, and sustenance phases retroactively justified the origination phase as worthy of attention.

Finally, the working definition of creativity, comprised of the twin components of unconventionality and viability, offers a useful conceptual framework for understanding the process of social change under study. Diamond and the program participants were conscious of the unconventional nature of the bicommunal approach from the outset of their activities. But the viability was still to be demonstrated in the origination phase. It was their value commitment to grassroots-based reconciliation and transformation that sustained their belief in its viability that later came to be demonstrated over the years. Through the evolution, acceptance, and sustenance phases, some local and international stakeholders came to acknowledge the viability of the bicommunal activities. It was through this gradual process of communal acknowledgment that unconventionality became creativity.

The Helsinki process: tapping the potential of a small neutral state (Klaus Törnudd)

Klaus Törnudd was one of the Finnish representatives in the Helsinki process,[35] a series of multilateral diplomatic consultations hosted by Finland in 1973–5 for thirty-five European and North American states to reduce international tension in the Cold War. The Finnish government also hosted a six-month informal preparatory talk in 1972–3 that determined procedural details including the agenda, participants, and ground rules for the substantive discussion to follow. The sustained consultation mechanism, known as the Conference on Security and Cooperation in Europe (CSCE), grew out of the Helsinki process of 1973–5 and continued until 1995, when it was transformed into a permanent international body, the Organization for Security and Cooperation in Europe (OSCE). Törnudd was a member of the Finnish delegation for the Helsinki process from September 1973 to August 1974. During that time, he had the rank of counselor and was in charge of the "third basket" of issues, namely, human contacts, information exchange, cultural interaction, and educational cooperation. In particular, Törnudd held the responsibility for chairing an informal working group on cultural interaction for the Helsinki Final Act, the comprehensive package of agreements signed by the thirty-five participating states in 1975.

In the interview, Törnudd explored creativity within the historical context of the Helsinki process. He defines creativity as all types of efforts to reach common agreement on wordings in the documents that subsequently became parts of the Helsinki Final Act. More specifically, Törnudd views creativity as a process of bringing up new formulas, phrases, and words – or even arguments and interpretations relating to certain words or phrases – which helped to persuade other parties.

Törnudd does not consider the Helsinki process and its follow-up negotiations as an example of conflict resolution in a conventional sense. In his view, the process was designed to gradually reduce tension and build confidence between the participating states. It was not meant to resolve any underlying conflicts. His definition of creativity therefore has to be viewed in the specific context of diplomatic negotiations for confidence building and conflict mitigation.

The conflict addressed by the Helsinki process was the Cold War, with emphasis on its European front and its inseparable link to North America. During the Cold War, Finland remained interested in promoting détente, the relaxation of tension between East and West. Détente was in the national interest of Finland because international tension could have exacerbated its negative effects on Finland, a country pursuing a policy of neutrality due in part to its vulnerability to Soviet pressure.

There were many issues that had built up the tension between the East and the West: the arms race and the ensuing mutual distrust; the division of Germany and the absence of a peace treaty defining the outcome of World War II; the ideological confrontation between pluralist democracy on the one hand and communist-governed dictatorship on the other; and the difficulties of promoting person-to-person contacts and exchanges.

The main goal of the Soviet side in the Helsinki process was to achieve recognition by the West of the European borders established as a result of World War II. An important side issue for the Soviet Union was to increase certain types of economic exchange. For the Federal Republic of Germany, it was imperative to establish the principle that borders could be changed peacefully by mutual agreement. For the Western countries in general, it was important to use this opportunity to create and expand openings in the iron curtain, improve personal exchanges, and facilitate a free flow of information.

As a neutral host country, Finland maintained a relatively low profile on most of these questions. Finland was principally committed to the success of the conference, its follow-up activities, and its long-term effects on stability and détente in Europe. To the advantage of Finland, the conference opened an opportunity to enhance the status of the neutral, non-aligned participating states as facilitators through such roles as chairing working groups, drafting meeting agendas, and introducing compromise proposals. Reflecting on how the Helsinki process contributed to Finland's own national interest, Ambassador Max Jakobson, a senior Finnish colleague of Törnudd and one of the most influential intellectual architects of the Helsinki process, writes:

> In July–August 1975 the Conference on Security and Cooperation in Europe (CSCE) adopted its Final Act in Helsinki. In Finnish eyes, the gathering of 35 heads of state or government in the Finnish capital was the grand finale of Finland's long labours to gain international recognition of its status as a neutral country. Finnish neutrality, President Kekkonen noted, was firmly embedded into the European structure.
>
> (Jakobson 1998: 81)

The Helsinki process of 1973–5 took a distinct form of diplomatic interaction, with the following procedural features:[36] (a) Finland as a relatively small state hosted the process in the middle of the global superpower rivalry; (b) all thirty-five participating states, from Monaco to the US, were given equal status, unlike in the UN Security Council – based on this principle, consensus-building was used for decision-making without vetoes being exercised by the privileged superpowers,[37] and working committees were chaired by all states in rotation; (c) the procedural arrangements were not constrained by the Cold War military alliances, at least in terms of formal diplomatic principles; and (d) three "baskets" of agenda, namely, security, economics, and human rights, were adopted to discuss diverse issues simultaneously and comprehensively, rather than in a conventional piecemeal fashion.

Törnudd considers the Helsinki process highly creative because it introduced new problems to the international agenda and developed new methods and concepts in inter-state relations, despite the political tension of the Cold War. For example, the invention of confidence-building measures (CBMs) was an innovation that has come to be accepted and developed elsewhere in the world. The concept of CBMs has been further developed in the context of the OSCE since 1995. CBMs today ensure permanent transparency in military matters throughout the OSCE member states. The CSCE also made it legitimate to take up certain issues in such areas as human contacts, family reunification, cultural exchanges, and transmission of information in subsequent bilateral and multilateral relations. Since these subjects were covered in the Helsinki Final Act of 1975, it subsequently became impossible to dismiss problems in these areas as "interference in internal affairs." The consensus method used in decision-making meant that all participating states were committed to all decisions and all parts of the Final Act. This marked a distinct difference from resolutions in the UN, where representatives advocating minority positions do not feel committed at all after votes are cast to make decisions against their minority views. The attention given to the follow-up process of the Final Act, for additional discussions and its actual implementation, was also an innovation. The process featured a sustained and evolving mechanism of continuous dialogue in which the participating states could raise questions again and again on issues that they had already discussed, until all representatives could come to feel that their concerns were given adequate attention. These procedural and substantive developments illustrate the parallel processes of evolution, acceptance, and sustenance of the creative changes that have grown out of the Helsinki process.

Because this episode offers a useful empirical basis for theory-building, the following analysis is necessarily detailed in terms of not only elucidating theoretical insights, but also elaborating its historical background one step further. Insights drawn from the analysis include such enabling factors as the pursuit of national interests, values and needs, the roles of actors seeking social change, and the function of leadership in creative processes.

Reflecting on the historical and regional context of the conference, Törnudd observes that the Soviet proposal to hold a multilateral security conference was brought to international attention on at least two occasions long before the Helsinki process started. The first time was in 1954, when the Soviet Union suggested that a fifty-year treaty should be drawn up for signature by all European states and it should be administered by a permanent institutional mechanism. This proposal was not acceptable to the Western states, as they were not at the time prepared to recognize the newly established German Democratic Republic. Moreover, the proposal did not include the US as a participant. It also failed to reflect the security needs of many Western countries that relied heavily on the North Atlantic Treaty Organization (NATO). The second occasion was in the mid-1960s, when the Soviet Union proposed to convene a European security conference in order to confirm the existing borders in Europe and build a framework for large-scale East–West economic cooperation.

By the late 1960s and early 1970s, there emerged more readiness to accept this idea in the West, due in part to West Germany's new policy, "Ostpolitik," which led to the mutual recognition of the two German states in 1973. The Soviet Union accepted the long-contested participation of Canada and the US in the proposed conference. The scope of discussion was expanded by incorporating such issues as human contacts and information exchange. All these problems and questions were gradually worked out first in bilateral discussions and later in multilateral consultations in the early 1970s, under the leadership and support of the Finnish government.

Considering these changes in the overall political context, Törnudd observes that the prospect of the participating states on all sides satisfying their respective national interests was a key enabling factor for the Helsinki process to emerge. It is inferred from this observation that pursuit of self-interest is not antithetical to the emergence of creative acts, particularly when means can be devised to make diverse interests mutually compatible. However, a closer look at what underlies the national interests reveals deep-seated values and needs such as the fundamental desire for security and survival. In the Finnish case, the desire for security and survival was pursued through the sustained struggle for neutrality that had evolved from its tumultuous history and memory of communist threat. As Törnudd's senior colleague Jakobson (1998) notes, the Soviet invasions of its sphere of interest, such as Hungary in 1956 and Czechoslovakia in 1968, reminded the Finnish leaders that their security and survival depended on how effectively they could carry out their neutrality policy and establish the geopolitical stability of Europe as a whole. A working assumption derived from this reflection is that the desire to fulfill what one cares about deeply engenders commitment and ingenuity conducive to creative change, stretching perceived boundaries of conventionality and possibility. Such a deep-seated aspiration is deemed consistent with the pursuit of self-interests because the former provides a historical and epistemological context from which the latter can emerge and develop.

Having looked at the trend of historical and regional change and the importance of interests and values, one can now shift attention to the social role of creators as another enabling factor. Although Törnudd was not directly involved in the preparatory phases of the Helsinki process before his involvement in 1972, the Finnish historical records that he has at his disposal illustrate how the intertwined process of incipience and origination developed in the late 1960s. The idea of convening a comprehensive multiparty conference on security in Europe had grown gradually through a series of initiatives, exchanges, and consultations. The Finnish initiative to host the conference was first conceived at a working lunch on April 29, 1969, in which President Kekkonen consulted Ambassador Max Jakobson, who at that time was Finland's Permanent Representative to the UN in New York. Records also show that sometime before the working lunch, the Soviet ambassador in Helsinki had reminded President Kekkonen of the Soviet interest in convening a pan-European security conference. During the working lunch, Kekkonen and Jakobson came to share the understanding that Finland should not simply give an answer to the Soviet Union, but should rather take its own initiative and even offer to host the conference. After the lunch, the idea was further elaborated in the Ministry of Foreign Affairs. As early as May 5, 1969, about a week after the meeting, the Finnish memorandum on this matter was ready for distribution.

The author's attempt to interview Ambassador Max Jakobson to inquire about the exact nature of his conversation with late President Kekkonen in the working lunch on April 29, 1969 has been unsuccessful. However, Jakobson reflects on this subject in his writing as follows:

> [I]t was on my suggestion that the Finnish government decided to take an initiative of its own by proposing that the security conference be held in Helsinki, the only European capital where both German states were represented on an equal footing
>
> (Jakobson 1998: 81).

It is inferred that the act of creation, at least within the context of the Helsinki process, was made possible partly because of the unique role of Finland as a neutral party in the polarized international relations. In this context, it is important to note that the Soviet Union had repeatedly expressed its desire to hold a pan-European security conference since the 1950s. Not until the Finnish initiatives started in the late 1960s, however, did the Soviet vision come to fruition. Although the effectiveness of the Finnish leadership has to be understood in the overall context of its relationship to the regional and historical trends of Ostpolitik and détente, it is clear that the Soviet Union's inability to initiate the process was inseparable from its role as a superpower pitted against another superpower. As demonstrated in many other conflict episodes under study, the social role assigned to the initiator of the creative action played a decisive function in turning the seemingly impossible vision into a reality and in shaping the unique nature of the action. No less important than the social role was the capacity of the Finnish leaders to make use of its unique role for the creative change.

Finally, the episode illustrates that the procedural and substantive creativity demonstrated in the Helsinki process came out of the same roots: the fundamental desire to fulfill the needs and values that mattered to the parties deeply. The innovative procedural rules devised in the informal preparatory talks in 1972–3 featured comprehensive agenda-setting, equality among all participating states, and communication outside the bipolar framework of the Cold War. Innovative outcomes developed through years of CSCE consultations included the invention of confidence-building measures for transparency and fear reduction. Both types of creative act grew out of the commitment of the Finnish leaders and other key stakeholders to fulfilling their deep values and needs for survival, security, and functional coexistence.

The Peru–Ecuador border dispute: transcendence with a quantum jump (Johan Galtung)

Johan Galtung is internationally recognized as one of the founding fathers of contemporary peace research, education, and practice. He is currently the director of TRANSCEND, a peace and development network for conflict transformation by peaceful means. Galtung has mediated over forty-five major conflicts around the world. According to Galtung, creativity is a jump, with the view to "channeling conflict energy toward new, innovative ways of satisfying basic human needs for all."[38] The task requires "experience, sheer intelligence in the IQ sense, the capacity to internalize vast amounts of emotional/cognitive material and to make that quantum jump to a new image/perspective with sufficient clarity, combined with the word-smith's ability to find the right words" (Galtung *et al.* 2002: 156). Galtung illustrates his understanding of creativity by referring to his consultation efforts as an independent mediator and consultant for Peru and Ecuador in 1995 and 1998.[39]

During the interview, Galtung did not describe the conflict in detail. In his writings, too, his mention of the background of the Peru–Ecuador conflict is necessarily brief. For example, a generic description of the case is found in his recent writing as follows:

> By the classical logic of the state system now celebrating its 350th anniversary since the Treaty of Westphalia, each piece of land, clearly demarcated, belongs to one and only one state. But what if two or more states claim the same piece of land, for instance because there is not only one *divortium aquarum* (watershed) but two, or a possible border river comes and goes? The classical answer is a war to arrive at a "military solution," and this is what Ecuador and Peru did in 1942, 1981 and 1995, following the 1941 war.
>
> (Galtung *et al.* 2002: 264)

To supplement this generic description of the Peru–Ecuador conflict, some additional background is provided,[40] based on Simmons (1999) and Marcella and Downes (1999). The conflict over sovereign control of the border area surfaced in the early 1820s, when Peru and Ecuador gained independence from the Spanish Empire, which had left many borders undefined in South America. Dozens of military confrontations occurred intermittently on the border between the two countries throughout the nineteenth and twentieth centuries, including the war of 1941. The 1941 war ended with the signing of the 1942 Rio Protocol, which was to draw a border by consolidating Ecuador's loss of territory as a result of its confrontation with Peru in 1936. However, in 1946 the Ecuadorian government claimed that the geographic information which formed the basis of the Rio Protocol was false. In 1960, Ecuador officially declared the demarcation scheme invalid, not only because of the false geographic information but also because of the threatening political environment in which Ecuador had to accept the Rio Protocol. In the wars of 1981 and 1995, Ecuador asserted its sovereign access to the disputed border area in the Amazon, including navigational routes from its domestic waters to the Atlantic Ocean. Peru remained committed to the "status quo" defined by the Rio Protocol, claiming its sovereign access to the border area. While coping with the 1995 war and its aftermath, the Peruvian government was desperately in need of diverting military expenditure to socio-economic reforms, including the urgent task of tackling the two million percent inflation that its economy had suffered in 1985–90.

A group of four guarantor states – Argentina, Brazil, Chile, and the US – intervened to deflect the bilateral tension soon after the 1995 war, in accordance with the dispute settlement clause in the Rio Protocol. The four states pursued shared interests in de-escalation of the regional arms race and creation of a stable economic environment for regional trade, investment, and growth. Drawing on numerous bilateral negotiations between Peru and Ecuador, the guarantor states arbitrated a final settlement in 1998 that established a border area. The agreement, the Act of Brasilia, was to establish two contiguous demilitarized natural parks, one for Peru and one for Ecuador, with a demarcated boundary separating the two along the zone disputed in the 1995 war. In addition, Ecuador was to be granted permanent access to a 1 km^2 private property in Tiwinza, inside the sovereign territory of Peru as a symbolic gesture to honor Ecuadorian soldiers who fought hard and died there. On navigation and commerce, Ecuador's right to use two non-sovereign areas of the Amazon tributaries was guaranteed, allowing Ecuadorian ships to travel directly from Ecuadorian domestic waters to the Atlantic Ocean.

Galtung began to play an active role in mediating the conflict in 1995, when he was invited to Ecuador to talk with the country's ex-president. Galtung proposed that a binational zone with a natural park be established in the disputed border area, instead of drawing a border line as intended by both parties.[41] The basic image of Galtung's vision was incorporated into the 1998 agreement.

The TRANSCEND method that Galtung applied on this and many other occasions has evolved from his philosophy of conflict. Galtung defines conflict as goal incompatibility. He sees pursuit of goals as inherent in human life, and observes that some goals of individuals and groups appear as mutually compatible but others contradict one another. To overcome a contradiction, Galtung first identifies the parties and their goals through one-on-one dialogue. He then distinguishes between legitimate and illegitimate goals, the former being aspirations for fulfilling four basic human needs, namely, survival, wellbeing, freedom, and identity. His approach focuses on resisting illegitimate goals nonviolently and bridging legitimate goals with creativity and empathy. When there are two primary parties to the conflict, he places one party's legitimate goals on the X-axis and the other's on the Y-axis within the Cartesian space in order to envision ways to make seemingly incompatible goals mutually compatible. He refers to this process of discovery as transcendence, which he views as a special form of the Hegelian synthesis of a thesis (a goal placed on the X-axis) and antithesis (a goal placed on the Y-axis). When there are more than two parties, his diagnosis does not fit within the Cartesian space and becomes more holistic and intuitive while following the same logic of making goals mutually compatible. Galtung drew an example of the "peace diagram" (Figure 2.1) applied to the conflict between Peru and Ecuador, both trying to gain sovereign control over their border area.

The five points on the peace diagram refer to possible outcomes of the conflict. Point A refers to Ecuador's total victory over Peru in securing the disputed border area, and point B is Peru prevailing over Ecuador. Galtung believes that it is precisely this either–or mentality, or dualism, that must be challenged and transcended to handle conflict creatively. Point C refers to fulfillment of neither Ecuador's nor Peru's initial goal. Galtung terms it a negative transcendence, equivalent to the negation of the negation in the Hegelian dialectics. Point C can be interpreted as hypothetical UN administration of the territory in which neither side retains sovereign control. It could also mean giving the territory to indigenous inhabitants in the area. Point D is a compromise, like dividing the territory using a ceasefire line, so that each side can get a portion of what it wants while conceding the rest to the other side. Point E is a positive transcendence, where both Peru's and Ecuador's goals are fulfilled in the form of a binational zone administered together. Galtung proposed option E as the basic image of a possible solution while combining other elements such as transitional administration by the UN.[42] The 1998 Act of Brasilia reflected Galtung's positive transcendence

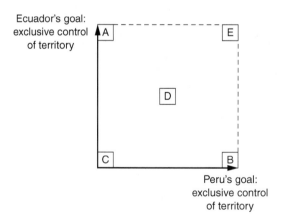

Figure 2.1 Peace diagram for transcendence.

as a blueprint, supplemented and modified by a number of compromises negotiated by the parties.

Asked about possible precursors of his binational zone proposal and the process of its origination, Galtung indicated that he did not draw on any analogies from other situations, but he simply interpreted his diagram for the Peru–Ecuador context. He recalls that it took him "exactly five seconds" to come up with the solution and it came to his mind even before his meeting with the former Ecuadorian president. Galtung (2004) describes how he explained his thinking process of origination to the ex-president. The quoted portion illustrates how he verbalized the meaning of the diagram:

> I have a little method, and this is to listen to what has not been said, to listen to the inaudible. Neither you, nor your colleague, has said anything about why one has to draw a border, probably because you think it is too evident. You are probably both of the opinion that every square metre on this our earth belongs to one and only one country. And it is like that, almost 100%. The method consists in identifying axioms of faith which are not to be discussed, not even to be formulated, and then start touching them, tinkering with them, shaking them, inserting the word "not", negating them so that everything becomes more flexible. As a general rule this will lead us to something that can be changed. But, as you pointed out yourself, it can easily become too creative, precisely because it is touching the articles of faith.
>
> (Galtung 2004: 80)

Galtung's binational zone proposal appeared to have gained momentum toward acceptance through his meetings with the Ecuadorian ex-president and his colleagues in 1995. In 1998, Galtung was again invited to Ecuador to give a lecture to commemorate the ninety-ninth anniversary of the country's military academy. Galtung spoke in front of forty generals and admirals. They wanted him to talk about the proposed binational zone, and spent three hours asking him detailed questions. Galtung sensed that the meeting was the opportunity in which real decision-making was taking place about the adoption of the proposal. They had not communicated their intention to Galtung, but it was apparent in the atmosphere of the meeting. The participants asked him extremely good questions, some with the "what if" rhetoric. Galtung was aware that the Ecuadorian leaders were willing to sign a peace agreement in September 1998, and they had even written its text already. The text contained the date and the place of signature, and a clause on a proposed revision to the agreement five years from signing the 1998 treaty. But the only point missing in the text was the solution itself. In Galtung's view, that good idea had already been there with them since the dinner party of 1995, in which the former president met with him. But the idea had to be subjected to the critique of the generals and admirals, or the real "bosses," according to the Ecuadorian ambassador to the UN who invited Galtung to the 1998 meeting.

Galtung's approach to the Peru–Ecuador conflict illustrates his TRANSCEND method. Using the working typologies and assumptions of the present study, its key features are described as: (1) outcome-oriented (suggesting substantive resolution options, not just processes); (2) agency-led (with a conflict worker generating possible solutions based on one-on-one dialogue with parties); and (3) paradigm-breaking (transcending the parties' shared frame of mind, axiomatic and unquestioned). Galtung supplements these essential features with procedural (as inseparable from outcome) and paradigm-accepting (trying not to be too creative) elements. However, Galtung rejects the possibility of systemically generated creativity because he believes that collectivity tends to discourage individual innovativeness through peer pressure, especially in conflict. To the extent that Galtung's approach is devised explicitly for the purpose of envisioning creative *outcomes*, it is distinguished from many other interviewees' methods that place primary emphasis on *processes*.

Galtung maintains that for successful conflict transformation, there needs to be not only transcendence, but also the parties' willingness to accept and sustain the vision. Thus his approach is formulated succinctly as: conflict transformation = transcendence + acceptability + sustainability, resembling the five-phase model developed in the present study. Galtung argues that for a transcendence option to be acceptable and sustainable, the solution needs to be creative, but not too creative – that is, within the carrying capacity, cognitive and emotive, of the parties. He also stresses that the solution has to be communicable to the parties, using up to four simple evocative words to formulate it. In the Peru–Ecuador case, for example, options included a "binational zone," a "condominium," and "joint sovereignty."[43]

From a psychological perspective, Galtung reflects that a process of transcendence is highly intuitive, and much of it takes place in the subconscious and unconscious. In the interview, he described this inner process as follows:

> you have an enormous amount of elements emerging in your mind, and in the beginning things look totally chaotic. And suddenly, like a lightening, something comes to you that captures all the elements and puts them all together, making them compatible.

Galtung (2004) further elaborates on the inner process of creation, by appeal to unique metaphoric expressions:

> Creativity is located in the border land between the intellectual and the emotional. Knowledge and emotions push together and suddenly the transcendence is there, the same way it happens to creative people in the arts of architecture and engineering. The word "arts" is important here, very often justified. A good idea starts like an emotion in the guts aching for some release, working itself up, arriving in the head-brain where it is verbalized and sent back again to the gut-brain producing a feeling of orgasmic release. Just like true love it does not happen that often. But when it happens it is enormous.
>
> (Galtung 2004: 94)

Galtung believes that creativity is learnable up to a certain point despite its highly intuitive nature, and beyond that point the ability comes with extensive experience. He observes that although there is no formula for creativity, there are some "jumping boards" that help envision creative outcomes in a given context, including the following four methods described by Galtung (1979; 2004).

The first method involves conceptualizing an *alternative world*, or a social context of the conflict different from what it actually is in empirical reality. This resembles a physicist asking, "What if gravity worked differently?" Galtung (1979) falls short of elaborating his idea fully, but one can illustrate his point with a recent example.

There has been talk of gradual de-militarization of state territories for collective security, especially after the two World Wars. Since the establishment of the UN, the vision has been expressed to bring national defense forces, or at least a portion of them, under transnational command for conflict prevention, peace-keeping, and other concerted tasks. Today the vision is far from practical, despite the end of the Cold War. Underlying the gap between the vision and the reality is the centuries-old structure of state sovereignty as a barrier to alternative security paradigms. Galtung's "alternative worlds" method invites one to ask such questions as: "What if de-militarization *worked* as a realistic national and international policy? What if a transnational security system were to work in empirical reality? What would the world look like then?" These questions help explore conditions under which the vision might become a reality, formulate hypotheses about how it might come about, and think about alternative empirical worlds in general.

In June 2004, Galtung visited Iceland in support of the presidential candidate Thor Magnusson, whose campaign platform included converting the American military base in Iceland into the headquarters of a UN peace-keeping force.[44] Magnusson's plan was to invite nations aspiring to abolish their national military to sign a contract to be protected by the UN force for a relatively small annual fee. In his lecture, delivered at Reykjavik University on June 9, 2004, Galtung furthered Magnusson's vision and proposed:

> The Keflavic base at the disposal of the UN is a model that could be copied around the world and multiply the potential for effective peace-keeping by having the troops pre-stationed. And how about making NATO the peace-keeping arm of the UN, giving force to the UN resolutions while at the same time steering NATO?[45]

Though Magnusson eventually lost the 2004 election and Galtung's vision failed to be realized on this occasion, the campaign opened up imaginative thinking and drew public attention to it. The episode illustrates how Galtung's "alternative worlds" method may apply in reality, at least as a platform for initiating a long-term campaign for creative social change.

The second approach outlined by Galtung (2004) is the heuristics of "this reminds me of…" or analogizing. Galtung distinguishes between two types of analogizing, identity and isomorphism (structural identity). *Identity* in this context refers to a simple comparison between two or more cases, such as a comparison between an adolescent in need of independent space in his household and a nation wanting to gain autonomy within the state to which it belongs. Identity could also mean drawing similarities and differences between cases of the same level of analysis, such as autonomies in the Åland Islands within Finland, and Greenland within Denmark. Used in dialogue with conflict parties, this form of analogy-building can be used to point to future scenarios beyond confrontation. Galtung points out, however, that critical differences between cases have to be kept in mind when building analogies. *Isomorphism* refers to comparison between relationships, that is, A's relationship to B as compared to X's relationship to Y. To illustrate isomorphism, Galtung (2004) contrasts a binational zone with two neighbors sharing their garden, with space and time as criteria for comparison. Spatially joint administration of a border area may work for two countries as well as for two neighbors despite the different levels of analysis. Time-wise, however, the two relationships differ critically. For example, average terms of office held by heads of state who administer their countries' border area are usually shorter than time periods of private land ownership. Moreover, while private landowners may buy or sell their properties and they may accordingly choose to move in and out, neighboring countries cannot "move out" of their territories irrespective of the rises and declines of their regimes and governments that have signed the joint-ownership agreement. Thinking through these possibilities helps the parties realize that analogies drawn from other cases have commonalities as well as critical differences in terms of temporal and spatial arrangements. Therefore, Galtung suggests using isomorphism not only for generating possible solutions, but also for exploring unexplored problems of the options under consideration. He recommends checking a seemingly attractive option at another conflict level, asking questions like "What would this mean if the problem was not between classes in society, but between regions in world society, or between husband and wife? Is there something we should watch out for that we have been unaware of?" (Galtung 2004: 95)

The third method that Galtung (2004) suggests is combining known elements in a new way in terms of time and space. Application of this method is illustrated by his proposal to reverse the conventional sequence in which a ceasefire, negotiations, and a vision for handling the conflict are pursued, usually in this order. Galtung suggests the exact opposite, namely, first a vision, then negotiations, and finally a ceasefire – or better yet, three processes at the same time. His rationale is that parties who believe in the chance of winning or otherwise making honorable sacrifices are not willing to lay down arms unless they are persuaded by a workable plan to end the military confrontation through negotiations or other means of communication. Galtung thus believes that visions for ending violence must be presented first in order to enable negotiations to start, followed by a ceasefire and disarmament. Changing the temporal sequence may appear creative but not too creative because its basic components are already well-known to the stakeholders involved. Likewise, changing spatial arrangements tends to stimulate creativity, and typically a modest level of creativity. An example of such spatial creativity is the gradual shift in the location of a kitchen in the house, from the periphery (for example, the backyard) toward the center of family activities over the past century, due in part to the change in the status of women in family life.

The fourth method described by Galtung (2004) is making the parties' axioms of faith explicit. On the spiritual and psychological level, this means making the parties in protracted conflict realize that they are trapped in the DMA syndrome, that is, *dualism* (the world is divided into two camps, with no neutrals), *manichaeism* (those who do not side with the good are all evil), and *armageddon* (the evil succumb only to violence). To do this, deep dialogue has to be launched to help the parties realize that there are more than two parties involved, and that convincing the other side that "our side" is not born permanently evil is no less difficult than the other side convincing "our side." The dialogue should then proceed to let the parties know that there *are* similar situations in which constructive solutions have been found. Applied to a Marxist class struggle, for example, the approach would involve helping parties realize that the conflict at hand is not only about the division between bourgeoisie and proletariat, but also about gender, generation, religion, and other possible social layers and influences. Another example of application is the Peru–Ecuador case, where both parties had never questioned why they needed to draw a border line, instead of creating a border zone. The axiom of faith for Peruvians and Ecuadorians was the Westphalian tradition of exclusive sovereignty over every square mile of state territory. The key to uncovering axioms of faith lies in finding unspoken, unquestioned commonalities hidden in the parties' belief systems. Galtung views his peace diagram as a tool to discover axioms of faith embedded in the conflict paradigm.[46]

Finally, building on the last two methods, Galtung offers a hypothesis about the relationship between creativity and culture. His thesis is summarized as follows:

> [T]he creative act may not introduce any new element at all, only put them together, in space and time, in a new way. Spatial arrangements and time orders that have been taken for granted are challenged. For that reason it is particularly easy to be creative in cultures with very definitive views on correct spatial orders; there is so much to challenge. A culture firmly dividing the world in center and periphery, assuming causality to flow from center to periphery rather than vice versa ... and conceiving of time as linear with clear views on what comes before and what after ... invites creativity. But if such unlinear ideas are firmly entrenched, as they are in Western culture, we would also have to expect considerable resistance.
>
> (Galtung 1998: 30)

To illustrate this hypothesis, Galtung offers an example from a macro historical perspective:

> [I]f *cause* = *center* = *God*, and *effect* = *periphery* = *Nature* + *Man*, the latter created in His image, then such ideas as democracy, secularism and evolution stand out as revolutionary. The first of these vested power with

the people/periphery, like a country without a capital. The second made God a periphery, suggesting that He was created by Man in Man's image. And the third was that Man was an emanation from Nature by competition, like Adam Smith arguing that out of this process came the best of all worlds.

(Galtung 1998: 31)

The hypothesized relationship between creativity and culture helps to conceptualize the dynamics of a paradigm shift for conflict transformation. One can draw on Galtung's hypothesis and generate a proposition on incipience and origination: the more deeply cultural norms are entrenched in society defining conventional temporal and spatial arrangements, the more clearly a creative mind can identify a conflict paradigm (for example, the center–periphery dichotomy) to transform. Its implications for evolution, acceptance, and sustenance are still to be explored, however, for this study falls short of addressing them comprehensively.

Interlude (2): reflections on intermediaries' creativity

The analysis of the nine episodes has generated a range of working propositions on the nature, origination, and other aspects of conflict resolution creativity. This interlude summarizes them succinctly in preparation for a synthetic theory-building exercise to be conducted in Chapter 3. As stated in the previous interlude, these propositions represent no more than conceptual building blocks, still to be examined in terms of internal and external validity across distinctly different empirical contexts.

A racial conflict in Tajikistan – Majid Tehranian:

1   Appealing to the parties' deeply held moral foundations helped them create their inner shifts.

An American labor dispute – John Smith (pseudonym):

1   The unconventionality of rule-breaking stood out because of the well-established rules of mediation in place.
2   The mastery of conventionality gave rise to the need and capacity for inventing the unconventional action.
3   Thorough paradigm-accepting practice opened a path to paradigm-breaking, in a manner analogous to Thomas Kuhn's thesis on scientific revolutions.
4   Contingency-based thinking determined whether, when, and how to break boundaries of conventional practice.

The civil war in Sierra Leone – Abdullahi Said Osman:

1   The commitment to principles such as unity and joint action encouraged a new mode of action to emerge.
2   Creativity emerged from the combined effect of local conventional knowledge and its unconventional application.

The Indonesia–Malaysia–Singapore conflict – John Burton:

1. In-depth conflict analysis led to a creative resolution.
2. The commitment to establishing conflict resolution as a legitimate discipline of academic inquiry and social action opened the way toward Track-Two diplomacy.

An Israeli–Palestinian problem-solving workshop – Herbert Kelman:

1. The discovery emerged from an intuitive, experiential, and contingency-based learning process.
2. Unexpected revelations and chance were welcomed within the framework of purposive action.
3. The whole picture of the discovery became clear only in retrospect.

Estonian–Russian psychoanalytic dialogue – Vamik Volkan:

1. Parties played with symbols and metaphors to humanize each other and create new relationships.
2. Revealing the parties' unconscious helped them experience creative ways of addressing traumas.
3. Providing an informal and inviting context helped them reveal and deal with collective traumas.
4. Transitional experience in childhood shapes the balance between illusion and reality.
5. Collective traumas distort the balance but effective use of metaphors can help parties adjust the balance constructively.
6. Precursors of creative resolutions begin forming in the unconscious even *before* conflict analysis.

The Cyprus conflict – Louise Diamond:

1. The tenacious commitment to grassroots-based transformation broke new ground in the practice of bicommunal peace-building.
2. Persistent action in evolution, acceptance, and sustenance validated origination in retrospect.
3. Gradual acceptance by key stakeholders authenticated the project's viability retroactively.

The Helsinki process – Klaus Törnudd:

1. Convergence of diverse national interests enabled the innovative multilateral dialogue to emerge.
2. The unique role of Finland as a small neutral state made it possible to offer space for the dialogue.
3. Finnish and other leaders' need for coexistence shaped both substantive and procedural creativity.

The Peru–Ecuador border dispute – Johan Galtung:

1 The application of the "peace diagram" enabled the quantum leap to emerge.
2 A creative transcendence requires communicability and acceptability/sustainability as enabling factors.
3 Conceptualizing an alternative reality to the given empirical reality contributes to envisioning creative solutions.
4 Analogizing through identity (A to B) and structural identity (A:B to X:Y) stimulates creativity.
5 Combining known elements in a new way in terms of time and space generates creativity.
6 Making the parties' axioms of faith explicit helps them realize alternative approaches to conflict.
7 One can find much room for creativity in societies in which the notion of time and space is fixed.

As noted in the first interlude, there emerged no clear patterns of systematic differences between conflict parties' and intermediaries' creativity in terms of how it first appears. Like conflict parties' creativity, intermediaries' creativity involves restructuring and reshaping how conflicts are understood and dealt with, challenging conventional modes of thinking and behavior, and persisting with the commitment to the new vision despite risks and oppositions. However, because the two types differ with respect to the *sources* from which creative initiatives emerge, the way they evolve and gain acceptance differs. Intermediaries' creativity is generated outside the circle of immediate conflict stakeholders. It is then introduced into the circle while at the same time, it is constantly shaped and reshaped by the stakeholders' input. Therefore intermediaries' creativity is "creativity from outside." Whether the unconventional and potentially viable initiatives can gain momentum depends on the parties' willingness, or "buy-in," to own them. On the contrary, conflict parties' creativity is generated by the parties themselves. It is "creativity from within." Because at least one of the parties has already demonstrated ownership of a given resolution option through the origination phase, conflict parties' creativity, if put into action, tends to gain at least some level of recognition and generates impact on the conflict situations immediately. The most likely initial impact is reactive devaluation, or the attitude of the adversaries to view the new ideas with distrust and treat them as being not as worthy as they potentially are.

To illustrate creativity from outside, Burton's problem-solving workshops on the Southeast Asian conflict and Galtung's binational zone proposal are considered. One of the co-facilitators and consultants in Burton's workshops recalls that no response was received for months from the heads of the respective governments to which Burton wrote a letter of invitation.[47] Because of the long wait, Burton was upset and some of his colleagues either gave up or even forgot about the project. It was only after their additional lobbying activities with the

Indonesian and Malaysian high commissioners in London that they finally secured support from both heads of state. In Galtung's example of outcome creativity, the first obstacle he faced in 1995 was the Ecuadorian ex-president's reaction – "too creative" – to his proposal to establish a Peru–Ecuador binational ecological park in the disputed border area. Galtung's discussion in 1998 with Ecuadorian generals and admirals who thoroughly critiqued his proposal appeared to have lowered the long-standing hurdle for acceptance. These and other cases of intermediaries' creativity suggest that the key to the unconventional initiatives that have gained momentum lies in the conflict parties' "buy-in," which often results from the intermediaries' tenacious persuasion. Without the parties' willingness to own the initiatives, the ideas, however creative in theory, could have been lost – and in fact, they would not have become the subjects of this study in the first place.

Creativity from within the circle of primary conflict stakeholders is illustrated by Henderson's Environmentalists for Full Employment movement and Johnston's episode on "accidental pregnancies", discussed earlier in this chapter. In Henderson's case, creativity was demonstrated in the form of an NGO network bridging pro-environmentalists with pro-employment advocates. Because Henderson was a pro-environment NGO worker herself, her idea immediately caught the attention of her environmentalist sympathizers, started generating impact on the national level, and gradually involved pro-employment sympathizers through the expanding NGO network. Although it is not clear from Henderson's episode whether reactive devaluation from pro-employment advocates posed a serious challenge to her campaign, opposition from within Henderson's potential allies was substantial. She reflects, for example, that some elitist environmentalists accused her of spreading communism. Similar group dynamics were observed in Johnston's case. Her creativity was demonstrated when her clinic hired teens in order to supplement its professional staff, who had been working hard to stop the teens' "accidental pregnancies." Because of Johnston's influential role as the clinic supervisor, her act of creativity generated an immediate and decisive impact on shifting the value conflict between the staff and the teens toward collaboration, however reluctant. As in the case of Henderson, the level of possible reactive devaluation from the teens is hard to infer, but the major opposition to Johnston's initiative came from within her clinic staff, who did not want to give up their long-held assumption of accidental pregnancies. The two episodes echo other incidents of conflict parties' creativity, or creativity from within. This type of creation tends to generate immediate impact on the conflict situations and invite reactive devaluation from their opponents, as well as from their own in-group constituents resisting change.[48]

Although the two types of creativity are conceptually distinguished for typology development, this distinction is hardly unambiguous in reality. This is particularly evident when an actor in conflict plays a dual role, both as a conflict party or stakeholder with vested interests and as a self-declared intermediary. This third and hybrid type of creativity is the subject of the next section.

88 *Exploration*

Episodes of creativity demonstrated by actors playing a dual function

Overview

The two episodes that illustrate the creativity of actors working in a dual function, both as a conflict party and intermediary, are summarized in Table 2.3.

The two cases are considerably different in many important ways, but they both demonstrate a dual function of a conflict party playing the role of an intermediary. As a conflict party, Boulding was a parent in relation to her five children trying to get more allowances from her and her husband. As an intermediary, Boulding convened and moderated family dialogues to transform the allowance question constructively. On the contrary, Saunders, as a senior US diplomat, was assigned to work with State Secretary Henry Kissinger to broker ceasefires between Israel and her Arab neighbors while at the same time, managing US–Soviet relations and restoring US access to Arab oil resources. The episodes described by the two interviewees share the duality of roles, and they are therefore placed in the same conceptual category for analysis.

Episodes of creativity demonstrated by actors playing a dual function

Children–parents dialogue: transferring the Quaker method from a community to a family (Elise Boulding)

Elise Boulding is a Professor Emerita of Sociology at Dartmouth College in New Hampshire and former Secretary-General of the International Peace Research

Table 2.3 Summary of the two episodes of creativity demonstrated by actors playing a dual function

Interviewee	Region and time	Role	Episode	Definition
Elise Boulding	Michigan, 1950s	Parent, conflict party, and dialogue moderator	Together with her husband Kenneth, introduced the method of Quaker business meetings to monthly dialogues with their five children, in order to allocate allowances and build a community within the family	Seeing things differently for conflict transformation
Harold Saunders	Middle East, 1973–4	Diplomat, negotiator, and mediator	Created the first "peace process" after the October 1973 war between Egypt, Israel, and Syria with US state secretary Henry Kissinger. Reshaped and interacted with the regional and global political context to carry out step-by-step shuttle diplomacy	Coming up with an approach that is not derived from existing models

Association. She defines creativity as the ability to see things in totally different ways. Boulding regards creativity as a component of conflict transformation that involves looking at a conflict from many different angles and putting various elements together to generate a fresh perspective. Despite many years of her professional life as a pioneering peace researcher, she selected a personal conflict episode from her family life to illustrate her understanding of creativity. The conflict was about how to allocate allowances among her five children. Her role in transforming the conflict was described as a mother and as a convener and moderator of a series of monthly family meetings that started in the mid-1950s, when Elise, her husband Kenneth Boulding (who was also a renowned peace researcher and who passed away in 1993), and their five children lived together in Ann Arbor, Michigan.

As a Quaker family, the Bouldings held periodic "Quaker *family* meetings for business" to tackle the problem of children's allowance allocation. Inspirations for this idea came from the Quaker practice of business meetings called "meetings for worship for business." Like Quaker business meetings in community settings, their family meetings started with silent worship followed by the sharing of the meeting agenda. Each child proposed what he or she thought to be a fair amount of allowance. Boulding introduced the idea that her husband's work outside their family life, her work as a mother and housewife, and their children's shares of household tasks all made their livelihood possible and functional. They then made a list of household tasks such as washing dishes, putting away groceries, tidying up rooms, making beds, sweeping the walk, and shoveling snow in winter. At each meeting, each child would accept one of the jobs. Amounts of allowances were decided according to the children's contributions to the household as well as to their needs.

The conflict involved at least two levels of tension that had to be transformed. One was the competition among the five children vying for more allowances, with each claiming what he or she regarded as a fair amount in relation to the other four. The other was the tension between the parents and the children, where the children as dependents negotiated to gain as much as possible from the parents, their providers. The family meetings were intended to transform this competitive relationship into a more mutual, communal one in which everybody's needs were expressed and met. The shift enabled the children to sense that they were contributing to the functioning of the household, instead of feeling that the parents did all the work and the children simply depended on them. There was subtle bargaining among the children for a little more or less in amount, but generally there was peaceful acceptance of the amounts allocated in the meetings. She was the main facilitator of the process, and her husband Kenneth took minutes of the meetings. Boulding believes that the action was creative because her family had never heard of the Quaker business meeting method applied to children's allowance allocation within a family. Conceptually, creativity was derived from shifting the levels of analysis from the local community to the family.

In Quaker business meetings at the community level, participants take turns to express their opinions. They sometimes disagree with one another but trust that out of periods of silent waiting, solutions emerge based on a new shared understanding of the problem at hand. In her *Cultures of Peace: The Hidden Side of History*, the publication recommended to supplement the interview, Boulding elaborates on the procedure and philosophy of Quaker business meetings as follows:

> Quakers ... in the absence of authority figures, developed a special consensus approach to decision making based on the "sense of meeting," as members sought divine guidance on what was to be done in the face of conflicting views of participating individuals. The refusal to use voting procedures and majority rule meant that decisions could not be taken until either all members reached agreement or dissenters were willing to "stand aside." What is particularly interesting about the consensus method is that it respects the presence of conflict and allows for the full airing of differences. It also depends on a disciplined spiritual maturity of members of the community, a common acceptance of collective inward illumination of the group, and great skill in intellectual discernment and interpersonal and intergroup communication. This is a tall order for any group, and therefore great importance is given to the religious education of the children of a Meeting. They must be prepared not only to carry on the consensus process within their Meeting but also to carry Friends' testimonies into the larger society in an active pursuit of social and economic justice and peace.
>
> (Boulding 2000: 99)

Both her writing and the present interview have made it clear that the creative application of Quaker business meetings into the family setting reflected both a great deal of conventionality derived from centuries of Quaker traditions, on the one hand, and the innovative transfer of public conscience into a more personal, intra-familial setting, on the other. Although the transfer generated unconventional, creative behavior within the family, the actual conduct of meetings drew on the conventionality and continuity of what the Boulding family had already been doing in public settings. It is inferred that the successful origination and evolution of Boulding's Quaker family meetings are attributed in part to the continuity of everyday behavior that was carried into this particular act of creation.

The episode also illustrates the link between value commitment and creativity. Underlying Boulding's desire for community-building was the deep spiritual pledge that she and her husband made when they married in 1941 during World War II. During the war, Kenneth faced difficulties as a conscientious objector and a British citizen living in the US. Sensing the bitterness of the war in daily life, the two deepened their shared conviction that raising their children to be peace-makers and developing their family as a peaceful community would contribute directly to world peace. The fact that Kenneth worked at the Economic and Financial Section of the League of Nations, which was temporarily located at Princeton University in New Jersey, and that they were both deeply involved in local, national, and international civil society activities helped them see the link between their family life and global society.

Closely related to her pledge in her marriage was her value commitment to respecting children as equal partners of adults. The initiation of the Quaker family meetings reflected this value commitment, which she shared with her husband. In Boulding's view, transforming her own family was a step toward challenging the structure and culture of today's age-segregated society, which she criticizes as follows:

> The problem is that the practice of social grouping by age has been carried to an extreme, leaving very few common social spaces in which child–adult friendships can develop. Think, reader, if you are under eighteen, who your over-thirty friends are. If you are over thirty, think who your under-eighteen friends are. Many preteens and teens have never had a serious conversation with an adult who was not a relative, a teacher, or someone else with special relationship for the young ... there is an underlying attitude, particularly in the One-Third World, that contributes to the pervasive separating out of children and adults, an attitude of disrespect for children and their capacities, masked by the provision of much specialized attention in carefully designated settings. Some of this disrespect comes from patriarchal authority patterns, some from a dislike of the unexpected – something children can be guaranteed to introduce into adult settings – and some from a basic social denial, a refusal to face a future different from the present, a future that will belong to and be shared by those who are now children.
> (Boulding 2000: 141)

Boulding's vision for transforming the dominant mode of relationships between children and adults parallels the broader theme addressed in *Cultures of Peace*, that is, nurturing partnership for peaceable diversity in society. She presents this theme as an antidote to the far-reaching paradigm of domination of men over women, hegemonic identity groups over "minorities" within and across states, the state and capitalism over civil society networks, urbanized centers over rural peripheries, the wealthy One-Third World over the less-wealthy Two-Thirds World, and humans' sociosphere over nature's biosphere. The significance of Boulding's Quaker family meetings is better understood in the broader context of her value commitment to nurturing partnerships in society.

Reflecting on Boulding's pledge in her marriage and her commitment to partnership-building in society, it is inferred that the kernel image of her creative approach had already been in store in her and her family's value system even *before* the conflict over allowance allocation was recognized as such. While her ability to reframe the competitive conflict into community-building was essential, it is no less important to emphasize that the basic template for the act of reframing had already been forming for some time. Appealing to this basic template, or her "big picture" and mission in life and society, Boulding was able to crystallize her act of creativity.

Finally, by reframing the competition into community-building, the Bouldings introduced new dimensions into the family dialogue. The allocation of household tasks, the subject that had been deemed totally unrelated to allowance allocation, came to be viewed as directly related to the allowance question. The *right* of each child to gain as much as possible was transformed into the *responsibility*-based understanding of the family as a community. The children's total dependency on the parents declined, at least symbolically, as interdependent partnership among the seven family members grew. A lesson learned from this episode is that the introduction of new seemingly unrelated dimensions, if performed appropriately, can uplift the parameters of the conflict from confrontation to constructive relationship-building, while at the same time staying focused on the "original conflict" – in this case, the issue of allowance allocation.

Kissinger's shuttle diplomacy in the Arab–Israeli conflict: principled flexibility for a "peace process" (Harold Saunders)

Harold Saunders views creativity as a process of coming up with an approach that is not derived from an existing model of conflict resolution. As Director of International Affairs at Kettering Foundation and President of the International Institute for Sustained Dialogue in Washington DC, Saunders has extensively practiced public peace-making between parties to racial and ethnic conflicts in different parts of the world. In the 1970s, he was Deputy Assistant Secretary and Assistant Secretary for Near Eastern and South Asian Affairs in the US State Department. As a senior diplomat who had worked closely with Secretary of State Henry Kissinger, Saunders illustrated his understanding of creativity by describing the US-led peace process after the war of October 1973 between Israel, Egypt, and Syria.

In June 1967, Israel launched a sweeping attack on Egypt, Syria, and Jordan, seized the whole of the Sinai Peninsula, and declared a victory. From the viewpoint of Egypt and Syria, which formed a united front against Israel, the war of October 1973 was meant to clear the stigma of the Arab defeat in 1967, which strengthened their sustained commitment to rejecting Israeli statehood. Surrounded by its Arab neighbors, Israel struck back in an attempt to secure its survival and reaffirm its identity as a nation. It soon regained a portion of the territory around the Suez Canal on the Egyptian front and used it as leverage in the subsequent ceasefire negotiations. The US government deployed a delegation headed by then Secretary of State Kissinger to the Middle East for mediation. Kissinger's team embarked on a *negotiation process* first with Egypt and then with Israel in order to devise a strategy to disengage Israel and its Arab neighbors from the long-standing military confrontations. Underlying Kissinger's initiatives was the US desire to have the Arab states lift their oil embargo on the US and to reduce Soviet influence in the Middle East in order to accelerate the momentum for détente.

According to Saunders, the US delegation demonstrated creativity in two ways. One was an open-ended political process that proactively and incrementally changed the overall political context in which its mediation activities unfolded. The second was the introduction of step-by-step shuttle diplomacy as a new method of negotiation and mediation in inter-state conflict.

As soon as Kissinger's shuttle diplomacy produced the first disengagement agreement between Israel and Egypt in January 1974, the US delegation decided to refer to their initiative as an Arab–Israeli *peace process*, going beyond the *negotiation process* which they had embarked on earlier. This first agreement created a new political environment in which Syria began negotiations with Israel, culminating in the disengagement agreement in May 1974. Inspired by the peace process unfolding step by step, the king of Saudi Arabia told Kissinger that if Kissinger could promise to establish an Israeli–Syrian disengagement agreement drawing on the Egyptian–Israeli agreement, then the Saudi government would support lifting the oil embargo on the US. While traditional diplomatic initiatives such as UN-led mediation efforts made little progress, Kissinger's approach marked a creative departure because it framed the plan of action broadly in order to change Arab–Israeli relations fundamentally.

Among many theoretical implications derived from this episode, three lessons deserve attention in an effort to explore what enables conflict resolution creativity to emerge and evolve. First, as Saunders pointed out, thinking broadly about negotiations and mediations within the framework of a continuous peace process opened the door for working differently to the way most negotiation experts would prepare for their engagements. Saunders observes that the peace process offered a context that was large enough to make negotiators and mediators think expansively about how to shape and reshape the inter-party relations fundamentally. Attempts to change relationships through a continuous political process opened doors for issues and possible actions at all levels of society, beyond conventional inter-governmental relations. The key was the openness to let the process generate its own energy and continuously discover subsequent steps in a flexible yet principled manner.

Second, Saunders reflects that probing into the heart of a conflict sparks creativity. In the broad context of the Middle East conflict, it was challenging to define exactly what the real problems were, what needed to be accomplished as a first step, and what obstacles had to be overcome and how. Coming up with the right answers to these questions required creativity. The approach needed was more complicated than the conventional way of finding out both sides' positions and mediating them. In a political context as broad as the Middle East conflict in the mid-1970s, responses to the problems had to be broad, yet focused enough to assure long-term effectiveness. Learning from this and other cases, Saunders observes that naming the essence of a conflict within a peace process sparks a creative approach. This also indicates that an adequate analysis and articulation of the underlying problem contribute to generating creative solutions, particularly in such complex contexts as the Arab–Israeli conflict.

Finally, it is inferred from Saunders' reflections that analogical thinking informed Kissinger's diplomacy in the Middle East. From the beginning of the Nixon administration, Kissinger had seen the management of the US–Soviet relations from a global and historical perspective. It was clear to Saunders that

Kissinger kept the image of a possible US–Soviet disengagement process in mind when coping with the Middle East crisis. Although the nature of Kissinger's experiential learning was far more complex than this study can handle, it is at least hypothesized that some elements of Kissinger's experience in détente diplomacy – such as his commitment to sustained systemic change and step-by-step confidence-building – helped him think about analogous measures taken in the Middle East.

Interlude (3): reflections on creativity demonstrated by actors playing a dual function

The analysis of the two episodes has generated a range of working propositions on the nature, origination, and other aspects of conflict resolution creativity. This interlude summarizes them succinctly in preparation for an integrative theory-building exercise to be conducted in Chapter 3. As stated in the previous two interludes, these propositions represent no more than conceptual building blocks, still to be examined in terms of internal and external validity across distinctly different empirical contexts.

Children–parents dialogue – Elise Boulding:

1. The application of the method of community meetings to a family setting, across levels of analysis, generated a new mode of dialogue.
2. An earlier spiritual pledge of marriage had prepared a cognitive template for the creative action that came to be adopted.
3. The family dialogue reflected a broader value commitment to nurturing partnerships in society.
4. Introducing seemingly unrelated dimensions of inter-party relations into dialogue helped to reframe the conflict and opened up new possibilities of resolution.

Kissinger's shuttle diplomacy in the Arab–Israel conflict – Harold Saunders:

1. The peace process paved the way toward unexpected discoveries that had evolved within the framework of principled flexibility.
2. Naming and articulating the essence of the conflict helped to generate creative solutions.
3. The exemplary image of the US–Soviet disengagement process provided a source of inspiration for envisioning the Middle East peace process.

Having considered conflict parties' and intermediaries' creativity earlier, one may infer that the creativity of the actors playing a dual role has the characteristics of both types, namely, creativity from within the circles of primary conflict parties and immediate stakeholders and creativity from outside. However, the two cases reviewed in this section appear to suggest that such an inference is hardly tenable.

Boulding's episode describes the conflict between the two parents and their five children over allowance allocation and depicts a simple yet evocative image of how the dual function may be played out for conflict resolution creativity. In this episode, it is the mother who introduced the creative initiative into the family, thus generating immediate impact on the seven parties' relationship to the conflict. The parents had the vested interest in raising the children in the way they wished. They also had the resource, money, of which the children wanted to have a fair share. However, despite being a "conflict party" herself from her children's point of view, Boulding utilized her capacity as a parent to convene and facilitate family dialogues among the seven, with her husband serving as a note-taker from time to time. Her role was that of an intermediary, though not entirely impartial. If the children had been much older and independent from their parents, there could have been more resistance to the parent's suggestion; thus the presence or absence of the children's "buy-in" could have been a more salient issue. Therefore the episode shows some elements of both conflict parties' creativity (with immediate impact on the conflict) and intermediaries' creativity (with the buy-in problem and the constituency issue taken care of almost automatically, thanks to the existing close-knit relationships within the family).

Saunders' episode is significantly more complex than Boulding's in terms of conflict dynamics, but the two episodes have some attributes in common. As a member of Kissinger's shuttle-diplomacy team, Saunders contributed to the mediation of the Arab–Israeli conflict. While playing the role of an intermediary in the Middle East, the US government was a major party to the Cold War, of which the Arab–Israeli conflict was an essential component. In this case, the creative initiatives came from within the conflict stakeholders, namely, from the US State Department in general and Kissinger's negotiation team in particular. Their impact on the Arab–Israeli diplomatic relations was immediate and substantive because Kissinger's shuttle diplomacy drew heavily on the US superpower status. Despite the strong leverage Kissinger and his team could exercise, however, they still had to make conscious efforts to *earn* the conflict parties' "buy-in" to advance their vision, through intensive negotiation and tenacious persuasion.

It is clear that the two cases under study are far from sufficient as an empirical basis for theorizing how the origination phase and the evolution–acceptance process may interact with one another in the hybrid type of conflict resolution creativity. A conclusion drawn from this exercise is thus highly tentative and necessarily speculative in nature. In the hybrid category, the dual effects of creativity from within and outside interact with one another in such a complex manner that the likelihood of evolution and acceptance depends on various contextual factors, such as how close or distant the actors' existing relationship is to the conflict parties they try to influence.

3 Theory-building

A comparative case analysis for identifying emerging themes and building on enduring concepts

Comparative analysis (1): emerging themes across the sixteen episodes

Introduction

The sixteen episodes of conflict resolution creativity have been explored in Chapter 2 to generate working propositions, in preparation for theory-building. Chapter 3 builds on these empirical findings in two different ways. First, the working propositions are systematically compared in order to identify patterns of thinking and social interaction that may account for how creativity emerges across different contexts of conflict work. This exercise will involve inductive reasoning and provide the focus of the first part of the chapter, comparative analysis (1). The second part, comparative analysis (2), will go beyond inductive reasoning to seek commonalities between cases. It will build on four enduring concepts of social science introduced earlier, and apply them as a heuristic device to consciously expand the cognitive horizon of what appears empirical and feasible, in search of unexplored pathways to conflict resolution. The four concepts are: (a) the longitudinal nature of creativity (the five-phase model); (b) the outcome–process typology; (c) the system–element link (levels of analysis); and (d) the relevance of paradigms. The sixteen episodes under study will provide an empirical basis on which each of the four concepts will be refined and developed for theory-building in the realm of conflict resolution creativity.

The present section, comparative analysis (1), will discuss the results of a systematic comparison of the fifty-nine themes derived from Chapter 2. The comparative analysis will reveal both distinct features and evocative similarities across the sixteen episodes, with respect to the nature and origination of creativity.[1] It will identify six emerging patterns, each exemplified or illustrated by three or more themes drawn from different episodes. These patterns are: (a) analogizing; (b) value commitment; (c) combining known elements in a new way; (d) unconventionality out of conventionality; (e) discoveries in retrospect; and (f) contingency-based, principled flexibility. As discussed earlier, these common themes are by no means more significant or "representative" than less common ones, considering the unique methodological choice adopted for data collection

Theory-building 97

and analysis. However, since the clustering of three or more emerging themes derived from categorically different contexts appears to offer a particularly useful starting point for theory-building and reflective practice, it deserves attention. While the six emerging patterns will be discussed in this section to highlight the core findings, the remaining un-patterned themes have to be reserved for a future inquiry that might be stimulated by this study.

Analogizing

Analogizing is a process of sensitizing one's mind across contexts. More specifically, it involves transferring what is learned in one social context to another and exploring relationships between the different contexts, including their similarities and differences. For the present purpose, a context refers to any conceptually definable category of objects, ideas, or phenomena under observation. The types of contexts and cross-contextual sensitization illustrated by the episodes include, but are not limited to:

- *Across temporal (historical) contexts*: This requires exploring the applicability of what was learned in the past to a future situation. In the Oslo peace process, for example, both Pundak and his senior colleague and the chief Israeli negotiator Yair Hirschfeld had consciously utilized models of negotiation and lessons learned from their past Israeli–Palestinian dialogues. Among them was the "proximity talks" that Hirschfeld had held in 1989 with Palestinian representatives in the Netherlands through the mediation of the Dutch government. Because it was illegal to have direct Israeli–Palestinian contact at that point, the Israelis stayed at one hotel, the Palestinians at another hotel, and they exchanged ideas through the shuttle diplomacy of Dutch mediators. The experience in this and other unconventional activities helped the Israeli team, as well as perhaps the Palestinian side, think creatively about how to design the Oslo process.
- *Across spatial (geographic) contexts*: This involves transferring lessons learned in one geographic context to another. For example, Awad observes that one of the precursors of the Palestinian villagers' nonviolent action in 1985 was the sustained grassroots dialogues he had held in Palestinian villages to prepare for such action. In those grassroots dialogues, Awad told the villagers how Gandhi worked with fellow Indians to remove the British from India and how nonviolent movements of women, students, and labor unions had made a difference in different parts of the world. For many Palestinian villagers who had long remained silent despite their lands being taken by Israelis, the examples of nonviolent resistance taking place elsewhere were a novelty. They encouraged the villagers to consider the possibility of practicing nonviolent action in their localities.
- *Across areas of specialization in the practice of conflict resolution*: An area of specialization refers to a set of practices addressing a certain type of conflict-related issue, such as labor–management relations, racial tension,

commercial transactions, environment, and international security. To build analogies across areas of specialization, one applies features selected from one area to another. In the example of Palestinian villagers' nonviolent protest, Awad highlighted such features as grassroots empowerment and participants' unity as essential not only in women, students, and workers movements, but also in Palestinians' resistance to territorial occupation.

- *Across levels of analysis*: This involves transferring insights generated at one level of analysis to another. Conceptually, four levels of analysis are distinguishable – micro (interpersonal), meso (within a society smaller than a nation and/or state), macro (international), and mega (between transnational entities and civilizations). Boulding applied the Quaker business meeting method to her family dialogue, thereby introducing insights gained at the meso level (the local Quaker community) to the micro level (her family of seven people).
- *Across relationships between subjects under observation*: This corresponds to isomorphism, described by Galtung. He illustrates it with a hypothetical example of a binational zone for peace compared with two neighbors sharing their garden.[2] The key question is: How does country A's relationship to country B compare to neighbor X's relationship to neighbor Y? In theory, one may utilize the formula $A:B = X:Y$ for exploring relationships not only between conflict parties, but also between two comparable sets of *any* concrete entities or abstract conceptual categories (for example, relationships between conflict resolution outcomes and processes). In practice, however, one's capacity to hold complex and abstract relationships in mind is not boundless and therefore limits the extent to which isomorphism is applicable in reality.

The five types of analogizing may overlap significantly in a given context of conflict resolution practice, and they are by no means distinguishable from each other in many cases. Nor are ways of analogizing limited to these five approaches.

Value commitment

Value commitment is a normative aspiration for realizing an alternative reality to the conflict at hand, with or without empirical underpinnings or precedent to support its viability. It directs one's attention to more constructive, and more "peace-prone," conditions still to be achieved. If there are analogous experiences that guide and inspire the social and epistemological process toward the perceived alternative, they would support its plausibility. But even without precedent, the uncharted terrain may be traveled when the "creator" and the advocates believe in the intrinsic value of making such a commitment.

The nature and sources of such value commitment vary. Boulding's attempt to apply the Quaker business meeting method to monthly family dialogues was inspired by her and her husband's spiritual pledge to build communal partnerships at all levels of society, starting with their own family. Johnston's decision to hire teenagers as partners with the clinic staff was derived from her professional ethics as a public health worker to serve public needs, instead of imposing her needs on the public. Henderson's Environmentalists for Full-Employment movement evolved from her aspiration to create a more sustainable economy by challenging the growth-based paradigm that tolerated unemployment and poverty. Burton's pioneering Track-Two initiatives were motivated by his philosophical search for a new "conflict resolution" paradigm as an antidote to the dominant paradigm of power politics.

These and other cases under study illustrate that the value commitment may evolve from religiosity, ethics, ideology, philosophy, and belief systems of other types.[3] In other words, it comes from *normative* visions shaping what ought to be, with or without the support of empirical underpinnings, or what is. Another dimension of the value commitment is its *future*-oriented nature inspired by, but essentially independent of, the past. It is stimulated by the exploratory and imaginative mode of opening up possibilities, going beyond the analytical mode of explaining and detailing what has occurred in the past. These observations invite important questions that need answering. For example, what kinds of value commitment contribute to conflict resolution creativity? Would all kinds of value commitment serve the purpose, including that of, say, suicide bombers and airplane hijackers aspiring to achieve what they believe is an ideal world? And why does value commitment appear to be a necessity for conflict resolution creativity? These and other questions will be addressed in the in-depth case study of satyagraha's emergence in Chapter 4, while a more systematic, comprehensive treatment of such complex questions has to be reserved for future inquiry. For the moment, it is noted that the kind of value commitment conducive to conflict resolution creativity appears limited to one aimed at overcoming violence, direct and/or structural. To endure the inevitable process of risk-taking, the value commitment needs to be based on a belief in its intrinsic value rather than an instrumental one.

Combining known elements in a new way

Conflict resolution creativity is stimulated by combining known elements in an unconventional manner. The elements are considered either essential aspects of the conflict or aspects that appear to be seemingly unrelated to it, or a combination of both types. Some of the episodes under study have demonstrated that the key to this process is coming up with a new integrative principle that offers a new coherence for the component elements to work together. As suggested by Galtung, a distinct feature of this approach to creativity is that the new vision generated by it is likely to be perceived as creative but not excessively so, for the conflict parties are already familiar with the essential components of the vision.

In Boulding's episode, community-building within her family became possible when she combined the issue of allowance allocation with familiar household tasks such as washing dishes, putting away groceries, tidying up rooms, making beds, sweeping the walk, and shoveling snow. Before the family meetings started, these household tasks were considered unrelated to allowance allocation. But when they are combined for the purpose of community-building in the household, these known elements began to bear different meanings with a different coherence. Despite the newness of their meanings, they were not too new to the family, for all of them had been familiar everyday phenomena. Likewise, Henderson's Environmentalists for Full-Employment movement became possible by linking environmental NGOs with labor unions under the then innovative principle of sustainable development. The "dots" she connected were familiar actors in American society, but the principle under which they were encouraged to work together marked a creative shift. Galtung discusses similar social processes in more general conceptual terms and suggests that shifting known temporal and/or spatial arrangements enables one to generate creative solutions to the problems at hand. As mentioned earlier, his examples include the reversal of the typical temporal sequence in which a ceasefire, political negotiations, and a vision for possible resolution emerge, as well as the spatial shift of the kitchen from the periphery to the functional center of the household.

The examples of Boulding and Henderson suggest that integrative principles that guide creative linking can be derived from the kinds of value commitment outlined earlier and elaborated later. With respect to the nature of creativity, it is plausible that this approach makes the resulting ideas communicable to the parties because of their familiarity with their component elements. Whether the visions are acceptable and sustainable, however, is a more complex question that has to be reserved for future inquiry.

Conventionality and unconventionality (continuity and change)

To be usefully creative, unconventional approaches have to be devised based on an extensive understanding of conventional rules and boundaries that frame people's expectations. Knowledge, experience, and expertise per se do not guarantee creativity, but they appear to help "creators" identify where the boundaries lie, which problems are outside the boundaries, and when and how to break them in order to devise viable resolution options.

In Smith's episode, the unconventional procedure that he adopted for labor mediation might have been neither conceivable nor workable if it had not been for his expertise and experience in having handled some 2,000 disputes before. His thorough understanding of American labor mediation was a necessary if not sufficient condition for breaking the institutional boundary of acceptable practice without provoking a crisis. This episode suggests a paradox. It is the thorough knowledge of conventional rules and boundaries within a given system of practice that enables one to envision how to break the conventionality. In other words, workable out-of-the-box solutions are likely to be generated when one thoroughly knows what is in the box and what it means to step out of it. In Smith's case, the capacity to identify the perceived boundary of the conventional practice as such, to recognize an "anomalous" problem pushing the boundary as such, and to step out of it in search of workable solutions appears to have been cultivated partly through years of routine puzzle-solving activities within the boundary of his profession.

Osman's episode on Sierra Leone also illuminates the link between conventionality and unconventionality, but from a different angle. For locals in Freetown, it was their conventional knowledge that the Pope's local representative was in a position to communicate directly with the RUF leaders who had been inaccessible to the central government. The seemingly unconventional conciliation activities orchestrated jointly by the OAU, the UN, and the Commonwealth became possible due in part to their use of the conventional channel of local communication in a new way.

These two episodes share attributes echoing the reflections on the Oslo peace process by Pundak, who aspired to work within the body politic and national consensus while trying to "push the envelope to its utmost." All three practitioners were aware of a boundary – professional, institutional, and socio-political – and stretched it or otherwise broke it while trying not to cause irreparable damage. Their capacity to recognize conventionality appears to be an essential requisite to be not only creative, but also *usefully* creative within their local epistemological contexts.

Discoveries in retrospect

According to some practitioners, the process of origination becomes fully recognizable only after it is successfully translated into practice through evolution and acceptance. In other words, those spearheading the creative shift tend to be unable to account for the nature of their conflict work holistically and articulately in its midst. This also indicates that creativity requires a tenacious validation and social learning process for evolution and acceptance in order to make the origination phase worthy of recognition in retrospect.

In the bicommunal reconciliation activities promoted by Diamond, it was only after many years of grassroots capacity-building and applied practice that the local authorities in Cyprus, the US and European governments, the UN, and various funding agencies came to recognize bicommunalism as a viable approach to peace-making. As illustrated by Falk's failed attempts to make the US government consider the North Vietnamese peace proposal, Diamond's bicommunal approach *could* have been rendered politically irrelevant or have simply disappeared if it had not been for the years of her and her local colleagues' tenacious mobilization efforts for evolution and acceptance.

While the episodes of Diamond and Falk highlight the need for validation efforts, Kelman's reflections on Israeli–Palestinian dialogues direct one's attention to another reason why the origination phase is hard to identify in the midst of its formative process. His discovery of legitimate representation and mutual recognition as a key principle for Israeli–Palestinian conflict resolution unfolded gradually and incrementally. He observes that it took the parties two decades to internalize this principle as an essential requirement, with the Oslo peace process of 1993 as a symbolic culmination point in their historical learning process. However, because the status of the PLO and Chairman Arafat was far from clear as of 1971, particularly from the Western perspective, Kelman's growing, if still nebulous, insight into legitimate representation and mutual recognition required not only a turbulent validation process, but also a gradual learning process for his audience – as well as for himself. In short, it requires combined effects of "vindication" by the leading creators, on the one hand, and social learning by their audience, on the other, to make the creative initiatives worthy of sustained impact and attention in historical hindsight.

Contingency-based, principled flexibility

Three episodes under study suggest that conflict resolution creativity emerges from sustained tension between two orientations of thinking and action: flexibility and directionality. This tension is described as principled flexibility. On one end of the spectrum, the epistemological process of creation has to be flexible enough to continuously open up unexplored possibilities that need to be explored. On the other end, the process cannot be so carelessly open-ended and unbounded as to lose basic directionality in an effort to search for creative alternatives. It requires recognizing a "big picture" that offers a sense, however nebulous, of which questions to ask in the process of searching, and what else has to be done to "move forward." Although such a "big picture" is hard to define schematically without a clearly identifiable context for it, it is at least inferred from the episodes under study that its image encourages expanding – rather than limiting – the definition of the conflict at hand, as well as possible solutions to it. Examples of a "big picture" include the perceived need for the Middle East peace process to go beyond a series of bilateral disengagement agreements (Saunders) and the historical significance of legitimate representation and mutual recognition discovered through small university-based dialogues between Israelis and Palestinians (Kelman). These searching processes were open-ended and flexible, yet at the same time guided by some sense of broad directionality.

A corollary of principled flexibility is the need for a contingency-based process. It is described as the unfolding of future possibilities and concrete steps shaped by the ones experienced immediately before them. In other words, the emerging possibilities and steps to be taken are contingent on the preceding ones. This observation is hardly non-obvious intuitively; but it is the explicit awareness of it and the moment-by-moment readiness to *consciously* utilize this awareness that is salient in conflict resolution creativity.

Saunders's observation of the Middle East peace process as facilitated by Kissinger's shuttle diplomacy illustrates conflict resolution creativity informed by contingency-based, principled flexibility. According to Saunders, what the US delegation envisioned was an open-ended political process. The team had started with general directions of desired political change in mind, but kept the door of future possibilities open to explore specific steps to be taken. As the US mediators took each step, they came to see new possibilities unfolding in a manner previously unimaginable. Examples of unforeseen developments include the Israeli–Syrian disengagement and the Saudi king's offer to consider the possibility of lifting the oil embargo against the US. Saunders observes that these developments created momentum that the US team could not have foreseen. Efforts made toward reaching each of the disengagement agreements gradually reshaped the overall political environment in which the mediators and the conflict parties interacted with one another, opening up unexpected possibilities. One of the key enabling factors for generating tangible political impact, it is inferred, was the US team's principled flexibility to welcome and seize "chance" factors as they arose.

Similar processes are observed in Kelman's and Smith's episodes, albeit on a much smaller scale. Kelman's commitment to the Burtonian framework of problem-solving guided his discovery of legitimate representation and mutual recognition as an operational principle. However, the content of his discovery had evolved step by step through his flexible, exploratory search for a participant from the PLO, as well as through a whole range of challenges and opportunities that his participation opened up for other Palestinian participants and their Israeli counterparts. Likewise, Smith's unconventional decision to make a one-time offer for settlement was guided by a set of conjectures drawn from his extensive experience and intuition, including his prognosis that a further lapse of time without settlement would trigger a serious social crisis. Yet his conjectures built up in his mind through an exploratory inquiry into the unique social circumstances surrounding the dispute, instead of their being predetermined by his prior mediation experience. The "big picture" for Smith was to avert the coming crisis of irreversible consequences, going beyond the professional commitment to settling the assigned case within the rules prescribed by mediation handbooks. These, and possibly other episodes under study, illustrate social processes where the sustained dynamic balance between flexibility and directionality facilitates the unfolding of unexplored possibilities step by step.[4]

Comparative analysis (2): theory-building based on the working typologies and concepts

Introduction

The first stage of comparative analysis has generated the six common patterns of creation, that is, analogizing, value commitment, combining known elements in a new way, unconventionality out of conventionality, discoveries in retrospect, and contingency-based, principled flexibility. These emerging themes represent what has actually occurred in empirical realities across different historical, geographic, and relational contexts, suggesting the possibility of similar changes that may take place in other contexts. The second stage of comparative analysis goes beyond discovering patterns of empirical reality and actively seeks to generate unexplored theoretical possibilities stimulated by empirical examples. Theory-building draws on the four working concepts that have offered general directions to the present inquiry, namely, the longitudinal nature of creativity (the five-phase model), the outcome–process typology, the system–element link[5] (levels of analysis), and the relevance of paradigms.

The rationale for the second stage of analysis is both philosophical and practical. One of the hallmarks of creativity for conflict resolution is the twin task of envisioning and actualizing an unseen future which, by definition, is neither foreseeable nor predictable based on empirical data, or what has already happened in the past. For actors in conflict seeking constructive ways forward, empirical data offers a guide. But the knowledge of the past is far from sufficient as a source of inspiration to cope with their unique local context that necessarily differs from any seemingly analogous situations known to them. Therefore, the kind of methodology useful for creative practice across contexts is a set of general heuristics which is derived from empirical illustrations as a point of departure and which, at the same time, guides the actors' conscious efforts to see what they have never seen and work the way they have never worked. The present discussion seeks to take a first step, however modest and necessarily speculative, toward constructing such heuristics.

The first working concept to be explored is the longitudinal nature of creativity, suggesting a holistic picture of its hypothesized life cycle through incipience, origination, evolution, and beyond. The three other concepts illuminate origination, the main focus of this study.

The longitudinal nature of creativity

The five-phase model hypothesizes a transition from incipience (kernel ideas present but still to be integrated), origination (integrated for application), evolution (shaping and reshaping), acceptance (recognized as a new rallying point for change), and sustenance (a new reality anchored with sustained momentum). The model is significant for both practice and evaluation. For practice, it serves as a heuristic tool to consciously search for possible pathways in a given context of conflict resolution. For evaluation, it offers a working template to reflect on the paths taken so far and make adjustments to move forward.

The model was introduced at an early stage of data collection to explore the longitudinal nature of creativity through interviews. To make explicit the author's working framework for data collection, the graphic image of the model (Figure 1.2) was presented to each interviewee after he or she had outlined an episode of creativity. Generally the interviewees acknowledged its usefulness, with some notable exceptions.[6] Reflecting on their feedback, as well as on a range of longitudinal shifts found in the sixteen episodes, it is concluded that the scope and extent of theoretical inferences made from the available empirical data are modest. The purpose of the present discussion, therefore, is limited to refining the working model to enhance its usefulness, illustrating it with a typology of different examples, and presenting unexplored pathways discovered in the course of analysis that may not fit into the model. As such, what follows is intended to neither affirm nor infirm the hypothesized longitudinal nature of creativity because of the limited amount of available data.

In the course of the interviews and data analysis, it has become increasingly clear that the initial five-phase model requires revision to account for a broader range of creative processes than it can adequately capture. A revised and simplified working model is graphically presented as Figure 3.1.

The revised image incorporates important discoveries through the study of the longitudinal nature of creativity. First, the five hypothesized phases may overlap both empirically and conceptually in a significantly more complex, indistinguishable manner than that in which they were initially formulated. For example, in Diamond's episode, the establishment of the Bicommunal Steering Committee made up of Turkish and Greek Cypriots marked an essential hallmark of the origination phase. Yet its incipience phase, building up through grassroots-based training for capacity-building, was characterized by her active support for conflict transformation and bicommunal coexistence. In this respect, the origination phase of bicommunalism as a movement was already in the offing during incipience. Moreover, the features and stakeholders of bicommunal work gradually emerged and grew with the participation of the media, youth, educators, and other stakeholders, though not in a linear, stage-like fashion from origination to evolution. The revised model makes more explicit the overlapping nature of the hypothesized phases, illustrated graphically by the three overlapping circles.

Second, the evolution, acceptance, and sustenance phases tend to be intertwined even more inseparably and intricately. The revised model takes this into account and shows that acceptance and sustenance are special, though not necessarily inherent, attributes of evolution, which corresponds to a much broader category of phenomena than these two. In other words, acceptance and sustenance are subtypes of evolution that may or may not materialize in a given local context of creation, for the manifestation of these subtypes depends on the depth and breadth of evolution. In the Cyprus case, Diamond identified the interrelated signs of acceptance and sustenance, such as the gradual recognition of bicommunal work by European funding organizations and the sustained local ownership of the bicommunal movement in the form of a bicommunal choir,

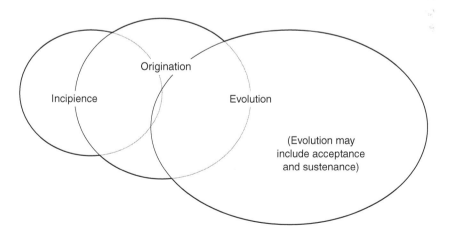

Figure 3.1 The longitudinal nature of creativity: a revised working model.

folk dance group, and villagers' reconciliation activities. These and other signs of acceptance and sustenance had evolved through the continuous shaping and reshaping of the national and international context that the bicommunal movement attempted to influence. Third, despite their overlapping nature, the three major phases of incipience, origination, and evolution unfold in that sequence, for without incipience, there could be no origination, and without origination, no evolution.

Like the original model, the revised model is intended to account for a wide range of creative processes for conflict resolution. Yet in the course of comparing the sixteen episodes, it has become increasingly clear that the comparison holds if, and only if, one chooses to view the episodes as *conceptually equivalent* to one another. In other words, the model may be useful to account for cases only when cases fit into the model in a manner conducive to cross-contextual comparison, with the danger of tautology looming. These critical reflections invite a question: methodologically, how should one identify and define a longitudinal process of creation most appropriately in a given empirical context which the model is employed to account for? Because this question has implications not only for the longitudinal model, but also for the other working assumptions and typologies that will be examined shortly, it deserves more careful treatment before an attempt is made to answer it. Two examples illuminate the significance of this question.

The first of these concerns *levels* of analysis,[7] which may be illustrated by the Helsinki process. The interview with Törnudd was held with the assumption that the working lunch of April 1969 was the beginning of the origination phase that continuously developed throughout the early 1970s. The theoretical choice was made to focus on the procedural features of the conference, such as the principle of equality, as an act of creativity. Consequently, the Soviet proposals to hold a pan-European conference, which had first emerged in the 1950s but failed to materialize, were considered part of the incipience. On the other hand, the preparatory activities and actual negotiations that culminated in the Final Act of 1975 were considered part of evolution, with distinct features of acceptance and sustenance emerging concurrently. They continuously evolved through the establishment of the OSCE in 1995 and beyond. However, having participated in many rounds of follow-up negotiations, Törnudd, from an individual negotiator's perspective, also illustrated the longitudinal nature of creation on a much smaller scale, focusing on logrolling and the tactical use of package deals among representatives within each round. Presumably each process of "smaller creativity" had its origination phase, followed by evolution and preceded by incipience. The comparison between the longer and shorter timeframes, which in this case correspond to the higher and lower levels of analysis, respectively, highlight the relative and selective nature of what are considered "cases" of creativity, which the model is applied to account for.

The second illustration of the debate relates to how to define *units* of analysis. Smith points out that in complex labor mediations, there are typically multiple primary issues that concern conflict parties. In his view, negotiations on each of the issues have a longitudinal process and, accordingly, multiple flows associated with multiple issues which overlap within a single case. He observes that since the working model has only one integrated flow from incipience to evolution, it may not adequately capture multiple flows within a complex case. Methodologically, the question is whether each of the issues within a single complex case should be regarded as a unit of analysis or, alternatively, a case as a whole should be seen as a unit.

To treat multiple "cases," broadly defined, as conceptually equivalent and compare them systematically, such challenges to the model's applicability as the ones illustrated by Törnudd and Smith have to be overcome. To meet these challenges, the methodological choice adopted in the present study is to frame each of the conflict episodes and the longitudinal phases thereof according to the way in which each interviewee as an informant conceptualized the longitudinal flow, or multiple flows if so preferred, from his or her subjective standpoint and at his or her "eye level" of analysis. This flexible approach to conceptualizing units and levels of analysis is both inevitable and justifiable. For, in general methodological terms, any attempt to analyze a conflict presupposes a judgment as to which parties and aspirations should form its foreground from particular observers' standpoints, while treating numerous other actors and aspirations, on the same level or different levels of analysis, as its background. The relative nature of the Helsinki process illustrates this point clearly. Moreover, the suggested methodological choice would invite individual actors in conflict to put themselves in the interviewees' positions and think through creative pathways to conflict resolution. This methodological approach is supported by the observation that actors in conflict always have particular roles and perspectives and therefore they, like the sixteen informants, have to work from their subjective and selective starting points.

To compare the cases systematically, a typology of longitudinal processes is constructed using the working model as an evaluative template. Focusing on the extent to which creative processes transitioned from one phase to another, four prototypes are conceptualized in Box 3.1, with examples given in parentheses where possible.

Box 3.1 Four types of longitudinal processes of creativity

Type A: The process failed in the transition from incipience to origination. (No example found, for this is inherently a hypothetical pathway.)

Type B: The process failed in the transition from origination to evolution. (Example: the US–Vietnam War described by Falk.)

Type C: The process failed in the course of evolution. (Example: the Oslo process described by Pundak. Also, the first satyagraha campaign in South Africa, which will be discussed in Chapter 4.)

Type D: The process succeeded through evolution and developed further. (Examples: the Helsinki process described by Törnudd, "accidental pregnancies" by Johnston, and family dialogues by Boulding.)

The four types of pathways are defined on the premise that through origination, there emerges an unconventional yet viable mode of thinking and action on the part of one or more parties, with explicit initiatives taken to apply the mode to practice. Therefore, Type A shows hypothetical scenarios where an incipient process has been building up, but it has yet to form a well-integrated and applicable mode of action and perception that may guide tangible social change. No examples are reported by the interviewees because creative modes can be described as such only after they are made manifest through origination.

Type B describes situations where new modes of thinking and action have emerged, at least form the informants' point of view, but have failed to enter the evolution phase. Theoretically, a case of this type is perceived in the given epistemological context as high on unconventionality and low on viability, or more precisely, the gap between unconventionality and viability appears to remain wide and insurmountable. Falk's 1968 visit to North Vietnam on behalf of the American peace movement illustrates this type. The new mode of thinking and action that he aspired to generate was intended to shift the US superpower's attention from power-based to rights-based relationships with North Vietnam, beyond the on-going asymmetrical warfare. Although the North Vietnamese proposal for the settlement of the conflict that Falk brought back in 1968 attracted significant media attention, it failed to evolve further and generate tangible impact on US policy.

Type C conceptualizes creative processes that have passed the origination phase, begun to evolve into concrete steps toward social change, but subsequently tailed off without gaining sustained momentum. Theoretically, a case of this type illustrates a greater extent of progress than Type B in terms of reducing the perceived gap between unconventionality and viability. The Oslo peace process described by Pundak exemplifies this type. It started as an unofficial channel of Israeli–Palestinian communication in January 1992, employing a new mode of negotiation procedures conducive to a new mode of resolution options. It evolved into the official status by May 1993 and paved the way toward international recognition as a formal Declaration of Principles in September 1993. Despite the significant efforts made toward acceptance, sustained momentum for implementation failed to grow, as evidenced by the Palestinian uprising in the fall of 2000 and the years of acrimonious gestures on both sides building up to its outbreak.

Finally, Type D represents a process of social change reaching the sustenance phase. Theoretically, a case of this type becomes a reality when a sustainable means is found and actualized to cope constructively with the tension between unconventionality and viability, with the former giving way to an emerging sense of conventionality over time. The historical development of the Helsinki process into the institutionalized security frameworks, CSCE and OSCE, illustrates phenomena of this type. Other examples include the communal partnership between the parents and children through monthly family dialogues (Boulding), and the sustained collaboration between the teens and public health professionals to tackle the teen pregnancy issue (Johnston).

To make it useful in practice, the typology requires further refinement and elaboration, beyond the scope of the present study. For example, a deeper empirical understanding would be essential as to what factors account for a successful transition from incipience to origination, origination to evolution, and beyond. Another important area of inquiry concerns under what conditions such a transition is likely to occur. Answering questions of this magnitude would require a far greater number of cases than there are for this study. For the moment, therefore, a preliminary attempt at theory-building may go no further than recapitulating hypothesized enabling factors identified in the preceding case studies that appear to facilitate a transition from one phase to another. Those factors are: (1) the capacity for integrating incipient elements in a coherent manner for concrete, practical application (for origination); (2) the capacity for communicating the vision persuasively and widely, making necessary adjustments along the way, and countering resistance from the inertia of the status quo (for evolution); and (3) the capacity for generating broad-based recognition and sustained momentum, for example, by building supportive norms and institutions (for acceptance and sustenance, as part of evolution). A working hypothesis under consideration is that the actors' clear awareness of these hypothesized factors – (1), (2), and (3) – would provide them with a roadmap to creation and help them envision and actualize longitudinal steps proactively, while anticipating inevitable difficulties that they are bound to encounter along the way.

Beyond typology development, the comparative analysis has revealed pathways of creative change that fail to be captured within the scope of the revised longitudinal model. These pathways indicate longer-term consequences of "failed" attempts, especially ones categorized as Type B (failures to transition from origination to evolution) and Type C (failures in the course of evolution). For example, Volkan's episode on Estonia illustrates a Type B process that led to creating yet another pathway. In July 1994, Volkan and his colleagues at the CSMHI organized a local community party in the Estonian town of Klooga, where the Estonian Army, like its Soviet predecessor, routinely performed dangerous target practice. The CSMHI team invited both Russian and Estonian-speaking national leaders and their families to the party, hoping that during the event, they could see and hear firsthand the danger facing the local residents in Klooga, a town that many officials based in the nation's capital, Tallinn, had never visited. Volkan's creativity was procedural and methodological: it involved translating the collective unconscious, "hidden scripts" of chosen traumas and glories, into concrete ways that were visible and understandable to conflict parties. The community party marked an origination phase, but it failed to evolve further and attain the intended goal of enabling the national leaders to sense the need for taking policy action to stop the daily "bombing" practice. However, this community event and follow-up activities supported by the CSMHI helped to sensitize the local residents' awareness of the serious problem. The locals eventually took the matter in their own hands, collected hundreds of signatures to organize a petition addressed to the Estonian president, and effectively brought the military exercises to an end. Their collective action, both unconventional and viable, originated at least in part from the CSMHI-sponsored community party, which "failed" to create its intended effect but helped to generate another pathway toward origination and beyond. The two different yet interrelated pathways to creative social change are presented as Figure 3.2.

Similar patterns of social change may arise from Type C cases as well. As will be demonstrated later, the first satyagraha campaign of 1906–14 led by M. K. Gandhi and other Indian community leaders in South Africa illustrates phenomena of this type. The satyagraha movement, despite its unprecedented achievement in repealing anti-Asiatic laws by January 1914, failed to evolve further as soon as Gandhi left South Africa for the last time in July 1914. While the satyagraha movement emerged and expanded in India for decades to follow, the social change of the Gandhian type virtually disappeared in its birthplace. According to Hunt (1990), however, in 1952, nearly forty years after Gandhi left the country, conscious efforts were made again to revive satyagraha in South Africa for a civil resistance campaign led in part by Gandhi's son Manilal.[8] From a long-term historical perspective, a "failure" in satyagraha's evolution was evident after Gandhi's departure; yet its potential for civil society mobilization had remained intact, resurfacing decades later as both a new and old basis for another origination phase to manifest. Assuming that the decades of its dormancy became part of the incipience phase leading up to the 1952 movement, the two pathways, one indicating a disappearance and the other a reappearance, are presented as Figure 3.3.

These examples of longer-term social change illustrate that those which appear to be "failed" initiatives of creation, whether they are of Type B or C, or possibly of other types still to be discovered, plant seeds for further social changes, conventional or unconventional. This expanded vision of creation is accounted for in part by the observation that "failed" attempts could help generate an unexplored mode of *value commitment* (for example, the Klooga residents' determination to stop military exercises), *analogizing* (for example, Manilal Gandhi's attempt in 1952 to revive his father's method), and other forms of enabling influence. It is also inferred that past "failed" attempts help reduce the perception of unconventionality in the eyes of those making analogous efforts in a new context, for such attempts are not "unprecedented" any longer. From a practical standpoint, these observations invite actors in conflict to broaden their time horizons, allowing them to recognize and build on potentially useful effects of past "failures."

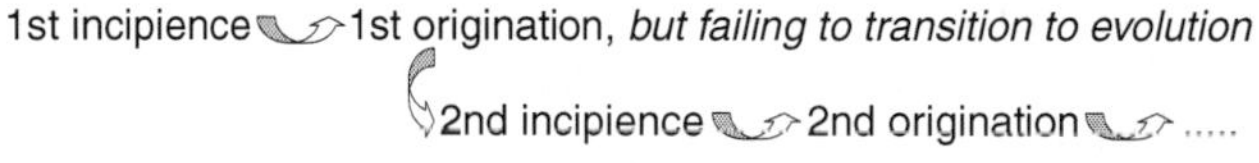

1st incipience ↝ 1st origination, *but failing to transition to evolution*
    ↳ 2nd incipience ↝ 2nd origination ↝ .....

Figure 3.2 A Type B phenomenon contributing to an alternative pathway.

1st incipience ↝ 1st origination ↝ 1st evolution, *but later tailing off*
    ↳ 2nd incipience ↝ 2nd origination ↝

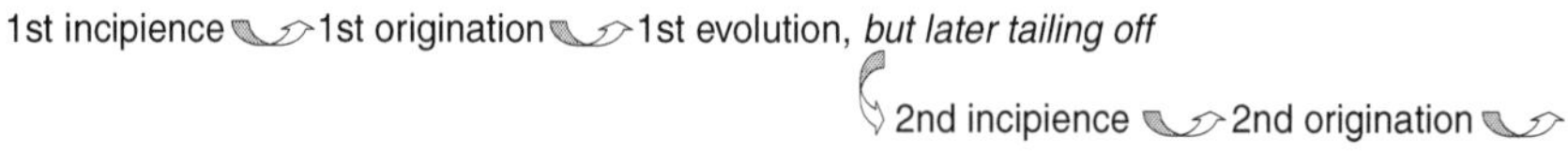

Figure 3.3 A Type C phenomenon contributing to an alternative pathway.

Outcome and process creativity

Outcome creativity is the capacity for breaking through a conventionally accepted reality of an inter-group difference that shapes the conflict at hand. Importantly, outcome creativity concerns the capacity to do something about *the conflict itself*. Process creativity, on the other hand, refers to the capacity for generating an unconventional yet viable procedure that marks a distinct departure from the way conflicts of similar kinds have been handled before by their stakeholders.[9] Process creativity concerns the capacity to devise procedural *means* by which to address the conflict. It does not follow, however, that procedurally creative means necessarily lead to outcome creativity. The definition simply indicates that procedurally creative approaches are unconventional in terms of the ways in which conflicts are handled, for example, by re-opening communication channels between parties in an innovative manner – regardless of whether viable resolution outcomes, unconventional or not, can actually come out of them.

Examples of outcome creativity under study include the episodes of Galtung and Henderson. Galtung's proposal for establishing a binational ecological zone was intended to transform the substantive difference between Peru and Ecuador, instead of devising procedural means by which to think about how to tackle the difference. Many of his procedural steps, in the form of Track-One and Track-Two consultations with senior policymakers, were not necessarily unconventional. Yet the proposed outcome was a paradigm shift, urging the conflict parties to transcend the conventional notion of demarcation – from a border line to a border zone, from linear to spatial. His proposal was also meant to encourage the parties to overcome the traditional Westphalian notion of exclusive territorial sovereignty and to entertain the possibility of joint-sovereignty, or a condominium, of symmetrical type. Significantly, the basic outline of the proposal was adopted as part of the 1998 peace accord for implementation.

Henderson's grassroots mobilization campaign, Environmentalists for Full-Employment, illustrates both process and outcome creativity; yet the latter particularly deserves mention for its long-term implications. The question she tackled was how to overcome the conflict, which manifested in US society in the 1970s as a policy dilemma, between pro-environment and pro-job advocates. The NGO-based mobilization activities she initiated aimed at bringing those opposing parties together on the innovative platform of sustainable economy, shifting people's attention from the present generation to the combination of the present *and* future generations.

Process creativity is illustrated by the episodes of Törnudd and Burton. As Törnudd emphasized, the Helsinki process was not intended to manage – let alone resolve – the Cold War in Europe in a substantive sense. Its primary goal was to initiate and improve processes of communication between the concerned European states, joined by the US and Canada, resulting over time in the evolution of CBMs. The process creativity under the leadership of Finland was evident in the institutional arrangements for the conferences, including multilateralism beyond bipolarity, the equal status of all participants – from micro city-states to the two superpowers – in rotating chairpersonship and voting, and the comprehensive packaging of interrelated political, economic, and human rights issues instead of handling discrete problems in the traditional piecemeal fashion.

Burton's informal problem-solving workshops illustrate another form of process creativity, one that marked a departure from formal diplomatic bargaining constrained by public pressure. Burton, like other researcher-practitioners interviewed, claims that creative procedures of the kind designed in 1965–6 stimulate conflict parties' and third parties' outcome creativity, for example, by way of shifting the parties' mutual distrust and fear toward a joint exploration of common security. But this suggested link between process and outcome creativity is far from evident given Burton's and others' cases under study. From a broader philosophical perspective, however, Burton's procedural creativity has implications for outcome creativity because it was part of his larger aspiration for building the new discipline, conflict resolution, as an antidote to the influential paradigm of power politics. Yet implications of this philosophical, cross-disciplinary conflict, which has been taking place mainly among Western-trained conflict professionals and concerned policymakers, have to be discussed outside the scope of the present inquiry.[10]

These examples make it clear that despite the overlap between the two types of creativity, they do differ significantly in nature. The difference lies between how to transform the conflict itself (outcome creativity) and how to approach the conflict parties in terms of spatial, temporal, relational, and other arrangements in which the conflict can be dealt with (process creativity). This distinction has at least two implications for the practice of conflict resolution. First, the ability to generate creativity, be it process-oriented or outcome-oriented, is inextricably linked to the capacity to understand what the conflict is about. For outcome creativity, the capacity for coming up with an unconventional yet viable reformulation of the conflict is essential. This notion of reformulation is termed differently according to the practitioners' preferences and depending on the contexts of practice. Examples of preferred terms include transforming (Lederach 1995), transcending,[11] dis-embedding/re-embedding,[12] reframing,[13] re-centering,[14] and reshaping.[15] Despite the differences in the prefixes used – trans- (beyond) and re- (again, in a better way) – there lies an essential commonality in the nature of the conscious – and perhaps beneath the conscious, too – that searches for outcome creativity: that is, the need for perceiving the conflict *differently* than before and/or than other actors involved in the same conflict. Whether the reformulation enters one's consciousness and becomes readily available for articulation before, during, or after the origination phase of creativity depends on the contexts of practice; but it needs to be registered in the conscious sooner or later in order for the substantive difference to be transformed and evaluated as such.

On the contrary, process creativity emerges with or without the willingness and capacity to reformulate the conflict substantively. For example, Burton's Track-Two initiatives did not presuppose any concrete image of how to reformulate the conflict between Indonesia, Malaysia, and Singapore.[16] His general theoretical framework had been in search of a case, and indeed any promising case, in which he could "test" his conflict resolution approach. Once articulated and replicated, the act of process creativity becomes a *method* of practice, just as Burton's informal problem-solving method was modified and applied to the Harvard graduate seminar (Kelman) and the Oslo process (Pundak).[17]

There are also cases in which an act of process creativity is inspired by overarching principles that compel a substantive reformulation of the conflict, illustrating the inherent interrelatedness of process and outcome creativity. For example, Boulding's Quaker family meetings were inspired by her religious aspiration for community-building at all levels of society, starting with her family of seven individuals. The spiritual principle that informed her act of process creativity also helped her reformulate the conflict between the parents and the children over allowance allocation. The new theme that had emerged from the reformulation was how to allocate household tasks among all seven family members, make their contributions to the family visible, and distribute allowances among the children according to their contributions. In this context, whether process creativity stimulated outcome creativity or the other way around appears to be an insignificant question, for both types of creativity co-arose interdependently, driven by the initiator's deep value commitment.

The second implication of the outcome–process typology concerns whether and to what extent the conflict parties need to take ownership of the suggested act of creativity of one type or another. As illustrated by the episodes of Galtung, Henderson, and, in a unique sense, Boulding, implementation of outcome creativity requires the parties' sustained commitment to acting on the reformulated version of the conflict, that is, an alternative reality. In practical terms, this means that the parties need to start changing the conventional patterns of behavior (such as violence) and attitude (like animosity) that reinforce the destructive potential of the conflict in which they have been locked. In contrast, process creativity can be carried out with or without such commitment to tackling the underlying difference itself. As illustrated by the Helsinki process (Törnudd) and the informal problem-solving method (Burton), process creativity requires the parties to commit themselves to initiating the process, but not necessarily to substantive outcomes that may result from it. Procedural commitment may help to generate outcome creativity, and it may even pave the way toward stimulating additional commitment necessary to apply the product of outcome creativity to practice. But such a phenomenon is a possible consequence of process creativity, not a prerequisite for generating process creativity per se. Therefore, it is argued that to be useful and effective, outcome creativity requires the parties' commitment to a reformulated reality of the conflict, while process creativity requires only the procedural commitment to entering a new form of inter-party communication and/or relationship-building.

These two implications concerning the need to reformulate conflicts and the nature of commitment are hardly non-obvious to the eyes of experienced conflict workers. But they are far from trivial when one analyzes the interviewees' comments on the process–outcome typology. Most of their feedback echoes the well-accepted framework of thinking on this subject, and it can be summarized succinctly as follows: process and outcome are interdependent and complementary to one another, and both types of creativity are necessary for conflict resolution. However, what is revealing is what they have *not* said: why is it that the sixteen researcher-practitioners of diverse backgrounds voluntarily selected episodes in which process creativity is salient but outcome creativity is obscure, with the notable exceptions of Galtung and Henderson? In other words, while the general theoretical comments which they verbalized converge on the complementary and indispensable nature of both process and outcome creativity, why did their self-reported episodes fail to spread more evenly across the two types? Of interest is the way these scholar-practitioners' attention is drawn more spontaneously to process, and much less to outcome, when asked to select the best illustration of conflict resolution creativity out of numerous others experienced in their long careers.

Any attempt to answer questions of this complexity would be necessarily speculative, due in part to the non-representative collection of cases that inform the study. One plausible answer could well be that the clustering of fourteen process-oriented episodes out of the total sixteen is coincidental. Another possibility is that from a bird's eye perspective, most of these Western-trained, English-speaking scholar-practitioners under study, despite their multicultural and multidisciplinary backgrounds, are inclined to think in similar ways – or more conservatively stated, they have not been sensitized to think of creativity with as much emphasis on outcome as on process. This speculative note is echoed by Galtung's reflections on American professionals in conflict work, with a twist:

> A typical American approach is extremely low on outcome creativity and very high on process creativity. For example, many Americans are good at organizing tables, making seating arrangements, suggesting "you should play his role and he should play your role," and so on.... Many diplomats devote their energy to process management including seating arrangements. However, they are poor in outcome creativity partly because they leave it to politicians and partly because they are not trained to create outcomes. The most creative people are Buddhists, Jewish rabbis, women, architects, engineers, and artists, though not necessarily in this order. All these people are breaking through conventional reality. On the contrary, one can almost guarantee that men in conventional natural sciences and conventional social sciences of the American and behavioral type are uncreative because they speak within their paradigms and stick to them.[18]

Stimulated by critics like Galtung, one is tempted to ask a question for future inquiry: has there been an emergence of shared expectations, and perhaps a professional culture, among Western-trained researchers, practitioners, and policymakers advocating the premise of impartiality in outcome, gratifying the intrinsic value of bringing parties together for talks and relationship-building, but remaining unaware of how consciously and systematically to explore ways to reformulate the conflict with outcome creativity? On this last point, some attempts have already been made for building theories and methods, such as interest-based principled negotiation (Fisher *et al.* 1991), integrative agreement (Pruitt 1987), lateral thinking (De Bono 1970; 1985), and the peace diagram for transcendence (Galtung 2004). Though useful for generating outcome creativity, these approaches have been criticized for their emphasis (or overemphasis) on rational, intellectual reasoning, failing to pay adequate attention to symbolic, relational, emotive, and subconscious/unconscious factors indispensable for generating sustained commitment of conflict parties to suggested outcomes. Much work, therefore, needs to be done to devise more holistic methods for stimulating outcome creativity and putting it into practical use.

System and element (levels of analysis)

Creativity for conflict resolution concerns how to understand levels of analysis. Conceptually, four levels of analysis are distinguished: (1) micro, or the individual level; (2) meso, or the sub-national and societal level, namely below the national and state level and above the individual level; (3) macro, or the national and state level; and (4) mega, or the transnational/regional to the global level. In reality there are sub-layers within each. For example, the meso category is comprised of a wide range of collectivities, all the way from a large-scale resistance movement (such as the RUF in Osman's episode on Sierra Leone) to a family (as in Boulding's episode on allowance allocation). The four levels often overlap, forming a complex web of relationships. Therefore, the four-level model is suggested as nothing more than a point of departure for understanding the level-of-analysis question as it relates to inter-group conflict.

For conflict resolution, the distinction between the four levels is important because it helps explore fundamental questions: At what level does creativity emerge in a given context of inter-group conflict? If states are parties to what may be termed a mega conflict (as in the Cold War), could a creative shift for conflict resolution emerge at the mega level through, say, the structure of polarity in international relations, or at the macro level of initiatives spearheaded by one or more states involved? In short, what level of interactions generates creativity in a given context of inter-group conflict? At the parties' "eye level," or a level higher or lower than that?

This discussion is formulated more comprehensively using the interrelated concepts of system and element.[19] A system refers to a network of interrelated parts with its boundary, imagined or real, separating itself from its outer environment. A system maintains its stability, dynamic or static, by fulfilling a set of requirements such as adaptation to the outer environment, inner coherence, and momentum toward realizing functions essential for its viability. Because of its collective nature, the concept applies to the meso, macro, and mega levels, while the micro level, not collective in nature, is excluded from consideration. Generally, the higher the level of analysis is, the more abstract and intuitive the understanding of a system becomes, for abstraction demands making theoretical inferences about phenomena that one cannot experience firsthand.

On the other hand, elements are component parts that constitute a system. Because a system refers to a network of actors involved in a conflict in this study, elements correspond to actors in conflict, such as parities, stakeholders with vested interests, and intermediaries. Given the four levels of analysis, a mega system is comprised of macro actors (and/or lower levels), a macro system of meso actors (and/or lower), and a meso system of micro actors, namely, individuals. Thus the lowest level where a system is formed is meso and the highest level where elements (actors) interact is macro. From this premise emerge three types of system–element link across the four levels of analysis, summarized in Figure 3.4.

The system–element framework is a *meta*-concept because it bridges any one of the three pairs of levels. For theory-building, this framework is useful because the present study encompasses micro/meso (for example, allowance allocation for children) to macro/mega conflicts (for example, the Helsinki process). From a practical standpoint, the concept helps actors (elements) in conflict direct their attention to the systemic context of which they are part, raising their awareness one level above their horizon, or their "eye level," in order to open up a bird's eye view of their patterns of thinking and behavior.

Despite the theoretical and practical relevance of the framework, its applicability has to be critically reviewed at least in one important respect. Reflecting on such cases as described by Boulding (allowance allocation) and Törnudd (the Helsinki process), one realizes that creative pathways to future possibilities are conceptualized in the minds of particular *individuals*, namely, Boulding as a mother and Max Jakobson as a Finnish ambassador and adviser to President Kekkonen, respectively, in these examples. Logically, this observation is self-evident: the individual, unlike collective actors (functioning as elements) at the meso level or higher, is the only category of actors endowed with the unity of body, mind, and spirit capable of conceptualizing empirical realities of conflict, as well as future possibilities beyond them. In other words, the individual is the only element capable of independent thought and action while collective actors, to a large extent, are products of abstract thinking and conceptual categorization. Therefore, the hypothesis that creativity emerges from collective actors at the meso, macro, and/or mega level appears to be empirically untenable. This observation coincides with the views of such interviewees as Smith, Galtung, and

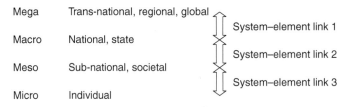

Figure 3.4 Four levels of analysis and three types of system–element link.

Volkan, who maintain that it is always *somebody* who initiates creative changes, regardless of the levels of analysis that require attention for the actual task of conflict resolution.

On what basis, then, could the equivalent status be assigned to all three levels of actors, from micro to macro? The answer, in short, is practical expedience, reflecting how individuals in conflict tend to interpret inter-group relations. For example, the American delegation led by Kissinger attempted to mediate the inter-state conflict between Israel, Egypt, and Syria after their war of October 1973. According to Saunders, it was Kissinger as an individual, with his state-sponsored status, that designed the grand strategy of a step-by-step peace process and shuttle diplomacy. This attempt to break through the conventional reality of conflict was first crystallized in Kissinger's mind. But from the Israeli and Arab perspectives, it was the US as a macro collectivity that generated and carried out the strategy by interacting with other states. This and other episodes of inter-group conflicts, meso and above, illustrate that the human tendency to attribute a generalized image to collectivities in conflict, especially a group "on the other side," comes to the foreground in adversarial relationships. It is also observed that the intra-group distinction between self and others as individual constituents, so clearly pronounced as to be self-evident "on *our* side," recedes into the background when faced with collective actions taken by "the *other* side." Regardless of which particular individual within the collectivity has first crystallized the vision of future possibilities and what strenuous efforts of consensus-building might have been required to make the individual's vision a collective position, the resulting act of creation introduced into the inter-group relations is deemed collective, particularly in the suspicious eyes of "the other side." Given the unique intra- and inter-group dynamics inherent in inter-group conflicts, therefore, it is both logical and useful to start with the working assumption that both individual and collective actors have the capacity to generate visions for conflict resolution.

Another important reason for assigning the actor's status across the levels of analysis is that creative pathways to change may emerge as a result of shifting levels of attention upward or downward, knowingly or unknowingly. In Boulding's episode, the path to community-building in her family opened up when the allowance allocation issue, which could have generated mild yet sustained tension between the parents and the children, the two small subgroups, was transformed into the new question as to how the seven individual family members could contribute to a functional household through partnership. Although the shift that had actually taken place in this episode appeared more consequential than intentional in Boulding's mind, it nevertheless suggests that shifting levels of analysis in one's mind can serve as a useful step for generating creative shifts. Therefore, in order to secure maximum flexibility in one's cognitive space, it is useful to hypothesize conceptual equivalence across the individual and collective levels of analysis and be prepared to oscillate between them.

Having defined the four levels of analysis and the three types of system–element link, one may explore the central question under consideration: in a given context of inter-group conflict, where does creativity originate, at the system or element level? The question is formulated with the explicit purpose of echoing a long-standing social scientific debate about whether social change emerges from the bottom-up or from the top-down, the former corresponding to the view that the element level ultimately matters as a source of change and the latter to the view that the system level matters.[20] This scholarly debate has practical implications for actors in conflict, questioning what level or levels of social interactions they should pay attention to in order to discover and act on ways to break through conventional realities.

In order to explore how the system level may account for creative change, an attempt is made to operationalize "systemic change" in more practical terms. As discussed earlier, a system is a bounded network of actors, individual or collective, brought together into interlocked relationships of conflict. To infer that a system creates a constructive, alternative reality is to argue that the bounded network of actors and their relationships evolves over time in a self-adjusting, self-generative way, with norms and institutions enabling the actors' interactions to open up a creative pathway to conflict resolution. In other words, the thesis under consideration is that context creates, not the actors within it, and that the creative function of the context remains essentially unchanged, even if the actors playing certain roles within it are replaced by other actors. In the interviews, no practitioners advocated positions analogous to this line of reasoning. Nor is there any illustration found in the sixteen cases under study in support of this thesis.

Theoretically, however, advocates of the free market system and the democratic political system would see their judicious applications to practice as approximations, if imperfect, of such self-adjusting, self-generative systems.[21] In addition, local mechanisms for dispute-handling, ranging from the Hawaiian reconciliation process (*ho'oponopono*) to the Somalian inter-clan dialogue (*shir*), are considered another category of social systems which may be utilized for envisioning future possibilities through, however paradoxical, the commitment to conventional norms and institutions.[22] Metaphorically, social creation at the system level resembles processes where a group of dancers improvise a performance by sensing each other's moves and a pair or trio of jazz musicians improvise music through seemingly spontaneous interactions. Although theoretical possibilities of systemic creativity have been explored and metaphoric illustrations given, this discussion necessarily remains speculative and inconclusive within the scope of this study.

On the contrary, the origination of creativity is more cogently accounted for at the element level. As noted earlier, Smith, Galtung, and Volkan observed in the interviews that it is only the element level, and more precisely the individual level, that can create. Smith and Galtung, in particular, view that the system of which the individuals are part may be open or closed to the individuals' creativity, but the system per se is fundamentally incapable of creating and actualizing future visions. Many examples are found that illustrate creative shifts generated at the element level, either micro, meso, or macro (with mega being a theoretical impossibility and thus excluded), such as Diamond's bicommunalism movement initiated at the micro level yet gradually affecting the meso conflict between Turkish and Greek Cypriots.

A review of the cases under study and the interviewees' reflections, therefore, suggests that the element level provides more promising ground for conflict work in search of creativity, with the system level providing a context of such work. However, beyond this dichotomous debate between system and element, top-down and bottom-up directionality, a new possibility of theory-building emerges, one that seeks to account more clearly for the *relational* nature of creation at the element level while interacting more consciously with the system level. This possibility is inferred from the Helsinki process. It is formulated as a hypothesis and model, hereafter termed *interdependent origination*, suggesting its explanatory potential for the origination phase of creativity.[23]

Interdependent origination refers to a social and epistemological process where two or more actors, micro, meso, or macro, separately seek to realize potentially creative ways of resolving or otherwise coping with their conflict, but each side alone is incapable of making it a reality without the support of unsympathetic others, either adversaries or other stakeholders. In other words, the model seeks to describe a situation in which actors involved in inter-group conflict come to co-create an unconventional yet viable resolution option through symbiotic and synergetic effects of coordinating their interactions, despite their obvious tension and hesitation to do so. The resulting process of generating creative resolution options is interdependent in nature, for the actors with divergent aspirations need each other to co-create an alternative reality that one side alone is unable to actualize.

Interdependent origination is contrasted to what may be termed *independent* origination, the phenomenon perceived and advocated by some interviewees. The latter implies that there is always an actor, typically an individual, who single-handedly conceptualizes an alternative reality to the conflict at hand and works to realize it despite resistance from other actors and the social context as a whole. Interdependent origination does not contradict independent origination in that the former, like the latter, presumes that independent actors initiate acts of creation. But interdependent origination addresses a new and more comprehensive question: What if more than two independent actors, across lines of division, come up with what they consider unconventional yet viable resolution options – which might be referred to as exit strategies, olive branches, or otherwise – and interact with one another over time?

Metaphorically, the tense yet functional relationship emerging between actors in conflict resembles aikido, a form of Japanese martial arts. In aikido, the opposing sides attempt to read and redirect each other's energy and flow of movement for non-aggressive engagement, unlike in karate or judo. Like interdependent origination, aikido as a form of human interaction requires understanding its unique system of communication, comprised of such factors as the institutionalized rules and expectations about non-aggressive engagement, the measured square space of a tatami mat, and the time limit that set boundaries of interactions. Also analogous to interdependent origination is the role and awareness of the individual actors in aikido, with each aspiring to actualize an endgame of his or her own, but being unable to create any interactions without the kinesthetic energy generated by the other side. However, unlike in interdependent origination, aikido is necessarily zero-sum in nature, with winning being the only desired outcome.

The Helsinki process described by Törnudd illustrates interdependent origination. Its systemic context was the international bipolar structure, and was mega in scope. At the element level, European and North American states, macro collectivities, interacted to shape part of the bipolar system. Tracing the kernel ideas that led to the Helsinki process, one realizes that it is the Soviet Union, not Finland, that first proposed a pan-European security conference as early as 1954. In the mid-1960s, seizing the mood of détente, the Soviet Union again accelerated its effort to convene a European conference of its own preferred type, with the explicit goal of confirming the existing European borders and developing East–West economic cooperation. Predictably, the Western states remained cautious, setting preconditions for their possible participation, such as the Soviets' reconfirmation of Berlin's legal status and its acceptance of the US and Canada as participants.

It was in this context of dynamic tension that the Finnish government performed aikido. As Max Jakobson, then Finnish Ambassador to the UN and an influential architect of President Kekkonen's neutrality policy, later described, Helsinki at that time was "the only European capital where both German states were represented on an equal footing" (Jakobson 1999: 81). The small Nordic state built on the rare confluence of the systemic momentum toward détente, the converging security needs of the European and North American states, and its diplomatic capacity as a neutral convener for the Eastern and Western camps and the non-aligned states. In so doing, Finland as an independent actor within the international system also sought its own interest in maximizing its national security, particularly in relation to the neighboring Soviet Union. It is inferred that this fusion of the Soviet, Finnish, and others' initiatives opened up the unprecedented multilateral process of East–West consultation, where unconventional yet viable arrangements, ranging from the comprehensive packaging of diverse issues to the equal status of all participating states, became an empirical reality.

The evolving relationship between this small Nordic state and the Eastern and Western blocks was filled with tension, but was uniquely symbiotic and synergistic. The Soviet Union alone, despite its superpower status and years of international lobbying efforts, could not initiate a European security conference for geo-political and structural reasons. Likewise, the Western camp alone would not have done it by convincing the Eastern camp. Finland, with its unique status of neutrality and access to both German states, could bring the Eastern and Western camps together, along with other non-aligned and neutral states. However, it is equally noteworthy that given the historical inertia rooted deeply in the bipolar structure of the superpower politics, Finland alone could not have realized its role as a convener *unless* the Soviet Union had campaigned for its own vision of pan-European coordination prior to 1969 and started engaging the

Western camp regarding the exploration of possible conditions under which a mutually acceptable process could be initiated. This inference is consistent with the fact that in the lunch meeting between President Kekkonen and Ambassador Jakobson on April 29, 1969, these two key leaders agreed to accept the Soviet proposal in principle, but also decided to proactively redirect the growing political momentum toward initiating a new kind of East–West dialogue hosted by Finland. Historically, when the two opposing camps and Finland were entering into the cautious process of co-creating something unconventional yet viable against the backdrop of the sustained bipolar confrontation, they did so amidst symbiotic and synergetic tension. For these reasons, the Helsinki process exemplifies interdependent origination.

Modeling after the Helsinki process, the three essential features of interdependent origination are hypothesized in more general terms:

1   *Tension*: actors entering the process of interdependent origination are adversaries, concerned stakeholders, and/or self-declared intermediaries with vested interests. They are in a relationship of tension or even hostility. But two or more actors now separately seek to try out what they believe to be viable ways to cope with the conflict, despite the sustained tension. The relationship between the actors resembles that of adversaries in aikido, while it is distinguished from the relationship between collaborative improvisers co-creating a group performance.
2   *Symbiosis*: two or more actors wanting to realize their own ways of coping with the conflict cannot put them into practice on their own individual initiatives because of the very nature of the conflict system in which they interact. They therefore need to utilize and build on what each other are aspiring to initiate, despite the tension and possible distrust. This process is analogous to adversaries in aikido trying to utilize each other's kinesthetic energy for effective engagement.
3   *Synergy*: the interactions and perspectives emerging from the adversarial yet symbiotic coordination, if channeled constructively, amount to a breakthrough of the kind that each actor has been unable to envision and actualize single-handedly. This resembles the aspect of aikido where two adversaries move together into an unforeseen, unexpected direction as a result of the two kinesthetic movements fusing to co-create a new synergistic flow of energy.

In short, interdependent origination is a form of *relational creativity* derived from symbiotic and synergistic tension. The hypothesized process of creation is quintessentially relational because it arises from interactions between two or more independent actors, instead of one prominent actor spearheading it despite resistance from all the rest. Empirically, interdependent origination, in its prototypical form, rarely occurs in reality. And the rarity of such occurrences is illustrated by the fact that none of the sixteen cases under study, with the notable exception of the Helsinki process, illustrates this working model. One can argue, however, that many of the cases in which two or more actors sought to realize their respective conciliatory visions, unconventional or not, reflect at least some elements of tension, symbiosis, and synergy. For example, in Boulding's episode on a method of family dialogue, which was introduced to transform the subtle yet sustained tension between the parents and children, the symbiosis between their approaches to coping with the tension was evident because of their existing family ties. A synergy emerged when the children's needs of allowances and the parents' desire for integrating both the children's needs and all seven family members' responsibilities were brought together to form a new basis for building communal relationships in her family. Boulding's case, however, differs from interdependent origination in its prototypical sense, for the shift occurred largely because of the parents' vision, with the children being in a relatively passive position to follow, accommodate, and occasionally resist the parents' suggestion. Unlike in the Helsinki process, the dynamic tension between different actors pursuing alternative visions was not salient in Boulding's episode, for somewhat predictable reasons.

Having articulated one exemplary case that illustrates the model, as well as one more case on the fringe of its applicability, one comes to realize that interdependent origination is but *one* subtype of relational creativity. There are potentially numerous other subtypes in the universe of relational creativity that the sixteen cases under study fail to illuminate. It is also plausible that such possible subtypes may not be conceptualized adequately in terms of the three variables, namely, tension, symbiosis, and synergy. Although other versions of relational creativity may not be explored systematically within the scope of this study, articulating at least one subtype goes a long way toward demonstrating that relational creativity of one kind or another is possible, not impossible. It is expected that this starting point of inquiry would contribute fruitfully toward discovering and theorizing other pathways of relational creativity, while assigning independent origination rightful status in both creativity research and conflict work.

To conclude the discussion on the system–element link in general and interdependent origination in particular, four implications for practice deserve mention. They are especially significant from individual actors' perspectives and suggest areas of future inquiry into relational creativity. First, interdependent origination is inherently an outsider's, or etic, perspective. From the viewpoint of the actors within the system, or the emic perspective, their interactions are unlikely to look symbiotic and synergistic even when they appear to exhibit these qualities from the etic perspective. This is analogous to adversaries in aikido fighting with one another without thinking consciously about how their adversarial moves might at times work together to create synergetic flows of their kinesthetic energy. A question emerges in the spirit of creative exploration: What if the actors choose to be conscious of this model of creativity when they interact with one another in search of ways to cope with their conflict? The awareness of the model, if utilized constructively, would expand a range of potentially useful approaches to making "our side's" efforts more workable, by tapping into the momentum generated by the "other side's" initiatives. Therefore a conscious shift from the etic to the emic understanding of conflict and the reflective capacity to oscillate between these two levels is essential and useful for practicing interdependent origination.

Second, the awareness of the model and the capacity to oscillate between the etic and emic perspectives presuppose the kind of conflict analysis that pays due attention to the system–element link. A systemic context helps to shape both constraints and expectations about what kinds of relationships may unfold and whether and how symbiotic and synergistic tension may arise from interactions between actors in conflict. Viewed from each actor's perspective at the element level, conscious efforts to understand the system as an overall context of social conflict and to articulate what the systemic dynamics means from an emic perspective are both essential for envisioning concrete steps toward interdependent origination. This reasoning is supported by the Helsinki process, in which the Finnish leaders' conscious efforts to build on the bipolar system and the unique status of neutrality that Finland sought were among the essential factors that enabled interdependent origination to unfold.

Third, to generate interdependent origination, each attentive actor's initiatives form an indispensable part of it. But their individual initiatives are not sufficient by themselves to constitute a relational process of interdependent origination as an organic whole. This means that in historical hindsight, each actor's contribution is so essential that the relational process would not materialize without the respective actors' initiatives, large or small, central or peripheral. Yet the fundamental paradox of this inherently relational phenomenon is that from each actor's perspective the image of the whole remains a potential reality *until* it is actualized, and perceived to be actualized, in the collective conscious of those involved. This observation is also illustrated by the Helsinki process. At each historical moment of diplomatic initiatives, ranging from the Soviet proposal of a pan-European conference in 1954 to the Finnish decision to host the process in 1969, to the subsequent formation of CSCE and OSCE, each of the primary actors spearheading social change was envisioning certain desired effects. But each actor taking a particular step remained unsure and exploratory, in the midst of the particular action being taken, about what the cumulative and interactive effects of the respective actors' individual initiatives might amount to in their synergetic totality. Considering this incremental, evolutionary nature of interdependent origination, one finds a plausible link between interdependent origination and contingency-based, principled flexibility; the latter was defined earlier as an emerging theme and illustrated by such episodes as the Middle East peace process (Saunders), the Israeli–Palestinian problem-solving workshop (Kelman), and labor negotiation and mediation in the US context (Smith). The question to be explored is whether and how contingency-based, principled flexibility facilitates a conscious step-by-step search for symbiotic and synergistic tension.

Fourth and final, when exploring conflict resolution creativity in general and interdependent origination in particular, one realizes that the higher the level of analysis under consideration is, the more abstract one's thinking becomes. A comparison between Boulding's family dialogue episode (micro/meso) and the

Helsinki process (macro/mega) makes this point clear. The comparison between these two cases also serves as a reminder that varying degrees of abstract thinking illustrated by the sixteen episodes indicate that a higher level of analysis demands more theoretical and intuitive thinking, for it limits the scope of direct, tangible experience in which a particular individual could be involved. This reflection underscores the significance of further theory-building on interdependent origination, as well as on other possible subtypes of relational creativity, particularly for the practice of conflict resolution in large-group conflicts.

Paradigms

This study started with the goal of exploring the applicability of paradigm-accepting and paradigm-breaking creativity in the light of Thomas Kuhn's thesis. As will be explained shortly, it was found that the Kuhnian sense of paradigm is not directly applicable to conflict resolution creativity. However, using the Kuhnian theory as a heuristic basis, a more applicable framework of thinking has emerged from an in-depth look into the sixteen cases and their theoretical implications. What follows is a preliminary sketch of the new framework, consistent with the exploratory nature of this study, aimed at generating useful hypotheses for future research and practice.

Reflecting on the historical trends in natural science, Kuhn described a paradigm as an organization of community practices. More specifically, a paradigm is "an entrenched point of view and a corresponding set of practices that organize the efforts of a community of investigators to emulate exemplars" (Nickles 1999: 335). Careful reflections, supported by empirical evidence obtained in this study, reveal that the Kuhnian sense of paradigm is inapplicable to conflict resolution creativity for a number of reasons, including:

- *The absence of relevant communal relationships*: In a given context of inter-group conflict, a community in the Kuhnian sense is indefinable. In many episodes under study, there are self-declared third parties intervening in inter-group conflicts, attempting to apply theories and methods generated in what they perceive to be a field of peace/conflict research and practice. But their sense of a professional community, imagined or real, is conceptually different from the universe of collective subjectivity in which the conflict parties themselves understand what *their* problems are. Exceptions are found where these universes overlap significantly; for example, Diamond pursued a grassroots-based transformational approach in Cyprus instead of an elite-based transactional approach popularized in her professional community, while by so doing, she contributed to bicommunalism in the local conflict setting, drawing on her unconventional professional method. In such cases of professional–local overlap as Diamond's, even the most imaginative and flexible attempt to apply the Kuhnian sense of stakeholder communities would fail, for Kuhn's theory appears incommensurate with far more complex phenomena of overlapping collective consciousness.

- *Lack of consensus on what counts as facts, theories, and methods*: Because of the highly structured nature of communal practices in natural science, it is possible for many, if not all, community members to agree on what counts as facts, theories, and methods, often corroborated with mathematic precision. In contrast, in social science in general and conflict resolution in particular, such consensus is hardly achievable, given the ambiguity and subjectivity of community practices in a given local context of inter-group conflict. For example, what might be regarded as essential concepts in almost any inter-group conflict, such as peace, justice, equality, and conflict resolution, could become a subject of persistent disagreement in a given geographic and historical context; so do relevant "facts" to operationalize such concepts, as well as concrete methods to put these concepts into practice. In short, the metaphysical, ontological, and methodological foundations of conflict work are too ambiguous to be reliable and useful in a given local context of practice.
- *Ambiguity of paradigm shifts*: Because of these reasons, a paradigm shift in the Kuhnian sense is neither recognizable nor definable in any meaningful manner in conflict work, except in a purely metaphorical sense of helping conflict parties imagine a quantum leap for social change.

Yet it is precisely this metaphoric value of the Kuhnian concept that offers promising grounds for theorizing qualitative shifts in collective consciousness. Elaborating this heuristic aspect of Kuhn's theory and reformulating the aforementioned inapplicable aspects fundamentally, one may devise a more useful and qualitatively different concept, *conflict paradigm*, as a step toward theorizing conflict resolution creativity. A conflict paradigm is defined as a systematic entrenchment of perceptual and interactive patterns inherent in conflict. The underlying premise of this concept is that from a bird's eye perspective, any conflict, large or small, complex or simple, is a social system shaped by certain regularities, however chaotic they might look, in terms of the ways in which its constituents interact with one another and form perceptions about their interactions. Importantly, a conflict paradigm is *not* meant to describe what might be considered a paradigmatic phenomenon within conflict professionals' communities, such as Burton's problem-solving dialogue method that came to be emulated by Kelman, Pundak, and other professionals. The concept is devised to focus primarily on conflict parties' interactions and perceptions; for example, the conflict paradigm in Burton's episode was comprised of the perceptual and interactive patterns enacted by Indonesians, Malaysians, and Singaporeans among others involved.

Theoretically, a conflict paradigm is a unique application of the system concept discussed earlier in relation to the system–element link. It is conceptualized for the specific purpose of generating outcome creativity. A conflict paradigm is distinguished from the general concept of system, for it seeks to illuminate entrenched perceptual and interactive patterns as a foreground while treating the rest of the systemic factors as a contextual background. However, it is analogous to the system concept in that it is a meta-concept applicable to different levels of analysis, depending on the particular ways in which actors choose to understand their conflict.[24]

Before carrying the metaphor of a Kuhnian paradigm further and elaborating the proposed concept of a conflict paradigm in detail, an attempt is made to compare these two perspectives more systematically in order to understand where the latter stands in relation to the former. Table 3.1 highlights the apparent differences between the two, as well as some evocative similarities.

Table 3.1 Comparison between a Kuhnian paradigm and a conflict paradigm

	Scientific paradigm (Kuhn)[*]	*Conflict paradigm (in a given local context of inter-group conflict)*
Constituents	Highly disciplined community comprised of scientists, universities, funders, journal editors, and industries seeking applications of useful findings	No overarching "community" of the like-minded exists because conflict parties and attentive stakeholders are usually adversarial. But the parties are entrenched in a system of interdependence and certain patterns of social interaction
Aims	Advancement of relevant theory and application, mainly through "puzzle-solving" exercises that conform to shared worldviews and standards	Attainment of the respective parties' aspirations, expressed or hidden, described in such terms as goals, positions, interests, needs, and values. Typically each party aspires to prevail over adversaries through its own goal attainment
Means (to attain the aims)	Scientific methods, such as experiments, perceived as viable by the community	Direct violence, economic sanction, containment, bargaining, non-recognition, discontinuation of communication, and other means that the parties consider viable
Internal dynamics	Rewarding rule-conforming discoveries, marginalizing anomalies, rebelling with new discoveries, resisting rebels, etc.	Manifestation, escalation, polarization, enlargement, entrapment, stalemate, dehumanization, etc.[†]
Longitudinal process for systemic transformation	Normal science, discovery of anomalies, crisis, revolution, emergence of a new science (and normal science again)	Incipience, origination, evolution, and beyond

Notes
[*] Table entries in this column are derived from the author's interpretation of Kuhn (1996).
[†] See Rubin *et al.* (1994) and Mitchell (1981) for these and other concepts of conflict dynamics.

Because a scientific community ordinarily pursues more or less common goals, it tends to induce convergent interactive patterns within it. On the contrary, actors interlocked in a conflict paradigm pursue what may appear to be contradictory aspirations. Therefore, actors in conflict tend to avoid convergence in relationship. Despite this apparent difference, the two concepts share a similarity. They both describe a social system of interdependence shaped by a set of means for goal attainment (unilateral or collaborative), inter-agency dynamics, and a longitudinal process for transformation. In other words, one can conceptualize both phenomena as a system of dynamic internal coherence and interactive patterns. The similarity in the longitudinal nature invites a deeper look into the possible usefulness of the conflict paradigm concept in order to generate creativity through paradigm shifts.

Epistemologically, systems thinking of the kind illustrated by Table 3.1 makes it possible for analysts, practitioners, and parties to make sense of a conflict as a bounded phenomenon to observe and act on. For example, the notion of Protracted Social Conflict (PSC), developed and popularized by Azar (2002) and others, has evolved from the observation that an inter-group conflict remains entrenched when a set of conflict parties interact in self-reinforcing spirals of distrustful, coercive gestures against one another over a sustained period of time. The Israeli–Palestinian conflict and the Cold War are two of the most well-known examples of PSC. Another explanation of the perceptual and interactive patterns that sustain inter-group conflicts is offered by Volkan from a psychoanalytic perspective. He suggests that untransformed violent conflicts inevitably manifest as collective psychoanalytic processes, ranging from purification of self-image to the re-enactment of chosen traumas and glories,[25] as he described in his Estonian–Russian conflict episode. Although Volkan's theory, unlike PSC, looks primarily at the collective behavior and perception of each large group on its own, it serves as at least a partial explanation of perceptual and interactive patterns between two or more regressed groups in untransformed conflict.

Reflecting on these theoretical insights into conspicuously violent phenomena, a question is raised: In order to see perceptual and interactive patterns that give organizational coherence to a conflict system, must one wait until the conflict escalates to the level of intensity with which Azar and Volkan are concerned? The answer is no, for every untransformed inter-group conflict has the potential for escalation, and entrenchment is enough of a theoretical reason to infer that momentum for behavioral and perceptual regularities *does* build in any conflict, already protracted or not, violent or not. Therefore, if equipped with right theoretical and methodological insights, the careful observer – whether an intermediary or a self-reflective conflict party – should be able to discover regularities underlying a given conflict paradigm regardless of whether the conflict is currently at an emergent, still-to-be-violent stage or a protracted, violent stage.

Building on the preceding discussion, the hypothesis under consideration is now spelled out systematically, first in conceptual terms and then with concrete examples for illustration. What generates and possibly reinforces the patterns, regularities, and iteration inherent in a conflict paradigm is a set of deeply entrenched perspectives, codes of behavior, and relational and structural inertia that the opposing parties practice in *common*, knowingly or unknowingly.[26] A paradox emerges that the conflict derived from differences and animosities is inherently a system of deep commonality. Out of this deep commonality arises the reluctant interdependence that binds conflict parties within the same temporal, spatial, and relational context, so long as the conflict matters to them. For example, two neighboring groups may share an assumption that a certain territory located between them is valuable, territorial sovereignty is exclusive, and the territory, once taken by one side, will be in its possession forever. As they persistently work to prevail over one another, typically interlocked in action–reaction spirals, the shared assumption becomes entrenched in their collective conscious, and sometimes even acculturated deep down. The entrenched commonality, in turn, reinforces their perceptual and interactive patterns and sustains their conflict paradigm. Viewed from the perspectives of those inside the conflict paradigm (or an emic perspective), expectations about future possibilities become bounded, for the same patterns that shaped the trajectory from the past to the present, if unbroken, are likely to shape the future.[27] The conflict paradigm becomes *the* reality, both empirical and conventional, in the collective conscious of its constituents, narrowing their perceived capacity to envision alternative realities beyond conventionality.

Therefore the first step toward breaking the conflict paradigm and generating creative possibilities for the future is to discover the entrenched perspectives, hidden codes of behavior, and relational and structural inertia, and then articulate them with sufficient clarity and simplicity. The second step is to open up ways to reformulate the perspectives, codes, and inertia in a more peace-prone yet pragmatic and acceptable manner, helpful to guide a creative shift.

To illustrate this hypothesis and explore it further, five conflict episodes under study are revisited and summarized in Table 3.2. The table shows: (1) essential perceptual and interactive patterns that shaped each of the five conflict paradigms; (2) alternative realities made possible by breaking the existing patterns; and (3) types of heuristic pointers that guided, or could have been used to guide in hindsight, a systematic search for the entrenched perspectives and the underlying patterns, in an effort to explore ways to de-entrench them.

The table entries are generated by operationalizing the three concepts – conflict paradigms, alternative realities, and heuristic pointers – in each of the five cases. To describe a *conflict paradigm*, one must look first at primary parties, their aspirations, their actions and interactions, and, if helpful, other selected elements of the conflict from a bird's eye perspective (namely, an etic perspective, empathetic yet detached), as if to pull oneself out of the web of interlocked relationships and take a panoramic, holistic view of it. Then a question is asked: Underneath the conspicuous differences shaping the conflict, what shared perspectives, perhaps so obvious as to be forgotten, remain unquestioned or unquestionable, thereby interlocking the parties in their unwanted interdependence? In short, what is the grammar of the conflict language at work?

In the episode of Johnston, the conflict paradigm, unquestioned and unquestionable, was upheld by the "common sense" of the clinic staff, the funding agency, and other stakeholders that teenagers' pregnancies were accidental. Deeply entrenched in the "common sense," according to Johnston, was the exclusive authorship of the problem-solving process designed and implemented by the well-educated medical professionals. Similar cases of systemic entrenchment were discussed by Boulding (parents superior to children), Diamond (intercommunal division inevitable), Galtung (commitment to a border line), and Henderson (employment at the cost of the environment).

Table 3.2 Conflict paradigms, alternative realities, and heuristic pointers: five selected cases

Interviewees (episodes)	Conflict paradigms	Alternative realities (achieved or at least introduced to practice)	Types of heuristic pointers
Boulding (childrens' allowances)	An emerging division between the children and parents; allowance allocation as a focus	A family of seven as a community; joint management of household responsibilities as a focus	Time (being trans-generational); relational structure (shifted from vertical to horizontal)
Diamond (Cyprus)	Inter-communal division (top-down, elite-based; transactional negotiation)*	Bicommunalism; (bottom-up, grassroots-based; transformational reconciliation)*	Relational structure (from separate to joint, hierarchical to horizontal)
Galtung (Peru–Ecuador)	Border line to divide; exclusive territorial sovereignty	Border zone to share; joint territorial sovereignty	Space (from one- to two-dimensionality); relational structure (Westphalia challenged)
Henderson (sustainable economy)	Focus on growth and the present generation; pro-environment versus pro-labor	Focus on sustainability and future generations; Environmentalists for Full-Employment	Time (from the present to the future); relational structure (from separate to joint)
Johnston (teen pregnancies)	Accidental pregnancies presumed as a reality; clinic staff as problem solvers	Intentional pregnancies accepted as a reality; staff–teen partnership	Time (with a trans-generational dimension); relational structure (from vertical to horizontal)

Note
*Here the table entry describes perceived shifts within what Diamond saw as conflict professionals' community, which coincided with desired changes within the conflict paradigm that she tackled in Cyprus.

An *alternative reality* is operationalized in terms of a new set of perceptual and interactive patterns made possible by de-entrenching the perspectives – either purposefully, "by chance," or by a combination of both – and reshaping them in a manner more constructive and acceptable to the parties. For the present purpose of illustration, whether the new patterns have actually been implemented (as in the case of Galtung's binational zone) or they have been launched into the stakeholders' collective conscious to trigger desired changes (as in Henderson's NGO network) is not as important as the fact that they have all penetrated some aspects of the conflict paradigms that need transformation.

At Johnston's clinic, the teens' remark, "This isn't accidental," became a shocking revelation to the staff, who had already secured funding for the stated goal of reducing accidental teen pregnancies and invested significant energy on that premise. Johnston's willingness as the supervisor to accept the teens' perspective reshaped not only the perceived problem, but also possible solutions, resulting in the clinic's decision to hire qualified teenagers as partners of the professional staff. Analogous attempts to envision and actualize alternative realities were described by Boulding (parents and children forming a functional community), Diamond (grassroots bicommunalism beyond elite-led separation), Galtung (a binational border zone instead of a border line), and Henderson (sustainability through the Environmentalists for Full-Employment).

Finally, *heuristic pointers* are explained and operationalized. The role of heuristic pointers is to direct one's attention to different categories of potentially relevant phenomena. In theory, a pointer may be any conceptual category, or a variable in social scientific terms, that serves as a heuristic bridge and catalyst between the empirical reality and potential realities. These pointers are intended to help search for hidden perspectives and underlying patterns inside and outside the conflict paradigm, like the bird's eye searching for patterns across terrains (but never forgetting that there are underground rivers, the vast expansion of open skies above the bird's head, unseen terrains spreading in all directions beyond the horizon, the terrains washed away in the past and long forgotten, and most importantly, what lies entrenched inside the bird's mind).

Reasoning inductively from the cases under review, one can formulate at least three types of heuristic pointer that appear to be generally applicable across contexts. Within each type, multiple subcategories need to be invented from conflict to conflict, from context to context. The three generic types are:

- *Concepts related to time (temporal heuristics)*: Identified and expressed in such terms as: conventional clock-time and calendar-time; generations (e.g., Boulding, Johnston); progression from the past to the present to the future (e.g., Henderson); birth–rebirth cycles; psychoanalytic stages of life from childhood to adulthood; and human, ecological, and geological timescales (e.g., Henderson, at least in part).
- *Concepts related to space (spatial heuristics)*: Identified and expressed in such terms as: local, regional, and global; territorial, trans-territorial, supra-territorial, and non-territorial;[28] center and periphery; and point (origin), line

Theory-building 131

(one-dimensional), zone (two-dimensional), and solid (three-dimensional) (e.g., Galtung).

- *Concepts related to relational structure (relational heuristics)*: Describing how relationships are structured and conceptualized in terms of: (1) human relationships, namely, Self's group identity in relation to Others' (e.g., Diamond), whether vertical or horizontal, equal or unequal, essential or marginal, exclusive or inclusive, dependent, independent, or interdependent;[29] and (2) human relationships with non-human entities, namely, Nature (e.g., Henderson) and the transpersonal (e.g., Boulding).

These three types inevitably interact and overlap with one another. The time–space (or history–geography) matrix provides a stage for Self's interactions, through a group or as an individual, with Others, be they human, non-human (Nature), or super-human (God), and often all three at the same time in an intricate entanglement.

In theory, a heuristic pointer is useful for its methodological promise: it is that which these pointers can point to that makes perceptual and interactive patterns persist and helps uphold the conflict paradigm intact. Therefore dislodging the systemic entrenchment and re-lodging the web of relationships somewhere else safer and acceptable to the parties opens up alternative realities. In practice, however, the pointers in Table 3.2 were not necessarily recognized consciously by the practitioners, parties, or other stakeholders when they were in the middle of breaking through the conflict paradigms knowingly or unknowingly.

In Johnston's case, for example, she and her clinic staff had been unaware of the fact that the teenagers were intentionally getting pregnant. It was the shocking encounter with the moment of the teens' self-expression that forced the staff to be silent and reflective of the unarticulated value conflict. Moreover, even after the value conflict surfaced to her consciousness, she did not guide her reasoning purposefully, as far as discernible from the author's interview with her, in search of ways to break through the entrenched assumption of accidental pregnancies. Her intuition stimulated by the shock, her recollections of analogous experiences in the past,[30] and her value commitment to professional ethics all appear to have played a much more important role in coming up with the solution than systematic reasoning of the kind suggested here. The salient heuristic pointers of the temporal and relational types are crystallized by the outside observer from the etic perspective, mainly for the purpose of evaluation in hindsight.

On the contrary, Galtung's episode illustrates a *conscious* search for entrenched perspectives and alternative realities by way of operationalizing what might be considered heuristic pointers, particularly those of the spatial type. With the use of the Hegelian dialectics laid out on the Cartesian space, it took Galtung "exactly five seconds," as he recalls, to come up with the image of a binational ecological park. In Galtung's case, therefore, his peace diagram method, which has the built-in mechanism of mobilizing heuristic pointers, consciously guided his reasoning to conceptualize an alternative reality and, by implication, the nature of the entrenched Westphalian tradition sustaining exclusive territoriality.[31]

If a continuum is constructed with a conscious breakthrough of Galtung's type at one end and an "unplanned" discovery of Johnston's type at the other, the three other cases – Boulding, Diamond, and Henderson – could be placed somewhere in the middle, perhaps somewhat closer to Galtung's side. The continuum stimulates imagination and raises a question: Reflecting on the five pathways to alternative realities, what could one infer about the use of heuristic pointers for breaking conflict paradigms *consciously*? Empirically, cases such as Johnston's indicate that the conscious use of heuristic pointers is never a prerequisite for discovering alternative realities. Nor is it necessary to be aware of the conflict paradigm in which one is entrenched. Empirically, parties and intermediaries may come across a vision of alternative realities serendipitously as if "by chance," or perhaps even literally by chance, without the conscious use of heuristic pointers or any other tools of creativity.

However, having articulated the heuristic pointers which appear to have held the key to the five pathways in hindsight, one is inclined to ask: What if all five practitioners *did* use the three types of heuristic pointers consciously and systematically, engage others in dialogue for naming their conflict paradigms, and search explicitly for alternative realities? In addition, what if they were conscious of hypothesized pathways from conflict paradigms to empirical realities, and even some of the examples in Table 3.2, *before* coming up with their alternative realities? Although it is not possible to answer these counterfactual questions, there is at least one point that can be made beyond doubt: once the hypothesized mechanism of conflict paradigms enters one's awareness, the conflict under consideration and future possibilities beyond the conflict never look the same as before. The suggested method in general and heuristic pointers in particular are useful not only for evaluating pathways taken already, but also for envisioning pathways still to be taken.

To envision future scenarios still to be realized, heuristic pointers have to be used flexibly yet systematically to guide one's attention from one type of phenomena to another, just as a bird's eyes looking in all directions. With a panoramic view of the parties, their aspirations, their ways of interactions, and other relevant factors in a given context of conflict, one may explore the nature of systemic entrenchment by asking such probing questions as:

- What are the temporal, spatial, and relational dimensions characteristic of this conflict? What types of dimensions do not appear salient or taken for granted in this particular conflict, in comparison with other familiar cases?
- How do the parties perceive and describe these dimensions under consideration? More importantly, how do they *not*?
- What if the parties' understandings of these dimensions were negated instead of being kept intact as unspoken codes of conduct? What if they were reformulated one way or another in a qualitatively different manner, for example, by replacing these dimensions with other hypothetical dimensions?
- What would the negations and reformulations mean, respectively, in this particular context of conflict? What would the reality look like provided such altered perspectives were translated into practice?

- What if other dimensions from each of the three types, which have not so far entered the parties' awareness, were brought to their attention?

Finally, a conscious appeal to heuristic pointers to transcend conflict paradigms is bound to generate what may appear to be unconventional pathways to alternative realities, particularly from the perspective of those resisting change. To make the origination phase viable, the unconventional visions must find a receptive audience to make them an empirical reality. Although this discussion on conflict paradigms is necessarily simplified for clarity as if the exploratory process could take place in one's mind single-handedly, the suggested method must be translated into dialogical, communicative processes, even across lines of tension. For this purpose, the working model of interdependent origination, among other approaches, offers a useful starting point for envisioning how conflict paradigms may be transcended successfully through relational creativity.

Summary of empirical findings and theoretical insights

To conclude the comparative analysis of the sixteen episodes, the core empirical findings and theoretical insights are summarized. The summary is offered in a concise bullet-point format, suggesting a working template for reflective practice and further inquiry. It also serves as a template for the case study of satyagraha to follow.

Findings in comparative analysis (1): the six emerging themes

Analogizing

- Analogizing is a process of sensitizing one's mind across contexts. It involves transferring what is learned in one social context to another and exploring relationships between the different contexts including their similarities and differences.
- Types of analogizing vary according to variables under consideration. They include such contexts as: (1) time (history); (2) space (geography); (3) areas of specialization in practice (for example, labor–management relations compared to environmental issues); (4) levels of analysis (for example, a local community compared to a family); and (5) relationships between subjects under observation (isomorphism, that is, A's relationship to B compared to X's relationship to Y).

Value commitment

- Value commitment is a normative aspiration for realizing an alternative reality to the conflict at hand, with or without empirical underpinnings or precedent to support its viability.
- Sources of value commitment include religiosity, ethics, ideology, philosophy, and other belief systems that encourage normative, future-oriented, and exploratory processes.

134 *Theory-building*

Combining known elements in a new way

- Combining known elements in an unconventional manner stimulates creativity. Elements under consideration may be either essential aspects of the conflict or aspects that appear seemingly unrelated to it, or a combination of both types.
- The key to this process is coming up with a new integrative principle that offers a new coherence for the component elements to work together.

Unconventionality out of conventionality

- To be usefully creative, unconventional approaches have to be devised based on an extensive understanding of conventional rules and boundaries that frame conflict parties and stakeholders' expectations.
- The awareness of perceived outer limits of practice – professional, institutional, socio-political, and otherwise – is a prerequisite for stretching them or even breaking them without provoking irreparable problems in the process.

Discoveries in retrospect

- According to some practitioners, the process of origination becomes fully recognizable only after it is successfully translated into practice through evolution.
- This epistemological process is enabled by the combined effects of both validation by those spearheading change and social learning by their audience.

Contingency-based, principled flexibility

- Conflict resolution creativity emerges from principled flexibility, or a searching process that is open-ended and flexible, yet at the same time guided by some sense of broad directionality and purpose.
- A corollary of principled flexibility is the need for a contingency-based process, defined as a continuous exploration of future possibilities and concrete steps that draw consciously on preceding actions and unfolding events.

Findings in comparative analysis (2): the five working concepts

Creativity of parties, intermediaries, and actors playing a dual function

- No salient difference is found between conflict parties' and intermediaries' creativity in terms of origination. But the two types are different with respect to the ways they evolve and come to gain acceptance by stakeholders in conflict.
- Conflict parties' initiatives by definition involve creativity from within the circles of immediate stakeholders. It generates some level of communal

recognition and impact on the conflict situations, most probably through reactive devaluation and resistance felt by opponents.
- Intermediaries' initiatives involve creativity from outside the circles of immediate stakeholders. It requires parties' "buy-in" to gain recognition and generate impact on the conflict situation.
- Creativity in the hybrid category is still to be explored. Preliminary indications are that the dual effects of creativity from within and outside interact with one another in such a complex manner that evolution and acceptance depends on various contextual factors, such as the actor's existing relationship with the conflict parties they try to influence.

The longitudinal nature of creativity

- The revised model hypothesizes a transition from incipience (kernel ideas present but still to be integrated) to origination (integrated for application), to evolution (shaping and reshaping). Evolution is a comprehensive process that may include acceptance (recognized as a new rallying point for change) and sustenance (a new reality anchored in society, with sustained momentum).
- Drawing on the revised model, four prototypes of longitudinal processes are suggested: Type A – the process fails in the transition from incipience to origination; Type B – the process fails in the transition from origination to evolution; Type C – the process fails in the course of evolution; and Type D – the process succeeds through evolution and develops further. It is hypothesized that a greater capacity for carrying the sustained tension between unconventionality and viability generates greater impetus for a transition from one phase to another.
- Creative processes occur outside the suggested model of longitudinal processes as well. What appears to be "failed" initiatives of creation, whether they are of Type B or C, or otherwise, may plant seeds for further social change, conventional or unconventional. This realization invites actors in conflict to broaden their time horizons, encouraging them to explore ways to build on potentially useful effects of what may be considered past "failures."

The outcome–process typology

- Outcome creativity is the capacity for breaking through a conventionally accepted reality of an inter-group conflict. Process creativity, on the other hand, refers to the capacity for generating an unconventional yet viable procedure that marks a distinct departure from the way conflicts of similar kinds have been handled before by their stakeholders. The two types are complementary to, and inseparable from, one another. But the critical difference lies between how to transform the conflict itself (outcome creativity) and how to approach the conflict parties in terms of spatial, temporal, relational, and other arrangements in which the conflict can be dealt with (process creativity).

- For outcome creativity, the capacity for coming up with an unconventional yet viable reformulation of the conflict is essential. On the other hand, process creativity emerges with or without the willingness and capacity to reformulate the conflict substantively.
- To be viable, outcome creativity requires the parties' self-motivated commitment to a reformulated reality of the conflict. Process creativity requires only the procedural commitment to entering a new form of inter-party communication and/or relationship-building.
- A question has emerged for future inquiry: Has there been an emergence of shared expectations, and perhaps a professional culture, among Western-trained researchers, practitioners, and policymakers advocating the premise of impartiality in outcome, gratifying the intrinsic value of bringing parties together for talks and relationship-building, but remaining unaware of how consciously and systematically to explore ways to reformulate the conflict with outcome creativity?

The system–element link (levels of analysis)

- Conceptualizing the four levels of analysis, micro, meso, macro, and mega, in terms of three sets of system–element link is important to explore what level of interaction generates creativity in a given context of conflict. A system refers to a network of interrelated parts with its boundary, imagined or real, separating itself from its outer environment. It shapes a context of a given conflict. On the other hand, elements are component parts, equivalent to individual or collective actors for the present purpose, that constitute a system.
- Findings suggest that creative change is inherently bottom-up, arising at the element level and influencing the systemic context to make the change possible.
- Interdependent origination conceptualizes a subtype of bottom-up change and describes a creative process where actors involved in inter-group conflict come to co-create an unconventional yet viable resolution option through symbiotic and synergetic effects of coordinating their interactions, despite their apparent tension and hesitation to do so. Aikido is a metaphor of this, and the Helsinki process an exemplar.

Conflict paradigms

- Thomas Kuhn's theory on scientific paradigms is inapplicable to conflict resolution creativity in a given local context of practice, for the latter lacks communal relationships of the kind that bind a scientific discipline. But Kuhn's theory offers a useful metaphor for designing a new method of practice, building on a new concept termed *conflict paradigm*.
- A conflict paradigm refers to a systemic entrenchment of perceptual and interactive patterns inherent in social conflict. The concept presupposes that

from a bird's eye perspective, any conflict, large or small, complex or simple, is a social system shaped and sustained by certain regularities, however chaotic they might look at first glance, in terms of the ways in which its constituents interact with one another and form perceptions about their interactions. A conflict paradigm is a unique application of the system concept, the latter being described in the context of the system–element link, and suggested for the specific purpose of generating outcome creativity.
- The suggested method helps actors in conflict transform their conflict paradigm into an alternative reality. An alternative reality, in the present context, is defined as a new set of perceptual and interactive patterns made possible by de-entrenching the perspectives – either purposefully, "by chance," or by a combination of both – and by reshaping them in a manner more constructive and acceptable to the parties.
- A search for alternative realities is stimulated by heuristic pointers, defined as evocative conceptual categories, or variables, that serve as a heuristic bridge between empirical and potential realities. These pointers are intended to help search for hidden perspectives and underlying patterns.
- Three types of heuristic pointers are suggested as particularly useful to explore alternative realities across contexts: (1) *time*, as in temporal shifts from the past to the present to the future, and across human, ecological, and geological timescales; (2) *space* in such terms as territorial, trans-territorial, supra-territorial, and non-territorial; and (3) *relational structure*, referring to both human–human relationships, for example, dependent, independent, or interdependent, and human relationships with Nature and the transpersonal.

4 Illustration

A case study of the first satyagraha campaign in South Africa from 1906 to 1914

Introduction

Having explored a range of working themes and concepts derived from the sixteen episodes of conflict resolution creativity, this chapter will illustrate how some of the suggested propositions may be applied to account for the emergence of the first satyagraha campaign in South Africa from 1906 to 1914. To the extent possible, the present case study will seek not only to discover new theoretical insights that have not been illuminated by the sixteen episodes, but also to integrate distinct enabling factors for creativity within the unique context of satyagraha's emergence.

As will be elaborated later, satyagraha, which is literally translated as "holding on to truth,"[1] refers to a distinct form of nonviolent civil disobedience. In the Gandhian tradition of moral politics, it is defined more specifically as a nonviolent means by which to manifest soul-force and self-suffering in order to restore irreducible essentials of human livelihood, without depriving opponents of theirs. The present case study is an attempt to illuminate the social and epistemological process through which this distinct form of collective action came into being, with emphasis on its origination phase in South Africa.

One of the primary reasons for selecting satyagraha's emergence for the stated purpose is its theoretical relevance, in view of the findings derived from the earlier stages of this study. In the course of the discussion to follow, it will become clear that the selected case cogently illustrates some of the key working propositions that have emerged from the sixteen episodes and helps to refine them further for conflict work. Another reason for selection is the intrinsic significance of satyagraha in the history of conflict and peace research and applied practice. The movement emerged on the fringes of Western civilization and European colonialism at the beginning of the twentieth century. Its enduring relevance as an instrument of strategic peace-making, however, outlived the century of mass violence and continues to shape the political lives of under-represented masses throughout the world. Attempts to apply its principle, or at least part of it, have been made at various stages of South African, Indian, and American history; its exemplary image continuously inspires grassroots movements in occupied territories in the Middle East, former socialist countries in Eastern Europe, and emerging democracies in Latin America. Inquiry into its social and epistemological origin is evocative and suggestive by itself. In addition, it is emphasized that the study explores satyagraha in South Africa, not in India, for it seeks to understand its *origination* phase. Satyagraha, as will be demonstrated later, had already matured in South Africa as a clearly definable process of political creation in the latter half of the 1900s, and evolved in various forms in the early 1910s. Importantly, the crystallization of this method in South Africa grew in a manner inseparable from Gandhi's self-awareness and religiosity, which were then carried over to India, along with the method itself.

Considering the illustrative purpose of the present case study, distinct conceptual features of satyagraha's origin may be spelled out at the outset, applying the working propositions and typologies articulated so far. Impressionistically, its unique characteristics are described as:

- *A conflict party's creativity*: the Indian community as a marginalized group, seeking redress from the South African government and European stakeholders involved in the Indian politics.
- *Process creativity*: concerned primarily with what procedural means ought to be applied to approach the conflicts at hand, with implications for outcome creativity.
- *Creativity generated at the element level, or agency-led creativity:* Gandhi and fellow satyagrahis seeking social change "from the bottom-up" by way of resisting social systems and structures of colonial rule in place.
- *Type C, in terms of its longitudinal nature*: the social and epistemological process of political creation reaching the evolution phase, yet failing to attain sustenance after Gandhi left South Africa in 1914.

Other profiles of the case will be described later, as they will constitute the essential part of the case analysis. In addition to outlining these features, it is worth re-emphasizing that the study of satyagraha as a case presupposes a comprehensive, holistic understanding of *conflict resolution* creativity as discussed in the introductory chapter, for satyagraha aims to make suppressed conflicts visible, rather than resolving them in a prototypical sense of peaceful resolution. However, the case is selected for illustration because the method seeks to realize an unconventional yet viable process by which to approach a conflict at hand, at least from its advocates' perspective.

Methodologically, the present case study neither confirms nor rejects the working propositions that have been articulated so far. Its aim is limited to theoretical refinement, clarification, and elaboration, with the view toward contributing to further inquiry and applied practice. For data collection, relevant archival documents were consulted as much as possible as a primary source of information, yet quality secondary sources also provided supplementary insights. The data analysis was qualitative and exploratory. Yet it was bound, to the extent possible, by the systematic search for consistency between different sources of information, as well as for possible regularities and patterns across observed events and phenomena from which potentially generalizable inferences were drawn.

Finally, an overview of the chapter is presented. First, Gandhi's life, from his birth in India in 1869 till his departure from South Africa in 1914, will be chronicled briefly. The biographic sketch of his personal history will offer a useful window of opportunity to understand satyagraha's social history, of which his life was both a reflection and a driving force. Second, the socio-economic, political, and psychological background of the case will be outlined from a broad historical perspective. This section will serve as a conflict analysis, illuminating the historical context from which satyagraha as a method of conflict work emerged. Third, profiles of primary stakeholders within the South African Indian community will be described. Because the selected case illustrates a conflict party's creativity, the analysis of the three socio-economic subgroups, merchants, indentured laborers, and ex-indentured workers and professionals, is considered an essential requisite for understanding what intra-communal processes and dynamics made this distinct form of political creation possible. Fourth, based on these preparatory discussions, the emergence of satyagraha will be described longitudinally. In order to demonstrate changes and continuities that had dynamically unfolded through the campaign, the eight-year period will be divided into four cumulative stages for analytical clarity. Fifth, the working propositions on value commitment, paradigm shifts, and analogizing will be applied to illustrate satyagraha's emergence, in addition to articulating an additional, unexplored theme, which probes the evocative link between creativity and identity transformation. An attempt will be made to explore how two of the most salient features of satyagraha, value commitment and analogizing, interacted with one another within its social and epistemological context. The final section will summarize key findings in the case study, with the view toward making them explicit as a contribution to future inquiry and practice.

Gandhi's life before mahatmaship: a biographic sketch

Consistent with the overall objective of this inquiry, the present case study explores the social and epistemological process of satyagraha's emergence as the primary unit of analysis, while treating the personal histories of its principal architects as embedded sub-units. The rationale for this methodological choice is that conflict resolution creativity is quintessentially a relational and social phenomenon, of which no single individual can ultimately claim exclusive authorship. As will be demonstrated throughout the present case study, this working assumption applies to the origin of satyagraha, of which Gandhi is widely regarded as the principal, and even exclusive, creator. In the mixture of fact and mythology about his image as a mahatma, or a great soul, the popularly held assumption that Gandhi single-handedly *created* satyagraha tends to be uncritically accepted in today's society, particularly in the West. This study will refute such a Gandhi-centric mythology about satyagraha's origin. At the same time, however, it will demonstrate the essential role of Gandhi's leadership as a social and epistemological phenomenon, reflecting South African Indians' communal history and identity, which found a coherent expression through the Gandhian struggle.

The biographic sketch of Gandhi's life needs to be viewed in this context of critical evaluation. Over-representation of Gandhi's individual creativity is avoided, for his contribution to satyagraha is appreciated as a historical and communal experience. It is in this qualified sense that one may appreciate the personal history of Gandhi's life as a window of opportunity to explore the social and epistemological history of satyagraha's origin. With this overall objective in mind, the biographic sketch to be provided in this section is necessarily selective. It highlights critical incidents and experiences that appear to have shaped the ways in which Gandhi contributed to satyagraha's origination at different stages of his life – from his childhood and adolescence in India to his student years in England, to his legal practice in South Africa before satyagraha's advent, to his newly discovered vocation as a conscientious law-breaker.

Mohandas Karamchand Gandhi was born on October 2, 1869 in Kathiawar, the peninsular portion of the present state of Gujarat, located in northwestern India. By the time of his birth, the British had already ruled India for two and a half centuries. The imperial and colonial worldview had been entrenched deeply in the collective mindset of many Indians. From ordinary Indians' perspective, the historical context in which M. K. Gandhi was born was the least conducive to a prospect that some day in a foreseeable future, British colonial rule would come to an end.

Mohandas was born as the third son of Karamchand Gandhi, prime minister of the small princely state of Porbandar, located in the Kathiawar peninsula. Though his birthplace was on the periphery of India's national politics, his family's prestigious lineage in the locality and his Bania, or trading caste, background were conducive to his adolescent aspirations for advanced education and upward social mobility.[2] His early exposure to the multi-religious atmosphere on the Arabian Sea coast and his parents' openness to different faith traditions enabled him to experience the lively confluence of Hinduism, Jainism, Islam, Zoroastrianism, and other religions during his childhood and adolescence. Gandhi's (1993) autobiography, written in his mid-fifties, describes what this early exposure meant to him, at least in retrospect:

> I got an early grounding in toleration for all branches of Hinduism and sister religions. For my father and mother would visit the *Haveli*[3] as also Shiva's and Rama's temples, and would take or send us youngsters there. Jain monks also would pay frequent visits to my father, and would even go out of their way to accept food from us – non-Jains. They would have talks with my father on subjects religious and mundane.
>
> He had, besides, Musalman and Parsi friends,[4] who would talk to him about their own faiths, and he would listen to them always with respect, and often with interest. Being his nurse, I often had a chance to be present at these talks. These many things combined to inculcate in me a toleration for all faiths.
>
> (Gandhi 1993: 33)

At the awakening of Gandhi's religiosity during his childhood, the exemplary image of devotion set by his mother, Putali Ba, played an important role. Because she was a committed member of a small local Vaishnava community that aspired to blend the Koran and Hindu scriptures into a coherent whole, Hindu–Muslim harmony was imbued in the most intimate part of young Gandhi's spiritual universe, of which his inviolable closeness to his mother constituted an essential pillar. Through Putali Ba's religious observance and numerous other influences surrounding him, Gandhi as a child and adolescent grew accustomed to the spiritual practice of fasting, oath-taking, vegetarianism, and non-killing, all becoming hallmarks of devoted satyagrahis' life years later. Implications of Gandhi's spiritual development, including his immersion in Kathiawar's local religiosity, will be elaborated later, in the context of exploring the nature of value commitment to creating satyagraha.

Gandhi married Kasturbai Makanji in 1882, when they were both thirteen years old. Their marriage followed the will of their parents and elders, and it reflected the traditional customs of Kathiawar. The first of their four sons, Harilal, was born in 1888, when Gandhi was eighteen; the last one, Devadas, was born in 1900, when he was thirty. Gandhi's life in South Africa, which began in 1893 at age twenty-three and came to a close in 1914 at age forty-four, was a continuous struggle, first to establish himself as a bread-earner and householder and later to seek oneness of his personal and public life as a leading satyagrahi. Behind the scenes of his struggles in public work, which will remain the central focus of this case study, were his personal struggles, including his unsuccessful attempts to build trust and functional family relationships with his first son Harilal.

From 1888 to 1891, Gandhi studied law in London in order to become a barrister.[5] From age nineteen to twenty-one, he immersed himself not only in legal studies and the English language, but also in various forms of Western secular influence – elocution, dance, violin, French, and British clothing. While his belief in British imperialism grew, with lasting impact on his style of public work in South Africa, he also began studying Oriental religions more consciously in London than ever before. One of the most important sources of religious inspiration for him was his encounters with British members of the Theosophist Society, a newly established group dedicated to the study and practice of selected elements of Hinduism and Buddhism. At the request of his Theosophist friends in late 1889, he helped them read the Sanskrit text of *Bhagavad Gita*. Through this experience, for the first time he read this sacred Hindu scripture, which would later become an infallible guide to his life and public work. Gandhi also began to make conscious efforts to study Buddhism around 1890–1. In short, his education in London not only prepared him professionally as an English-speaking barrister, but also built his identity philosophically as a non-sectarian Hindu, increasingly more curious about Oriental spirituality and Occidental modernity. The spiritual pilgrimage he started in earnest in London would later intensify in South Africa, and gradually shaped his style of public work in his thirties and beyond.

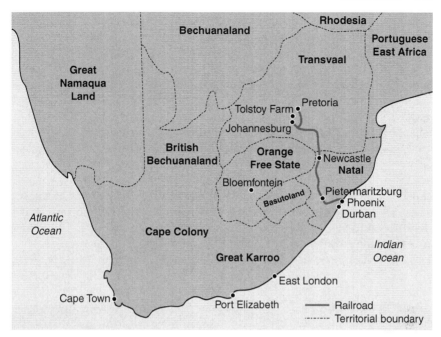

Figure 4.1 Map of South Africa before 1914.

In the summer of 1891, Gandhi sailed back to India as a young barrister. He was eager to report to his mother about his educational achievement, only to learn that she had already passed away. Until early 1893, Gandhi tried unsuccessfully to practice law in Kathiawar courts. In April 1893, upon his elder brother's recommendation, Gandhi decided to work for one year as a commercial lawyer in Natal, South Africa for Dada Abdullah and Co., one of the most prominent Indian companies in the region at that time. Gandhi's primary motive for taking up this short-term assignment in Natal was to seek a new experience as a hired legal representative of the commercial giant from Gujarat, his home region. However, his encounters with racial discrimination in South Africa made him reflect seriously on issues related to human dignity and justice and eventually think beyond the narrow confines of his initial career interest.

According to his autobiography, the twenty-four-year-old Gandhi accidentally learned in April 1894 about the Natal legislature's plan to consider eliminating Indians' franchises on racial grounds when he was attending his farewell party in Durban on the eve of his return voyage to India. Then and there, he decided to cancel his trip and petition against the proposed legislation. In August 1894, the Natal Indian Congress (NIC) was established to protect and advance the welfare of Indians in South Africa in general and the commercial interests of Natal-based merchants in particular,[6] with Gandhi appointed as its first honorary secretary at age twenty-four. Gandhi's involvement in South African regional politics thus began in Natal.

For the next seven years, until late 1901, Gandhi spent much of his time in Natal as a lawyer, political organizer, lobbyist, social and health worker, and in miscellaneous other capacities. Despite the broad range of activities in which he was involved from age twenty-four to thirty-two during this period, his public work was dedicated primarily to drafting and delivering petitions for constitutional protest. Many of his petitions sought to challenge discriminatory legal practices against South African Indians, especially Natal-based merchants. Importantly, these petitions presupposed Gandhi's acceptance of the colonial and imperial legal framework, in which white supremacy and Indians' relative inferiority remained unchallenged. This style of legal and political activity reflected Gandhi's fundamental confidence in and loyalty to the British Empire, despite his awareness of anti-Indian policies in Natal and elsewhere. His imperial loyalty was demonstrated most symbolically from late 1899 to early 1900, when he risked his life to serve the British on the frontlines of the Anglo-Boer War as a leading member of the Indian Ambulance Corps.

At the end of 1901, Gandhi returned to India at age thirty-two, with the intent of settling there permanently. Upon returning, he began appealing to prominent Indian National Congress (INC) leaders in order to elicit their support for South African Indians' struggles. His appeals, however, failed to find a receptive audience in the Indian political circles, preoccupied with their own domestic affairs. In the meantime, he tried in vain to establish himself as a lawyer, first in Rajkot, Kathiawar and then in Bombay. Through these personal and professional struggles, he had become exhausted and severely ill by March 1902 – even to the extent that his doctor advised him to "take complete rest" for two to three months.[7] When he received a cable in November 1902 from South African Indians recalling him for urgent political work there, he did "not yet feel strong enough for the mental strain" that his advocacy work in South Africa was due to demand him. Thus Gandhi's stint in India in 1901–2 set a stage for a personal and professional crisis in his life, revealing both his inner urge for attaining political relevance prematurely on the scene of India's national politics, on the one hand, and his frustration caused by his inability to fulfill his political aspirations, on the other. It is inferred from this observation that the renewed commitment to public work that Gandhi would demonstrate upon returning to South Africa was attributed in part to this sobering experience of failure in his motherland in his early thirties.

In December 1903, Gandhi returned to South Africa. By February 1904, he had decided to settle down as a lawyer and public worker based in Johannesburg, the hub of Indian commercial and political activities in the Transvaal. What awaited Gandhi there was the apparent deterioration of socio-economic conditions facing fellow Indians, as a result of the British taking over the Transvaal government from Boers after the war of 1899–1902. From the Indians' perspective, the British failed in the post-war period to address their grievances under Boer rule, which the Indians expected the British to tackle immediately in exchange for their wartime service and costly sacrifice for the Empire. Instead, the British-led administration in the Transvaal seized this opportunity to consolidate white-only rule and proactively implemented policies of anti-Asiatic discrimination in such areas as inter-state migration, issuance of trade permits, and segregation of bazaars for Indian traders. Given this economic and political crisis facing the Indians in the Transvaal and elsewhere in South Africa, Gandhi's public work as an experienced petitioner intensified in the mid-1900s. Importantly, however, his method of public work and his political ideology during this period, particularly before the advent of satyagraha in late 1906, still remained within the confines of constitutional protest, reflecting his aspiration to be an effective petitioner but not necessarily a revolutionary law-breaker.

In addition to earning public confidence in the South African Indian community as a lawyer and public worker, Gandhi also began to assume new roles in his social life that would generate a lasting impact on the way satyagraha was to emerge and evolve. One of the new roles he assumed was that of a professional journalist. In June 1903, the South African Indian community's weekly *Indian Opinion* commenced publication in Durban under the initiatives of its proprietor, Madanjit Vyavaharik. Upon his returning to India in October 1904, Gandhi began to assume full responsibility for the day-to-day operation of the *Indian Opinion*, while he had to intensify his effort to write articles on public affairs regularly. As will be elaborated later, his role as an opinion leader through the weekly journal would become an important rallying point for the satyagraha movement to emerge and evolve.

Another role Gandhi began to play was that of a principal householder in communal settlements. In October 1904, he read John Ruskin's *Unto This Last: Four Essays on the First Principles of Political Economy* and decided to practice the virtues of simple communal life described in the book. Toward the end of 1904, he purchased ten acres of land near Durban and established the Phoenix Settlement, an experimental colony for ideal community life centering on collaborative manual labor. He then transferred the operational base of the *Indian Opinion* from Durban to the Phoenix Settlement, where the printing of the weekly continued without using machines. Another experimental settlement, the Tolstoy Farm, was to be established in mid-1910 on the 1,100 acres of land near Johannesburg, when Gandhi was devoting much of his time to public work in the Transvaal. In historical hindsight, it is inferred that Gandhi's experience as a householder and leader in creating microcosms of communal life, joined by settlers of diverse backgrounds, contributed toward realizing macrocosms of multi-religious and multi-lingual coexistence in South Africa and later in India. In terms of more immediate consequences of these experiments, the settlers' spiritual commitment to satyagraha would soon be tested and prove genuine and firm in late 1913, when Gandhi decided to bring women from these settlements to the frontlines of the satyagraha struggle in order to expand the movement's constituency base.

Soon after these new roles and tasks were introduced into Gandhi's life, another critical incident occurred, shaping his outlook on both public work and personal life in an important way. In the spring of 1906, the Zulu "rebellion" broke out against the British-led Natal government. Gandhi organized an Indian

Ambulance Corps and served the Natal government, which was en route to consolidate the white supremacist rule over the already marginalized native Africans. Witnessing the British "man-hunt" of defenseless Zulus, Gandhi reflected deeply not only on the brutality of the British conduct, but also on the implications of his risky public work for his family life. What came to his mind while serving on the frontlines was the need to transform his personal life decisively, by observing celibacy (brahmacharya) and voluntary poverty for life. As soon as the Corps was discharged from service in July 1906, he returned to the Phoenix Settlement, shared his realization with his closest friends, and took a vow to this effect, inviting others to do the same on their own accord. In Gandhi's mind, taking a vow of celibacy and voluntary poverty meant relinquishing his worldly desires, particularly the ones arising from his attachment to his family and children and to his wealth. By relinquishing those desires, he aspired to dedicate his entire being selflessly to risky public work. Step by step, his spirituality and inner resolve matured, preparing him to express his identity through the new method of public work, satyagraha.

On September 11, 1906, some 3,000 Indians gathered in Johannesburg and took a mass pledge of nonviolent civil resistance to a proposed anti-Asiatic law in the Transvaal. With the advent of satyagraha, the micro history of Gandhi's life would gradually merge into the social and epistemological history of satyagraha. As will be described in the sections to follow, the eight-year history of satyagraha in South Africa was the Indian community's collective experience in which Gandhi played an indispensable leadership role. By way of interacting with this communal process, Gandhi as a Western-styled lawyer representing wealthy merchants gradually transcended his initial commitment to constitutional protest, and eventually discovered his new vocation and identity as a conscientious law-breaker and revolutionary nationalist for Indians of all socio-economic and regional backgrounds. It is on this social and epistemological process that the discussion will now focus, paying due attention to critical incidents in Gandhi's life from 1906 to 1914 as part of the broader communal experience.

Conflict analysis: the economic, political, and psychological context of satyagraha's emergence

To contextualize the satyagraha campaign of 1906–14 in the social and epistemological setting in which it emerged, it is essential to analyze the social conflicts facing the primary actors involved in it. The objective and scope of the conflict analysis are illustrated by a hypothetical yet practical question: supposing that there had been an impartial yet empathetic conflict worker familiar with all major parties to the conflicts, with intimate knowledge of their aspirations, expressed or hidden, around the mid-1900s to the early 1910s, what would an outline of his or her conflict analysis look like? To keep the scope of analysis manageable, influential constituencies within the Indian, Boer (Afrikaner), and British communities in South Africa will be considered primary conflict parties.

Other domestic actors such as the indigenous African, Colored (mixed-race), and Chinese communities, as well as concerned foreign nations and governments such as India and Great Britain, will be considered a secondary yet important part of the larger historical context of analysis. The period under study marked not only satyagraha's origination and evolution, but also the historical transition of the South African nation from the destruction and traumas left by the Anglo-Boer War of 1899–1902, toward the emergence of the Union, integrating the four divided republics under British or Boer political influence. Geographically, analysis will focus primarily on the Transvaal and Natal, the central stages of the satyagraha campaign, while events in the Cape Colony and Orange Free State (OFS) are considered secondary and in the background.

What follows is a bird's eye view of socio-economic, political, and cultural–psychological undercurrents shaping the sustained large-scale conflicts in which satyagraha found its historical roots. Analysis of each of the three topics will be necessarily brief, for its aim is limited to providing relevant background information that helps to understand how the first satyagraha campaign illustrates the applicability of selected working hypotheses on creativity.[8]

From a long-term historical perspective, underlying the socio-economic forces that the first satyagraha movement challenged was Euro-centric, capitalist expansionism and fundamentalism, particularly its manifestations crystallized by British colonialism in the late nineteenth century and the early twentieth century.[9] Its effect was expansionist because British colonialism, far exceeding in scope its Dutch predecessor that had reached the Cape colony in the mid-seventeenth century, wove South Africa irreversibly into its global capitalist structure, with wide-ranging consequences on the international role of South Africa's modernizing economy. It was, at the same time, fundamentalist because the Euro-centric capitalist structure penetrating the South African economy was driven by ever-growing pursuits of high returns from capital input. Such pursuits were expanded even to the point of justifying, and at times ignoring, excessive human sufferings as a necessary cost of supplying cheap, disposable labor.

In South Africa, capitalist expansionism and fundamentalism manifested in the form of colonial exploitation of different kinds, including slavery and its contemporary liberalist offspring, an indentured labor system. Driven in part by the British missionary zeal for interracial equalization, slavery was abolished as an official policy in the Cape in the early nineteenth century, despite the resistance of Boers, who trekked north and northeast in search of land and freedom from British influence.[10] In Natal, however, despite the abolishment of slavery, British colonialists continuously sought cheap labor to meet the rising demands of production in their sugar and tea plantations and thus introduced an indentured labor system in 1857.[11] Starting in 1860, numerous shipments of Indian workers under a five-year contract, most of them departing from Madras and Calcutta, found their way to Durban.[12] With the migration of poor Indian laborers came a smaller number of Indian entrepreneurs, who successfully built trading relationships not only with Indian migrants but also with Europeans and non-Europeans. By the end of the nineteenth century, many Europeans came to view these wealthy Indian traders as a serious threat to their economic welfare and survival, first in Natal and later in the Transvaal. Thus, during the few decades leading up to the satyagraha campaign, Indians had emerged on the South African scene both as "haves" in competition with European traders and as "have-nots" whose livelihood depended solely on feeding the burgeoning capitalist enterprises with cheap labor.

In the second half of the nineteenth century, South Africa underwent another decisive experience that expanded and deepened its socio-economic structure of capitalism, with far-reaching global ramifications. Diamonds were discovered in 1867 in the OFS, followed by the discovery of gold in 1886 in the Transvaal. These discoveries, combined with large coal deposits found in Natal and the Transvaal adding to the Natal coalmines already in operation, led to the "mineral revolution," paving the way toward South Africa's rapid industrialization and urbanization. The rise of the Transvaal Rand (mining region) was particularly significant. By 1898, for example, the Transvaal became the largest single gold producer, accounting for 27 percent of total production in the world; by 1914, the year the first satyagraha campaign came to an end, its share rose to as high as 40 percent.[13] With the dramatic expansion of an exploitable resource base, the South African economy became an arena for unprecedented capital investments, not only in mineral extraction, but in railways, international steamship services, telegraph communication, commercial agriculture, and other kinds of socio-economic infrastructure. Industrialization grew in tandem with urbanization, accelerated by a massive influx of European migrant workers called Uitlanders. Many Uitlanders were British and settled in the Transvaal Rand. From the traditional Boers' point of view, Uitlanders were generally considered de-Christianized, opportunistic profit-seekers, threatening the centuries-old Calvinist, agrarian virtues that defined the Boer identity. This British–Boer tension, running deep in the unresolved socio-economic, structural problems between them, survived the war of attrition from 1899 to 1902, which ended in a pyrrhic British victory. The continuous influx of "uncivilized" Indians, not only in Natal plantations and coalmines but also in the Transvaal and Natal urban settings, appeared – in the eyes of humiliated Afrikaner nationalists – as yet another degrading effect of what were essentially British capitalist enterprises.

Another long-term consequence of industrialization and urbanization was the surge of organized labor movements spearheaded by European syndicalists, setting examples for other racial groups in South African society. Against the background of sustained economic deprivation among urban white workers, syndicalist movements for unionization, resisting the Union government's restrictions and employers' control, grew increasingly radical and even violent. Radical syndicalism became particularly salient and widespread in the early 1910s, when Gandhi, for the first time, mobilized indentured Indian laborers for satyagraha. By then, many white rulers, both Afrikaner and British, had come to fear that proletarian consciousness might become a new rallying point for poor workers of different racial backgrounds, possibly even native Africans, to form either a united front or separate fronts against the European ruling class.[14] This European fear played an important role in the timing and fashion in which the satyagraha campaign came to an end in early 1914.

Considering the political environment of the first satyagraha campaign, one may describe an overarching theme of the historical period in question as state-making, at least from the European rulers' perspective. In legal and administrative terms, state-making, following the 1909 South African Union Bill, took the form of establishing a federal framework to bring the Cape Colony, the OFS, the Transvaal, and Natal together into unified statehood under a single constitution. In more substantive terms of political relationship-building, state-making was one of the means by which to facilitate "conciliation" between the British and Boers after the war of 1899–1902. In addition, it also reflected the long-term aspirations of the British imperial government to incorporate a unified nation of South Africa firmly into its global strategic alliance against potential threats, such as Germany and its colonial outposts in Africa and elsewhere.[15]

Several years into the post-war reconstruction process, the inter-group animosity between the British and Boers remained tense. In addition, the steps toward "conciliation" taken by such Boer architects for state-making as Louis Botha and Jan Christian Smuts, the latter being the primary counterpart of Gandhi in his final negotiations with the government, infuriated still vengeful Afrikaner nationalists in the OFS and elsewhere. Afrikaner nationalism surged vocally during the local elections held in each of the four states between 1906 and 1907, as groundwork for the subsequent Union-building. Brought into the constitutional framework of power-sharing in 1910, Afrikaner nationalist politicians, deeply resenting the proposed "imperialist" scheme of conciliation and bilingualism, confronted the Botha administration in the Union government. Afrikaners' intra-communal division became most salient in March 1913, when Prime Minister Botha removed the prominent Afrikaner general and Justice Minister, James B. M. Hertzog, from his cabinet. Defying the Botha administration openly outside the cabinet, Hertzog successfully rallied broad-based support from dissatisfied Afrikaners and formed a Nationalist Party in January 1914. It was at this height of Afrikaner nationalism and intra-communal schism that the satyagraha campaign reached its climax in the form of the Great March, toward the end of 1913.

While state-making for Anglo-Afrikaner conciliation institutionalized white supremacy, it consolidated the exclusion of non-white constituencies from institutional politics at the same time. From the perspective of the white ruling class, it was imperative to keep native Africans, who constituted the largest part of South Africa's population, under law and order as a precondition for white-based state-making. That being an absolute priority, grievances raised by Asiatics for want of civil and commercial rights remained secondary or even marginal in the eyes of the Union statesmen preoccupied with their urgent, overriding need for state-making and Anglo-Boer "conciliation" – at least until satyagraha forced them to pay attention, most notably in the early 1910s. From the standpoint of non-white leaders of different racial groups, state-making sharpened the contrast between those hoping to survive within the constitutional politics and others left with no choice but extra-constitutional recourse to seek political survival. The Colored, with the limited franchise granted to influential constituencies in the Cape, stayed on the former course; native Africans and Asiatics were driven to take the latter. In this sense, satyagraha as an institutionalized means of law-breaking was born against the backdrop of white-based law-making for conciliation.

Finally, the cultural and psychological context of satyagraha's origin is considered. At its core lay tension, entanglements, clashes, and transformations of group identities, accentuated by defining, and at times traumatizing, experiences of the respective communities in conflict. Some communal identities were centuries old and others just emerging. These identities evolved around nationalism, regionalism, civilization, religion, caste, and class, depending on the unique histories and carriers of the communities' meaning-making patterns. Nationalism, or loyalty to a nation, became a particularly salient factor in South African identity politics, especially for some sections of Boers and Indians at the wake of the twentieth century. As a form of cultural legitimizer and de-legitimizer, nationalism is defined as a collective identity shaped and reshaped by historical experiences and memories, and bounded by a shared attachment to the same motherland, language, religion, origination myth, and/or other carriers of meaning-making processes, often inherited from generation to generation.[16]

For the formation of Afrikaner nationalism, which became an important part of satyagraha's historical background, the Anglo-Boer War of 1899–1902 played a decisive role. The war claimed the lives of about 34,000 Boers, civilian and non-civilian, and 22,000 British and Empire soldiers, with no less than 14,000 African lives lost in its midst.[17] As the Boers turned to guerrilla tactics to resist the advancing British troops by early 1900, the British adopted a scorched-earth strategy, burning some 3,000 Boer farms and destroying their livestock. About 28,000 Boer civilians, most of them women and children, died from epidemics after being incarcerated in overcrowded "concentration camps" set up by the British. These Boer civilian deaths claimed about 10 percent of the Boer lives in the two republics fighting against the British, namely, the Transvaal and the OFS.[18]

These statistics fall far short of illustrating the depth of humiliation engraved in Boers' collective consciousness. Unhealed traumas found expressions in monuments, religious ceremonies, war epics, and other cultural carriers reflective of nationalistic emotions. One symbolic example of these psychological phenomena was the ceremony held on December 16, 1913 to unveil a monument in Bloemfontein, the capital of the Orange Free State, to remember the women and children who had died in the concentration camps. The construction of the monument was funded by donations from all parts of the country. The date of the ceremony was set on Dingaan's Day, a national festival of thanksgiving commemorating Boer trekkers' epic victory over Zulu king Dingaan's forces in the famous "Battle of Blood River" on December 16, 1838. The emotional speech delivered by General Smuts, who by then had become one of the most influential politicians in the Union and Gandhi's counterpart in the on-going negotiations over the Indian question, appealed deeply to Afrikaner heroism, patriotism, and Calvinist purity, in search of paths to self-preservation and "inter-racial peace" – with the British.[19]

While humiliated Boers deepened their attachment to their Afrikaner motherland and cultural heritage, the British ruling class and businessmen in South Africa, let alone more transient migrants such as Utilanders, remained attached to the British motherland and identity, many living in Anglophone townships. Within their imperial worldview of different versions, ranging from relatively liberal ideologies of Cape-based urban residents to more conservative views held by Natal-based plantation owners, their British motherland remained in the center; for many of them, South Africa was but a peripheral outpost under the colonial influence of London. While the British continuously expanded imperial control over this mineral-rich outpost through war and conquest, most decisively during the Anglo-Boer War, they had come to face an increasingly serious obstacle of their own making – an "Asiatic invasion." The problem became most salient by the end of the nineteenth century in Natal, where the British colonialists sought to procure a cheap labor force urgently, and later spread to the Transvaal.

With the introduction of the indentured labor system in Natal in the mid-nineteenth century, shipments of Indian workers began to flow into the port of Durban. In 1893, Indians in Natal – 46,000 in total – outnumbered 45,000 Europeans.[20] From the Europeans' point of view, these foreign Asiatics added to the overwhelmingly large non-white population in Natal, some 470,000 Africans. The Asiatic population remained larger in size than the European around the time of satyagraha's origination and evolution: 101,000 Asiatics compared to 97,000 Europeans in 1904, and 133,000 Asiatics to 98,000 Europeans in 1911.[21] In addition to being outnumbered, Europeans also faced commercial competition with a growing number of Indian entrepreneurs,[22] most of them skilled, wealthy Muslims from Bombay, whose presence was perceived widely as threatening Europeans' economic livelihood. In the Natal parliament and other arenas of state policymaking, the European fear of being outnumbered and outmaneuvered by Asiatics was voiced vehemently and persistently,[23] echoed in the white-run press and public opinion.

Psychologically, the deep-seated fear of the British colonialists, left outnumbered at the peripheral outpost far from their motherland, was driven in part by their shared sense of perpetual insecurity and the need for survival in the "uncivilized" land.[24] Their growing fear also reflected and thickened the perceived boundaries between *we-ness* and *they-ness*, where "they" as "uncivilized" non-Europeans – native Africans, the Colored, and Asiatics alike – must be controlled and prevented from venting their frustration and "we" as civilized Europeans, both British colonialists and local Boers, must always remain on guard over their untamed animality. During the satyagraha campaign of 1906–14, the Europeans' emotions ran particularly high not only in Natal, but also in the Transvaal and elsewhere, for they witnessed the unprecedented level of revolutionary potential in the violent strikes led by white (mainly English) syndicalists, on the one hand, and the nonviolent alternatives invented by Indians, on the other, both setting disturbing examples to inspire native Africans and the Colored who might follow suit.[25]

Profiles of Indian stakeholders in the satyagraha campaign

Before describing satyagraha's emergence longitudinally, its principal advocates and participants within the South African Indian community are briefly profiled. Reflecting the unique history of Indians' arrival and settlement in South Africa throughout the latter half of the nineteenth century and the early twentieth, there emerged three distinct socio-economic groups within the community. Each group was made up of individuals of diverse religious, regional, linguistic, and caste backgrounds. The three socio-economic groups are: (1) merchant entrepreneurs; (2) indentured laborers; and (3) ex-indentured Indians as well as their colonial-born descendants. During the satyagraha campaign, these groups strove to achieve both overlapping and contradictory aspirations that reflected their long-standing grievances, socio-economic or otherwise in nature. Because satyagraha's emergence paralleled the dynamic divergence and convergence of these three groups attempting to realize their aspirations, the profile of each group deserves attention. In this context of intra-communal relationship-building for satyagraha, constraints and strengths that defined Gandhi's role, first as a hired representative of elite merchants and later as a more independent community leader, will become clear in the discussion to follow.

Indian merchants started migrating to Natal in the mid-1870s, over a decade after the first shipment of indentured laborers arrived in 1860. They established solid entrepreneurial bases mainly around Durban, gradually extended branches in the urban interior, first in Natal and later in the Transvaal, and subsequently built well-structured commercial networks of interdependence with small traders through property rentals and credit. As of 1904, some two years before the Indian struggle officially began, there were 1,225 merchants of this type in Natal and 581 in the Transvaal,[26] who could afford to obtain trade licenses issued by the government. Swan (1985) estimates that these wealthy merchants, some 1,800 in total, each earned over £300 a year, compared to the average annual income of £12–18 earned by a free (not indentured) Indian of that time. This suggests that the monopoly by a privileged few was deeply entrenched in South African Indians' socio-economic relations, with significant implications for the internal politics of satyagraha to be elaborated shortly.

Most of these prominent merchants were Gujarati-speaking Muslims from western India, particularly around Bombay, and were commonly dubbed "Arabs" by Europeans unfamiliar with them. By the 1890s, the resentment of Europeans in Natal against competitive Indian merchants found concrete political expressions in the form of government regulations on trade licenses and bazaar locations, both of which were indispensable for Indian merchants' livelihood. Drawing on their financial and political clout, the Indian merchants repeatedly petitioned the state governments of Natal and the Transvaal, as well as the Union government after 1910, to secure their rights to commerce, with little success.

As mentioned earlier, Gandhi was hired in 1893 as a commercial lawyer by Dada Abdullah and Co., one of the most influential Gujarati merchant groups in Natal. Based in Durban, the company had fifteen branches spread in South Africa and had been carrying out regular commercial transactions in India, England, and Germany in the 1890s,[27] posing a significant threat to European competitors. Gandhi arrived at Durban in order to meet the company's urgent need to hire a full-time lobbyist to protest against increasingly severe government restrictions on Indian trade. As a British-educated barrister from Gujarat, Gandhi, though still only twenty-three, was uniquely suited to offer legal services, where his language skills in both English and Gujarati and his cultural awareness of Gujarati traders' manners were useful for the merchants who hired him. Gandhi entered local politics in Natal in mid-1894 in his capacity as the first honorary secretary of the NIC. He spent the next twenty years on lobbying, conventional legal practice, and spiritually motivated public service, first in Natal and later in the Transvaal, except for a stint in India from October 1901 to December 1902. These two decades of legal and political work coincided with his growing commitment to religious studies and practice.

For the purpose of understanding satyagraha's origin, it is important to note that the deepening of Gandhi's religious awareness, as well as his disillusionment with the British inability to fulfill the imperial ideals of equality and equity for Indians, had gradually come to shape his identity as a moral leader and conscientious law-breaker. Through the weekly journal, *Indian Opinion*, that began publication in June 1903, his political and spiritual discourse came to be publicized widely and systematically within the South African Indian community and beyond. More on Gandhi's identity transformation and its effects on satyagraha's epistemological origin will be discussed later.

While Muslim merchants from Bombay and other western Indian regions worked to secure their share in the British-led project of capitalist expansionism and colonialism, others occupying the lowest level of India's socio-economic strata continued their influx as indentured laborers into South Africa in the late nineteenth and the early twentieth century. The laborers were employed to supply cheap and efficient labor for sugar and tea plantations in southern Natal and coalmines in the north.[28] A majority of them were Tamil-speakers from southern India with diverse Hindu backgrounds, with a whole range of caste backgrounds from Brahmin to outcaste,[29] all sharing the urgent economic need for escaping abject poverty in the areas of their origin. It is estimated that the indentured laborers shipped to Natal from the two Indian ports of departure, Madras and Calcutta, numbered about 150,000 for the entire period of shipment from 1860 to 1911.[30]

According to the 1857 law introduced in Natal, indentured laborers were to gain independence on completion of their five-year contract. The law also stated that freed laborers were to be granted a free return passage to India or alternatively given a plot of land to stay in South Africa. However, the new immigration law of 1895 required time-expired workers to either return, re-indenture, or pay the £3 tax to gain independence. The revised law reflected Europeans' fear of being outnumbered by free Asiatics, and it was intended to either bind the Indians under indenture continuously or to make them leave on their own. For the majority of time-expired ex-indentured laborers, neither returning nor paying the £3 tax was an affordable option. They were therefore compelled to re-indenture out of necessity. Government statistics show that the rate of re-indentured laborers continuously rose as a general trend throughout the 1900s and the early 1910s,[31] when the satyagraha struggle emerged and grew. For example, in 1904 about 7 percent of time-expired indentured laborers chose to re-indenture. The rate of re-indenture rose to 54 percent in 1908, and to 95 percent in 1912, a year before Gandhi and other leading satyagrahis led thousands of indentured laborers in Natal to strike and march, in order to abolish the £3 tax. Consequently, as of 1911, some 79,000 indentured laborers, or 52 percent of the total 152,000 shipped from India since 1860, were either compelled or chose to stay in South Africa even after their contracts had expired.[32] In psychological terms, the significant rate of indentured and re-indentured laborers who committed suicide reflected a prevailing sense of hopelessness among them.[33] Despite the gravity of the laborers' suppressed grievances, they were neither included in the platform of Indians' organized politics nor supported by elite merchants, for the latter distinguished themselves from the "uncivilized" indentured laborers in their own struggle against Europeans' racial prejudice, except on rare occasions where the merchants' interests coincided with those of the laborers.

A great majority of the ex-indentured Indians remained in the lower strata of Natal's economy, occupying such positions as small farmers, hawkers, fishermen, and shopkeepers. By the mid-1900s, however, a small group of well-educated white-collar professionals emerged from these Indian masses, with distinct "colonial-born" consciousness and organizational capacities to give political expression to it. Having received Western education, mostly at Christian missionary schools, this emerging cohort of colonial-born professionals came to occupy such positions as lawyers, accountants, civil servants, journalists, teachers, interpreters, clerks, and petty entrepreneurs.

Konczacki (1967) estimates that as of 1904, there were a little over 300 such ex-indentured or colonial-born professionals, whose average annual income was around £65, which corresponds to one-fifth of that of the average merchant and five times as much as the average indentured laborer's. Unlike merchants, the colonial-born professionals identified with South Africa as their home. Yet they generally maintained their cultural affinity with the Tamil or other mother language(s), as well as the religious beliefs brought from India, mostly Hinduism but also Islam, Christianity, and other faith traditions. Through Western missionary education, they also attained proficiency in English, and some of them came to adopt Christianity, thus losing their Indian family names. With their growing political awareness and organizational skills, the new elite established their own political associations in Natal, such as the Hindu Young Men's Association (HYMA) in 1905, the Natal Indian Patriotic Union (NIPU) in 1908, and the Colonial Born Indian Association (CBIA) in 1911. Unlike merchant organizations such as the NIC and the Transvaal-based British Indian Association (BIA), both of which exercised decisive influence on satyagraha, these new elite groups lacked a solid financial basis. They also distinguished themselves from the merchant politics, as they actively sought to expand their constituencies among Indian laborers or at least to express sympathies to their grievances. Based on their ex-indentured background, they advocated the repeal of the £3 tax, greater educational opportunities, issuance of trade licenses, and more generally, a removal of structural barriers that kept the ex-indentured from attaining upward social mobility. As will be illustrated later, the new elite's ex-indentured Tamil background played a decisive role in expanding satyagraha's constituency beyond Gujarati Muslim merchants, as well as in mobilizing the long-neglected masses of indentured and ex-indentured laborers. At the same time, however, the distinct aspirations and backgrounds of the new elite and the underclass from which they had emerged remained vulnerable to political manipulation and radicalization, the factor that heightened the merchants' concern when the satyagraha movement successfully attracted mass mobilization toward its end around 1913–14.

The longitudinal process of satyagraha's emergence

Having described the economic, political, and psychological contexts, as well as the profiles of the Indian merchants, indentured laborers, and colonial-born new elite, the analysis will now turn to how satyagraha as a distinct method of conflict work emerged and evolved within the South African Indian community, with emphasis on its longitudinal process. By tracing the movement's major campaign issues, its primary advocates, and the geographic locations of key activities undertaken, the eight-year process, which formally started in September 1906 and came to an end in April 1914, is roughly divided into four stages, as will be described shortly. The issues that surfaced in the form of government policies and Indian grievances reflected protracted conflicts between them, with deep roots in the structural violence of different kinds. In order to understand satyagraha as a method of conflict work, this section will not only summarize the major issues shaping each of the four stages, but also illuminate some of the root conflicts underlying them and the measures adopted by satyagrahis to cope with these conflicts. By following the movement's longitudinal development, one will be able to see how satyagraha as a social and epistemological process had emerged and grown step by step, by way of interacting with – and at times even provoking – Indian–European conflicts manifesting one after another. Parenthetically, it is noted that because the present case study looks at satyagraha as an example of creative conflict work, it will focus selectively on such conflict-related phenomena as are related *directly* to its social and epistemological origin.[34]

The first stage of the campaign started in the Transvaal and lasted for less than a year and a half, from September 1906 to January 1908. What triggered the

Indian protest was the Draft Asiatic Law Amendment Ordinance, which the Indians called the "Black Act," published on August 22, 1906 by the Transvaal government, now under British rule after Boers' defeat in the war. Reflecting the British commitment to assuring an orderly transition of this former Boer republic to Responsible Government soon to be established, the Draft Ordinance aimed to ban future Indian immigration to the Transvaal and request those who currently resided there illegally to leave. To this end, it required all Indians in the Transvaal, men, women, and children over eight years old, to receive a new certificate of registration at the Asiatic Department, an organization created specifically for this purpose. Upon receiving a certificate, every Indian was to bear the legal obligation to carry it all the time and be prepared to present it to officials and policemen at any time on their request. Failure to comply with this law was to subject the defaulters to fines, imprisonment, and even deportation. What infuriated the concerned Indians was not only the strictness with which this measure of racial exclusion was imposed, but also the requirement of ten finger impressions to be obtained from each registrant for an identification purpose (see Figure 4.2 for the application form for registration). The Indian leaders interpreted the requirement of ten fingerprints as an indication of the government's intention to reduce the status of free Indians to that of criminals.[35] For the concerned Indians, this discriminatory requirement posed an unprecedented threat to their honor and self-preservation, and it was considered more urgent than such long-standing issues as the segregation of marketplaces and the restricted issuance of trade licenses.

Attended by some 3,000 Indians, the mass meeting on September 11, 1906 at the Empire Theater in Johannesburg marked the formal beginning of the nonviolent protest movement. The central driving force of this mass mobilization campaign was Gujarati Muslim merchants, particularly the leaders of the Hamidia Islamic Society. The Society was established in July 1906 as a Johannesburg-based Muslim benevolent organization and was comprised of several hundred members at the time of the meeting.[36] The proposal for deliberate, systematic jail-going was presented to the emotionally charged audience by the Society's founder and first president, Haji Ojeer Ally and seconded by Haji Habib, a fellow Gujarati Muslim and chairman of the BIA's Pretoria Branch. Indicating an early sign of broad-based mass mobilization, this merchant-led meeting was attended by Tamil-speaking workers, hawkers, and small traders, many of whom were employees or debtors of the merchants, or otherwise part of their extensive commercial and social networks.[37] A review of the meeting's minutes reveals that a small portion of the meeting time was allocated to a few politically unknown Tamil speakers, whose main task was to convey the contents of prominent merchants' Gujarat and English speeches to Tamils in attendance.[38] Among such Tamils representing the lower-income constituency was Thambi Naidoo, who would become a leading satyagrahi within the next few years and, in 1913, helped to expand the virtually collapsed Gandhian movement to the masses of Tamil-speaking indentured laborers in northern Natal.

[FACE]
APPLICATION MADE FOR REGISTRATION OF AN ASIATIC ADULT

Name in full .... Race ....
Caste or Sect .... Age .... Height ....
Residence .... Occupation ....
Physical description ....
....
....
Place of birth ....
Date of first arrival in the Transvaal ....
Where resident on 31st May, 1902 ....
Father's name .... Mother's name ....
Wife's name .... Residing at ....
Sons and Male Wards under the age of 8 years ....

Name	Age	Residence	Relation to Guardian

Signature of Applicant ....
Signature of person taking application ....
Date .... Office ....

[BACK]
Name ....
Right Hand Impressions

Thumb	Index	Middle	Ring	Little

Left Hand Impressions

Thumb	Index	Middle	Ring	Little

Simultaneous Impressions

Left Hand	The four fingers	Right Hand	The four fingers

Impressions of Adult taken by .... Date ....

Figure 4.2 Application form for registration of an Asiatic adult.

Note
An actual kinesthetic experience of giving ten fingerprints on the designed sections of this form would enable one to vicariously sense the kind of humiliation that might have been felt by the South African Indians, who were required to follow this mandatory procedure. This form also enables one to infer the mindset of the European government officials who designed its layout and most probably even pilot-tested its use by placing their own fingers on it. The form is adapted from Gandhi (1962, vol. 7:501).

Parenthetically, it is worth noting that in this epoch-making meeting, Gandhi's role was supplementary at best to Ally, Habib, and other Gujarati merchants, who presented a series of major resolutions to the audience and received enthusiastic applauses. As a lawyer, lobbyist, social worker, and editor of the *Indian Opinion*, Gandhi had already come to be viewed as a leader in the Indian community, at least to the point of being granted an allotted time for a speech among a dozen other speakers. Yet the minutes of the meeting clearly show that he was not a main drawcard. It is inferred from this and the overall background of the merchant-led mobilization efforts that at the point of satyagraha's advent, Gandhi was still in a transitional process of emerging as a political leader, gradually departing from his initially designated status as a hired representative of elite merchants.

Epistemologically, the public oath-taking was important for satyagraha's emergence because it crystallized the collective process of deliberate, systematic jail-going as a means of nonviolent civil disobedience. Amidst its ritualistic fervor, it conceptualized, articulated, and communicated a collective form of self-sacrifice and suffering unambiguously, despite being unconventional from the standpoint of many Indian participants and certainly that of non-Indians. Beyond its conceptual and epistemological significance, what distinguished this mass pledge of resistance from many similar pledges made in the past by politically active Indians, albeit on smaller scales, was that this time, it was implemented in practice. In terms relevant to the present study, the oath-takers' potential reality gradually unfolded as a new empirical reality.

Under Responsible Government, inaugurated on March 21, 1907 in the Transvaal, the draft anti-Asiatic law was immediately adopted as Act 2 of 1907 as early as March 23. After the government's repeated calls for Asiatic registration, 545 residents out of some 7,000 in total offered to register by the end of November 1907.[39] Yet the majority remained firm not to register. On December 28, 1907, the government started arresting the movement's leaders. By the end of January 1908, some 2,000 were sent to jail as a result of active defiance of Act 2 of 1907 or other related anti-Asiatic laws that the government strictly applied during this period.[40] It was against this background of the Indians' unprecedented collective commitment, which, however, was offset by a number of defaulters and other signs of weaknesses, that a compromise was negotiated and agreed upon in early February 1908 between Smuts, Gandhi, Naidoo, and Leung Quinn, chairman of the Chinese Association, which had earlier joined the Indians to form a united Asiatic front. The compromise brought a truce to the struggle and closed its first stage. The proposed settlement suggested that the Indians secure dignified treatment by registering *voluntarily* to fulfill the government's need for controlling Asiatic immigration, in exchange for a repeal of Act 2 of 1907. In an effort to fulfill this settlement, Indians organized another mass mobilization campaign, this time for community-wide voluntary registration, with the effect that by early May 1908, some 8,000 Indians completed applications for registration.[41]

The second stage of the campaign was built on the first, and it lasted for another year and a half from May 1908 to June 1909 in the Transvaal. On

May 12, 1908, three days after the Indian voluntary registration campaign came to an end, the government announced that Act 2 of 1907 would be retained. The government further required that those entering the Transvaal after May 9 be now obliged to register under Act 2 just as the law had initially stipulated before the compromise. In addition, the subsequent negotiations between Smuts, Gandhi, and other leaders to save the short-lived truce reached a deadlock by late June 1908, with Gandhi declaring a resumption of satyagraha. The renewed campaign added to its platform new objectives, such as the refusal to comply with Smuts' demand to ban the entry of educated Indians, whom he regarded as potential satyagraha leaders, into the Transvaal from Natal or any other state.

One of the salient shifts that took place at an early stage of the second campaign was the decline of merchants' support, which they attributed to the confusion arising from the government's "betrayal" of Gandhi and other committed satyagrahi leaders. Under the influence of increasingly reluctant merchants, small traders forming part of their credit networks also withdrew from the frontline of the struggle. With many prominent merchants leaving, the movement grew increasingly more moralistic and less commercially driven, compared to its initial phase. This shift was symbolically illustrated by the fact that by December 1908, some 2,000 Indians in the Transvaal, out of about 7,000 in total, went to jail. Importantly, most of these jail-goers were hawkers who responded to Gandhi's moral call for self-sacrifice.[42]

Another salient shift in the movement involved the invention of symbolic and evocative actions to expand its constituents and uplift their morale. For example, to seek hawkers' support for defying the trade license requirement, which presupposed registration under Act 2 of 1907 as a prerequisite, committed merchants such as Essop Mia, a senior member of the Hamidia Islamic Society, volunteered to hawk themselves publicly without permits, in an effort to provoke the government to arrest them.[43] Another gesture of symbolic collective action was the burning of permits issued by the government. In a mass meeting on August 18, 1908, attended by some 3,000 Indians and Chinese, about 1,500 registration certificates and 500 trade licenses were burnt in protest, following the repeated public calls to collect those documents, as well as a house-to-house collection tour organized by leading satyagrahis (Swan 1985: 171).

Despite these and other efforts, the movement soon collapsed. By February 1907, 97 percent of Asians in the Transvaal, mostly Indians, had taken out registration certificates in response to the introduction of Act 36 of 1908, which modified but essentially inherited the substance of Act 2 of 1907 (Swan 1985: 174). The crisis of the movement was due in part to the absence of leadership, for leading satyagrahis, including Gandhi, underwent multiple prison terms, particularly between late 1908 and early 1909. The leaderless character of the movement became more salient and decisive at its second stage, when Gandhi and Haji Habib, chairman of the BIA, left for a deputation in London in late June 1909, not to return till the end of that year.

Looking at the first two stages of the satyagraha campaign longitudinally, it is observed that in broad outline, its first stage illustrates *origination*, for the kernel images of self-suffering and nonviolence came to be integrated and articulated as a concrete method of conflict work. The second stage is considered an extension of this *origination* phase for the most part, with emphasis on concrete applications of the principles already declared in the first stage. The second stage, however, also marked an entry into an *evolution* phase, with different issues, aspirations, and constituents joining and leaving, shaping and reshaping the movement through continuous expansion and decline.

In addition, looking at the first two stages from the viewpoint of conflict analysis, the determination of the European policymakers to have the Indians registered in the late 1900s reflected the shared needs of the British and Boers to consolidate their demographic and socio-economic control over the non-white population. Given their overriding needs at that point, the Asiatic Law Amendment Ordinance was part of their preparation for white-only state-making, post-war "conciliation," and unchallenged imperial hegemony in the mineral-rich Transvaal. Solid control over Indians in the Transvaal was imperative, for their continuous influx into the state – which, for Indians having taken refuge in Natal during the war, meant nothing but post-war repatriation – was bound to expand the threatening "Asiatic invasion," as well as more commercial competition with Europeans struggling to recover from the economic devastation. The surge of nationalism among the still-humiliated Afrikaners accelerated not only their tension with the British in the capitalist-dominated mining industry and in the politics of post-war conciliation, but also with the "inferior," un-Christianized race imported into their Calvinist Boer state as an additional disturbance. Satyagrahis' jail-going did not transform these socio-economic, political, and identity crises. Instead it made them even more visible through public protests, media coverage, and parliamentary discussions, to the effect that the Indians, unlike the Colored and native Africans, could nonviolently yet effectively introduce their case on the political platform for sustained national and international attention.

The third stage of the movement featured an extended period of negotiations and diplomacy for nearly four years, from December 1909 to September 1913. The arena of main activities remained the Transvaal, whose central status in South African politics was consolidated through the inauguration of the Union of the four states in 1910. Upon Gandhi's return in December 1909 from a failed mission of protest in London, he barely found 100 active satyagrahis remaining for continuous engagement (Swan 1985: 225). With the decline and split in his merchant constituency, satyagrahis' primary means of protest was political negotiations, particularly between Gandhi and Smuts, whose new official status as Union Minister of the Interior inadvertently elevated his Indian counterpart's to chief representative of the whole Indian community in the Union. Drawing on the second stage of the campaign, the Gandhi–Smuts negotiations focused mainly on Act 36 of 1908 and other regulations restricting Indian immigration.

The single most important event that took place during this politically quiet period for satyagrahis was Gopal Krishna Gokhale's tour around South Africa from October 22 to November 23, 1912. Gokhale was a member of the Viceroy's Council in India, and was by far the highest-ranking Indian dignitary to be received in South Africa at that point. His visit responded to Gandhi's long-standing invitation, and aimed to study South African Indians' grievances, in addition to discussing matters of mutual concern with European leaders and other stakeholders in Indian politics. During his visit, Gokhale organized meetings with indentured laborers and inquired about their work conditions firsthand, thus arousing in their mind a sense of political awareness, on which the final stage of satyagraha would draw to expand its constituency base. Gokhale also negotiated with Smuts and other high-ranking officials in the Union over Indians' grievances on November 14, 1912. The negotiation resulted in what Gokhale considered, and Gandhi unreservedly accepted as, the South African officials' promise to repeal the £3 tax imposed on Indian laborers who had completed their terms of indenture.

A subtle yet important transformation in Gandhi's self-awareness was in the offing during Gokhale's tour. Gandhi's diary on December 1, 1912 notes that as he saw Gokhale off to India at Dar-es-Salaam on the final day of the tour, Gandhi, who had been in Western attire for nearly two decades throughout his life in South Africa, wore an Indian dress for the first time in his adulthood.[44] It is inferred that Gokhale's tour brought Gandhi, as his guide, closer to the laborers, who had been completely left out of satyagraha until then, and sensitized Gandhi's mind to start identifying with the neglected underclasses through Gokhale's mentorship.

Another critical incident during the third stage was Justice Malcolm Searle's judgment on Indian marriage, given in the Cape division of the Supreme Court on March 13, 1913. The judgment stated that the wife of a polygamous marriage was to be prohibited from entering South Africa to join her husband even if she were his only wife to accompany him. Gandhi and other leading satyagrahis interpreted the Searle judgment as an attack on Indian religions, on the ground that the judgment placed Christian monogamous marriage above Hindu and Muslim equivalents, reducing non-Christian Indian wives to concubines and their children to illegitimate minors.[45] Calls for renewing an organized protest to nullify the Searle judgment were made by the whole spectrum of South African Indian leaders throughout April 1913 and beyond.

Gandhi, like Natal and Transvaal merchants, spent the next five months petitioning the Union government to restore the rights of Indian wives. He also sought to repeal the £3 tax, which had remained unheeded by the Union Minister of the Interior despite what the Indians saw as the government's promise to Gokhale. In mid-September 1913, Gandhi formally declared that the negotiations had failed and thus the satyagrahis were now compelled to renew their pledge of resistance, this time with a much broader scope of issues and constituents to be involved.

The fourth and final stage of the campaign thus started. It lasted for seven months, from September 1913 until its conclusion in April 1914, shifting the geographic focus of its activities to Natal, where the long-neglected underclass was mobilized for the first time. The satyagraha pledge communicated to the government and the press included not only the marriage and tax issues, but also such long-standing issues as immigration restriction and trade licenses that concerned merchants and the new elite.[46] Despite the heightened concern on the part of merchants, particularly those of the NIC, they generally remained skeptical about the effectiveness of the satyagraha method, and eventually split into those who preferred to seek conventional, constitutional redress and others who chose to support the Gandhian movement financially, morally, or otherwise.

The campaign commenced on September 15, 1913 with only sixteen committed satyagrahis from the Phoenix Settlement near Durban, twelve men and four women, proceeding on foot to cross the Natal–Transvaal border illegally without permits. These satyagrahis, mostly Gujarati-speaking family members and relatives of Gandhi, were arrested at the border as planned, and they were sentenced to three months' imprisonment with hard labor on September 23, 1913.

While the Phoenix party was mobilized and successfully imprisoned, another party of eleven female volunteers at Tolstoy Farm, six of them carrying babies and one pregnant, joined the movement in response to Gandhi's call for action. Unlike the Phoenix party, most of these women were Natal-born Tamils and spoke the same language as the majority of indentured laborers in Natal coalmines and plantation farms. Although they crossed the Natal–Transvaal border illegally, they failed to be arrested. These women then proceeded as planned to Natal coalmines, joined by Thambi Naidoo, a veteran Tamil community leader and Gandhi's trusted associate, and several other male satyagrahis along the way. In Newcastle, one of the principal urban centers in the Natal coalmine district, the enlarged party of satyagrahis successfully mobilized indentured laborers to suspend work in order to advance the cause of repealing the £3 tax. Describing this mobilization process in response to a press interview that appeared in Johannesburg-based *Rand Daily Mail* on October 22, 1913, Gandhi was quoted as stating, "The presence of these brave women who had never suffered hardship and had never spoken at public meetings acted like electricity, and the men left their work." (Gandhi 1966, vol. 12: 246). As a result of their mobilization effort, these satyagrahis were finally arrested and imprisoned in late October 1913.

As the arrests of women became news and widely communicated by the press, they invited emotional responses from previously indifferent Indians in both South Africa and India.[47] In historical hindsight, one realizes that at this critical juncture of the satyagraha movement, Gandhi's closest personal ties with a few dozen members of the Phoenix Settlement and Tolstoy Farm became a symbolic rallying point for effective mass mobilization. Thus his personal history of householdership and the movement's evolutionary process merged in confluence, reflecting the increasingly personalized nature of Gandhian moral politics characteristic of its final phase.

The labor strike that had started on October 16, 1913 grew exponentially. Within two weeks, 4,000–5,000 indentured laborers stopped working (Swan 1985: 245). As a chief architect of the movement, Gandhi was not prepared for such a rapid expansion of labor stoppage. The unexpected success in constituency expansion generated an urgent need for sustaining such a large number of undisciplined laborers and their impoverished families in good order. Time pressure accelerated the sense of urgency for some form of improvisation to cope with the crisis.

While the Union government bought time to wait for the costly movement's collapse under its own weight, the coalmine owners and other employers of Indian laborers faced an imminent possibility of financial disaster. On October 25, 1913, they gathered to talk with Gandhi at the Durban Chamber of Commerce. In the meeting, Gandhi expressed his willingness to advise the laborers to resume work as soon as the promise made by Smuts and other leaders to Gokhale to repeal the £3 tax could be honored. He also justified the strike's adverse consequences on the European entrepreneurs on the grounds that the white-only government and the European businesses had long prevented Indian laborers from attaining freedom after indenture, and therefore the mine owners had been complicit in the sustenance of the unjustifiable £3 tax (Gandhi 1928: 265–6). Emotional exchanges between Gandhi and the European employers eventually led the latter to present an ultimatum to the Indian strikers, with the intent of coercing them back to work or else depriving them of daily rations.

On October 29, 1913, when the ultimatum was expected to be issued, Gandhi, Thambi Naidoo, and other leading satyagrahis began an organized march with some 4,000 strikers from Newcastle toward the Natal–Transvaal border, in order to seek mass arrests by the government. Smuts waited for a possible collapse of this Great March. But as the "Asiatic invaders" crossed the border and entered the Transvaal, special trains were arranged to transport them back to Natal's coalmines, and the strikers followed this arrangement.

In the meantime, the indentured laborers' strike and the Great March coincided with European proletariats' general strike in January 1914, which demanded the undivided attention of the Union government. The combined effect of these and other uncoordinated events compelled the government to establish a special committee of inquiry into Indians' grievances,[48] in line with the strong public appeal and suggestion made by Indian Viceroy Hardinge. The committee's recommendation incorporated the feedback from unofficial negotiations between Gandhi, Smuts, and a few intermediaries, and culminated in the Indian Relief Bill of April 1914. The Bill, in effect, repealed the £3 tax and legalized the immigration status of Indian wives outside monogamous Christian marriage.

Gandhi left South Africa in July 1914 for the final time. Many Indian merchants became deeply frustrated by Gandhi's compromise with Smuts that became the 1914 settlement, for it left their primary concerns, such as the trade license and bazaar location issues, unresolved. With Gandhi gone and the merchants' disillusionment deepened, satyagraha rapidly lost momentum in South Africa. What remained was a shared memory of communal experience and precedent, which was to be invoked many years later as a symbolic reference point for future popular movements arising in South Africa.

Looking at the third and fourth stages longitudinally, it is observed in broad outline that the third stage illustrates an extension of the *evolution* phase that had already begun in the second stage, for the satyagraha campaign continued to suffer from a lack of merchants' united support, while expanding its scope to include the marriage and £3 tax issues toward its end. This continuous evolutionary process of shaping and reshaping the movement was amplified by its subphase, *acceptance*, illustrated symbolically by Gokhale's visit, which forced the movement's powerful adversaries, including high-ranking Union officials, to accept satyagrahis' grievances as no longer ignorable or marginal. While the fourth and final stage furthered the degree of *acceptance* through such high-profile events as Indian Viceroy Hardinge's intervention in the South African crisis, it also illustrated the inability of the movement to carry on the evolution phase much longer. With Gandhi out of sight and the intra-communal tension among Indians untransformed, the possible transition to a *sustenance* phase remained unfulfilled, at least in the immediate future.

Finally, examining the last two stages of the campaign from the viewpoint of conflict analysis, it is argued that satyagraha addressed two levels of deep-rooted structural problems, however imperfectly. On the first level, it sought to make the inequity of unchallenged patriarchy visible through women's participation on the frontline. Both the Indian and European politics during the period under study were male-dominated. The Searle judgment, with its apparent religious and racial connotations, compelled the male Indian leaders to reclaim their female companions' honor as inseparable from their own. Gandhi's decision to include female satyagrahis in what became a highly visible campaign, particularly in 1913–14, was driven by this. Yet satyagraha, as a method of conflict work and social mobilization readily available by then, provided a symbolic means by which to challenge and de-entrench the male-dominant political discourse that had been prevalent not only among Europeans, but also among Indians themselves.

Another level of deep-rooted problems was socio-economic in nature. Through work stoppage and other selected means, satyagrahis, knowingly or not, exposed the long-undisturbed status quo of capitalist fundamentalism, which had assumed the form of indentured labor in South Africa. Justified by the colonialist ideology of white supremacy and racial discrimination, this system of government–industry relations had kept massive externalities, including human suffering, from surfacing to attain political visibility. The satyagrahis' nonviolent strike in northern Natal and the subsequent Great March fell far short of transforming such a deep-rooted form of structural violence; they even provoked confrontations, particularly with European mine owners, employers, and the South African government. However, satyagrahis succeeded in articulating their unique version of justpeace – the intersection of social justice to correct the past and proactive peace-making to establish a better future – against the background of white proletariats' industrial militancy at its height.

Selected working propositions on creativity and their explanatory potential

Four working propositions on conflict resolution creativity are applied to illustrate satyagraha's emergence. They concern identity transformation, value commitment, paradigm shifts, and analogizing. The proposition on the relationship between creativity and identity transformation is added as a unique contribution of the present case study to creativity research. After discussing the applicability of each proposition, an attempt will be made to illustrate how value commitment and analogizing shaped and reshaped one another in a dialectical relationship, suggesting possible interactions between other enabling factors in more general terms.

Parenthetically, it is noted that these four propositions are illustrative only, in view of the overall objective of this case study to refine and elaborate at least some of the working concepts that have emerged from the preceding comparative analysis of the sixteen cases. However, it is also acknowledged that these four propositions are selected purposefully, for they appear to highlight some of the most indispensable enablers and hallmarks of satyagraha's emergence – without which this unique method of conflict work, it is inferred, would not have come into existence in the first place. For brevity of discussion, the remaining working propositions that this case study fails to incorporate have to be reserved for future inquiry, for the purpose of further theoretical refinement and elaboration.

Identity transformation: from a Western-styled legal representative to an Indian nationalist leader

Analysis of the first satyagraha campaign reveals an additional working proposition, one that has not been explored so far in the comparative study of the sixteen cases. The proposition concerns the role of identity transformation, particularly that of Gandhi in the present context, as a quintessential enabler of creativity and social change. Identity is the self-awareness of who one is in relation to others. It reflects one's experience of belongingness shared by others within the same universe of communal relationships.

In an effort to explore a holistic meaning of identity, Eric Erikson, in his seminal psychoanalysis of Gandhi's inner struggle, defined the term as "a process 'located' in the core of the individual and yet also in the core of his communal culture, a process which establishes, in fact, the identity of those two identities" (Erikson 1969: 22). Erikson's definition echoes the suggested proposition that seeks to capture the unique dynamics of satyagraha's origination. Satyagraha, as a social and epistemological process, emerged and grew in part as a reflection of Gandhi's continuous learning and personal transformation in the ever-changing historical context, which in turn shaped and reshaped his identity. The continuous transformation of his self-awareness generated new ways of problem identification, cultivated untapped capacities to reinterpret existing challenges, invented unexplored approaches to resolution, and brought to his attention the need for building partnerships with potential constituents who had previously been left out. To the extent that the dynamic synchronicity of his identity transformation and its communal context helped to create not only the new mode of conflict work but also the tangible form of dispute settlement in 1914, Gandhi's identity as a leader represented part of the evolving *communal* identities shared by the Indian satyagrahis and other sympathizers, consistent with Erikson's definition.

Gandhi's identity transformation in South Africa was a multifaceted process that manifested on many interrelated levels of his inner being and its outer extension. Five of them deserve mention as they directly influenced the way he led the satyagraha campaign and interacted with it.

1. *Organizational and professional role*: Gandhi started his South African experience in 1893 as an English-speaking legal *representative* whose primary task was to advocate the interests of Indian commercial elites in Natal, taking up similar responsibilities later in the Transvaal. During the campaign of 1906–14 and particularly toward its very end, he had become a moral and political *leader* himself through his community service for all Indians in South Africa, including indentured laborers and women.

2. *Ideology and spirituality*: Gandhi first arrived in South Africa in 1893 as a British liberal imperialist, fresh from his legal training in London from 1888 to 1891. He maintained, or at least acquiesced in, his identity as a British subject until his struggle as a satyagrahi gradually transformed him to become an Indian nationalist, even to the point where by the late 1900s, he claimed the unsurpassed superiority of Indian civilization to Western civilization.[49]

3. *Race*: Throughout this South African experience, Gandhi was not only an imperial segregationist but also a racial purist, distinguishing his Indian "race" from others, especially those of Europeans and native Africans. With the deepening of his moral conviction toward the end of the satyagraha campaign in South Africa, his identity as a more universalistic humanist transcending racial and other divides began to emerge, at least in a nebulous, embryonic form.

4. *Socio-economic class*: Gandhi started his career as an elitist lawyer for the upper to middle classes of Indians and remained essentially elitist in many respects until around 1913, when he first decided to work consciously and systematically for the lowest class, indentured laborers.

5. *Region of origin*: Born and raised in the northwestern coastal region of Kathiawar, Gujarat, Gandhi started his life and career in South Africa with the support of what may be considered a distinctly, if not exclusively, Gujarati-speaking community. As he gradually transcended his identity as a representative of commercial elites through the campaign, he renewed his self-awareness as a pan-Indian nationalist. With the expanded sense of self-consciousness, he strove to serve not only Gujaratis, but all Indians, including Tamils, mostly indentured laborers and their colonial-born descendents in Natal, from the southern province of Madras and its vicinity.

In short, Gandhi's identity transformation in South Africa, reflected in the transformation of his social movement, was a shift in his self-awareness from an interest-based, law-abiding petitioner to a value-based, law-breaking revolutionary, with a consistent commitment to nonviolent means to achieve his ends. Importantly, however, there were kernel elements of his identity that remained unchanged throughout his South African experience. For example, his discriminatory and segregationist stance vis-à-vis native Africans persisted, reflecting racial prejudices shared by many Indian immigrants and their colonial-born descendants at that time. While accepting white supremacy in South Africa, he, together with fellow Indian leaders, insisted that the white-dominated government refrain from treating Indians the same way as native Africans, whom he called "Kaffirs" and "Negroes." On the contrary, his openness to different religious traditions had stayed consistent throughout his South African experience, and later in India as well. Inheriting his mother's religious practice from her small Vaishnava community that aspired to unify Hindu scriptures with the Koran, Gandhi worked closely with both Hindus and Muslims.[50] His closest co-workers and advocates for the satyagraha movement also included committed Christians of both European and Indian origin.

These hallmarks of his personal identity, some fluid and others stable, helped to shape the unique attributes of the satyagraha movement as a social and epistemological process, which in turn reshaped the context of his identity transformation. The dialectical interplay between Gandhi's identity transformation and its dynamic context continuously made and remade the boundaries of the Indian communal consciousness within which certain types of paradigm shifts were envisioned, value commitments pledged, and analogies drawn. When his transformed identity fused into satyagrahis' collective consciousness by the end of the campaign in South Africa, Gandhi as a moral symbol became part and parcel of the Indian communal experience itself – a process that barely started in South Africa but later grew exponentially through his ascendance to mahatmaship in India.

Value commitment: perceiving the intrinsic worth of public work and transcending instrumentalism

Value commitment involves striving toward what *ought to be*, beyond *what is* or *what was* in the reality of conflict at hand. Satyagraha as a conflict-handling mechanism had gradually come into existence through the evolution of Gandhi's *intrinsic* value commitment to community service in general and conflict work in particular, challenging and transcending the pervasive belief in political *instrumentalism*. Instrumentalism presupposes that political means and ends are essentially extrinsic to one another despite their apparent interconnectedness, and that the means to be selected have to be instrumental to achieving the desired ends. The corollary of this position is the widely held belief, explicit or implicit in public discourse, that good ends not only justify necessary means by which to achieve them, but the justifiable ends assume moral priority over the means, including what might be ordinarily considered unjustifiable. In the history of political thought, different versions of instrumentalism were crystallized and popularized by such thinkers as Machiavelli and Bentham in the West and Kautilya in India. In the social and epistemological context of the first satyagraha campaign, political instrumentalism was practiced ubiquitously. For example, it manifested in the form of white supremacy which was deemed instrumental to law and order in South Africa, British imperialism to international stability, colonial exploitation to economic prosperity, and the use of force to peace and justice.

It was against these historical tides that Gandhi's political learning, through trial and error in South Africa, had gradually built up toward his religious conviction in the oneness of means and ends in public and conflict work. In his moral politics, carrying out just means was considered intrinsically valuable because the very act of striving for moral ends in conflict work through just means was, in and of itself, of the highest value, for which one must be willing to pay the ultimate price whenever necessary. As a leader of the movement, Gandhi, particularly since the mid-1900s, had striven to cultivate satyagrahis' intrinsic value commitment to nonviolent means, with varying degrees of success, against the deep culture and structure of political instrumentalism embedded in European-ruled South Africa and elsewhere.

The precursors of Gandhi's intrinsic value commitment were distinctly religious and cultural in a manner unfamiliar to Europeans and other stakeholders involved. A review of Gandhi's writings, supplemented by general insights into religious beliefs from which he learned, enables one to infer that by the end of the satyagraha campaign in South Africa, he, already in his mid-forties, had crystallized many of his moral principles derived from Hinduism, Buddhism, Jainism, and other traditions.[51] However, Gandhi, not being a theoretician but a practitioner, had not left a well-integrated, schematic account of his growing inner realization while he was in South Africa.[52] Therefore, what follows is an attempt to reconstruct it as coherently and succinctly as possible, supplemented by informed inferences about how Gandhi's learning in South Africa helped to shape the satyagraha movement in India.

Deeply anchored in Gandhi's religiosity were two intertwined strands of the connection between means and ends, rooted in his interpretation of Hinduism. They are tapas (purification) and moksha (self-realization) on one level and ahimsa (non-killing) and satya (truth) on the other. Although these two strands of spiritual orientations are derived from the shared heritage of Oriental religiosity and in no way separable from one another, it is observed that in Gandhi's and committed satyagrahis' worldview, the tapas–moksha connection tended to claim attention in their individual, spiritual life, and the ahimsa–satya link helped to shape their public, political life. Table 4.1 summarizes the relationship between these concepts succinctly.

Table 4.1 Means and ends in Gandhian religiosity

Means	*Ends*
Tapas (purification, self-suffering)	*Moksha* (spiritual freedom, enlightenment)
Ahimsa (nonviolence, love of all beings)	*Satya* (truth)

Tapas refers to moral fervor, that which burns up impurities. The word literally means warmth or heat. Applied to the quest of self-actualization, it signifies self-suffering through purificatory action, austerities, and penance as a path to strive for the ideal. In his memoir *Satyagraha in South Africa*, Gandhi (1928: 16) describes his image of tapas metaphorically: "Real suffering bravely borne melts even a heart of stone. Such is the potency of suffering or *tapas*. And there lies the key to Satyagraha." The ultimate aim of tapas, and that of private and public life as a whole, is to attain moksha, translated variously into such terms as self-realization, enlightenment, salvation, and freedom from life and death. Muc, the root of the word moksha, denotes releasing and setting free. Linking the twin concept of tapas and moksha may evoke in one's mind the image of water, the substance that evaporates and fuses into air when sufficiently heated, illustrative of life's transience as well as continuity beyond the inevitable end of one's lifetime.

In 1925, eleven years after he had left South Africa, Gandhi, having established his mahatmaship firmly in India by then, introduced his autobiography to its readers as follows:

> What I want to achieve, – what I have been striving and pining to achieve these thirty years, – is self-realization, to see God face to face, to attain *Moksha*. I live and move and have my being in pursuit of this goal. All that I do by way of speaking and writing, and all my ventures in the political field, are directed to the same end.
>
> (Gandhi 1993: xxvi)

The clarity of the religious conviction declared by the fifty-six-year-old mahatma was still in the making in South Africa. But his intensive learning process, including his immersion in religious literature during his multiple prison terms and his moral and political writings such as *Hind Swaraj* in 1909, demonstrates the path of his religious pilgrimage, set out irreversibly toward a spiritual evolution of mahatmaship.[53]

In theory, tapas is a means toward the ultimate end of life, moksha. But in reality, moksha is an ideal goal-state for which one must continuously strive throughout one's lifetime, by way of practicing tapas each moment. Therefore, tapas and moksha are inseparably fused into the cultural and psychological actuality of the dedicated Hindu community servant; for him, each act of self-suffering and purification for moral causes is an immediate, tangible assurance of spiritual freedom attainable within one's lifetime, with karmic implications for the afterlife. In short, moksha is attainable only partially and experientially at each moment of striving through tapas.

The relationship between tapas and moksha is mirrored in the parallel interconnectedness between ahimsa and satya. Ahimsa, which literally means non-injury, non-killing, and nonviolence, encompasses a wide variety of locally adopted religious practices and concepts that involve renunciation of any thought, word, and action intended to harm living beings. Ahimsa permeates

Indian religiosity broadly and deeply, with both shared and unique applications practiced in Hinduism, Buddhism, and Jainism (Iyer 1973). The Jain tradition of ahimsa, which pervaded the local culture of Kathiawar in which Gandhi was born and raised, sets particularly strict requirements in life, maintaining that non-killing is an absolute duty for Jain devotees in their effort to relieve their lives from inevitable cycles of birth and rebirth[54] (Dundas 2005).

Building on his childhood and adolescence immersed in the local Jain tradition and other spiritual influences, Gandhi developed his own praxis of ahimsa step by step throughout his adulthood. In the course of his religious pilgrimage that became particularly conspicuous during his legal studies in London and intensified further in South Africa during satyagraha's formative years, Gandhi gradually crystallized his faith in the absolute sanctity and interconnectedness of all lives. His faith in ahimsa reflected his worldview that all lives were created according to rta, or the all-encompassing, eternal, and infallible cosmic law upholding the moral equilibrium and coherence in human life as well as the whole universe. For Gandhi, therefore, unconditional respect for all living beings – even including adversaries inflicting violence (himsa) on him and fellow satyagrahis – was both an inviolable principle and a sacred duty to be fulfilled in the spirit of devotional self-suffering, tapas.

The ultimate end of life dedicated to ahimsa is satya, or truth. It also denotes being real, existent, valid, sincere, pure, and effectual. The word satya is derived from the word sat, which literally means being. Philosophically sat refers to the ontological reality of phenomena independent of epistemological attempts to interpret it. The most divine manifestation of sat is described as Sat, the Absolute Truth, which reflects the universal, eternal cosmic law, rta. Gandhi believed that satya, validated and sustained by Sat at its existential roots, was an ideal end-state, unreachable and unattainable in an ultimate sense. Yet he maintained that satya was a moral end for which one must strive continuously, for he believed that one would be able to gain at least a glimpse of satya experientially in every earnest action to pursue it. In his worldview, the immediate and ultimate test of one's commitment to satya was one's ability and willingness to practice ahimsa through self-suffering, with unconditional trust in the cosmic and moral order, in which every living being, a friend or foe, played an indispensable part.

Just as tapas is a means to strive for moksha, ahimsa is a means to seek satya. However, because of the very nature of satya as an ultimately unreachable end, satya in practice is one and the same as ahimsa, the means through which one can realize part of satya at least from one's subjective, experiential perspective; in other words, realization of satya is revealed as authentic only in relation to one's subjective sense of truthfulness – which falls far short of the more holistic, divine, and absolute Truth that lies far beyond human comprehension. For this reason, Gandhi's faith in the oneness of means and ends, tapas and moksha, ahimsa and satya presupposed respect for multiple relative truths perceived by different actors, in accord with the "Many-pointed Doctrine" in Jainism and analogous, at least impressionistically, to the Western epistemological tradition of relativism.[55] Paradoxically, his respect for many-ness was anchored in the deep awareness of Sat, the absolute ontological existence, around which relative truth claims converge and diverge. In Gandhi's mind, the devotion to many-ness called for humility when sharing a perceived truth with others, for his claim of truth might be just as partial and fallible as others'.

In Gandhi's worldview, the infallibility of the means–ends connection was reinforced by his faith in karma, the ethical law of cause and effect inherent in life and the cosmos. In *Hind Swaraj* written in 1909, he illustrated his understanding of karmic causality metaphorically:

> [Dismissing the connection between the means and the end] is the same as saying that we can get a rose through planting a noxious weed. If I want to cross the ocean, I can do so only by means of a vessel; if I were to use a cart for that purpose, both the cart and I would soon find the bottom. "As is the God, so is the votary" is a maxim worth considering. Its meaning has been distorted, and men have gone astray. The means may be likened to a seed, the end to a tree; and there is just the same inviolable connection between the means and the end as there is between the seed and the tree. I am likely to obtain the result flowing from the worship of God by laying myself prostrate before Satan. If, therefore, anyone were to say: 'I want to worship God, it doest not matter that I do so by means of Satan' it would be set down as ignorant folly. We reap exactly as we sow.
>
> (Gandhi 1997: 81)

Gandhi's faith in infallible ethical causality enabled him to dedicate his life to adopting moral means, with or without assurances of achieving desired ends. It was an ultimate value commitment to the law of karma, which he believed would bring about just ends, either within his lifetime or thereafter, so long as he remained truthful to the just means that he could opt to take. In his worldview, whether a cause-and-effect relationship between his action and desired results could be fulfilled was a matter to be decided by God, which he equated with Truth presiding over karmic retribution. His faith in just means remained consistent throughout his life in South Africa and beyond, illustrated by his reflections on the Great March of 1913, written in the mid-1920s:

> We are merely the instruments of the Almighty Will and are therefore often ignorant of what helps us forward and what acts as an impediment. We must thus rest satisfied with a knowledge only of the means, and if these are pure, we can fearlessly leave the end to take care of itself.
>
> (Gandhi 1928: 289)

Furthermore, the same principle of karma led him to believe that attempts to pursue asatya, or untruth, would always fail in the long run no matter how irreversible they might appear in the short run. Therefore, what he should care about as a votary of God and an imperfect human being was whether he was striving unflinchingly for tapas and ahimsa as a pathway to moksha and satya.

Having outlined the intrinsic nature of Gandhi's personal commitment to nonviolent leadership, one may now explore how it shaped, or at least interacted with, the social and epistemological process of satyagraha's creation. In relation to the European ruling elite and its constituencies, the satyagraha campaign, converging and diverging around Gandhi's value commitment, defied their law-and-order mentality instrumental to white supremacy and stability in South Africa. What had conventionally upheld this mentality was the deeply entrenched, and thus virtually unquestionable, perspective shared by both the ruling elite and the ruled that *self-preservation* was an irreducible need of everybody. Satyagraha broke this political axiom by appeal to an elevated sense of religious consciousness, in varying degrees of success from stage to stage, from campaign to campaign.

Writing on Indians' unfulfilled potential for nonviolent action in *Hind Swaraj*, Gandhi (1997: 94–5) remarked, "That nation is great which rests its head upon death as its pillow. Those who defy death are free from all fear." In the same chapter of this 1909 booklet, Gandhi stated even more provocatively:

> But a passive resister[56] will say he will not obey a law that is against his conscience, even though he may be blown to pieces at the mouth of a cannon. What do you think? Wherein is courage required – in blowing others to pieces from behind a cannon or with a smiling face to approach a cannon and to be blown to pieces? Who is the true warrior – he who keeps death always as a bosom-friend or he who controls the death of others? Believe me that a man devoid of courage and manhood can never be a passive resister.
>
> (Gandhi 1997: 93)

Consistent with these remarks, Gandhi and committed fellow satyagrahis repeatedly subjected themselves to imprisonment, hard labor, and other forms of punishment sanctioned by the South African government. Underlying their value commitment was their willingness to accept self-suffering, and even possible death, as their religious duty to practice tapas. This heightened consciousness of death as part of life's eternity was derived from their aspiration to cultivate fearlessness, with faith in inviolable karmic pathways to satya and moksha. Imprisonment deprived them of freedom in social life, but it gave them spiritual freedom attainable only through purificatory acts of self-suffering. From the dedicated satyagrahis' point of view, the European rulers' political rationalism derived from their self-preservation instinct was only a relative truth and as such, it was far from absolute in light of the satyagrahis' religious commitment to Sat, the Truth. In this sense, satyagraha emerged as a social and epistemological process through which the Indians' intrinsic value commitment to restoring the ancient cosmic law and order sought to redefine the seemingly absolute status of the contemporary secular law and order, which had been instrumental to Western-dominated colonialism and imperialism.

Finally, the effect of Gandhi's intrinsic value commitment on the Indian constituents, some supportive and others adversarial, needs to be examined.

Although the method of satyagraha in general and the means–ends connection in particular had evolved into a coherent whole within Gandhi's worldview by the time he wrote *Hind Swaraj* in 1909,[57] his approach to moral politics, let alone his religious faith in self-suffering, had hardly gained full support from other Indians in South Africa during the period of the satyagraha movement. Contrary to the image of the mahatma with which he would later come to be associated in India, Gandhi's status as a relatively young leader within the Indian community in South Africa was far from unchallenged and unparalleled, even until the very end of the movement in 1914. His identity transformation from commercial elites' legal representative to a more inclusive, independent leader, through the mass nonviolence pledge of September 1906 and the subsequent epoch-making events, shaped, and was in turn shaped by, the rises and falls of both secular and religious groups, reflective of dynamic leader–follower relationships evolving among South African Indians.[58] In order to contextualize Gandhi's intrinsic value commitment within the social and epistemological process of satyagraha's origination, one may briefly illustrate how his emerging leadership interacted with two of the most salient rallying points for Indians' communal relations, *class* and *religion*.

With the deepening of class consciousness in South African society accelerated in part by emerging labor movements, the socio-economic strata continued to divide Indians in the 1900s and 1910s. Among the three socio-economic groups with overlapping communal identities – the merchants, the indentured underclass, and the ex-indentured and their colonial-born descendants – the merchants remained decisively influential in shaping the satyagraha movement because of their financial and organizational capacity. During the campaign period, the merchant class in Natal demanded that the government liberalize the policy on trade licenses, while the Transvaal-based merchants protested against the proposed policy that would virtually confine them into segregated locations unsuited for competitive commercial activities. The repeated failures of both satyagraha and conventional petitioning to satisfy their commercial interests frustrated them and eventually led them to rebuke Gandhi's leadership openly.

Their frustrations and controversies surrounding Gandhi's commitment to satyagraha became particularly salient throughout the tumultuous year of 1913, when Gandhi actively sought to expand his constituency base in Natal beyond the merchant elite. His efforts to expand the constituency were intended to revive the then inactive satyagraha movement in order to repeal the Supreme Court decision of March 14, 1913 that rendered illegitimate the immigration status of Indian wives married according to Indian polygamous arrangements.[59] Another emerging focus of contention that occupied Gandhi's attention during this period concerned the urgent need to deal, as a matter of the Indian nation's honor,[60] with what he saw as the Union government's failure to repeal the £3 tax imposed on indentured laborers, despite the consent which Gokhale was thought to have obtained from Smuts and other high-ranking officials in November 1912. These were highly moral subjects, reflective of the deepening intrinsic commitment and identity transformation that Gandhi had come to realize by then. The ethical implications of these issues per se, however, fell short of arousing and uniting merchant elites, whose overriding priority was to attain commercial success on the British colonial frontier. On April 26, 1913, for example, the NIC met to discuss the organization's position vis-à-vis Gandhi's campaign, with some 500 people attending, including both veteran merchants and emerging colonial-born traders. In this meeting, they voted overwhelmingly to repudiate Gandhi's approach.[61] By the time Gandhi started organizing the massive labor strike by way of mobilizing thousands of indentured laborers in Natal, merchants' resentment against Gandhi's leadership peaked.[62] Consequently, Gandhi had to virtually abandon his former elite constituency base and hurriedly created a new merchant organization, the Natal Indian Association (NIA), comprised of emerging ex-indentured traders and other sympathizers, some fifty of them in total, willing to support the costly labor strike (Swan 1985: 250–1).

In addition to socio-economic interests and class consciousness, religious affiliations became yet another rallying point around which Indians' support for Gandhi's intrinsic value commitment grew and declined. Reflecting on the relationships during the campaign between Hindus and Muslims, two of the most populous Indian religious groups in South Africa as in India, Gandhi noted:

> There was for all practical purposes no Hindu–Muslim problem in South Africa. But it would not be claimed that there were no difficulties between the two sections and if these differences never assumed an acute form, that may have been to some extent due to the peculiar conditions in South Africa, but was largely and definitely due to the leaders having worked with devotion and frankness.
>
> (Gandhi 1928: 109)

His evaluation of Hindu–Muslim relations in South Africa appears consistent, at least in general terms,[63] with empirical evidence available, including the fact that many public meetings which attracted participants from diverse religious backgrounds were held almost interchangeably at venues of their regular faith-related activities.[64] Even more significantly, no evidence has been found, at least to this author's knowledge, that suggests that whatever differences made explicit between Hindus and Muslims during the satyagraha movement were attributed directly to the apparent differences between their scriptural messages per se. This is an important observation to make, for Gandhi's core values, formed primarily under the Hindu, Jain, and Buddhist traditions that presupposed karmic continuity of life and death, were clearly distinguishable from Muslims' commitment to the finality of life bounded by Allah's divine will. Despite the apparent theological differences, however, Gandhi's value commitment as a political discourse still offered viable common ground for Hindu–Muslim cooperation in South Africa.[65]

Although significant potential existed for inter-faith cooperation in the 1900s and 1910s, there were occasions where community leaders politicized their constituents' religious identities and mobilized them under polarizing slogans. Some of these polarizing activities went as far as rebuking the Gandhian value commitment altogether and threatening to divide the Indian community in general and the satyagraha movement in particular. One of the symbolic incidents that illustrate the divisive trends was the arrival of Swami Shankeranand, a highly revered Hindu missionary and brahmin from Punjab, at Durban in early October 1908.[66] Soon after his arrival, Shankeranand started a two-month tour around the Natal coastal districts, vigorously propagated Hindu revivalism, and strove to apply his religious principles to organize political activities in South Africa. By early 1909, Hindu political groups sprang up under his influence in Durban, Pietermaritzburg, and several other localities of Natal, attracting ex-indentured and colonial-born Indians, including the emerging elite class. The organizational slogan of Shankeranand and his committed followers was clearly divisive: anti-Muslim, anti-Congress, and anti-Gandhi. Their divisive approach not only challenged the Muslim merchants, but also split the new elite, including the Natal Indian Patriotic Union (NIPU), an organization established in March 1908 in Durban to address the needs of the colonial-born. Those who left the NIPU to follow Shankeranand organized a united front, declared that they alone could represent South African Indians, and denounced the NIPU and the NIC as illegitimate representatives.

It was against this background of Hindu–Muslim tension that a quarrel broke out between Shankeranand's Hindu followers and several prominent Muslims of the Congress in the Durban Mosque Market in late May 1909. Dissatisfied vegetable hawkers, petty cultivators, white-collar workers, and other Hindu sympathizers of the ex-indentured background rallied around Shankeranand in response. They organized a boycott of the Durban Mosque Market to carry out a "religious crusade" against the Muslims. On a more pragmatic level, they demanded a fair share of control over profits, only to be rejected by the Mosque trustees, who argued that their religion disallowed them to divert the Mosque's funds for the objective asserted by Shankeranand's group. Despite the joint arbitration efforts made by Christians, Muslims, and Hindus, the dispute escalated further, eventually to the extent that disgruntled Muslim traders and other concerned stakeholders opened an alternative market in August 1910 to continue business activities on their own. With the apparent failure of the boycott, Shankeranand's political influence declined rapidly and many of his supporters left the short-lived semi-religious movement in 1910 and thereafter.

Shankeranand's Hindu revival movement and the resulting tension between the colonial-born Hindu elite and the Muslim Congress members in Natal coincided with the period in which Gandhi's satyagraha campaign in the Transvaal reached the highest intensity, particularly toward the end of 1908, desperately trying to build undisturbed inter-faith unity. The incident symbolically illustrates that Gandhi's value commitment to satyagraha was far from unchallenged and unparalleled; he had to literally *earn* the political relevance of his religious commitment amidst intense rivalry, in order to prove his unconventional movement viable.

Having explored the socio-economic and religious contexts of Gandhi's leadership, one may come to argue that his value commitment, once translated into public action, became an ideal means and end for unconventional social change at best and a source of sustained communal tension at worst. Although the political viability of Gandhi's personal commitment was evaluated differently according to the stakeholders' socio-economic, religious, and other viewpoints, its function remained unchanged, at least in one respect throughout the satyagraha campaign: it never ceased to be a *rallying point* around which Indians' hope and despair, moral conscience and pragmatic interests converged and diverged continuously and dynamically. In Gandhi's own reflections during the 1908 struggle in the Transvaal:

> We consider this [significant achievement of mobilization and self-suffering] a victory of truth. We do not claim that every Indian adhered to truth in the course of the struggle. Nor do we claim that no one thought of his own interests during the campaign. We do, however, assert that this was a fight on behalf of truth, and that most of the leaders fought with scrupulous regard for truth.[67]

This social and epistemological function of Gandhi's intrinsic value commitment invites further inquiry into how conflict workers' own religiosity, or their consciousness of death (Erikson 1969), shapes the nature of creativity intended to transform structural violence, a subject to be explored in the discussion to follow.

A paradigm shift: transcending violent means to transform structural violence

Satyagraha illustrates process creativity, with implications for conflict resolution outcomes as well. Although the working thesis on conflict paradigms, developed earlier to generate outcome creativity, is not directly applicable to this case study of process creativity, the Kuhnian notion of paradigm shifts is still suggestive as a heuristic tool to illuminate the distinct nature of satyagraha's origination. For the present illustrative purpose, the meaning of a paradigm is not confined to an organization of community practices of the kind which Kuhn described in scientific terms. Instead, what one ought to bring to the foreground of attention is a paradigm's function as a prevailing *discourse* of social relations, that is, a social structure of meaning-making patterns within which actors' expectations converge and diverge, knowingly or unknowingly, with varying degrees of commitment to its perceived center of gravity. Systemic entrenchment of actors' perceptions and interactive patterns remains a common denominator among the Kuhnian theory, the conflict paradigm thesis, and the kind of discursive structure under consideration. On the other hand, what distinguishes between the suggested heuristic concept and a conflict paradigm, though both are inspired by the same Kuhnian theory, is that the conflict paradigm thesis is devised for the specific purpose of generating outcome creativity, whereas the suggested heuristic concept attempts to illustrate a broader scope of discursive patterns that contextualize conflict work in more general terms. Within this revised, yet still essentially Kuhnian, framework of exploration, paradigm shifts correspond to discursive shifts, where qualitatively different questions emerge and allow for qualitatively different answers to become relevant, instead of being discarded as irrelevant offhand. In the first satyagraha campaign, Gandhi's identity transformation shaped, and was shaped by, paradigm shifts, affecting religious and political discourses that had long remained unquestioned or otherwise unquestionable in the European–Indian relations in South Africa. The most fundamental among those shifts was the creation of proactive, practical, and nonviolent means to transform, or at least effectively protest, structural violence without resorting to the more conventional means of armed struggle.

As discussed earlier, structural violence is indirect violence generated by social repression and exploitation, where the dichotomy between victims and victimizers is hardly definable or meaningful. Structural violence tends to be accentuated and perpetuated by involuntary membership of marginalized identity groups into which one is born. The structural violence inflicted on the Indians in South Africa took the form of exclusive white supremacy and economic exploitation, which stood in the way of the Indians' attempt to fulfill such irreducible needs as security for legitimate existence, freedom of movement, respect for spiritual identity, and economic welfare. Historically, satyagraha had emerged from the social and epistemological context of structural violence, and it was devised as a nonviolent response to transform it. In 1909, Gandhi's conviction in satyagraha's capacity to transform structural violence, particularly its manifestations institutionalized in South Africa's law and order, was communicated clearly through his *Hind Swaraj*:

> A man who has realized his manhood, who fears only God, will fear no one else. Man-made laws are not necessarily binding on him. Even the government do not expect any such thing from us. They do not say: "You must do such and such a thing" but they say: "If you do not do it, we will punish you." We are sunk so low, that we fancy that it is our duty and our religion to do what the law lays down. If man will only realise that it is unmanly to obey laws that are unjust, no man's tyranny will enslave him. This is the key to self-rule or home rule.
>
> (Gandhi 1997: 92)

For Gandhi and his devoted supporters, satyagraha was a direct application of their intrinsic value commitment to large-scale conflict work and intended to transform structural violence, first in their inner spiritual realm, then in the secular, political struggle for social change.

A closer examination of satyagraha's unique historical context illuminates the nature of the paradigm being challenged. It also helps to explore how the satyagrahis worked to transform the paradigm, knowingly or unknowingly. During the 1900s and 1910s, a range of marginalized communities challenged the South African government in a protest against structural violence, economic, political, or otherwise. These communities included white syndicalists, native Africans, the Colored, and Indians. They all shared the perception that they were politically repressed, economically exploited, or at least marginalized in society. However, their responses to the problem varied according to their beliefs and the political opportunities open to them. For example, the Native Africans and white syndicalists, for different reasons, either chose violent means for redress outside constitutional politics or were inadvertently embroiled in state-sponsored violence. Put more empathetically, from their perspectives they were driven to use force as the last resort and the only available means by which to cope with the state-sponsored structural violence.

Industrial militancy was growing in scope and intensity while the Indian struggle was in full swing. As proletariat revolutionaries rapidly consolidated leadership among European migrant workers dissatisfied with their economic and sanitary conditions in urban and mining districts, they demanded the reluctant Union government to permit the laborers' right to form trade unions more freely. Violent confrontations between radicalized European workers and the government, the latter being supported by mine owners, spread throughout the Transvaal Rand in July 1913. The unresolved conflicts resurfaced in January 1914, culminating in an unprecedented general strike in the mines, railways, and other industrial lifelines throughout the Union. The imperial troops intervened to control violent mobs, while the indentured Indians' nonviolent strikes, which had lasted from October to December 1913, presented a sharp contrast to widespread industrial violence. To help the government and the public restore order, Gandhi deliberately suspended the satyagraha struggle in January 1914. The Indians' decision to aid their adversaries in the midst of the latter's hardship not only invited a mixture of curiosity and awe from the Europeans in crisis, but also demonstrated to them the unfamiliar principle of active nonviolence enacted against the backdrop of white workers' industrial violence.

Another scene of mass violence unfolded between the Europeans and the native Africans during the Indian struggles, as a continuation of centuries-old colonial repression. The Zulu "rebellion" of 1906 in Natal, which Gandhi as an eyewitness characterized as nothing but a British man-hunt of defenseless natives,[68] exemplified the brutality of the white supremacist policy. To the extent that the "rebellion," which had erupted in April of that year, was a response, at least in part, to the newly imposed poll tax on native Africans, the violent method of their resistance, let alone the violent measure of repression adopted by the British, presented an evocative contrast to the nonviolent method that the Indians were about to adopt in September of the same year. From a historical perspective, the "rebellion" also symbolized an end, at least for the time being, to the unending cycles of violence and counter-violence that the European rulers desperately strove to settle permanently, in order to direct undivided attention to the urgent task of Anglo-Boer reconciliation and Union-building.

Both the European workers and indigenous Africans underwent what they perceived as capitalist exploitation and state repression. They were both involved in mass violence, provoked or unprovoked, willingly or unwillingly, during the historical period in which satyagraha came into existence. Contrary to these two groups that became either victims or victimizers in the violent incidents, there were two other communities, the Colored and Indians, that underwent marginalization and exploitation but responded differently. These two communities generally used nonviolent constitutional means to address their grievances. However, the Indian satyagrahis, particularly after late 1906, came to place less importance on constitutional means, while the Colored stayed within constitutional politics.

Unlike the first-generation Indian migrants, the Colored held a distinct South African identity, for nearly 90 percent of them were born and raised in the Cape Colony during the historical period under study.[69] Because of their status as "mixed blood," succeeding European, Malay, Indian, and native African heritages, the Colored, like Indians, were classified by Europeans as neither completely white nor black. In the liberalist tradition of interracial power-sharing in the Cape, some 4 percent of the Colored residents enjoyed the franchise, which was still too restrictive for the "less civilized" Coloreds who failed to meet literacy and property qualifications. In 1902, the Colored succeeded for the first time in sending their elected representative, Abdullah Abdurrahman, a British-educated medical doctor, to a city council, and shortly thereafter to the Cape Provincial Council. Under the leadership of Abdurrahman and others, the Colored established the African Political Organization (APO) in late 1902, in order to achieve their long unfulfilled needs such as better access to quality education and expansion of the franchise in the Cape, with the view toward setting precedent to what they hoped to achieve in the Transvaal as well.

Although both the Colored and Indians were condemned to second-class status and they were both virtually left out of the white supremacist project of state-making after the Anglo-Boer War, the Colored, unlike voteless Indians, stayed within constitutional politics by retaining their franchise. The contrast between the two communities became particularly salient in 1909, when representatives of different racial communities, including Abdurrahman and Gandhi in close communication, were invited to London to discuss the South African Union Bill. Despite Abdurrahman's objection, the Bill became a law, to the effect that the newly established Union government was to be comprised of European representatives only. Seizing this critical moment, Gandhi successfully persuaded Abdurrahman to form a united Indian–Colored front for satyagraha. It turned out, however, that Abdurrahman's constituents, including teachers and businessmen, later prevented the two leaders' vision from being carried out. While the Colored constituents in the Cape adhered to the apparently ineffective but safer means of constitutional politics so as to challenge the exclusive state-making, the Indians' movement for nonviolent law-breaking in Natal and the Transvaal reached its climax, most symbolically through the Great March of late 1913, against the backdrop of widespread industrial violence.

Theoretically, the dilemma facing the four communities – the above three and the Indians – concerns what political *means* to adopt for redress. But the issue is also substantive and deeply existential in nature. This dilemma is formulated as a question: How should a marginalized community cope with the contradiction between the perceived *effectiveness* of its action and the *ethicality* thereof? The question resonates with the larger theme of enduring importance: How can one realize both peace and justice when they are presented as contradictory in a given context of structural violence?[70] In the eyes of the leaders of marginalized groups, well-organized violent means appear to be an effective way of realizing justice beyond the perpetual structural violence inflicted on them. On the other hand, nonviolent law-abiding means, however well organized and ethically appealing, appear ineffective as a method of attaining immediate results, in their fight against the deeply entrenched structural violence. This effectiveness–ethicality connection, parallel to the peace–justice link, remains evocative today, as it was in the historical context of satyagraha's origination.

Given this social and epistemological background, it is suggested that the creation of satyagraha marked a paradigm shift, for it demonstrated a concrete way of transcending this dilemma, which had been entrenched in the political axiom of dichotomous thinking, pervasive in the West as well as in the East. The structural violence facing European workers and native Africans was dealt with by massive direct violence, which in the eyes of the wielders of force, was necessary for effective redress regardless of its ethicality. The structural violence affecting the Colored, albeit in a more moderate form, was addressed by nonviolent – and thus perhaps ethical – means, whose effectiveness, however, was severely compromised because of their acquiescence in the racist political structure. Epistemologically, satyagraha emerged as a struggle to break this dilemma between effectiveness and ethicality, and by implication, peace and justice. It strove for *both*, by accepting self-suffering, even up to death, as a means to transform structural violence. As a political procedure, it advocated breaking laws embodying structural violence, by way of organizing proactive nonviolent means, while rejecting seemingly effective violent alternatives. In short, the creativity of satyagraha lies in the discovery of a concrete method to practice justpeace.

A systematic attempt to explore why and how this dilemma was transcended socially and epistemologically exceeds the scope of this case study, whose main purpose is to illustrate working propositions on conflict resolution creativity. Yet the preceding discussion on Gandhi's intrinsic value commitment leads to the inference that the moral conviction in the oneness of means and ends played an essential role in creating satyagraha as a method of justpeace. For political instrumentalism not only distinguishes between effectiveness and ethicality, but it even justifies suspending ethicality for the immediate purpose of securing prima facie effectiveness to attain perceived higher ends. However, this pathway to social change was closed to the devotee of Oriental faith, whose end in life was to follow the narrow path of tapas and ahimsa single-mindedly toward moksha and satya. In this unique philosophical and spiritual sense, satyagraha was not a product of creation – at least not in terms familiar to contemporary creativity researchers. Instead, satyagraha was a secular manifestation of an essentially religious pursuit, which its practitioners strove to apply strictly and systematically to the most unlikely context of political instrumentalism, thus generating an epistemological gap between themselves and their opponents. By appeal to Kuhnian heuristics, therefore, one may argue that the overcoming of this perceived inter-communal gap between the satyagrahis' intrinsic value commitment, on the one hand, and their adversaries' political instrumentalism, on the other, marked a paradigm shift in the offing.

Analogizing: learning across contexts for discovery and persuasion

Analogizing entails discovering and transferring relevant insights, consciously or subconsciously, across what the learner views as comparable contexts, be they temporal (historical), spatial (geographic), relational (isomorphic), or otherwise. As in the preceding discussion on value commitment, the analysis of this agency-led social process requires understanding Gandhi's personal learning in the foreground, for satyagraha emerged and evolved in a manner inseparable from his identity shift from a merchant representative to a moral, political leader, particularly after the mass pledge of nonviolent civil resistance declared by some 3,000 Indians in Johannesburg on September 11, 1906. In view of this historical context, the present analysis will first explore how Gandhi built analogies for his moral and political leadership during the few eventful years leading up to the pledge of September 1906. It will then briefly discuss how his cross-contextual learning contributed to, and interacted with, the emergence of satyagraha as a social and epistemological process.

A review of Gandhi's writings on the eve of satyagraha's advent suggests two prototypes of analogizing characteristic of his meaning-making patterns at that time. One was *analogizing for origination*, guiding his mind toward discovery-oriented learning that eventually led to the articulation of satyagraha. Discussion on analogizing in this study has so far focused on this first type. The other was *analogizing for acceptance*. Acceptance for conflict resolution creativity, as discussed earlier, is a distinct subtype and milestone of an evolution phase. Attaining acceptance involves developing a new rallying point of public attention around which stakeholders' interests, expectations, and moral values converge and diverge. In the context of satyagraha's development, Gandhi's analogy-building for acceptance was reflected in his repeated attempts to communicate his emerging value commitment widely and to persuade fellow Indians and attentive others to act on it. The weekly *Indian Opinion*, read by up to 3,500 subscribers,[71] became an essential vehicle for this purpose.

Having distinguished between the two conceptual types, however, it is emphasized that they were closely interconnected in a given practical context of Gandhi's analogy-building, as will be demonstrated shortly. The conceptual distinction is nevertheless useful because it enables one to evaluate the nature of Gandhi's learning at each juncture of satyagraha's development, in varying degrees of emphasis on either origination or acceptance, or both at the same time. The suggested typology also offers a way to trace longitudinal shifts in Gandhi's rationale for analogizing, from origination to acceptance as a general trend, as he began his conscious efforts around January 1904 to unite the Indian community for nonviolent law-breaking.

The historical context of the mid-1900s, when a critical transition took place from the incipience to the origination phase of satyagraha, shaped both Gandhi's learning processes and the Indian community's mobilization potential in an important way. In his *Indian Opinion* article on January 14, 1904, Gandhi urged Transvaal Indian traders to defy the government's recent instruction that required them to re-register for trade licenses under stricter, and possibly more arbitrary, conditions than previously expected. Despite Gandhi's repeated appeals for necessary "sacrifice," reflected in his emotional editorial series during the weeks to follow, his first public call for systematic law-breaking, jail-going, and honorable self-suffering failed to arouse the Transvaal Indian merchants, let alone less-active others in the community, into concerted action.[72] Importantly, despite this first call for law-breaking publicized in January 1904, his faith in legal recourse within the British state system had remained essentially unchanged, at least for some years to come. His faith in the system mirrored his loyalty to the Empire and his hope for better protection to be granted equally to white and non-white British subjects in South Africa, including Indians. Gandhi's disillusionment with the increasingly unmistakable betrayal by the British of the South African Indians, many of whom risked their lives to support the imperial forces during the Anglo-Boer War of 1899–1902 in anticipation of improved treatment after the war, grew stronger throughout the mid-1900s. His disillusionment, coupled with the crystallization of his moral discourse during this formative period, eventually led to his new identity as a committed law-breaker declared at the mass pledge in September 1906. His personal identity transformation and public failure experienced in 1904–6 was important for satyagraha's emergence, for it helped Gandhi shape his interpretive lenses through which to select, consciously or subconsciously, which contemporaneous events should be considered newsworthy and what analogies and moral lessons should be drawn from them, either for origination or acceptance.

Gandhi's sensitized mind appeared to have been searching for evocative analogies during these few intensive years leading up to the mass pledge in September 1906, and beyond that decisive event. Several dramatic popular movements emerging on the international scene during this period in turn supplied Gandhi and fellow Indians with stimulating sources of inspiration from which useful analogies were drawn. One of the most frequently mentioned sources of analogizing, reflected in the *Indian Opinion* in the mid-1900s, concerned the Bengalese boycott (swadeshi) of British goods. The boycott was intended to protest against Lord Curzon's British-sponsored proposal to divide Bengal into the eastern and western parts, in an effort to merge the eastern part, populated mainly by Muslims, into its northeastern neighbor, Assam, for administrative expedience. In his article "Will India wake up?" on August 19, 1905, twelve days after Bengalese leaders met in Calcutta to declare a general boycott, Gandhi wrote without concealing a surge of nationalistic fervor within him:

> Since this news [of the official approval of Lord Curzon's proposal] reached India, meetings are said to have been held in almost every village of Bengal.

> People of all communities have been participating in them. Even Chinese merchants seem to have taken part. These meetings are said to have been so impressive that long telegraphic reports have reached far-off South Africa. Resolutions challenging the Government were, for the first time it would appear, moved at these meetings. It appears to have been suggested in the course of the speeches that, if the Government did not take heed, Indian merchants should stop all trade with Great Britain. We must admit that our people have learnt these tactics from China.
>
> (Gandhi 1961, vol. 5: 44)

Unlike other sources of analogy-building that will be discussed shortly, Gandhi's report on Bengal on this particular occasion did not take the form of a well-articulated contrast to South African Indians. Yet judging from the very nature of the subject that pertained directly to their motherland, its political and moral implications, although interpreted variously by the readers and the writer, were necessarily comparative and analogical, in relation to their own struggle against white rule in South Africa.

In an attempt to explore possible implications of the Bengalese event for analogizing, three observations may be made. First, because of what Gandhi referred to as a rare or even unprecedented nature of the defiant resolution taken "for the first time it would appear," it is plausible that the Bengalese boycott had some effect on Gandhi's mind and stimulated his analogy-building for origination. This inference is consistent with the fact that he continuously studied, discovered, and reported on the unfolding of the Bengalese movement as well as on its background, as reflected in the series of his 1905 articles such as "Ishwarchandra Vidyasagar" (September 16, providing a biographic sketch of a Bengalese heroic educator and social activist), "The boycott" (October 7), "Brave Bengal" (October 28), "Divide and rule" (November 4), and "The heroic song of Bengal" (December 2).[73] Second, since the Bengalese event was unfolding while the Indians sought redress to their own grievances in South Africa, the nature of cross-contextual thinking at work was spatial in nature, with analogies drawn from one geographic location to another, namely from Bengal to South Africa.

Third, the analogical learning undertaken by Gandhi and possibly other Indians in South Africa was inspired in part by another evocative, contemporaneous event, one unfolding in China. In his article "The Chinese and the Americans" on September 9, 1905, less than a month before the above-mentioned report on Bengal was published, Gandhi noted that the Chinese were effectively boycotting American goods in their protest against the US government's "anti-Chinese laws" that excluded Chinese labor from economic competition. His acknowledgement of the Chinese influence on the Bengalese boycott is important, for it indicates that there were dynamic inter-regional interactions that provided a broader epistemological context of Gandhi's and other community members' analogical learning. Yet even more importantly, Gandhi drew the following moral lesson from this article on the Chinese boycott, written in his native Gujarati:

> where there is unity, there alone is strength, and also victory. This deserves to be carefully borne in mind by every Indian. The Chinese, though weak, appear to have become strong on account of their unity, thereby bearing out the truth of the Gujarati verse, "Thus do ants when united take the life of a fierce snake."

Unity was Gandhi's message, conveyed repeatedly to his principal constituents, Gujarati merchants. And his inquiry into the power of unity is elaborated further in a passage that follows the aforementioned portion of his article on Bengal:

> But if the people really act accordingly, there would be nothing surprising if our troubles came to a speedy end. For, if this is done, Great Britain will be put to great loss; and the Government can have no means of dealing with it. They cannot compel the people to carry on trade. The method is very straight and simple. But will our people in Bengal maintain the requisite unity? Will the merchants suffer for the good of the country?
>
> (Gandhi 1961, vol. 5: 44)

In addition to the need for solidarity, which failed to materialize among Transvaal merchants during Gandhi's first attempt to organize nonviolent lawbreaking in January 1904, he strove to articulate and communicate another essential political principle, the notion of voluntary servitude. It asserts that even the most powerful rulers lose their ruling power when the ruled refuse to serve and that the ruled, therefore, have the inherent capacity to transform oppressive political relations by suspending their assistance, cooperation, and obedience to the rulers (Sharp 1979). To the extent that this message unambiguously evoked the urgent need for merchants' unity and systematic noncompliance, it illustrated Gandhi's use of analogical images aimed at attaining communal acceptance of known principles.

In addition to the Bengalese and Chinese boycott movements, the people's uprising in Russia shaped Gandhi's analogical learning on the eve of satyagraha's advent. In his article "Russia and India" on November 11, 1905, Gandhi characterized the 1905 Russian Revolution as a model for Indians' action to challenge oppression by British rule. Significantly, the article goes much further in articulating kernel ideas of satyagraha's essence than any of the numerous articles on the Bengalese and Chinese boycotts written in the mid-1900s. It is doubly significant that this unambiguous, prophetic articulation of satyagraha's essence had already emerged in his mind as early as nine months before the Draft Asiatic Law Amendment Ordinance was published in the Transvaal on August 22, 1906, which became the immediate trigger of the September 1906 pledge. Because of its historical and theoretical significance, it deserves quoting at length, divided in two parts:

> The present unrest in Russia has a great lesson for us. The Czar of Russia today yields the most autocratic power in the world. The people of Russia

suffer numerous hardships. The poor are crushed by the weight of taxes, the soldiers put down the people, who have to submit to all the whims of the Czar.... The Russian people have suffered all this for years, but they have now reached the limit of their patience. They have struggled hard to end this tyranny, but in vain. They rose in rebellion and killed the Czars, but they could not secure justice. This time they have found another remedy which, though very simple, is more powerful than rebellion and murder. The Russian workers and all the other servants declared a general strike and stopped all work. They left their jobs and informed the Czar that, unless justice was done, they would not resume work. What was there even the Czar could do against this? It was quite impossible to exact work from people by force.... The Czar has therefore proclaimed to the people that they will be granted a share in government and that he will not make any laws without their consent.... For even the most powerful cannot rule without the co-operation of the ruled. If the Russian people succeed, this revolution in Russia will be regarded as the greatest victory, the greatest event of the present century.

(Gandhi 1961, vol. 5: 131–2)

Here an analogy is built on a comparison, one that is implied at least, between the two geographic contexts, Russia and India, with a clear message being sent to the Indian community in South Africa. Lessons learned by Gandhi from this event and communicated to fellow South African Indians include the superiority of nonviolence to violence and the applicability of the theory of voluntary servitude in practice. The article also indicates that Gandhi was both learning and sharing the unfolding of an unprecedented phenomenon with great interest, one whose moral significance was consistent with his emerging value commitment but which, considering his failure in January 1904, was still in need of empirical illustration to be viable and acceptable by his constituents' standard.

Following the passage quoted above, the article encouraged the South African Indian community to rise up for nonviolent law-breaking, by appealing to an evocative analogy:

In the caption to this article we have put Russia and India together. We have therefore to justify it by showing how India is concerned with the events in Russia. There is much similarity between the governance of India and that of Russia. The power of the Viceroy is no way less than that of the Czar. Just as the people of Russia pay taxes, so also do we; just as the Russian taxpayer has no control over the use of the money thus raised, so also the Indians have none; as in Russia, so in India, the military is all-powerful. The only difference is that the power of the state is rather more brusquely exercised in Russia than in India. We, too, can resort to the Russian remedy against tyranny. The movement in Bengal for the use of *swadeshi* goods is much like the Russian movement. Our shackles will break this very day, if the people of India become united and patient, love their country, and think of the well-being of their motherland disregarding their self-interest. The governance of India is possible only because there exist people who serve. We also can show the same strength that the Russian people have done.

(Gandhi 1961, vol. 5: 132)

In addition to the reiteration of unity, voluntary servitude, and selfless patriotic service, the article reveals two other critical insights. First, analogy-building applied here went beyond a simple cross-contextual comparison and consciously utilized isomorphism; it contrasted Russian masses' relationship to Czars with Indians' relationship to the British. Gandhi's reasoning process in this article is prototypical of the two-case comparison method that he routinely used.[74] He juxtaposed the two sets of relationships in order to point out apparent similarities and set a baseline for comparison, then singled out an evocative difference to show the relatively favorable position of Indians compared to Russians, and finally urged the Indians to fulfill their untapped potential revealed by the comparison. Viewed in the historical context of the mid-1900s, Gandhi's message conveyed by this isomorphism was clear: his unconventional and hitherto unaccepted vision of nonviolent law-breaking should be considered viable, as demonstrated eloquently by the analogous event in Russia. It is also inferred that his attempt at analogy-building for communal acceptance was by no means inconsistent with analogical learning for origination, which appeared to have been taking place concurrently in Gandhi's and fellow Indians' political consciousness. For their continuous learning of uncharted epistemological terrains – explored only vicariously through the Russian, Bengalese, and Chinese examples – would shortly find a compelling means by which to integrate many of the incipient principles into an actionable whole.

Second, that Gandhi attributed an exemplary image to the revolution, not just a popular uprising or rebellion, as early as 1905 is historically significant. Revolutions, particularly of the type unfolding in Russia as of 1905, involved overthrowing existing systems of governance. However, there exists sufficient evidence to suggest that such an unambiguous expression of revolutionary fervor was hardly consistent with the general pattern of imperialist perceptions and behavior demonstrated by Gandhi in much of the 1900s. For example, his loyalty to the Empire and British rule was reflected in his service as a Sergeant-Major in the Indian Ambulance Corps from June to July 1906, in support of the British repressive campaign against the Zulu "rebellion."[75] His faith in the ultimate goodness of British imperialism was also expressed repeatedly through his writings during this period,[76] including his message "Empire Day" on May 29, 1905. The article unreservedly praised the late Queen-Empress as a unifying symbol of all nations under the British flag and reflected Gandhi's imperialist ideology, as it stated, "The lesser persons who administered her power might make mistakes; injustice even might be committed in her name; but the people ever knew that the mistakes and the injustice come *not* from Victoria the Good."

Gandhi's appeal for applying "the Russian remedy against tyranny" under British rule contradicted his own imperialist ideology still active in late 1905.

His willingness to learn from the Russian Revolution thus leads to the inference that the possibility, however remote it might have seemed at that point, of overthrowing British rule had already entered his political consciousness as early as about a year before even the method of their first collective action took shape. It is also inferred that his willingness to carry the Russian analogy this far signaled his readiness to start questioning his liberal imperialist ideology. Epistemologically, this meant that the combined effect of the unconventional social change unfolding in Russia, on the one hand, and Gandhi's cognitive readiness to draw practical analogies from it, on the other, began to stretch the outer boundary of his imperialist worldview. This worldview expansion, it seems, prepared him and fellow Indians toward adopting systematic law-breaking due to emerge shortly.

Finally, having explored how Gandhi as an emerging leader learned analogically, the analysis will now turn to how his personal learning contributed to, or at least interacted with, the social and epistemological process of satyagraha's emergence. Discussion on this point is preliminary and necessarily speculative, for any attempt at demonstrating leader–follower relationships of this magnitude would become exceedingly more complex than what this study is meant to accomplish.[77] Also, archival evidence available for this purpose is limited. However, a brief mention may be made on at least three aspects of the campaign, stimulating an inference that Gandhi's analogical learning was not contained within his mind, but it began to be translated into concrete communal processes of creation. These illustrations concern intra-communal dialogues triggered by Gandhi's analogical learning on the eve of the public oath-taking in September 1906, the adoption of deliberate, systematic jail-going as a method of protest, and the possible epistemological origin of the Great March in late 1913.

The two *Indian Opinion* articles, "Criminal" and "Russia and India," both of which appeared on September 9, 1906, two days before the mass pledge taken in Johannesburg, indicate that Essop Mian, an influential Muslim leader in the Transvaal, contributed an article to its Gujarati section. In it, Mian raised a question as to how the present South African Indian situation could be compared to Russia. He was a prominent merchant and an official of the Hamidia Islamic Society, the primary organizational sponsor of the September 11 meeting. This Muslim leader's contribution of comparative insights to the Indian community's weekly journal offered Gandhi yet another timely opportunity to publicize his suggestion that the proposed nonviolent approach by Indians would be unquestionably superior to the violent means that the Russians had adopted, because of what Gandhi regarded as the "divine law" of means and ends. In the mass meeting on September 11, Mian as one of the main speakers again raised the Russian analogy, this time in front of some 3,000 enthusiastic Indians filling the Empire Theater.[78] Despite this circumstantial evidence, it would be premature to determine, based merely on this and other similar instances of intra-communal communication, whether and to what extent the community members had directly learned from Gandhi's attempt at analogy-building in the overall historical context of satyagraha's emergence.

Yet at least from Gandhi's perspective, a potential opportunity presented to him by other community leaders like Mian helped him rally the community's support around the kind of analogical learning growing in his mind.

Another plausible effect of analogizing by Gandhi, and possibly by other community leaders working closely with him, was observed in the epistemological process through which jail-going became an established method of resistance. In the mass meeting of September 11, Hajee Habib, a prominent Gujarati merchant and chairman of the Pretoria branch of the BIA, presented the proposal for jail-going to the audience, who had already been aroused by Mian and other leaders' speeches. In the record of the meeting publicized in the *Indian Opinion*,[79] Habib's remarks and the audience's reactions are described as follows:

> This Bill is most objectionable. If it is passed, I solemnly declare that I will never get myself registered again and will be the first to go to gaol. (Applause.) I recommend the same course to you all. Are you all prepared to take the oath? (The Assembly stood up to a man and said, "Yes, we will go to gaol!") Only by so doing shall we succeed. We tried this method in the days of the Boer Government also. Some 40 of our men were once arrested for trading without licenses. I advised them to go to gaol and not to seek release on bail. Accordingly, they all remained there without offering bail. I immediately approached the British Agent, who approved of our action and ultimately secured justice for us. Now that a British Government is in power, the time has come for us to go to gaol, and go we will.
> (Gandhi 1961, vol. 5: 442)

Habib's statement indicates that there had been precedent of systematically organized jail-going within the Indian community, albeit on a much smaller scale than in satyagraha, possibly prior to the outbreak of the Anglo-Boer War in 1899. How this Indian precedent might have helped to shape satyagraha's epistemological origin is far from clear, given the limited amount of evidence available. However, it is significant to note that at least one of the merchant leaders had experientially known deliberate, systematic jail-going as a possible method of resistance, for the shared knowledge possibly mitigated the sense of unfamiliarity and unconventionality on the part of other community members to follow suit.

Given this experiential background of the community, it is inferred that Gandhi's analogical learning on jail-going illustrated by the *Indian Opinion* articles was supplementary at best to satyagraha's emergence. In a protest against the poll-tax imposed on native Africans and Indians, Gandhi wrote in November 1905 on a recent meeting held by the Transvaal government's Chief Magistrate, in which a defiant native African representative reportedly stated, "The Government will have to line the roads of the Colony with gaols for the accommodation of the defaulters."[80] In addition, Gandhi's article on October 20, 1906 titled "Tyler, Hampden and Bunyan" praised three exemplary English figures of self-sacrifice in an effort to encourage Indians to keep the pledge that they had already taken over a month earlier.[81] In this article, Gandhi described Hampden's heroic revolt that culminated in people's refusal to pay what he considered an unjust tax, which had been imposed under King Charles's rule in the seventeenth century. Gandhi further noted that in the face of the united popular resistance to the tax, "It was realized [by the King] that thousands of people could not be sent to gaol."

Gandhi repeatedly referred to analogous jail-going episodes before and after the pledge on September 11, with varying degrees of emphasis on either origination or acceptance, or both. An important insight derived from these indications is that even before massive gaol-going became an empirical reality for the first time toward the end of 1908, Gandhi, through analogy-building, had already begun to see in his mind's eye at least a theoretical possibility of filling the jail with such massive popular presence as to render it dysfunctional as a system of punishment. As in the Russian analogy, how and to what extent the analogical learning evolving in Gandhi's mind, as well as that of other community members, shaped satyagraha's epistemological origin remains to be explored. However, what this inquiry has made clear is that the combined effect of analogous suggestive experiences, either vicarious or direct, helped to inspire and justify the potential of unconventional collective action to become an empirical reality.

The third and final example of possible social influence generated by Gandhi's analogy-building is highly speculative, yet reflective of the sustained relevance of analogical learning beyond satyagraha's origination phase. In his psychoanalysis, *Gandhi's Truth: On the Origins of Militant Nonviolence*, Erik Erikson (1969) explains how Gandhi came up with the image of the Great March of thousands of indentured laborers, which started on October 28, 1913 and headed toward the Transvaal border from Newcastle, Natal. After over a dozen Tamil-speaking satyagrahis successfully but unexpectedly drew these laborers en mass from Natal coalmines, Gandhi was suddenly faced with a dilemma as to how to secure a place for their refuge and how to turn these uninformed, untrained satyagrahi candidates into disciplined pilgrims who could reach the refuge in an orderly manner. The destination of the March that he chose was the Tolstoy Farm, his communal settlement near Johannesburg, two days' walk from Newcastle. The only affordable means of transportation available to them was on foot. In his psychoanalysis of Gandhi's preconscious, Erikson speculates the epistemological origin of the Great March as follows:

> Gandhi played with the idea of an Indian Trek as an indigenous gesture of manly protest which might reverberate in South African hearts. For ... Gandhi was deeply impressed with the Boers' fortitude in leaving their homesteads for the freedom of the open spaces; and it may well be that the famous Boer Trek provided one heroic model for the great March and for many marches since.
>
> (Erikson 1969: 213)

Consistent with Erikson's inference, there is sufficient evidence to demonstrate Gandhi's respect for pious Boers, sometimes contrasted to unfaithful British colonialists.[82] However, evidence is still to be found to demonstrate that Gandhi had actually drawn an analogy from historical Boer treks, particularly the well known Great Trek of over 10,000 Boers, who left the Cape Colony in the 1830s and headed north and northeast in search of economic, political, and spiritual freedom from British colonial influence. Despite the uncertainties surrounding Erikson's inference, one can hardly discard it offhand; nor can one afford to disregard unorthodox speculations of Erikson's kind in more general terms, precisely because of the unsettled uncertainties. For the unprecedented nature of the Great March is clearly distinguishable from all other strategies used during the eight-year campaign, and this originality invites one to suspect unconventional sources of inspiration. Besides, because this unprecedented March – be it inspired by Boer trekkers, Gandhi's own marching experience during the Zulu "rebellion," or other epistemological origins – became one of the immediate causes of the 1914 Gandhi–Smuts settlement, Erikson's view deserves further scrutiny.[83] What is less speculative, on the other hand, is Erikson's observation that the Great March of 1913 in South Africa became a crucial analogical basis for envisioning many Gandhian marches to follow in India, including the famous Salt March in March 1930.

Interactions between the working propositions: understanding value commitment and analogizing in context

In this case study, the working propositions of identity transformation, paradigm shifts, value commitment, and analogizing have been applied to explore theoretical implications of satyagraha's emergence for conflict resolution creativity. With the exception of the proposition on identity transformation, which has emerged as a unique attribute of the present case, the remaining three were deduced from the comparative analysis of the sixteen brief case studies conducted earlier. As discussed in the introductory chapter, the deductive thinking of the kind that generated the working propositions led to the enumeration of distinct theoretical statements, which are unavoidably "atomic" in nature and thus de-contextualized from the concrete cases that inspired to formulate them. The study of satyagraha's origination, then, is an attempt to recontextualize at least some of these discrete propositions in the wholeness of a single case, so that a conflict worker may envision how to translate the propositions into a given context from a holistic and practical perspective.

Intuitively one realizes that all four working propositions discussed so far, as well as many others that have not found sufficient space for discussion, are inseparably interconnected. Having discussed these four propositions (and having sensed many others in the background), however, it has come to attention that a particularly salient and evocative connection is identified in the present case between value commitment and analogizing, with important implications to be drawn from this connection. The attempt being made here to demonstrate the connection between these two propositions is illustrative in nature, for it aims to stimulate further inquiry into various unexplored connections between other working propositions, which the present case study has to leave out deliberately for brevity.

The analysis of satyagraha's origination and Gandhi's personal transformation has revealed that the movement was not only agency-led, but also morally and religiously driven at its very core, with varying degrees and kinds of materialistic and pragmatic motives inevitably interacting with its spiritual essence. While Gandhi's intrinsic value commitment, which came to be accepted or rejected by various stakeholders, continued to anchor the movement in its central, moralistic discourse, it was usefully *supplemented* by analogical learning for both origination and acceptance.

Significantly, the relationship between the value commitment and analogizing was dialectical and mutually reinforcing; yet it is also observed that in general terms, analogical learning provided no more than catalytic, facilitative influences on the formation of the value commitment, which appears to have been evolving in Gandhi's adult life for some time and shared with others with varying degrees of tangible impact to be generated. This observation drawn from the unique and specific context of satyagraha is suggestive for the purpose of exploring other cases of social and epistemological creation, because it illustrates the possibility that there is *an order of relative importance* among different enabling factors for creativity. In the present case study, an order of relative importance refers to a social and epistemological context in which certain enabling factors are generally considered relatively more influential than others, subject to possible longitudinal changes that may arise from their dialectical, dynamic relationships. Evidence suggests that in the context of satyagraha's origination, the intrinsic value commitment guiding Gandhi and other devoted satyagrahis generally took moral precedence over their analogical learning in terms of shaping and sustaining the movement, although the two factors were supplementary and by no means mutually exclusive.

In his 1909 booklet *Hind Swaraj*, Gandhi challenged fellow Indians advocating the need to expel the British from India by force. As a counterargument to them, he stressed that it was ultimately Indians themselves who chose to retain the British and remained satisfied for so long under British rule. To overcome the sustained deprivation of freedom in India, Gandhi proposed an alternative vision where Indians were to cultivate moral independence, so as to welcome the British in India to be assimilated and "Indianised" if they so desired. In a hypothetical dialogue with a critic who denounced Gandhi's vision as inconsistent with historical precedent and thus too unrealistic, Gandhi replied:

> To believe that what has not occurred in history will not occur at all is to argue disbelief in the dignity of man. At any rate, it behooves us to try what appeals to our reason. All countries are not similarly conditioned. The condition of India is unique. Its strength is immeasurable. We need not, therefore, refer to the history of other countries.
>
> (Gandhi 1997: 74)

It is noteworthy that Gandhi wrote *Hind Swaraj* on his return journey to South Africa by boat from his failed mission in London, where he had been entrusted by the South African Indian community to present its position to the British and other law-makers discussing how to establish white-only Union government. At the time of his writing this booklet, the unprecedented mass mobilization for satyagraha, which had reached its first peak late in 1908, had already declined, and his credibility as a community leader had hit its lowest ebb, as many influential merchants, disillusioned with the lack of tangible results despite their prolonged self-sacrifice, had already left Gandhi and the satyagraha movement. Given this historical context, Gandhi's explicit reference to his belief that self-rule (swaraj) was to be attained with or without analogous cases in the past or in other regional contexts deserves attention, for it illustrates the significant deepening of his intrinsic value commitment during this period of difficulty.

From a longitudinal perspective, this 1909 statement usefully compares to his *Indian Opinion* articles written immediately after the jail-going pledge of September 1906.[84] In those messages to the Indian community, Gandhi introduced numerous analogous incidents of grassroots-based resistance in South Africa and elsewhere during this period, as well as in the remote past, in an attempt to uplift the Indians' morale and prepare their minds to endure the unprecedented hardship due to come. His reliance on analogy-building for communal acceptance during this earliest phase of the movement presents a sharp contrast to his 1909 statement, for the latter, unlike the former, places his value commitment over the availability of precedent and, more generally, empirical likelihood of success.

This shift in moral priority reflected in *Hind Swaraj* appears to have thereafter remained firm and stable in his conviction. Recording his memory of the early phase of the first satyagraha struggle in South Africa many years later, Gandhi wrote:

> [As] Tolstoy observed, the Transvaal struggle was the first attempt at applying the principle of Satyagraha to masses or bodies of men. I do not know any historical example of pure mass Satyagraha. I cannot however formulate any definite opinion on the point, as my knowledge of history is limited. But as a matter of fact we have nothing to do with historical precedents. Granted the fundamental principles of Satyagraha, it will be seen that the [beneficial] consequences I have described are bound to follow as night the day. It will not do to dismiss such a valuable force with the remark that it is difficult or impossible of application. Brute force has been the ruling factor in the world for thousands of years, and mankind has been reaping its bitter harvest all along, as he who runs may read. There is little hope of anything good coming out of it in the future. If light can come out of darkness, then alone can love emerge from hatred.
>
> (Gandhi 1928: 173)

From this and other similar remarks that Gandhi had left, it is inferred that his "theory of unprecedented action" came to be internalized in his mind and translated into a series of unconventional actions in the years to come. Moreover, there are indications that Gandhi's emphasis on the intrinsic value commitment over precedent and analogous experience did not stay within his personal spiritual life, but it had begun to generate tangible impact on the collective experience of satyagrahis in South Africa. For example, the movement attained the unprecedented level of mass mobilization in late 1908 and at the end of 1913. The massive scale of jail-going, deportations, financial losses, and even martyrdom became an empirical reality on these occasions. This was due in large part to the active participation of hawkers and other lower-income Indians in the Transvaal for 1908 and indentured laborers in Natal for 1913. These satyagrahi candidates who generated decisive impact on the movement were mostly illiterate and belonged to the lower strata of the community's socio-economic hierarchy, in which the merchant elite occupied the highest position. From a socio-economic perspective, Gandhi's intensive analogical learning primarily influenced relatively wealthy and literate Indians, who could subscribe to the *Indian Opinion* and read the articles written only in English and Gujarati. On the contrary, his analogy-building for communal acceptance had little direct impact on the lower and underclass Indians, many of whom were Tamil speakers from southern India and their colonial-born descendants. While the lower and underclass Indians had their own economic, socio-political, and spiritual needs to realize through collective political action, those needs alone had never united them for systematic jail-going before satyagraha's advent. One may conclude, therefore, that the intrinsic value commitment of Gandhi and other devoted leaders offered them a central focus of public attention, around which these uninformed Indians rallied, even without substantial knowledge of analogous popular movements elsewhere that could have boosted their morale.

The satyagrahis' unique emphasis on the intrinsic value commitment over analogizing brings one's attention back to one of the central questions of the present study: how can one envision and actualize an unconventional yet viable alternative to the conventional reality of inter-group conflict at hand, by way of bringing the empirical reality a step closer to the envisioned potential reality? An answer emerging from the present inquiry into satyagraha's origin is highly idiographic and even unscientific: articulate a transcendent paradigm of nonviolent spiritual action with or without precedent to support its empirical viability, communicate the newly formed commitment widely through both words and personal examples of risk-taking, and strive to fulfill the commitment persistently until the proposed unconventional vision becomes a new empirical reality – or death relieves the practitioners from this unending task. This point deserves elaboration because it highlights the practical and theoretical significance of this case study.

In the course of satyagraha's emergence, attempts were made and precedents created to envision and actualize the potential reality of perceived justpeace, or the ideal intersection of ethicality and effectiveness, in the empirical, conventional reality of structural violence and colonial instrumentalism. What distinguished satyagraha's emergence from many other similar attempts by Indian and non-Indian communities in the past was that the satyagraha struggle *did* generate tangible effects, however transient and limited in scope, on the deeply entrenched racial conflicts at hand. The primary driving force of this historical and communal envisioning process was the intrinsic value commitment, translated into various actions for self-suffering, ranging from financial losses to jail-going to martyrdom. The irreducible essence of the potential reality that the satyagrahis aspired to realize was the non-negotiable and inherently nonviolent ideals, truth (satya) and self-actualization (moksha). The intrinsic value commitment, because of its irreducible, non-negotiable, and essentially religious nature, had to be applied in practice against all odds, with or without a moral boost that could have been derived from analogous episodes, as well as from other possible forms of empirical support for the vision's viability.

In terms of conflict resolution theory and practice, the value-based, ideal-driven nature of satyagraha's emergence was ideographic but suggestive, given its enduring significance in the contemporary history of conflict work. Metaphorically stated, the earliest experience of the satyagrahis was a struggle for penetrating the still-to-be penetrated corner of the empirical reality, with the unconventional theory of religiosity as a guide and evocative analogies as heuristics to explore how to apply their theory into practice. In this sense, the epistemological origin of this weapon of justpeace, which was to become a sustained focus of social scientific inquiry and applied practice, finds itself on the exact opposite of scientific objectivity.

Finally, having explored the relative importance of the value commitment over analogizing, it is emphasized that analogizing, for its part, also helped to reshape the value commitment, at least in a subtle manner. This observation underscores the earlier point that these two enabling factors of creativity were dialectical in nature. For example, Gandhi's reference to the Russian Revolution of 1905 consciously or subconsciously stretched and reshaped his cognitive boundaries, within which his loyalty to both Indian patriotism and liberal imperialism had long remained essential and unshaken. Psychoanalytically, one infers from this that the highly evocative image of the Russians' victory over their oppressive rulers, with the seemingly unprecedented empirical reality unfolding in Gandhi's own eyes, aroused his rebellious preconscious, even to the point of transgressing the cognitive boundaries set by his value commitment in political life. Importantly, the exemplary image of the Russian revolution, wrapped in Gandhi's moral and emotional fervor, was communicated to a few thousand readers of the *Indian Opinion* at the time of prolonged frustration shared by the Indian community. The Russian analogy surfaced and resurfaced from the political consciousness of some community leaders, particularly when dramatized by such rituals as the public oath-taking on September 11, 1906.

Summary of the major findings

This case study has illustrated how one may apply the four working propositions to shed fresh light on satyagraha's emergence. By so doing, it has contributed, at least in a modest manner, to exploring potentially generalizable insights into conflict resolution creativity.

As stated earlier, the selected propositions are illustrative only, and for the sake of brevity the present case study has purposefully left out other potentially useful propositions, such as combining known elements in a new way, unconventionality derived from conventionality, and contingency-based principled flexibility. In view of unexplored possibilities for further inquiry, it is emphasized that these other propositions deserve attention as a way of illuminating satyagraha's origin from different angles and taking the on-going discovery process in new directions.

At the same time, reflecting on the range of significant discoveries made throughout this chapter, one may argue that the selected propositions represent some of the most quintessential enablers and irreducible hallmarks of satyagraha's origin – without which this unique exemplar of process creativity would not have come into existence the way it did, with such enduring political and spiritual impact as is observed today. With this evaluation of the case in mind, the remaining part of the present chapter will summarize five lessons derived from the case study, in anticipation of future inquiry into conflict resolution creativity in general and satyagraha's origin in particular.

First, satyagraha came into being and evolved in a manner reflective of Gandhi's identity transformation. The agency-led process of satyagraha's origination resonated with continuous dialectical interactions between Gandhi's identity shifts and the shifts in South African Indians' communal experiences. Five interrelated processes of Gandhi's identity transformation that helped to shape satyagraha most cogently involved his shifts: (1) from a hired legal representative of elite merchants to a moral and political leader for all Indians; (2) from a British liberal imperialist to an Indian nationalist; (3) from a racial purist to a less committed purist, with early symptoms of his universal humanist tendency gradually emerging at the end of his activities in South Africa; (4) from an advocate for the upper to middle class, to Indians of all classes; and (5) from a Gujarati regionalist to an advocate for Indians from all regions, including Tamils from the south. Despite these shifts in his identity orientation, his acceptance of white superiority and black inferiority remained unchanged, and so did his respect for all known faith traditions, including Islam, Hinduism, Jainism, Buddhism, Christianity, and Zoroastrianism.

Second, Gandhi's intrinsic value commitment to the oneness of means and ends, transcending political instrumentalism, became a sustained rallying point around which satyagrahis' and other stakeholders' expectations, interests, and moral values converged and diverged throughout the campaign. The sense of oneness was derived from the religious belief in the fusion of tapas (purification) and moksha (enlightenment), as well as that of ahimsa (non-killing) and satya (truth). Consistent with the uniquely personalized blend of Hindu, Jain, Buddhist, and other religious influences that shaped his worldview, Gandhi aspired to practice tapas and ahimsa as a means, trusting the infallible cosmic law (rta) and moral causality (karma) to take care of the ultimate attainment of moksha and satya as desired ends. Yet his intrinsic value commitment to satyagraha had hardly achieved its status in the Indian community as a trusted principle of collective action against structural violence. Because politicization of class consciousness, religious affiliations, and other hallmarks of social identity continued to divide the Indian community, Gandhi and his fellow satyagrahis strove to earn popular support for their intrinsic value commitment in order to make it a unifying factor. Despite the sustained intra-communal tension, as well as the adversaries' obstruction, the persistent effort made by Gandhi and others to apply the intrinsic value commitment to practice presented an alternative reality in South African society, in sharp contrast to the conventional reality of colonial instrumentalism.

Third, since satyagraha exemplifies process creativity rather than outcome creativity, it is suggested that heuristic inspirations generated by the Kuhnian theory should be applied more expansively to illustrate the present case than the conflict paradigm thesis, introduced earlier, could illuminate in scope. Of interest in this expanded scope of inquiry is what kind of discursive shifts had taken place through the birth of satyagraha, as it sought to de-entrench the prevailing perceptions and interactive patterns of political instrumentalism, as well as of structural violence. A comparative perspective on the four marginalized groups during the period under study, namely, European proletarians, native Africans, the Colored, and Indians, reveals a dilemma that they all faced respectively, in their effort to challenge the state-sponsored structural violence of different kinds. The dilemma concerned how to seek redress both effectively and ethically in the course of their political resistance. Satyagraha initiated a paradigm shift, for it sought to create a practical method of nonviolent resistance to overcome this axiomatic dichotomy, which the other communities were either unable to transcend, unaware of, or simply unconcerned about.

Fourth, as reflected in his *Indian Opinion* articles and other writings, Gandhi analogically learned and communicated moral and political lessons from a range of geographic, historical, and relational contexts inside and outside South Africa, particularly on the eve of satyagraha's advent in the mid-1900s. His approaches to analogizing are categorized in two prototypes, one for origination and the other for acceptance. These two conceptual types were intertwined inseparably, however, in each concrete instance of his analogy-building effort. His failure in January 1904 to mobilize Transvaal Indian merchants based on his first public call for systematic law-breaking sensitized his mind to search for evocative analogies, possibly motivated by his deep yearning for a more promising occasion to arise, or to be created on purpose. He found convincing analogies for both origination and acceptance in such epoch-making events as the Russian Revolution and the Bengalese and Chinese boycotts that stirred the Indian and international public opinion in 1905. Kernel principles of satyagraha derived from and affirmed by these and other exemplary cases include solidarity, patriotic self-sacrifice, voluntary servitude, and nonviolence as inviolable means. In addition, preliminary evidence suggests that Gandhi's analogy-building effort for communal acceptance contributed, directly or indirectly, to inspiring and legitimizing such collective actions as systematic jail-going and demonstrative marching, sometimes facilitated by other leaders' analogous experiences and active support.

Fifth and final, these and other possible enabling factors for satyagraha's emergence are interrelated in a web of dynamic relationships. In addition, in a given context of conflict resolution creativity there appears to be an order of relative importance among these factors. What has emerged as a particularly salient relationship between interconnected factors in the present context is the one between the intrinsic value commitment and analogizing, with the former generating predominant influence over the latter. As an increasingly influential architect of satyagraha, Gandhi repeatedly stated the overriding importance of the value commitment as the movement's spiritual core, which he encouraged fellow satyagrahis to practice, regardless of the absence or presence of supportive precedent and empirical viability. At the communal level, Gandhi's emphasis on the value commitment over supportive precedent became a rallying point of the movement at its peaks in 1908 and 1913, successfully mobilizing lower and underclass Indians who had not been sensitized by the analogical lessons and inspirations that Gandhi had drawn and publicized persistently to motivate the community. The unique link between the two enabling factors inspires a search for a possible answer to one of the research questions that have framed the present inquiry as a whole: how can one envision and actualize an alternative reality beyond the empirical reality of inter-group conflict at hand? The answer that the satyagrahis found in their social and epistemological context was: to establish a new moral paradigm as a guiding "theory of practice" and apply it persistently, by way of learning from analogies to envision and legitimize concrete actions for practice. Finally, evocative analogies drawn from dramatic events that sensitized Gandhi and other community leaders, such as the Russian Revolution of 1905, appeared to have expanded the boundaries of their value commitment in a subtle yet important manner, suggesting that the two forms of creative influence shaped and reshaped each other dialectically.

5 Conclusion
Implications for research, practice, and pedagogy

Introduction and overview

The preceding chapters have sought to expand and deepen the understanding of creativity for conflict resolution. The present chapter will provide an opportunity to pose, reflect back, and look ahead. To this end, three steps will be taken.

First, it will offer a 360-degree review of the essential findings presented so far, asking: What lessons have been learned from this inquiry in broad outline? The reflective summary to be offered will be necessarily detailed, with the view toward identifying and crystallizing promising areas of future inquiry.

Second, an attempt will be made to demonstrate at least one concrete way of integrating and applying some of the study's essential findings to the context of conflict resolution dialogue and training. For this purpose, a working method of conflict work termed a "cross-contextual case study" will be outlined, with concrete examples illustrating how it applies to practice. This method, as well as the suggested steps to make it learnable and communicable through continuous refinement and needs-based adaptation, will help explore what kinds of additional research may be necessary and useful to complement both practical conflict work and pedagogic application.

Third, apart from the proposed "cross-contextual case study" method, there are numerous other ways to build on this study's findings in search of new directions in conflict and peace research, practice, and pedagogic application. Several of such future possibilities will be summarized in the form of research questions, for they appear particularly promising and theoretically evocative.

Summary of the key findings

This study has explored a question: How do creative resolution options and/or procedures by which to come up with resolution options first emerge, gradually evolve, and subsequently come to be accepted or rejected in a given social and epistemological context of inter-group conflict? Creativity is defined as unconventional viability, or a social and epistemological process where an actor or actors involved in the conflict learn to formulate an unconventional resolution option and/or procedure for resolution, and a growing number of others come to perceive it as a viable way of coping with the underlying problems from their collective and subjective point of view. This study has been undertaken with the view toward helping conflict workers and parties bridge the empirical reality of conflict (namely, what is and what was) with a potential reality of conflict resolution (namely, what can be and what ought to be). To this end, it has systematically explored ways in which one can come to see what one has never seen, for the purpose of envisioning and actualizing unconventional yet viable alternatives to a given inter-group conflict at hand.

Methodologically, the study has been exploratory, discovery-oriented, and qualitative, aimed at generating working typologies and hypotheses that one can examine and refine through future inquiry and experimental practice. The first of the two cumulative phases taken for inquiry was the comparative analysis of sixteen conflict resolution episodes of diverse professional, regional, and organizational backgrounds, each described by a leading researcher-practitioner. An in-depth interview with each of the sixteen researcher-practitioners revealed how the social and epistemological process in question came to resolve or otherwise cope with the conflict at hand, by way of invoking some elements of unconventional viability in the given local context. The sixteen episodes of conflict resolution creativity cover a broad spectrum of contemporary events such as: the Oslo peace process, the OAU's intervention in Sierra Leone, the first problem-solving workshop to address the Indonesia–Malaysia–Singapore conflict, the Helsinki process for moderating the East–West confrontation during the Cold War, the establishment of a binational ecological zone in the disputed Peru–Ecuador border area, and the US-based grassroots movement aspiring to achieve sustainable development beyond the dominant paradigm of economic growth.

Six themes have emerged from the systematic comparison of the sixteen cases, with each theme representing a hallmark and/or enabling factor for conflict resolution creativity illustrated by three or more cases of diverse backgrounds. These themes are:

1 Analogizing for sensitizing one's mind across contexts.
2 Value commitment to realizing an alternative reality to the conflict at hand, with or without empirical underpinnings or precedent to support the viability of the expressed vision.
3 Combining known elements in a new way.
4 Envisioning unconventional resolution options with a thorough understanding of what existing rules and normative boundaries are there to frame the conflict parties' and other stakeholders' expectations.
5 Anticipating discoveries to unfold in an unanticipated way and recognizing them in retrospect, particularly in the midst of concrete actions being taken to translate creative resolution options into practice.
6 Pursuing a sustained process of searching that is open-ended and flexible yet, at the same time, guided by some broad sense of directionality and purpose.

In addition to these themes that have emerged from the inquiry, five concepts of enduring significance in social science were introduced from relevant literature and the preparatory case studies conducted before this research project was formally launched. These ideas were used to explore possibilities of theory-building in conflict resolution creativity. The five concepts are: the roles assumed by actors in conflict, the longitudinal nature of creativity, the outcome–process typology, the system–element link (or levels of analysis), and paradigm shifts. These five concepts and the theoretical insights derived from them will be reviewed in some detail, for they point to promising directions of future inquiry.

First, the creativity of (a) conflict parties, (b) intermediaries, and (c) actors performing both functions at the same time was explored. In general terms, there emerged no categorical difference between the three types in terms of the nature of origination. However, preliminary indications suggest that when intermediaries attempt to apply their unconventionality to practice, their visions must be complemented by conflict parties' "buy-in" in order for evolution and acceptance to take shape. On the contrary, creativity originating through conflict parties' own initiatives tends to gain political relevance, generating more immediate effects on evolution and acceptance than intermediaries' creativity. Yet predictably, conflict parties' creativity faces difficulties when they attempt to overcome reactive devaluation derived from mutual distrust.

Either way, viability has to be *earned* through risk-taking and sustained commitment, two of the indispensable qualities that must be activated for generating primary constituencies' readiness to accept alternative realities to a given conflict at hand. This observation on the need for earning viability also appears applicable to the creativity of actors performing both functions at the same time. This preliminary observation, however, must be more empirically and rigorously examined by a greater number of case studies aimed at generating more comprehensive and conclusive insights into this multifaceted subject.

Second, to conceptualize the longitudinal nature of conflict resolution creativity, the proposed five-phase model, which hypothesizes incipience, origination, evolution, acceptance, and sustenance for the methodological purpose of data collection and analysis, was modified and simplified. The revised model highlights incipience, origination, and evolution as its main components, while it takes into account acceptance and sustenance as supplementary sub-categories of the evolution phase. Utilizing the revised model as a heuristic basis, four prototypes of longitudinal processes for conflict resolution creativity emerged from the comparative case analysis:

- Type A: unconventional processes failing in the transition from incipience to origination.
- Type B: unconventional processes failing in the transition from origination to evolution.
- Type C: unconventional processes failing in the course of evolution.
- Type D: unconventional processes growing out of evolution and developing further with sustained momentum.

Drawing on the preliminary indications derived from the present study, it was suggested that the degree to which a process of conflict resolution creativity successfully transitions from Type A through Type D corresponds to the extent to which the perceived gap between unconventionality and viability is minimized and transformed in the given social and epistemological context of conflict work. Yet this typological thinking by no means presumes linear progression from one longitudinal stage to another. The study illustrated, for example, how "failed" attempts to actualize alternative realities, as in the case of satyagraha's decline immediately after Gandhi's departure in mid-1914, could unexpectedly pave the way toward constructive social change that might unfold at some point in the future. This finding suggests the need for expanding time horizons of conflict work in order to identify, utilize, and evaluate long-term, multifaceted consequences of perceived "failures."

Third, the relationships between outcome and process creativity were explored. While outcome creativity requires the capacity to break through the conventionally accepted reality of a given conflict at hand, process creativity entails the capacity to develop procedural means by which to address the conflict. Simply put, outcome creativity concerns transforming the conflict per se while process creativity involves transforming ways of inter-party communication. That the two types are interrelated, dialectical, and complementary to each other is intuitively obvious, as mentioned explicitly by many interviewees. Yet the theoretical and practical implications of this typology are not.

For example, outcome creativity presupposes the capacity to understand what the conflict is about, as well as the capacity to reformulate the existing conflict paradigm into a workable alternative reality. Process creativity, on the other hand, may also be enhanced and facilitated by empirical conflict analysis, but it presumes neither the capacity to reformulate the conflict itself nor the readiness to articulate an alternative reality. Another critical difference between the two types concerns the need for conflict parties' self-motivated commitment to implementing resolution options derived from the conflict work under question. While outcome creativity requires their commitment to accepting the suggested alternative realities over time as their own, process creativity materializes when the parties commit themselves to the given unconventional modes of inter-party communication and relationship-building – which may or may not generate alternative realities in substantive terms.

Stimulated by the observation that fourteen interviewees out of the sixteen in total voluntarily chose to describe personal experiences of process creativity as the most fitting illustrations of their creative conflict work, a question emerged for critical reflection: Has there been an emergence of shared expectations, and perhaps a professional culture, among Western-trained researchers, practitioners, and policymakers advocating the premise of impartiality in outcome, gratifying the intrinsic value of bringing parties together for talks and relationship-building, but remaining unaware of how consciously and systematically to explore ways to reformulate the conflict per se with outcome creativity?

Fourth, the relationship between conflict resolution creativity and the system–element link was explored. Questions were raised for theory-building, such as:

How do unconventional yet viable alternatives to an inter-group conflict emerge across levels of analysis in a given social and epistemological context of social change? Do they evolve from the bottom-up, for example from the micro to the meso level, or from the top down, namely, the other way around? Self-reflections shared by many interviewees, consistent with the author's empirical findings in the comparative case analysis, indicate that conflict resolution creativity tends to emerge and evolve from the bottom-up, from a lower to a higher level of analysis, resisting systemic inertia that stands in the way of agents of creative change aspiring to rise up.

Beyond this general observation, the study also explored what processes of creative bottom-up change actors in inter-group conflict can consciously generate, using the Helsinki process as a heuristic basis for theory-building. Out of the exploration emerged the working hypothesis of interdependent origination. This concept is defined as unconventional viability arising from the symbiotic and synergistic tension between two or more parties seeking workable approaches to resolution from seemingly divergent points of view. More specifically, interdependent origination is a social and epistemological process where actors involved in inter-group conflict come to co-create an unconventional yet viable resolution option through symbiotic and synergetic effects of coordinating their interactions, despite their apparent tension and hesitation to do so. This working thesis illustrates one sub-type of relational creativity and evokes the image of aikido, rather than more combative forms of martial arts, such as karate and judo. Importantly, this relationship-centered approach to theory-building and applied practice is distinguished from the image of what may be termed "independent origination" – a widely held notion of creativity where an agent of change stands up single-handedly and spearheads a creative process despite systemic inertia and resistance.

Fifth and final, Thomas Kuhn's theory of paradigm shifts was introduced as a metaphor and its implications explored in search of useful heuristics for conflict resolution creativity. The exploratory inquiry led to the proposed method of conflict work aimed at identifying a conflict paradigm, envisioning alternative realities beyond the conflict at hand, and facilitating a transition from the conflict paradigm to alternative realities. A conflict paradigm is a systemic entrenchment of perceptual and interactive patterns inherent in social conflict. A search for a conflict paradigm in a given social and epistemological context is stimulated by asking a question: What is the grammar of the conflict language at work, which may appear in the eyes of the conflict parties to be so deeply entrenched, axiomatic, and perhaps even obvious as to be long forgotten and unarticulated?

An alternative reality, on the other hand, is an alternative set of perceptual and interactive patterns that evolve from de-entrenching the entrenched perspectives and reshaping them in a manner more constructive and acceptable to the parties. In order to identify conflict paradigms embedded in conflicts and envision alternative realities beyond them, a conscious and systematic approach to dialogue and reflection is suggested, with the help of temporal, spatial, and relational metaphors, termed heuristic pointers.

While the comparative analysis of the sixteen episodes conducted in the first phase constituted the main part of this study, the supplementary second phase was introduced to clarify, refine, and elaborate some of the working themes and proposed concepts. The emergence of the satyagraha movement in South Africa from 1906 to 1914 was examined in depth in order to illustrate how one may apply such working themes and concepts as value commitment, paradigm shifts, and analogizing to the analysis of this unique social and epistemological context of conflict work. The case exemplified the kind of process creativity which was generated from the bottom-up by one of the under-represented parties to the deeply entrenched economic, political, and psychological conflicts in South Africa, but which eventually tailed out with the departure of the movement's principal leader, M. K. Gandhi, in 1914.

From the case study emerged an additional working theme. It highlights the inseparable link between Gandhi's identity transformation and the drive of the movement toward its distinct vision of nonviolent social transformation, which was facilitated by the use of an unconventional form of conflict work. In addition, satyagraha's emergence illustrated how two of the working themes, value commitment and analogizing, shaped and reshaped one another over time. As a general trend, the satyagrahis' value commitment helped to shape the ways in which they built analogies from historical and contemporaneous events that inspired Indian nationalism and new moral politics.

A working model of conflict work that emerged from this case study is highly idiographic, scarcely scientific, yet evocative. It involves articulating a transcendent paradigm of nonviolent spiritual action with or without precedent to support its empirical viability, communicating the newly formed commitment widely through both words and personal examples of risk-taking, and striving to fulfill the commitment persistently until the proposed unconventional vision becomes a new empirical reality – or death relieves the practitioners of conflict work from this unending task.

Cross-contextual case studies: one way of integrating key findings for practice and pedagogic application

Throughout the present inquiry, it has been discovered and demonstrated that creative processes for conflict resolution are far from linear and rationalistic. This implies that conflict resolution does not always precede or presuppose a formulaic conflict analysis, as far as the cases under study are concerned. This finding does not necessarily contradict the empirical possibility and practical usefulness of resolution options derived from logical and rational analysis. However, it does suggest the need for understanding the analysis–resolution link much more flexibly and comprehensively than conventionally thought, anticipating and accepting the possibility that visions of resolution precede analysis, analysis precedes resolution, and the two even co-arise by shaping and reshaping each other dialectically and continuously. The expanded awareness of the analysis–resolution link opens up what may be considered less familiar modes of thinking that inform how to understand the past, envision the future, and bridge the two.

The rest of the discussion in the present chapter builds on this expanded awareness of the relationship between the potential and the empirical, as well as on other key findings. It outlines what future possibilities may unfold from these discoveries, particularly for research, practice, and pedagogic application. Emphasis on pedagogy is important, for the epistemological attributes of the enabling factors for creativity, such as analogizing and combining known elements in a new way, cogently demonstrate that some aspects of conflict resolution creativity are learnable and thus teachable. The heuristic tools and concepts devised through the present study are intended not only to stimulate conflict work and research, but also to supplement pedagogic methods for systematically learning and teaching how to activate creative potential inherent in individuals and communities of diverse backgrounds.

To translate the expanded awareness of the empirical–potential link into practice, a new method of conflict work termed *cross-contextual case studies* is introduced. The suggested method is a meta-framework for designing and facilitating conflict resolution dialogue and training intended to cultivate conflict resolution creativity. It utilizes unfamiliar conflict scenarios of the past and/or present as a heuristic guide to conflict resolution and the prevention of possible violence. The method is a meta-framework because it provides a generic conceptual template within which a range of heuristic tools and concepts can be introduced and integrated flexibly according to the varying needs of exercise participants. The suggested method is *cross-contextual* in nature because it invites exercise participants concerned about a particular context of social conflict (e.g., Ethiopia and Eritrea) into another context (e.g., Peru and Ecuador) that may be unfamiliar to them yet somewhat analogous to their own conflict in terms of its essential attributes (e.g., exclusive sovereignty claimed over a contested border area). The goal of the exercise is to provide a unique interactive space for creative brainstorming and dialogue in which the parties can distance themselves from their own conflict but jointly brainstorm how to transform its essential attributes using the scenario of somebody else's conflict. It is hoped that a carefully designed and facilitated process of cross-contextual learning will enable the parties to recognize their conflict paradigm form a fresh perspective and start envisioning an alternative reality.

Three types of cross-contextual case studies are suggested, with the concept of time used as a heuristic pointer, or a variable: contemporaneous, historical, and hypothetical. Each of the three types is elaborated with examples. First, a *contemporaneous case study* is designed to reflect on an on-going unresolved conflict unfamiliar to exercise participants. For example, for Eritrean and Ethiopian political influentials unfamiliar with Latin American politics in mid-1998, when the cross-border fighting began to escalate between these two neighboring African countries, learning about the contemporaneous Peru–Ecuador border dispute, still to be settled at that point, would have been stimulating. For the purpose of the proposed learning experience, elaborate details of the Peru–Ecuador conflict would not have been necessary for the Eritreans and Ethiopians. A mere outline of the Peru–Ecuador dispute, including basic information about who the primary parties were and what their salient issues and expressed aspirations were, would have sufficed, at least as a starting point of their learning process. In addition, it would have been useful to state explicitly at the outset of the exercise that its primary objective would have been to think as pragmatically yet expansively as possible and envision broad outlines of plausible resolution options without being constrained by the details of the dispute.

It is inferred that because of their unfamiliarity with the Peru–Ecuador conflict and the absence at that point of a solution in sight, the Eritreans and Ethiopians would have been challenged to envision and explore alternative realities to the Peru–Ecuador conflict, with possible effects of learning and transfer to their own conflict in the Horn of Africa. Depending on the needs and circumstances of the Eritreans and Ethiopians, the envisioning process could have been exercised separately or jointly, assisted or unassisted by a professional facilitator familiar with the Peru–Ecuador conflict and relevant social theory. A range of working typologies and propositions on creativity, such as analogizing, combining known elements in a new way, interdependent origination, and conflict paradigm, could have been utilized as heuristic tools for the exercise. It is plausible that because of the participants' unfamiliarity with the Peru–Ecuador conflict, they would have been able to play with both emotional detachment and intellectual affinity to the Peru–Ecuador case and its future possibilities, thereby walking through the kind of cognitive pathways that they dared not to walk through for the purpose of disembedding the systemic entrenchment in their own conflict. This method of conflict resolution dialogue and training drawing on the Peru–Ecuador conflict could have been useful as of mid-1998, not only for Eritreans and Ethiopians, but also for others facing analogous problems, such as the Japanese and Russians over the long-disputed status of the Kurile Islands located in the North Pacific Ocean.

Second, a *historical case study* is a method by which to reflect on a past, unfamiliar conflict where some elements of unconventional viability were effectively applied for resolution. As in contemporaneous case studies, conflict scenarios adopted for historical case studies need to be unfamiliar to those participating in the exercise. Yet unlike contemporaneous case studies, historical case studies look into past conflicts that have already been resolved or at least constructively addressed with creativity. An essential requirement for a historical case study is that the exercise participants ought to remain unaware of what the solution was to the conflict under study. For Eritreans and Ethiopians facing their border dispute in the late 1990s, for example, the historical conflict between Finland and Sweden over the status of the Åland Islands in the 1910s and 1920s was likely to be an unfamiliar event. The procedure of creative envisioning applied to contemporaneous case studies would have been transferable in principle to their attempt to reflect on the unfamiliar Åland dispute. On completing a thorough envisioning process, an important supplementary dimension of the exercise would have been introduced to the participants still grappling with inevitable uncertainties surrounding their proposed solutions to the unfamiliar conflict; the information to be added would have concerned, for example, how the

Finnish and Swedish had actually resolved the conflict through the arbitration decision of 1921 under the League of Nations and how their peace had been kept unbroken ever since despite the political turbulence that had swept the region during World War II and the Cold War. The fact that the Westphalian paradigm of modern statehood began to be reconsidered as early as the late 1910s in favor of envisioning cultural, political, and economic functions of state sovereignty would have been evocative for the Eritreans and Ethiopians, regardless of their willingness to consider the Åland model seriously in their political conscious. A similar exercise using the Åland Islands question or other analogous cases of "joint sovereignty" could have been used to stimulate dialogues on such recent contexts as the Peru–Ecuador border dispute and the Japanese–Russian conflict over the Kurile Islands.

Third, a *hypothetical case study* provides an opportunity to reflect on a hypothetical conflict scenario that integrates theoretically useful lessons drawn from two or more actual conflicts, contemporaneous or historical, or a combination of both. Exercises of this kind have already been popularized in the form of simulations, used commonly as an experimental research method and as a method of experiential learning. Depending on the needs and circumstances of exercise participants, a hypothetical scenario needs to be designed in such a way as to enable them to retain some level of emotional detachment from it, for example, by making sure not to incorporate the participants' own on-going conflicts and easily recognizable markers thereof. It is also important not to reveal how the conflicts embedded in the hypothetical scenario have actually been resolved, in order to prevent the participants from being predisposed toward thinking in line with what has already happened in empirical reality. Information control will remain essential until the participants complete their envisioning process on their own.

At the same time, subject matters covered by the hypothetical scenario must be unambiguously relevant to the shared concerns of the participants so that they can draw potentially transferable lessons from the exercise. For example, to tailor a hypothetical case study for Japanese and Russian stakeholders involved in the Kurile Islands dispute, potentially useful aspects of the historical Åland dispute and the contemporary Peru–Ecuador conflict may be selected and integrated for the purpose of designing a new conflict scenario. In the hypothetical conflict between countries A and B, surrounded by their neighbors C, D, E, and others, reference to a disputed territory in their border area would make the question of sovereignty explicit. Such reference would therefore appeal unambiguously to the participants' shared concern, albeit in general conceptual terms.

In addition to introducing general subjects of common concern, one can purposefully incorporate into the scenario suggestive (and perhaps unexplored) possibilities that are potentially applicable to the Kurile Islands dispute. In this particular instance, suggestive possibilities may be derived from, for example, the multifaceted understanding of sovereignty's functions in Åland and the binational ecological park established in the Peru–Ecuador border zone with the help of international monitoring systems. These suggestive ideas may form part of the initial script of the hypothetical scenario for the exercise, or alternatively they may be introduced in the context of a debriefing and deeper dialogue after the exercise participants have completed their envisioning process on their own. Irrespective of these procedural details, the key to the hypothetical case study method is the value of introducing into the participants' cognitive space what they might not have thought about on their own, as well as what might help them discover their systemic entrenchment by way of recognizing that there *are* alternatives. The use of heuristic tools, ranging from analogizing to conflict paradigm, is expected to help the participants envision such alternatives by activating their creative potential in their own unique ways.

It is parenthetically noted that the conceptual focus of cross-contextual case studies is by no means limited to territorial sovereignty, the subject chosen to illustrate the three types. The nature of issues to be addressed by this method is open to all kinds, from environmental conflict to labor dispute to the initiation of nonviolent civil resistance, so long as useful conflict scenarios can be found for the exercise to meet the twin requirement of unfamiliarity and experiential relevance. Moreover, the use of the cross-contextual case study method is not confined to the state level of analysis, but it is generally applicable to all levels, from micro to mega, and even across different levels of analysis.[1]

For the purpose of theory-building, it is emphasized that the three types of cross-contextual case studies share the same working assumption that the exercise participants' unfamiliarity with a given conflict, be it contemporaneous, historical, or hypothetical, can *substitute* for the unknowability of the future, at least from their subjective and experiential point of view. Because conflict resolution creativity is a social and epistemological process of shaping an unpredictable, unknowable future based on knowable elements of the past and the present, vicarious experiences in resolving unfamiliar conflicts through such carefully designed exercises would help prepare one's mind to explore how to shape unpredictable futures beyond the present reality of conflict at hand. Conceptually, this means that present unfamiliarity generated by this method serves as a theoretical equivalent and approximation of future unpredictability. The suggested theoretical equivalence between unfamiliarity and unpredictability appears to deserve attention, for it provides a potentially useful basis for exploring how creativity can be taught and learned consciously and systematically. This working assumption is also useful for practice and training in conflict prevention, which requires accepting future unpredictability as inevitable but still formulating concrete action to prevent theoretically inferred consequences of inaction from manifesting.

Finally, possible directions of future research activities need mention, in an attempt to refine and expand the use of the cross-contextual case study method. In general terms, more conscious and systematic efforts must be made to generate theoretical knowledge and empirical data that can be used as heuristic starting points and stepping stones, for the explicit purpose of envisioning unseen futures and exploring counterfactual alternatives to the violent past. This means transcending the monolithic, exclusive focus on the past and the present as well as on the empirical, descriptive, and analytical – which is sometimes viewed as a terminal end of social scientific pursuits. To stimulate conflict resolution creativity in practice and pedagogic application, through cross-contextual case studies or other means, more basic research needs to be conducted to discover, compile, and disseminate a greater number of "success stories" that illustrate at least some elements of unconventional viability.[2] It is also suggested that these carefully designed case studies and theoretical reflections shed light on how systemic entrenchments have been discovered and de-entrenched in various epistemological and social contexts of conflict, how practically useful analogies have been built and communicated effectively among key stakeholders, and how conflict workers and parties have come to envision and actualize what they had previously been unable to see in their mind's eye.

Questions for future inquiry

The method of cross-contextual case studies serves as a starting point for brainstorming a wide range of other possible ways in which the working typologies and concepts can be refined and applied. Going beyond the unique focus of this particular method, one may think of at least five areas of further inquiry as especially promising and theoretically evocative. Each of them is briefly outlined.

First, this study has at least indirectly addressed the multifaceted question of justice in its conceptual background. The question of justice has been interwoven throughout the discussion in such terms as ethicality, power asymmetry, and structural violence. However, the relationship between conflict resolution creativity and justice is still to be defined with sufficient clarify, in order to be useful for practitioners grappling with contradicting views of justice and injustice in their local contexts of conflict work. These reflections on the relationship between creativity and justice stimulate questions such as: What kinds of systemic entrenchment sustaining a conflict paradigm should be retained intact and what kinds need to be de-entrenched and transformed for peace? Do all forms of systemic entrenchment need transformation? Or are there any "just" and peace-promoting kinds that need no transformation?

Second, closely related to the question of justice is the nature of value commitment conducive to conflict resolution creativity. Because value commitment requires seeking normative aspirations that may or may not be empirically supported, it inevitably runs the risk of degenerating into extremism, fanaticism, and even political irrelevance. Therefore, an important question is raised: how can one distinguish between the value commitment to sustained peace-making of the revolutionary type (exemplified by satyagraha, at least in a qualified sense) and the fundamentalist commitment to what might lead to anti-peace? From the perspective of a conflict resolution practitioner and analyst, this distinction between generative and degenerative value commitment is far from clear. The ambiguity tends to deepen, especially in the midst of inevitable value contestation characteristic of epoch-making creativity and seismic social change. Assuming that peace is a sustained process of transformative capacity-building, inquiry into this question may be stimulated by asking: What kinds of value commitment enhance parties' capacities for transforming destructive potential of social conflict into constructive relationships, without depriving other parties of their capacities? On the contrary, what kinds of value commitment prevent the parties from envisioning and practicing transformative processes?

Third, conflict resolution creativity unfolds in a dynamic confluence of unconventionality and viability. This working assumption is derived in part from the observation that unconventionality and viability often appear as contradictory requirements, and therefore aspiring toward unconventional visions tends to limit the likelihood of their social and epistemological appeal to the given context of conflict work. An important question surfaces: How can one find an acceptable and sustainable balance between unconventionality and viability when envisioning an alternative reality to the conflict at hand? Because unconventional viability is a dynamic, ever-evolving communal experience, the balance has to be conceptualized in terms of a dynamic process, that is, a meta-equilibrium of kind.

One of the potentially useful ways of conceptualizing and operationalizing such a balance is to hypothesize an adequate level of "carrying capacity" that may exist in a given social and epistemological context of inter-group conflict. For the present purpose, carrying capacity is defined as the readiness in a given context of intra- and inter-communal relations for appreciating, accommodating, and applying what may appear to be unconventional yet potentially viable visions for resolving the conflict at hand. In highly speculative terms, one may infer from the case studies conducted in this inquiry that social factors conducive to generating carrying capacities include, but are not limited to:

- a shared experiential basis on which to build constructive analogies;
- sustained leadership willing to take risks;
- epistemological congruency between local meaning-making patterns and newly introduced visions for creative change;
- simplicity and communicability of the unconventional visions under consideration;
- openness of the social structures and institutions in place;
- availability of resources, including time to assimilate and actualize the suggested unconventional change.

Given this conceptual background, an important question is raised for future inquiry and applied practice: How can conflict workers and parties assess the nature and level of carrying capacity in a given social and epistemological context of inter-group conflict in which they seek to envision and actualize alternative realities?

Fourth, this study has explored conflict resolution creativity primarily at the conscious level, with emphasis on agency-led, bottom-up processes of social change. If the scope of inquiry is expanded to bring the unconscious to the foreground of attention, as Freud did in his analysis of dreams and fantasies, what additional insights into conflict resolution creativity might be generated? Of particular interest is whether and how the study of the *collective* unconscious sheds light on social and epistemological processes of constructive creation, not merely individual creation in which Freud and his contemporaries were primarily interested. This line of questioning is expected to fruitfully supplement the study of the collective unconscious undertaken by Vamik Volkan and his colleagues, who have looked primarily into destructive processes of inter-group conflict, but not constructive, creative ones.

Fifth and final, the present inquiry has purposely kept the role of culture in the background, in order to assure the manageability of data collection and analysis. Yet the working propositions derived from the case studies highlight the essential role of culture, for these propositions illustrate diverse patterns and processes of meaning-making within and across particular social and epistemological contexts of inter-subjectivity. For example, the case study of satyagraha has revealed that the creative social transformation attempted by the Indian community leaders emerged in the confluence and confrontation of divergent meaning-making patterns, including the white supremacists' adherence to colonial instrumentalism and the Indians' sacrificial commitment to life's irreducible essentials. Questions that may stimulate this line of reasoning include: How do cultural influences shape the ways in which unconventionality and viability merge in confluence, evolve over time, and come to be accepted or rejected in a given local context of inter-group conflict? How might creative processes emerge and evolve for conflict resolution when social groups with distinct cultural backgrounds are interlocked in conflict, with each seeking a way out from its own cultural standpoint? What roles can a conflict worker play in facilitating resolution processes between distinct cultural communities, by appeal to such heuristic tools and concepts as value commitment, analogizing, interdependent origination, and conflict paradigm? And importantly, how does the researcher's own cultural lenses and unarticulated patterns of meaning-making come to be reflected in his or her inquiry into conflict resolution creativity?

While these five questions exemplify ways in which the horizon of creativity research can be expanded for conflict resolution, the common core of these lines of inquiry lies in the commitment to building theories about how consciously and systematically one can create and multiply rare empirical phenomena, as well as ideal phenomena yet to be realized, that are conducive to overcoming violence and building peace. Such a vision of inquiry is distinct from, yet supplementary to, the primary focus of social scientific research that seeks to identify regularities and patterns underlying observable empirical realities.

If certain types of empirical reality, such as compelling examples of outcome creativity and transformation of entrenched conflict paradigms, are urgently needed for the fulfillment of human and social potential but there appears to be little historical precedent to support the viability of such a vision, social scientific pursuits may be directed consciously toward creating ways to bring the vision into fruition. Such a proactive approach to inquiry is what makes peace research a unique discipline, for it promotes a mode of social scientific thinking with an explicit value commitment to overcoming violence and building peace. This vision calls for theory-building that consciously and systematically guides practical action, by way of exploring unexplored pathways to conflict resolution. In the paucity of empirical data and precedent to substantiate the likelihood of success, theory becomes a principal guide to action, as in the case of satyagraha's origination.

Having witnessed how the last century of mass violence was slated into another century of tension and destruction, with the emerging discourse of the "war on terror" prevailing in the US and elsewhere, one can hardly overemphasize this purposive, creative function of social science, with the explicit value commitment to overcoming violence of all forms, direct, structural, and cultural. Lessons learned from numerous events of mass violence in the last century – from the Holocaust under Nazism to the Rwandan genocide, to the ethnic cleansing in the Balkans – accentuate the generative role of social science in general and peace research in particular. It is hoped that the preliminary attempts made in this study at articulating hypotheses on such themes as the longitudinal nature of creativity, interdependent origination, and conflict paradigms will become a constructive step toward articulating guideposts for effective action. Concerted efforts are urgently needed to advance these visions of both reflective and proactive social science.

Appendix
Questionnaire for researcher-practitioner interviews

Part 1: mandatory questions

The following eight questions were asked to all interviewees regardless of the nature of the conflict resolution episodes they chose to discuss.

1. **Career profile**: Please briefly describe the nature of your conflict resolution (or peace-building) practice, including the types of conflicts (or social settings) you focus on, the institution(s) you work with, the roles you play, and the geographic focus you may have.
2. **Conceptual definition**: In general terms, what is your understanding of creativity for conflict resolution? How do you define it?
3. **Case description**: Considering your extensive professional experience, what has been the most creative procedure and/or substantive outcome of inter-group conflict resolution that you have developed, experienced, or otherwise observed closely? (*If the interviewee is known to have created and implemented a particular approach or solution, the researcher may prompt him or her to use the experience to answer the following questions.*) The example you provide does not need to be an exemplary "successful" episode so long as you believe you can draw meaningful lessons from it. However, please indicate a process and/or outcome that you know very intimately because I will shortly ask you several follow-up questions specifically on the subject. To describe the experience of your choice, please first provide a brief description of the inter-group conflict, including its geographic scope and time period, the major parties and issues involved, and the role(s) you played. Second, please outline the creative procedure and/or resolution outcome applied in the context.
4. **Justification for case selection**: Concerning the example that you have just provided, why do you think the procedure and/or resolution outcome should be considered creative?

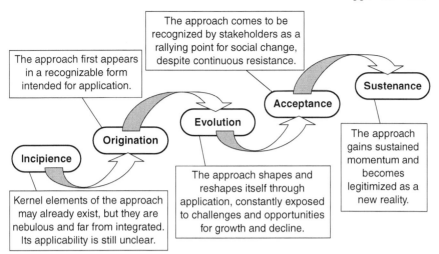

5. **Origination – enabling factors**: Please describe how the creative procedure and/or resolution outcome first appeared. For example, what social and individual factors enabled or facilitated the process to emerge?
6. **Origination – limiting factors**: On the other hand, were there any social and individual factors working against the creative procedure and/or resolution outcome to emerge? If yes, what were the limiting factors?
7. **Incipience**: Before the creative procedure and/or resolution outcome first appeared as a clearly recognizable form of social influence, had there been any precursor(s) to it? If yes, how do you characterize the precursors? For example, where had they been in store, under whose initiatives, and for how long? Or in fact, had the creative initiative first appeared without any precursors to speak of?
8. **Evolution**: Please describe in more detail how the creative procedure and/or resolution outcome evolved over time after it first appeared. For example, how did it grow and spread, or decline and contract in influence? How was it shaped and reshaped by other social forces, ideas, and/or movements? What were the enabling and limiting factors, respectively, for the procedure and/or resolution outcome to evolve over time?

Part 2: optional questions

The remaining questions were asked depending on the nature of the episodes selected. When the creative initiatives failed to evolve soon after the origination, questions on acceptance and sustenance were omitted. In addition, if answers to some of the theoretical questions (11 to 16) were already included in the interviewees' views expressed up to this point, they were omitted to avoid duplication.

9. **Acceptance**: Considering the way the creative process and/or resolution outcome evolved, how do you characterize the extent to which the initiative

was subsequently accepted or rejected by its immediate stakeholders? How about the extent of acceptance or rejection by those other than the immediate stakeholders in a much broader social context? On what ground do you think your assessment of acceptance or rejection is justified?

10 **Sustenance**: Did the creative procedure and/or resolution outcome gain sustained momentum and come to be well anchored over time in the socio-political context? (Depending on the interviewee's assessment of the conflict, modify this question for clarity by adding "even after the initiative gained a high level of social acceptance?" and/or "even after the conflict ceased to escalate.") To what extent did it become, or fail to become, part of a new social reality with sustained momentum? What social and individual factors sustained, or failed to sustain, the momentum over time? How and with what results? Why did the procedure and/or resolution outcome come to gain, or fail to gain, sustained momentum, considering both enabling and limiting factors at work?

11 **Generalizability of insights**: Speaking in more general terms and going beyond the particular conflict episode that you have just described, what factors do you think enable or hinder the early preparatory process (incipience), origination, evolution, acceptance, and sustenance of creative procedures and/or substantive outcomes for resolving inter-group conflicts? If appropriate, please add new insights to your earlier comments on the conflict episode. In addition or alternatively, please summarize and highlight the most important insights you have already described about enabling and limiting factors for conflict resolution creativity.

12 **Evaluating the framework of research under consideration (1)**: As illustrated by the five-phase model you have seen earlier, these interview questions are based on the working assumption that creativity for conflict resolution is an on-going social process involving an early preparatory process (termed *incipience*), *origination*, *evolution*, *acceptance*, and *sustenance*. In your view, to what extent are these five phases useful to understand creativity in conflict resolution and peace-building? If you find these phases not so useful, how would you like to modify them, or what alternative ways do you suggest to characterize the social process of conflict resolution creativity?

13 **Evaluating the framework of research under consideration (2)**: Another important assumption for this study is the idea of *paradigm shift*. More specifically, a creative process and/or resolution outcome is often considered *anomalous* by many stakeholders, particularly when the idea first appears. The anomaly is recognized as such partly because a pervasive paradigm or mode of thinking and social interaction discourages such an unfamiliar process to emerge. In your view, to what extent is this assumption applicable and useful to characterize creativity for conflict resolution? Is the awareness of a prevailing paradigm a compulsory prerequisite to a creative procedure and/or outcome for resolving inter-group conflict? Or does conflict resolution creativity emerge regardless of people's awareness of a prevailing paradigm? Please state your position on this debate and explain.

14 **Evaluating the framework of research under consideration (3)**: If you find the concept of paradigm not so useful to frame the understanding of creativity in conflict resolution, what alternative assumption(s) can be used?
15 **Eliciting insights for typology development (1)**: The present research project explores both process and outcome creativity; the former is defined as creativity used to devise the means by which to resolve conflict and the latter as creativity demonstrated in the substance of resolution outcomes. The example of creativity you discussed contains many elements of process or outcome creativity. (Choose one as appropriate. Then briefly give an example of the other type, referring to the Åland Islands question or satyagraha.) Do you think these two types of creativity differ in terms of the ways of thinking and social interaction involved? If so, how?
16 **Eliciting insights for typology development (2)**: This study also aims to explore conflict resolution creativity spearheaded by prominent individuals or "agents" (like M. K. Gandhi in satyagraha), on the one hand, and ones facilitated by social institutions or "systems" (like the League of Nations in the Åland Islands question), on the other. First, do you think this distinction is useful to understand conflict resolution creativity? Why or why not? Second, if you think this distinction is useful, do you see any difference between these two types in terms of the ways of thinking and social interaction involved? If so, how?
17 **Supplementary comments**: Is there anything else that I should have asked but I have not, in order for me to fully understand your views on creativity for conflict resolution?

Notes

1 Introduction: in search of points of departure and stepping stones

1 Cropley (1999) reviews contemporary literature on creativity research and identifies novelty, relevance, effectiveness, and ethicality as key elements of creativity in general terms. Although this framework of thinking offered one of the starting points at an early stage of the present inquiry, subsequent findings have helped to refine it substantially, generating the working definition described here.
2 Violence means harming and hurting the body, mind, and/or spirit. Direct violence is the kind of violence exercised by an actor or actors inflicting its harmful effect on a particular recipient or recipients. Structural violence is indirect violence. It is inflicted by political repression and economic exploitation, where the dichotomy between victims and victimizers is blurred, unlike in direct violence. See Galtung (1996).
3 In creativity research, the domain is defined as "a set of practices associated with an area of knowledge" (Gardner 1994: 152).
4 See Chapter 3 on paradigms.
5 Whether there exists a field of conflict resolution, comparable to other well-established traditional disciplines, is a question that needs answering on a different occasion. Yet controversies over this question are secondary in importance for the purpose of defining the scope of the present research.
6 LeBaron (2002) offers useful insights to conceptualize this point.
7 Inferred from Freud (1958), Jung (1964), Erikson (1969), and Winnicott (1953), among other contemporary psychoanalysts.
8 Reflecting on his first unofficial problem-solving workshop on the Indonesia–Malaysia–Singapore conflict in the mid-1960s, which became the first of what is today known as "Second-Track" dialogues, John Burton, a former Australian diplomat and a pioneering scholar-practitioner of conflict resolution, is explicit about the fact that he had already held an image of his untested method in mind and had been consciously looking for a conflict where his method could be "tested" with good chances of success. (See Chapter 2 for the episode of creativity offered by Burton.) Although Burton's and other practitioners' episodes discussed in this study do not necessarily reveal their preconscious, one can infer, from their explicit value judgments, that part of their resolution options had been building up for some time before they found conflicts as opportunities for applied practice.
9 These preparatory activities lasted from January 2003 till March 2004, followed by a full-blown study that came to a completion in March 2005.
10 Some of the findings from these interviews have already been summarized in the discussion on artistic and scientific creativity, in the preceding section on the scope of the inquiry.

11 Inspired by the author's interview with Ambassador John McDonald at the Institute for Multi-Track Diplomacy (IMTD) on June 6, 2003 in Arlington, Virginia.
12 A substantial revision to the five-phase model will be suggested in Chapter 3, especially in the section theorizing the longitudinal nature of creativity, based on the empirical findings that have emerged from data collection and analysis.
13 Parenthetically, there was one more working typology, exemplar-based and rule-based (or principle-based) creativity, which was suggested initially to guide the data collection process. Exemplar-based creativity is derived from concrete examples for creative social change, and rule-based (or principle-based) creativity by abstract principles. In the course of data collection and analysis, it was decided to incorporate this typology and related findings into the discussion on the other three working concepts, particularly paradigm shifts. On the other hand, the data analysis process resulted in the development of an additional typology, one that compares creativity exercised by conflict parties, intermediaries, and other types of actors playing the two functions at the same time. This additional typology will be elaborated later in Chapter 2.
14 The use of ideal types is inspired by Weiss (2002).
15 The summary of the Åland Islands question is based on Barrons (1968) and Mannerheim (1954).
16 The summary of the first satyagraha campaign is based on Gandhi (1928) and Swan (1985).
17 This description is meant to reflect the general nature of the campaign in broad outline. A more detailed description, including its rises and falls, will be presented in Chapter 4.
18 A large-N case study systematically compares a large number of cases, often selected as a sample of a larger universe of relevant phenomena, with the view toward explaining potentially generalizable principles and patterns related to the phenomena.
19 Clark (2002), particularly its introductory chapter on the Western worldview, offers a useful insight into the "atomizing" nature in knowledge construction in general and scientific thinking in particular.
20 Lijphart (1971) distinguishes between six types of case study methods: atheoretical, interpretive, hypothesis-generating, theory-confirming, theory-infirming, and deviant. Given Lijphart's typology, the first phase of this study is considered hypothesis-generating in nature and the second phase interpretive, for the second phase seeks to illustrate satyagraha through the interpretive lenses provided by the working hypotheses generated by the first phase.

2 Exploration: sixteen episodes of creativity

1 The US–Vietnam War (interviewee Richard Falk), an inter-racial conflict in Tajikistan (Majid Tehranian), and the Indonesia–Malaysia–Singapore conflict (John Burton) are categorized as Asian cases. This ad hoc categorization scheme is used only for the present purpose of overview, and it does not affect the rest of the analysis.
2 Likewise for the present purpose, the Estonian–Russian conflict (interviewee Vamik Volkan), the Helsinki process (Klaus Törnudd), and the Cyprus conflict (Louise Diamond) are categorized as European cases.
3 Parenthetically, as demonstrated throughout the analysis to follow, the broad range of cases under study has offered a useful empirical basis for exploratory comparative analysis, which has helped, by way of theoretical inference, to conceptualize the kinds of creativity that *fail* to be illustrated by any of the sixteen cases.
4 The term "episode" is used interchangeably with "case" in this study. The latter is defined earlier in the section describing the overall design of the study.
5 Various insights derived from Emerson *et al.* (1995), LeCompte and Schensul (1999), Robson (1993), Ryan and Bernard (2000), Stake (2000), and Vaughan (1986; 1992) informed the qualitative method of data operationalization and analysis.

6 Some of the interviewees offered only limited background information about the conflicts that they chose to discuss. To contextualize their conflict resolution episodes meaningfully, the author supplemented them with brief descriptions of the conflicts based on relevant literature whenever necessary. In selecting the supplementary sources, priority was given to the publications written or recommended by the interviewees themselves in order to reflect their views as accurately as possible.
7 This aspect of the theory-building exercise will be discussed in Chapter 3.
8 Question 4 (justification for case selection) in the Questionnaire for Researcher-Practitioner Interviews in the appendix.
9 These categories and their definitions will be presented in Chapter 3.
10 Parenthetically, it is noted that several schemes of categorization were devised as possible alternatives. They include levels of analysis of the conflicts (micro, meso, macro, and mega) and Multi-Track channels of conflict resolution practice (governments, NGOs, activism, research–training–education, and others described by Diamond and McDonald (1996)). But none of these alternatives offered a useful typology in which the sixteen cases would spread reasonably across categories.
11 For Falk, his opponent was the US government that he was trying to influence as a representative of the American peace movements and as a legal specialist who was entrusted by the North Vietnamese leaders to deliver their conflict settlement proposal to their US counterpart.
12 Johnston was a Visiting Professor of Conflict Resolution at George Mason University in Virginia at the point of the interview (January 2004). She is currently the Director of the Center for Conflict Management at Kennesaw State University in Georgia, USA.
13 The content of the North Vietnamese proposal of 1968 was not mentioned in the author's interview with Falk. The summary description here is based on Gene Roberts, "New anti-government alliance fails to stir public support in South Vietnam," *New York Times*, July 12, 1968 and Hedrick Smith, "U.S. visitor to North says group might be focus of a postwar regime," *New York Times*, July 9, 1968.
14 The content of the 1972 US–North Vietnam agreement and its possible consequences in 1973 were not mentioned in the author's interview with Falk. The summary description here is based on Ciment (1999: 1252–63).
15 The description of the accord is based on Goldschmidt (2002: 400) to supplement the interview.
16 The summary description of the economic cooperation plan was added by the author and reviewed by the interviewee for accuracy.
17 Pundak's view echoes that of Mary Clark, a biologist, human nature theorist, and conflict researcher, who defines creativity in conflict resolution as "breaking boundaries without causing crises." Clark was interviewed by phone on March 20, 2004.
18 This is an important point to be elaborated later in a distinctly different context of conflict resolution creativity – the emergence of satyagraha in South Africa, led by Gandhi and other Indian community leaders, analyzed in Chapter 4.
19 In the Peru–Ecuador conflict, Galtung offered consultation only to the Ecuadorian side upon its invitation. However, as will be explained more fully later, both the method of his intervention and the content of his advice (namely, the establishment of a Peru–Ecuador binational park) are considered impartial because the exact same proposal could have been offered to the Peruvian side given the right conditions. This inference is supported by the observation that in a number of analogous contexts of his conflict work during the past decades, Galtung has been consistent in his effort to play the role of an intermediary, holding a dialogue with one conflict party at a time and trying to meet with all sides of the conflict. Galtung's method of conflict work will be elaborated later.
20 This compares to the view of another interviewee, Johan Galtung, who argues that the more firmly people's expectations are set about the social structure and culture in

which they try to be creative, the more room they can find to conceptualize, if not to practice, creative alternatives to the status quo.
21 The notion of contingency-based practice for creativity was suggested by Professor Wallace Warfield, an experienced practitioner based at George Mason University's Institute for Conflict Analysis and Resolution (ICAR), with expertise in gang violence, racial conflicts, and other issues in American society. The interview with Warfield was held on January 16, 2004 in Fairfax, Virginia.
22 This working definition of creativity is the author's recapitulation of Burton's ideas expressed in the interview and in his writing. Burton had been suffering from ill health during the period of the author's correspondence with him in 2003–4, and some interpretive work was necessary and inevitable on the points that he was unable to elaborate at length. To write this section, the author drew heavily on Burton's writings, particularly his 1966 monograph *A Case Study in the Application of International Theory: Indonesia–Malaysia–Singapore*. The author checked the accuracy of his interpretations through correspondence with Burton in preparation for this case study.
23 Mitchell (2000) carried out an in-depth study of Burton's involvement in the conflict between the three countries. The description of the conflict, which was not detailed by Burton in the interview, is supplemented by Mitchell.
24 As early as January 1966, immediately after the first workshop, Burton had in mind some concrete suggestions for assuring the parties' security needs, as presented in his reflection paper. These suggestions include: developing a self-sustained mechanism for Malaysian self-defense; phasing out foreign bases, followed by a joint US–UK declaration for freeing the Malaysia–Singapore–Indonesia region from future foreign interventions; and establishing a regional security agreement intended to reassure Singapore's safety. The extent to which these and other possible resolution options generated by Burton and others were reflected in the final agreements in the summer of 1966 to formally end the conflict is still to be explored.
25 Most notably Johan Galtung, who maintains that in-depth analysis may reveal the past but creative images of the future come from, inter alia, the capacity to envision an alternative reality, but not necessarily from the knowledge of "data" about what has already happened. See the analysis of Galtung's intervention in the Peru–Ecuador conflict that follows.
26 Quoted from Burton's reflections written on the occasion of launching David Dunn's book, *From Power Politics to Conflict Resolution: The Work of John Burton* in June 2004 in Canberra, Australia. Burton shared these thoughts with the author with the intent of supplementing the interview for the present study.
27 This description is drawn from the same source as above.
28 Kelman (1997: 212) describes his method as a process where politically influential participants from both or all sides of the conflict meet

> in private, unofficial, academically based, problem-solving workshops designed to enable the parties to explore each other's perspective, generate joint ideas for mutually satisfactory solutions to their conflict, and transfer insights and ideas derived from their interaction into the policy process.

29 The PLO was formed in Cairo in 1964.
30 Insights gained from an interview with Susan Shields at George Mason University in Fairfax, Virginia on June 2, 2004. Shields is internationally renowned as a modern ballet dancer and choreographer.
31 This summary of the social background of the Estonian project is based on Volkan (1997).
32 The summary is based on Winnicott (1953) and the review written by Mitchell and Black (1995).
33 Western psychologists studying *individual* creativity place much emphasis on subjects of this type. While the inquiry into creativity, fantasies, dreams, and the unconscious

by such influential researchers as Sigmund Freud (1958) and Carl Jung (1964) forms an important part of the general theoretical background of this study, a fuller exploration of these psychoanalytic subjects in the context of *inter-group* conflict resolution has to be attempted on another occasion.
34 Examples of public mobilization activities in Cyprus are discussed in Diamond and Fisher (1995: 292–3).
35 Methodologically, the Helsinki process was pre-selected as a relevant case study subject by the present author based on his preliminary studies. Törnudd, as a renowned political scientist and long-term senior diplomat, was subsequently identified as an interviewee known to have substantial firsthand experience in the Helsinki process.
36 The procedural features of the Helsinki process described here were summarized by the author based on Freeman (1991: 58–9). The accuracy of this description was confirmed by Törnudd.
37 In theory, however, the consensus-based mechanism for decision-making meant that all participating states, from the superpowers to micro states, were *equally* entitled to veto anything on the agenda, as pointed out by Törnudd. Thus an element of unconventionality is found in the adherence to procedural equality among the participating states, but not necessarily to the absence of veto in decision-making.
38 A brochure titled *TRANSCEND: A Philosophy of Peace and Development*, the year and place of publication unknown.
39 Over the years, Galtung has worked extensively on the subject of creativity in conflict work. This section goes into some depth and length to capture not only what he discussed in the interview, but also his extensive writings related directly to the issues raised in the interview.
40 Galtung reviewed an earlier version of this case study, including the supplementary description of the Peru–Ecuador conflict inserted by the author. In the author's follow-up telephone interview with him on November 26, 2004, Galtung pointed out that details of what had happened in the history of the conflict were nearly irrelevant to the actual process of devising the resolution outcome. In his view, the details described here belong to the *past* but creativity for transforming the conflict concerns how to create a *future*; these details of the past did not affect the way he came up with the resolution option. This point is worth noting to illustrate Galtung's notion of time as a basis for creative transcendence. Therefore it is emphasized that the present description of the conflict reflects the author's, not Galtung's.
41 A more detailed ten-point plan is described by Galtung *et al.* (2002: 264–5).
42 His ten-point proposal is laid out in Galtung *et al.* (2002: 264–5).
43 See Galtung *et al.* (2002: 319) for more examples.
44 The information about Thor Magnusson's presidential campaign in Iceland is drawn from a TRANSCEND email circulation dated June 1, 2004, sent by co-director Dietrich Fischer. Magnusson's website is: www.althing.us.
45 A TRANSCEND circular email dated June 10, 2004, sent by Dietrich Fischer.
46 This subject is discussed in greater detail in Galtung (1977), "Science as invariance-seeking and invariance-breaking activity," and in Galtung (1998), which offers practical advice to conflict workers.
47 C. R. Mitchell's interview with one of the facilitators in London on November 20, 1987.
48 John Smith (a pseudonym adopted for the anonymous interviewee introduced earlier) distinguishes between intermediaries' and conflict parties' creativity based on his extensive experience as a labor mediator. He observes that representatives in labor–management negotiations tend to refrain from presenting creative resolution options early in the process for fear that their constituents criticize them as too compromising and weak. Experienced labor mediators, too, avoid sharing their best and most creative ideas with the negotiators for fear that the negotiators might reject them simply to demonstrate their firmness to their constituents and to their opponents.

3 Theory-building: a comparative case analysis for identifying emerging themes and building on enduring concepts

1 The methodology of comparative analysis is described at the beginning of Chapter 2.
2 See the analysis of the interview with Galtung in Chapter 2 for details.
3 Other cases illustrating value commitment include Awad (nonviolent resistance as an alternative to silent obedience), Törnudd (the Finnish aspiration for neutrality in the context of the East–West tension), and Osman (a joint appeal through inter-organizational unity instead of separate appeals).
4 Parenthetically there appears to be a trend in Western creativity research, spearheaded mostly by psychologists interested in art and science, to conceptualize creativity in terms of dialectical tension between two opposing psychological tendencies within the person. The author's thesis on principled flexibility is derived from the episodes under study but echoes this trend. Examples of this type of theory-building effort include insights contained in the flow theory of Csikszentmihalyi (1996) and the Janusian process of Rothenberg (1999).
5 Based on the discoveries made in this study, the term "agency" is replaced by "element." The latter connotes either individuals or collectivities, depending on the level of analysis where a "system" is conceptualized. A more detailed explanation will be offered in the section on the system–element link that follows.
6 As a psychoanalyst studying conflicts involving large political groups, Volkan observes that the model captures logical reasoning in negotiation and conflict resolution but fails to account for the unconscious. He argues that a rational model of this kind is not useful when societies are regressed and traumatized. Because the present study addresses the conscious behavior and perceptions as a foreground of creative practice and the subconscious and unconscious as its background, Volkan's criticism, though well taken, has to be dealt with on future occasions of inquiry. Other interviewees' criticisms and suggestions fall within the scope of the study and inform the discussion throughout this section.
7 The relationship between conflict resolution creativity and the levels of analysis will be more fully explored later in this chapter.
8 Hunt (1990) also mentions that similar civil disobedience movements were organized, for example, in 1919 by the predecessor of the African National Congress (ANC). But he observes that their political and epistemological link to satyagraha of the Gandhian type is still to be established empirically.
9 Similarity is a relative concept and has to be understood in a given local context of collective subjectivity. For the present purpose, it is sufficient to point out that a perception of similarity is derived from analogizing, defined and elaborated earlier in Chapter 3.
10 Questions for future inquiry include: What counts as creativity and creation within the epistemic community of conflict resolution scholars and practitioners, broadly defined? How does creativity emerge and evolve within the field? Thomas Kuhn's theory of scientific revolutions and paradigm shifts appears to offer a promising starting point of inquiry, and will be discussed more thoroughly later in Chapter 3.
11 Discussed in the analysis of Galtung's episode.
12 The concept of dis-embedding/re-embedding is introduced in Johan Galtung and Finn Tschudi's essay "Crafting Peace: on the psychology of the TRANSCEND Approach" in Galtung *et al.* (2002).
13 See Henderson's episode, for example.
14 Wertheimer (1945), discussed by Emery commenting on Burton's first problem-solving workshop.
15 The author's working thesis on reshaping, particularly in the context of cross-cultural conflict work, is found in Arai (2006).
16 Nor was Burton as an impartial consultant expected to reformulate the conflict substantively, especially before entering a dialogue with the parties. In this particular

instance, therefore, the very nature of process creativity made the consultants, if not the conflict parties, refrain from proposing possible acts of outcome creativity. The emerging norm of impartiality among professional conflict workers, especially those trained in the Western academic and professional contexts, has important implications for their awareness, or lack thereof, of the distinction between process and outcome creativity. This subject will be elaborated later in Chapter 3.
17 Parenthetically the method, then, gradually becomes conventional in the eyes of its regular users, although not necessary for conflict parties unfamiliar with it. The evolution of what was once an act of process creativity continues to be considered unconventional across historical and geographic contexts. However, this observation is *not* meant to suggest that the perception of process creativity in a given context of conflict is necessary or desirable for conflict resolution.
18 Quoted from the author's interview with Johan Galtung on April 3, 2004 in Manassas, Virginia.
19 In social science, the term "element" is often used interchangeably with "unit" and "agent", and "system" with "whole". The terms *system* and *element* are used in this inquiry because they describe the concepts under study most unambiguously.
20 An overview of this debate is presented in Hollis and Smith (1991).
21 On the function of democracy, democratic peace theorists build their argument in line with this thesis, demonstrating the role of civic norms and institutions as a sustained basis for managing contradictions within states and between them. See Brown *et al.* (1999).
22 On this point, the author is indebted to the insights drawn from his conversations with Manulani Aluli Meyer, a long-term *ho'oponopono* facilitator and professor of education at the University of Hawaii, Hilo and Abdullahi Said Osman, former Somali Ambassador to the UN.
23 The author acknowledges Ambassador Klaus Törnudd's valuable comments and constructive criticisms on the earlier version of this working hypothesis, as well as on his interpretation of the Helsinki process, which will be reflected in the discussion that follows.
24 This flexible and relative nature of the levels-of-analysis question is discussed earlier in the present chapter, in relation to the longitudinal nature of creativity. This discussion is applicable to conflict paradigms as well.
25 Volkan (2004) discusses these group processes in detail.
26 Parenthetically entrenched perspectives, codes of behavior, and relational and structural inertia parallel the three interrelated dimensions of conflict, namely, attitude, behavior, and contradiction, suggested by Galtung (1996: 70–3).
27 It is this perception, based on the premise of regularity inherent in social conflict, that enables parties, intermediaries, and observers to form a *prognosis*. Contemporary news reports on social conflicts are filled with prognostic comments of this kind. This perception and its underlying premise also make *counterfactual* analysis possible when interventions bring about a new reality as an alternative to what could have happened should the regularity remain unaltered. Thus the thesis under consideration has important implications for the practice of conflict prevention.
28 Territoriality is entrenched in the traditional sense of Westphalian statehood, where the livelihood of political collectivities is fixed to a bounded territory. Trans-territoriality has begun to emerge with the political, economic, and social integration of the European Union. Supra-territoriality is illustrated by homogenizing effects of globalization, most notably in instantaneous electronic communication, including its audiovisual application to the media. Non-territoriality is most salient when sovereignty is understood as a multifaceted political function, detachable – at least to a limited extent – from traditional territoriality, as in the Swedish-speaking autonomous region of Åland within the Finnish territory sustaining a cultural, political, and economic coexistence over the past three generations.

29 To conceptualize interpersonal and inter-group relationships, the simplest type of relational structure is A's relationship to B, with A and B defined as comparable entities. At a more complex level, relationships are multi-layered and interwoven, thus structured, as in hierarchical organizations. Relational structures grow significantly more complex because patterns of social interaction become multi-layered and multi-directional. Therefore this third type of heuristic pointer is meant to encompass a whole range of relationships and their imaginable structured forms, limited only by the human capacity to hold such ideas in mind without causing cognitive overload.

30 Asked to recall analogous experiences that might have stimulated her thinking, Johnston described the way she as a health professional helped a diabetic woman who could not read. When Johnston visited the woman's house, she realized that the woman had many different colors of nail polish. With the woman's permission, she marked food items and measuring cups with various colors of nail polish. That way the woman could remember that cereals should be eaten in half a cup each time, for the cereal box and the measuring cup were both marked with lavender nail polish. Johnston reflects that the common thread connecting this and other similar experiences is the search for something or someone that one can identify with and understand easily. Insights obtained through correspondence with Johnston on February 7, 2004.

31 In the interview, as in his writings in 1977 and 2004 on related subjects, Galtung emphasized the use of not only the positive transcendence analogous to the Hegelian synthesis (for example, meeting *both* Peru's *and* Ecuador's goals) but also the negative transcendence analogous to Hegel's "negation of the negation" (for example, meeting *neither* Peru's *nor* Ecuador's goals). Articulating both kinds of transcendence and exploring their implications in a given empirical reality appear helpful for discovering entrenched perspectives (for example, linearity of demarcation) and opening up alternative realities (for example, a binational zone for a positive transcendence and a UN-sponsored temporary trusteeship for a negative transcendence). The temporal, spatial, and relational types of heuristic pointers are automatically mobilized and integrated when following these reasoning processes.

4 Illustration: a case study of the first satyagraha campaign in South Africa from 1906 to 1914

1 According to Iyer (1973), satyagraha may also be translated as a relentless search for truth, a determination to reach truth, truth-force, and soul-force.
2 His family name, "Gandhi," literally means "grocer."
3 A temple of the Vaishnava faith tradition.
4 Musalman and Parsi refer to Muslim and Zoroastrian, respectively.
5 See Hunt (1978) for an in-depth analysis of Gandhi's experience in London and its impact on his life and work.
6 See Swan (1985). It is parenthetically noted that NIC's stated objectives were much broader than the advancement of Natal-based Indian merchants' interests. For example, its constitution stipulated the founders' explicit commitment to helping indentured Indian laborers in South Africa as well as the poor and helpless in general. The tension between Gujarati merchants' commercial interests and Gandhi's growing aspirations to serve less-wealthy Indians of diverse backgrounds will be discussed later, as an important theme in the financial and political dynamics of satyagraha.
7 "Letter to Parsee Rustomjee" dated March 1, 1902 in Gandhi (1960, vol. 3: 226–8).
8 For a more extensive description of the historical conflicts underlying the first satyagraha campaign, literature on Gandhi's South African experience, the British imperial policy in South Africa, Afrikaner nationalism, and a host of other subjects needs to be consulted. Some of the sources that contributed to the present conflict analysis are noted throughout this section, as well as in other sections of this chapter.

9 See, for example, Saunders and Smith (1999) on the British Empire in South Africa during the period under study.
10 Lovell (1956) details the historical tension between the British and Boer and describes how it helped to shape Afrikaner nationalism. Hancock (1958) explains Boers' treks from an economic standpoint.
11 Pachai (1971).
12 An extensive survey of Indian indentured laborers and their profiles is reported in Swan (1985).
13 These statistical figures are cited from Saunders and Smith (1999: 690).
14 Hancock (1962) provides useful insights into European rulers' fear. Empirically their fear was not entirely baseless. As Hunt (1990) points out, Gandhi and other leading satyagrahis were in fact approaching African, Colored, and Chinese leaders in South Africa in an effort to mobilize them for the Indians' nonviolent resistance movement against the newly established Union government. In this case, it is important to note that the South African Native National Congress (SANNC), later renamed the ANC, was formed in 1912, uniting native Africans from different regions for a protest against the Natives' Land Act, a segregationist policy in support of white-based state-making.
15 In 1884, Germany, under the expansionist policy of Bismarck, seized the west coast of Namibia, adjacent to the Cape Colony, to the surprise of many British policymakers. This event, among others, not only aroused the British fear of a possible further expansion by Germany, but also deepened the conviction that South Africa would remain indispensable as a strategic base for maintaining British hegemony. See Saunders and Smith (1999).
16 Insights derived from Isaacs (1975) and Anderson (1991) helped to conceptualize nationalism.
17 These estimates are cited from Saunders and Smith (1999: 617–18).
18 In contemporary African history, the ratio of the Boer death tolls to the entire population of their nation is comparable in magnitude to the 1994 genocide in Rwanda.
19 See Hancock and Poel (1966, vol. 3:139–48) for the speech Smuts delivered on this occasion, containing these and other relevant details. It is particularly noteworthy that when Gandhi systematically mobilized Indian women for the first time in the satyagraha movement in late 1913 for the purpose of restoring their nationalistic, religious honor in relation to marriage issues, Smuts, on his part, remained committed to his attempt to sensitize Afrikaner nationalism and religiosity, albeit with emphasis on reconciliation with the British, not with other racial groups.
20 These figures on the population of Natal in 1893 are cited from Pachai (1971: 19).
21 The 1904 and 1911 census results are found in Thompson (1960: 486). The above figures are approximations of the original numbers. In theory, Asiatics include not only Indians but also other immigrants from Asia, such as Chinese. But in reality, Asiatics in these years were almost entirely Indian.
22 As of 1893, for example, there were approximately 5,500 Indian traders, whose economic status was distinctly different from that of indentured laborers in Natal. See Pachai (1971: 19).
23 See, for example, a series of government investigation reports and anti-Asiatic countermeasures discussed in Pachai (1971).
24 These observations on the psychological orientations of Europeans, particularly those in the ruling class, are derived primarily from the analysis of the letters, many of them confidential, exchanged between Smuts and other senior policymakers in South Africa and Great Britain concerning the Asiatic question between 1907 and 1914. The letters are compiled in Hancock and Poel (1966, vols. 2–3).
25 These European sentiments are reflected in policymakers' correspondence, such as a confidential instruction to Smuts by Lord William Selborne, British High Commissioner for South Africa in 1905–10 and an architect of the Union, concerning the

possibility of the Indian example encouraging the Colored and educated native Africans to follow suit. See Hancock and Poel (1966: 361–6). Also suggestive is the statement in the Union parliament on February 26, 1914 made by Smuts, who at that point was Defense Minister and undergoing intensive negotiations with Gandhi to finalize their settlement, to justify his decision to deport some leading syndicalists back to Britain. Part of Smuts' statement, quoted from Hancock (1962, vol. 2: 369), reads:

> We are ... a small white colony in a Dark Continent. Whatever divisions creeping in among the whites are sure to be reflected in the conduct of the native population, and if ever there was a country where the white people must ever be watchful and careful, and highly organized, and ready to put down with an iron hand all attempts such as were made on the present occasion, that country is South Africa.

26 These figures are based on the number of trade licenses issued in 1895–1908 in Natal and the Transvaal, respectively, complied in Swan (1985: 266–79).
27 The profiles of the Company's chief merchant Abdullah Haji Adam, as well as other prominent merchants of the period under study, are described in Swan (1985: 6–8).
28 The starting monthly wages of male indentured laborers were: ten shillings for agricultural work; twelve to fifteen for mining; and twenty for the Natal Government Railway. Domestic servants' monthly wages were substantially higher, ranging from one to five pounds. Despite the range of monthly wages that varied according to the types of work, it is clear that the £3 tax introduced in 1895 on ex-indentured laborers was excessively demanding. See Swan (1985: 25–6) for more details on indentured laborers' wages and treatment.
29 Indentured laborers included not only Hindus, who constituted the greatest majority by far, but also Muslims, Christians, Sikhs, and others. Regionally, a smaller yet substantial number of laborers were also shipped from areas surrounding the eastern port town of Calcutta. See Swan (1985: 281–5) for the statistics on indentured labors based on ship logs and other archival sources.
30 This excludes 1866–74, when the indenture system was temporarily suspended. The statistics are cited from Swan (1985: 28).
31 See Swan (1985: 286–7) for relevant statistics.
32 These rounded figures are derived from Swan (1985: 1, 28).
33 See, for example, government records and an *Indian Opinion* article compiled in Bhana and Pachai (1984: 17–20).
34 For a more comprehensive description of satyagraha's origin, other sources have to be consulted. Especially useful for understanding Gandhi, satyagraha, and the Indian community in South Africa are: the first twelve volumes of *The Collected Works of Mahatma Gandhi*, Gandhi's autobiography, *Satyagraha in South Africa*, Swan (1985), Huttenback (1971), Pachai (1971), and Erikson (1969).
35 See Gandhi (1928: 93–4), as well as the *Indian Opinion* article titled "Criminal" on September 8, 1906 in Gandhi (1961, vol. 5: 411–12).
36 See the *Indian Opinion* article "Haji Ojeer Ally" dated October 6, 1906 in Gandhi (1961, vol. 5: 459–60).
37 Swan (1985: 121–2) provides useful details on the Indian socio-economic networks, based on her extensive archival research.
38 The minutes are publicized in "Johannesburg Letter" in the *Indian Opinion* on September 22, 1906 in Gandhi (1961, vol. 5: 439–43).
39 Swan (1985: 142). These figures are based on the available statistics of Asiatic registrants, mostly Indians.
40 Swan (1985: 142).
41 See the *Indian Opinion* article "Voluntary registration in the Transvaal," dated May 9, 1908 in Gandhi (1962, vol. 8: 222).
42 The *Indian Opinion* article "Balance sheet" on December 26, 1908 contains Gandhi's estimate of Indian jail-goers. See Gandhi (1968, vol. 9: 115–17) for the article. On the

role of hawkers and Gandhi's moral transformation during this period, see Swan (1985: 164–77). In addition, Gandhi's moral leadership will be elaborated later in the sections discussing value commitment and other working propositions.
43 "Johannesburg Letter," *Indian Opinion*, July 18, 1908 in Gandhi (1962, vol. 8: 367–70).
44 See Gandhi (1972, vol. 11: 415) for his diary of December 1, 1912.
45 See, for example, the *Indian Opinion* articles, "Hindus and Mohamedans beware" and "Attack on Indian religions," both on March 22, 1913 and found in Gandhi (1972, vol. 11: 496–7). See also, "The marriage imbroglio" on April 12, 1913 in Gandhi (1966, vol. 12: 14–15).
46 The campaign's objectives are articulated in the *Indian Opinion* article "An official statement," dated October 15, 1913 in Gandhi (1966, vol. 12: 239–41).
47 See "Women in jail" in Gandhi (1928: 257–60).
48 In October and November, 1914, spontaneous and apparently leaderless strikes of Indian indentured laborers emerged in sugar plantations of southern Natal, provoking cycles of violence and counter-violence between the Indians and the police. Although satyagraha leaders were not directly involved in organizing these activities in the south, the impact on the southerners generated by the northerners' strike and march was apparent and significant. The Union government was compelled to settle the dispute with satyagrahis not only because of the effectiveness of the latter's organized movement, but also because of the combination of both deliberate and unanticipated actions taken by the Indians and others.
49 Gandhi's 1909 booklet, *Hind Swaraj*, is the clearest articulation of his view on this subject.
50 Erikson (1969: 103–40) psychoanalyzes Gandhi's childhood and offers stimulating insights into how his parents helped to shape his character.
51 In order to explore the religious and cultural precursors of Gandhi's intrinsic value commitment presented here, a range of sources were consulted, including his own writings such as *Hind Swaraj* (*Indian Home Rule*) written in 1909, a series of letters and correspondence during his South Africa years compiled in *The Collected Works of Mahatma Gandhi*, an extensive analysis of Gandhi's moral politics and its religious and cultural background by Iyer (1973), a study of Gandhi as a martyr by Smith (1997), and a psychoanalysis of Gandhi and his cultural environment since his childhood by Erikson (1969).
52 His publication *Hind Swaraj*, comprised of twenty short chapters, comes closest to serving this purpose, only that blueprints of his emergent religious principles which came to shape his value commitment were still at an early stage of development and require well-informed interpretive work to be useful for the present study.
53 His reading list in jail around 1908–9 included the *Upanishads*, *Ramayana*, *Bhagavad Gita*, and numerous other Hindu scriptures, and his reflections on these religious subjects formed an essential part of *Hind Swaraj*. See Gandhi (1997: 5–9) for his reading list in jail.
54 The exact nature of Jain influences on Gandhi's religiosity is still to be explored. As mentioned earlier, Gandhi's parents practiced Hinduism in a local Vaishnavate community, and they did not necessarily follow Jainism of one form or another in a strict, religious sense. It is inferred, however, from Gandhi's writings and other sources that his mother Putali Ba's devotion to the local spiritual tradition, derived in part from the Jain spiritual heritage of Kathiawar, played an important role in forming Gandhi's early religious conscience. Also reflective of possible Jain influences on young Gandhi is his encounter upon returning from London with Shri Rajchandra Ravjibhai Metha, or Raychandbhai, a Jain devotee, poet, and jewelry trader, who captivated Gandhi's mind for his exemplary godly pursuits. In his autobiography, Gandhi (1993: 90) recalls that the spiritual guidance he had received from Raychandbhai, despite being only a few years older than Gandhi himself, left as much enduring impact on

his life as Ruskin's *Unto This Last* and Tolstoy's *The Kingdom of God is Within You*. Through his correspondence with Raychandbhai, Gandhi (1958, vol. 1: 91) as a young barrister in South Africa, asked questions like, "If a snake is about to bite me, should I allow myself to be bitten or should I kill it, supposing that that is the only way in which I can save myself?"

55 See Dundas (2005) for discussion on the Many-pointed Doctrine in Jainism. Erikson (1969) also discusses psychoanalytic implications of this principle for Gandhi's life.
56 The English terms, passive resistance and passive register, are rough translations of satyagraha and satyagrahi, respectively, in the original Gujarati text.
57 This inference is derived from his own reflections in Gandhi (1928: 212).
58 One of the most detailed accounts of the intra-communal political dynamics, processes, and structures is Swan (1985), who critically and empirically re-examined Gandhi's role in South Africa with emphasis on the emerging class consciousness. Swan's study forms a basis for the present analysis of Indians' intra-communal relations, supplemented by other sources.
59 Gandhi's *Indian Opinion* article "Attack on Indian religions" on March 22, 1913 urges Indians of all faith traditions to challenge the Supreme Court decision for the sake of Indian women's honor, as well as for their own.
60 Reflecting on the reason for adding the £3 tax issue to the campaign's objectives, Gandhi (1928: 249) wrote

> the breach of a promise, made to such a representative of India as Gokhale, was not only a personal insult to him but also to the whole of India ... it is impossible to pocket an insult offered to the mother country.

61 For details of this meeting, including the actual content of the decision, see Swan (1985: 239).
62 The public meeting in Durban on October 12, 1913, which was attended by many merchants and Gandhi himself, reportedly turned into a complete chaos, where a police intervention was called for to avert fist fights. See Swan (1985: 244–5).
63 Historical records indicate that adversarial relations did surface from time to time between Hindus and Muslims in South Africa in the 1900s, but they typically manifested in the form of acrimonious exchanges of words rather than physical violence. In his *Indian Opinion* article on May 27, 1905, for example, Gandhi took note of the antagonistic Hindu–Muslim correspondence in a journal published in Eastern Cape and appealed for de-escalation and conciliation. Examples of this nature suggest that there *was* a great deal of potential for serious inter-faith disunity, at least perceived as such in Gandhi's mind on the eve of satyagraha's advent.
64 This is consistent with the empirical findings of Swan (1985), who observes that members of Hindu, Muslim, Zoroastrian, and other religious associations, comprised mostly of merchants, frequently attended secular social activities open to all Indians and mixed with one another.
65 This observation is applicable not only to Hindus and Muslims of different denominations, but also to Christians (mainly colonial-born), Parsis (practicing Zoroastrianism), and others who supported or otherwise interacted with the satyagraha movement.
66 Shankeranand's episode summarized here is based on Swan (1985: 198–203).
67 Cited from his *Indian Opinion* article, "Triumph of Truth," on February 8, 1908 in Gandhi (1962, vol. 8: 60–2).
68 See Gandhi (1993: 315), for example, for his impressions of the Zulu "rebellion."
69 Hunt (1990) offers a useful analysis of the Coloreds' political participation as compared to Indians'. The present discussion on the Colored draws primarily on Hunt's analysis.
70 The classical debate over the just war doctrine, which attempts to define under what conditions and in what manner collectivities like nations are justified to use force as an divine instrument of peace, highlights the enduring importance of the peace–justice

connection in Western political thought. The just war doctrine is also a prototypical example of political instrumentalism discussed earlier.

71 As discussed earlier, the *Indian Opinion* started in June 1903 in Durban, and Gandhi assumed full responsibility for its costly, time-consuming operation by October 1904. According to Gandhi (1928: 131–4), its readership generally ranged from 1,200 to 1,500, and it reached some 3,500 when the movement attained the highest level of mobilization. Since there were about 20,000 literate Indians in South Africa, somewhere between 6 percent and 18 percent of the potential Indian readership followed Gandhi's moral and political perspectives weekly. Many others who could not afford to subscribe gathered weekly around a subscriber, who read aloud the news for them. It is inferred from this communal practice that small-group dialogues on topical issues spontaneously followed weekly news reading in various localities. The journal therefore offered an effective vehicle for widely communicating the discoveries from Gandhi's continuous leaning, through analogizing or otherwise.

72 This call for collective resistance in January 1914 may be considered part of the *incipience* phase of satyagraha, which is one essential aspect of the movement's longitudinal nature still to be discussed in this study.

73 All these articles are compiled in Gandhi (1961, vol. 5).

74 Gandhi's articles in the *Indian Opinion* applying two-case comparison, with varying degrees of isomorphic emphasis, abound. Examples of such articles written in the mid-1900s include, but are not limited to: "England and Russia: a comparison" (November 26, 1903), "Indian National Congress and Russian Zemstvos: a comparison" (the first part on January 14, 1905 and the second on January 21, 1905), "The Chinese and the Kaffirs: a comparison" (June 10, 1905), "Japan and Russia" (June 10, 1905), "The Chinese and the Indians in Singapore" (July 1, 1905), "The Chinese and the Indians: a comparison" (September 16, 1905), "Black and white men" (February 3, 1906), "Egypt and Natal: a comparison" (August 4, 1906), and "Russia and India" (September 8, 1906, titled the same as the above-cited November 11, 1905 article). These articles are compiled in Gandhi (1960, vol. 4; 1961, vol. 5). Whether this consistent pattern of thinking was routinized in Gandhi's mind through his early legal training in London and/or other developmental processes is still to be explored. Yet the pattern seems to suggest that analogizing played an essential role in Gandhi's political learning and communication with the general public.

75 Gandhi's (1961, vol. 5: 367–73) detailed report from the frontline, "Indian Stretcher-Bearer Corps," appeared in the *Indian Opinion* on July 28, 1906. The report concludes by stating, "the writer of these notes is able to confidently assert that the little band is capable of performing any work that may be entrusted to it," indicative of Gandhi's sustained effort to vindicate Indians' respectable status within the British-dominant political system in Natal.

76 Gandhi's *Indian Opinion* articles reflecting his liberal imperialist ideology on the eve of satyagraha's advent include: "India's service to the empire" (October 15, 1903), "India makes the empire" (August 20, 1904), "Long live the king-emperor!" (November 12, 1904), "Cable to king-emperor" (November 11, 1905) – which publicizes his birthday greetings – and "Empire Day" (May 26, 1906). These articles are compiled in Gandhi (1960, vol. 4; 1961, vol. 5).

77 The detailed historical analysis of Swan (1985) is exceptionally valuable in this respect, though Swan's main focus is on socio-economic relations within the South African Indian community. More work needs to be done on the *epistemological* dimension of satyagraha's origin as a valuable contribution to the Gandhian scholarship.

78 The meeting on September 11, 1906 was reported in "Johannesburg Letter," which appeared in the *Indian Opinion* on September 22, 1906. See Gandhi (1961, vol. 5: 439–43).

79 "Johannesburg Letter" on September 22, 1906, in Gandhi (1961, vol. 5: 439–43).
80 Quoted from "The poll-tax" on November 25, 1905 in Gandhi (1961, vol. 5:139–41).
81 See Gandhi (1961, vol. 5: 476–7) for the article.
82 See, among others, Gandhi (1928), particularly his sympathetic description of Boers in the "History" chapter of the volume.
83 Gandhi (1928) briefly mentioned many years later that the experience that he had gained by participating in the Anglo-Boer War and the Zulu "rebellion" helped him lead the Great March, but did not specify how his past experience might have inspired him to come up with the image of this unprecedented approach to mass mobilization and organized protest.
84 Most notable among these articles are "The duty of Transvaal Indians" on October 6, 1906 in Gandhi (1961, vol. 5: 461–3) and "Tyler, Hampden, and Butyan" on October 20, 1906 in Gandhi (1961, vol. 5: 476–7).

5 Conclusion: implications for research, practice, and pedagogy

1 This possibility is discussed earlier in the context of isomorphic analogizing, as in a comparison between two neighbors' sharing a garden and two countries sharing a border.
2 Reflecting on the seventeen cases reviewed in this study, one suggestion that comes to mind is the need for systematically teaching at least 50–100 cases of creative transformation in various historical, geographic, and relational contexts and at different levels of analysis, in a multi-year graduate degree program in conflict and peace studies. This suggestion is illustrative only, but the general point to be made is the urgent need for cultivating creative capacities for conflict resolution, not just skills for conflict analysis.

Bibliography

Anderson, Benedict. 1991. *Imagined communities: Reflections on the origin and spread of nationalism*. London: Verso.

Arai, Tatsushi. 2006. When the waters of culture and conflict meet. In *Conflict across cultures: A unique experience of bridging differences*, edited by M. LeBaron and V. Pillay. Yarmouth, Maine: Intercultural Press.

Azar, Edward. 2002. Protracted social conflicts and second track diplomacy. In *Second track/citizens' diplomacy: Concepts and techniques for conflict transformation*, edited by J. Davies and E. Kaufman, 15–30. Lanham, Md.: Rowman & Littlefield Publishers.

Barrons, James. 1968. *The Aland Islands question: Its settlement by the League of Nations*. New Haven, Conn.: Yale University Press.

Bhana, Surendra and Bridglal Pachai, eds. 1984. *A documentary history of Indian South Africans*. Cape Town, South Africa: David Philip.

Bondurant, Joan V. 1965. *Conquest of violence: The Gandhian philosophy of conflict*. Berkeley, Calif.: University of California Press.

Boulding, Elise. 2000. *Cultures of peace: The hidden side of history*. Syracuse, N.Y.: Syracuse University Press.

Brown, M. E., S. M. Lynn-Jones, and S. E. Miller, eds. 1999. *Debating the democratic peace*. Cambridge, Mass.: The MIT Press.

Buber, Martin. 1958. *I and thou*. New York: Charles Scribner's Sons.

Burton, John W. 1966. A case study in the application of international theory: Indonesia–Malaysia–Singapore. Paper prepared in January 1966 for the British International Studies Association's annual conference. London.

Center for the Study of Mind and Human Interaction (CSMHI), University of Virginia. *History, methodology and concepts of CSMHI*. www.healthsystem.virginia.edu/internet/csmhi/history&methodologycfm#history (accessed June 1, 2005).

Ciment, James. 1999. Vietnam: Second Indochina War, 1959–1975. In *Encyclopedia of conflicts since World War II*, vol. 4. New York, N.Y.: Sharpe Reference.

Clark, Mary E. 1989. *Ariadne's thread: The search for new modes of thinking*. New York, N.Y.: St. Martin's Press.

———. 2002. *In search of human nature*. London: Routledge.

Cohen, Raymond. 1993. Creativity in conflict resolution: Breaking the deadlock in international negotiations. In *International Relations and pan-Europe: Theoretical applications and empirical findings*, edited by F. R. Pfetsch, 517–24. Munster, Germany: LIT Verlag.

Coleman, Peter T. and Morton Deutsch. 2000. Some guidelines for developing a creative approach to conflict. In *The handbook of conflict resolution: Theory and practice*,

edited by M. Deutsch and P. T. Coleman, 356–65. San Francisco, Calif.: Jossey-Bass Publishers.
Cropley, Arthur J. 1999. Definitions of creativity. In *Encyclopedia of creativity*, vol. 1, edited by M. A. Runco and S. R. Pritzker, 511–24. San Diego, Calif.: Academic Press.
Csikszentmihalyi, Mihaly. 1996. *Creativity: Flow and the psychology of discovery and invention*. New York, N.Y.: HarperCollins.
De Bono, Edward. 1970. *Lateral thinking: Creativity step by step*. New York, N.Y.: Harper & Row, Publishers.
———. 1985. *Conflicts*. London: Harrap.
Diamond, Louise and Ronald J. Fisher. 1995. Integrating conflict resolution training and consultation: A Cyprus example. *Negotiation Journal* 11 (3): 287–301.
Diamond, Louise and John McDonald. 1996. *Multi-track diplomacy: A systems approach to peace*. West Hartford, Conn.: Kumarian Press.
Dundas, Paul. 2005. Jainism. In *Encyclopedia of religion*, edited by L. Jones, 4764–72. Detroit, Mich.: Macmillan Reference USA.
Einstein, Albert. 1995. *Relativity*. Amherst, N.Y.: Prometheus Books.
Emerson, Robert M., Rachel I. Fretz, and Linda L. Shaw. 1995. *Writing ethnographic fieldnotes*. Chicago, Ill.: The University of Chicago Press.
Emery, Fred. 1966. The rationalization of conflict: A case study. Paper presented at the CIBA Foundation on June 3, 1966. London.
Erikson, Erik H. 1969. *Gandhi's truth: On the origin of militant nonviolence*. New York, N.Y.: W. W. Norton & Company.
Faure, Andrew Murray. 1994. Some methodological problems in Comparative Politics. *Journal of Theoretical Politics* 6 (3): 307–22.
Fisher, Roger, William Ury, and Bruce Patton. 1991. *Getting to yes: Negotiating agreement without giving in*. New York, N.Y.: Penguin Books.
Fogg, Richard Wendell. 1985. Dealing with conflict: A repetoire of creative, peaceful approaches. *Journal of Conflict Resolution* 29 (2): 330–58.
Freeman, John. 1991. *Security and the CSCE process: The Stockholm conference and beyond*. New York, N.Y.: St. Martin's Press.
Freud, Sigmund. 1958. *On creativity and the unconscious: Papers on the psychology of art, literature, love, and religion*. New York, N.Y.: Harper & Row, Publishers.
Galtung, Johan. 1977. Science as invariance-seeking and invariance-breaking activity. In *Methodology and ideology: Essays in methodology*. Copenhagen, Denmark: Christian Ejlers.
———. 1979. On the structure of creativity. In *Papers on methodology: Theory and methods of social research*. Copenhagen, Denmark: Christian Ejlers.
———. 1996. *Peace by peaceful means: Peace and conflict, development and civilization*. London: Sage Publications.
———. 1998. Conflict transformation by peaceful means: The Transcend method. Training manual. Geneva: The United Nations.
———. 2004. *Transcend and transform: An introduction to conflict work*. London: Pluto Press.
Galtung, Johan, Carl G. Jacobsen, and Kai Frithjof Brand-Jacobsen. 2002. *Searching for peace: The road to TRANSCEND*. London: Pluto Press.
Gandhi, Mohandas K. 1928. *Satyagraha in South Africa*. Ahmedabad, India: Navajivan Press.
———. 1958–66. *The collected works of Mahatma Gandhi*, vols. 1–12. New Delhi: Publications Division, Ministry of Information and Broadcasting, Government of India.

——. 1993. *An autobiography: The story of my experiments with Truth*. Boston: Beacon Press.

——. 1997. *Hind Swaraj and other writings*. Edited by A. J. Parel. Cambridge: Cambridge University Press.

Gardner, Howard. 1993. *Creating minds: An anatomy of creativity seen through the lives of Freud, Picasso, Stravinsky, Eliot, Graham, and Gandhi*. New York, N.Y.: Basic Books.

——. 1994. The creators' patterns. In *Dimensions of creativity*, edited by M. A. Boden, 143–58. Cambridge, Mass.: The MIT Press.

Gerardi, Debra. 2001. Developing creativity and intuition for resolving conflicts: The magic of improvisation. http://mediate.com/articles/gerardi.cfm (accessed March 2003).

Ghai, Yash. 2000. Autonomy as a strategy for diffusing conflict. In *International conflict resolution after the Cold War*, edited by P. Stern and D. Druckman, 483–530. Washington, DC: National Academy Press.

Goldschmidt Jr., Arthur. 2002. *A concise history of the Middle East*. Boulder, Colo.: Westview Press.

Gruber, Howard E. 2000. Creativity and conflict resolution: The role of point of view. In *The handbook of conflict resolution: Theory and practice*, edited by M. Deutsch and P. T. Coleman, 355–65. San Francisco, Calif.: Jossey-Bass Publishers.

Hancock, W. K. 1958. Trek. *The Economic History Review* 10 (3): 331–9.

——. 1962. *Smuts: The sanguine years 1870–1919*. Cambridge: Cambridge University Press.

Hancock, W. K. and Jean van der Poel, eds. 1966. *Selections from the Smuts papers*, vols. 2–4. Cambridge: Cambridge University Press.

Hannum, Hurst. 1990. *Autonomy, sovereignty, and self-determination: The accommodation of conflicting rights*. Philadelphia, Pa.: University of Pennsylvania Press.

Hare, A. Paul and David Haveh. 1985. Creative problem solving: Camp David summit, 1978. *Small Group Behavior* 16 (2): 123–38.

Harris, Marvin. 1990. Emics and etics revisited. In *Emics and etics: The insider/outsider debate*, edited by T. Headland, K. Pike, and M. Harris, 48–61. Newburry Parks, Calif.: Sage Publications.

Hasegawa, Tsuyoshi. 1998. *The Northern Territories dispute and Russo-Japanese relations*, vol. 2. Berkley, Calif.: University of California at Berkeley.

Hechter, Michael. 1990. The emergence of cooperative social institutions. In *Social institutions: The emergence, maintenance, and effects*, edited by K.-D. Opp, M. Hechter, and R. Wippler, 1–5. New York, N.Y.: Aldine de Gruyter.

Hechter, Michael, Karl-Dieter Opp, and Reinhard Wippler. 1990. Introduction. In *Social institutions: The emergence, maintenance, and effects*, edited by K.-D. Opp, M. Hechter, and R. Wippler, 13–33. New York, N.Y.: Aldine de Gruyter.

Hiltebeitel, Alf. 2005. Hinduism. In *Encyclopedia of religion*, edited by L. Jones, 3988–4009. Detroit, Mich.: Macmillan Reference USA.

Hirsch, John L. 2001. *Sierra Leone: Diamonds and the struggle for democracy*. Boulder, Colo.: Lynne Reinner Publishers.

Hollis, M. and S. Smith. 1991. *Explaining and understanding International Relations*. Oxford: Clarendon Press.

Hunt, James D. 1978. *Gandhi in London*. New Delhi, India: Promilla & Co.

——. 1990. *Gandhi and the black people of South Africa*. Online historical document of the ANC in South Africa. www.anc.org.za/ancdocs/history/people/gandhi/hunt.html.

Huttenback, Robert A. 1971. *Gandhi in South Africa: British imperialism and the Indian Question, 1860–1914*. Ithaca, N.Y.: Cornell University Press.

Isaacs, Harold R. 1975. *Idols of the tribe: Group identity and political change*. New York: Harper & Row.

Iyer, Raghavan N. 1973. *The moral political thought of Mahatma Gandhi*. New York, N.Y.: Oxford University Press.

Jakobson, Max. 1998. *Finland in the new Europe*. Westport, Conn.: Praeger.

Jung, Carl G. 1964. Approaching the unconscious. In *Man and his symbols*, edited by C. G. Jung and M.-L. von Franz, 20–103. Garden City, N.Y.: Doubleday & Company.

Kelman, Herbert C. 1993. Coalitions across conflict lines: The interplay of conflicts within and between the Israeli and Palestinian communities. *Conflict between people and groups*, edited by S. Worchel and J. Simpson, 236–58. Chicago, Ill.: Nelson-Hall.

———. 1997. Group processes in the resolution of international conflicts. *American Psychologist* 52 (3): 212–20.

———. 2001. The role of national identity in conflict resolution: Experiences from Israeli–Palestinian problem-solving workshops. In *Social identity, intergroup conflict, and conflict reduction*, edited by R. D. Ashmore, L. Jussim, and D. Wilder, 187–212. Oxford: Oxford University Press.

———. 2002. Experience from 30 years of action research on the Israeli–Palestinian conflict. Paper prepared for a Program on Negotiation brown bag lunch on March 5, 2002 at Harvard University. Cambridge, Mass.

Konczacki, Zbigniew A. 1967. *Public finance and economic development of Natal, 1893–1910*. Durham, N.C.: Duke University Press.

Krippendroff, Klaus. 1980. *Content analysis: An introduction to its methodology*. Beverly Hills, Calif.: Sage Publications.

Kuhn, Thomas S. 1996. *The structure of scientific revolutions*. Chicago: University of Chicago Press.

———. 2000. *The road since structure: Philosophical essays, 1970–1993, with an autobiographical interview*. Edited by J. Conant and J. Haugeland. Chicago: University of Chicago Press.

League of Nations. 1921. *The Aaland Islands question: Report submitted to the Council of the League of Nations by the commission of rapporteurs*. Geneva: League of Nations.

LeBaron, Michelle. 2002. *Bridging troubled waters: Conflict resolution from the heart*. San Francisco, Calif.: Jossey-Bass Publishers.

LeCompte, Margaret D. and Jean L. Schensul. 1999. *Designing & conducting ethnographic research*. Walnut Creek, Calif.: Altamira Press, Rowman & Littlefield Publishers.

Lederach, John Paul. 1995. *Preparing for peace: Conflict transformation across cultures*. Syracuse, N.Y.: Syracuse University Press.

———. 1999. The challenge of the 21st century: Justpeace. In *People building peace: 35 inspiring stories from around the world*, edited by the European Center for Conflict Prevention, 27–35. Utrecht, the Netherlands: European Center for Conflict Prevention.

Lijphart, Arend. 1971. Comparative politics and the comparative method. *The American Political Science Review* 65: 682–93.

———. 1975. The Northern Ireland problem: Cases, theories, and solutions. *British Journal of Political Science* 5 (1): 83–106.

Lincoln, Yvonna S. and Egan G. Guba. 1985. *Naturalistic inquiry*. Beverly Hills, Calif.: Sage Publications.

Lovell, Colin Rhys. 1956. Afrikaner nationalism and apartheid. *American Historical Review* (January): 308–30.

Mannerheim, Carl Gustaf. 1954. *The memoirs of Marshal Mannerheim*. Translated by E. Lewenhaupt. New York, N.Y.: E. P. Dutton & Company.

Marcelia, Gabriel and Richard Downes, eds. 1999. *Security cooperation in the Western Hemisphere: Resolving the Ecuador–Peru conflict*. Miami, Fla.: North–South Center Press.

Meyer, Manulani Aluli. 2003. *Ho'oulu – Our time of becoming: Hawaiian epistemology and early writings*. Honolulu, Hawaii: 'Ai Pohaku Press.

Mitchell, Christopher R. 2000. The CIBA workshops 1965–66: A pioneering initiative in international problem solving. Draft working paper. Institute for Conflict Analysis and Resolution, George Mason University, Fairfax, Va.

Mitchell, Stephen A. and Margaret J. Black. 1995. *Freud and beyond: A history of modern psychoanalitic thought*. New York, N.Y.: Basic Books.

Mumford, Michael D. and Paige P. Porter. 1999. Analogies. In *Encyclopedia of creativity*, vol. 1, edited by M. A. Runco and S. R. Pritzker, 71–7. San Diego, Calif.: Academic Press.

Nickles, Thomas. 1999. Paradigm shifts. In *Encyclopedia of creativity*, vol. 2, edited by M. A. Ruco and S. R. Pritzker, 335–46. San Diego, Calif.: Academic Press.

Organization for Security and Cooperation in Europe (OSCE) Secretariat. *OSCE handbook*. www.osce.org. Vienna: OSCE Secretariat.

Organization of African Unity. 1995. Report of the Secretary General on the OAU fact-finding mission to Sierra Leone led by Assistant Secretary General Ambassador Abdullahi Said Osman, 7–23 February 1995. Addis Ababa, Ethiopia: OAU.

Orr, James. 1951. Calvinism. In *Encyclopaedia of religion and ethics*, edited by J. Hastings, 146–55. New York, N.Y.: Charles Scriner's Sons.

Pachai, Bridglal. 1971. *The international aspects of the South African Indian question 1860–1971*. Cape Town, South Africa: Struik (PTY) Ltd.

Payne, Robert. 1969. *The life and death of Mahatma Gandhi*. New York, N.Y.: Smithmark Publishers.

Pruitt, Dean G. 1987. Creative approaches to negotiation. In *Conflict management and problem solving: International applications*, edited by J. D. Sandole and I. Sandole-Staroste, 62–76. New York, N.Y.: New York University Press.

Risse-Kappen, Thomas. 1995. Ideas do not float freely: Transnational coalitions, domestic structures, and the end of the Cold War. In *International Relations theory and the end of the Cold War*, edited by R. N. Lebow and T. Risse-Kappen, 187–222. New York: Columbia University Press.

Roberts, Gene. 1968. New anti-government alliance fails to stir public support in South Vietnam. *New York Times*, July 12.

Robson, Colin. 1993. *Real world research: A resource for social scientists and practitioner-researchers*. Oxford: Blackwell Publishers.

Rothenberg, Albert. 1999. Janusian process. In *Encyclopedia of creativity*, vol. 2, edited by M. A. Runco and S. R. Pritzker, 103–8. San Diego, Calif.: Academic Press.

Rubin, Jeffrey Z., Dean G. Pruitt, and Sung Hee Kim. 1994. *Social conflict: Escalation, stalemate, and settlement*. New York, N.Y.: McGraw-Hill.

Runco, Mark A. 1999. Time. In *Encyclopedia of creativity*, vol. 2, edited by M. A. Runco and S. R. Pritzker, 659–63. San Diego, Calif.: Academic Press.

Ryan, Gery W. and H. Russell Bernard. 2000. Data management and data analysis methods. In *Handbook of qualitative research*, edited by N. K. Denzin and Y. S. Lincoln, 769–801. Thousand Oaks, Calif.: Sage Publications.

Saunders, Christopher and Iain R. Smith. 1999. Southern Africa, 1795–1910. In *The Oxford history of the British Empire*, vol. 3, edited by A. Porter, 597–623. Oxford: Oxford University Press.

Sharp, Gene. 1979. *Gandhi as a political strategist: With essays on ethics and politics*. Boston: Porter Sargent Publishers.

Simmons, Beth A. 1999. *Territorial disputes and their resolution: The case of Ecuador and Peru*. Washington, DC: United States Institute of Peace.

Smith, Hedrick. 1968. U.S. visitor to North says group might be focus of a postwar regime. *New York Times*, July 9.

Smith, Lacey Baldwin. 1997. *Fools, martyrs, traitors: The story of martyrdom in the Western world*. New York, N.Y.: Alfred A. Knopf.

Spector, Bertram I. 1995. Creativity heuristics for impasse resolution: Reframing intractable negotiations. *The Annals of the American Political and Social Science: Flexibility in international negotiation and mediation*: 81–99.

Stake, Robert E. 2000. Case studies. In *Handbook of qualitative research*, edited by N. K. Denzin and Y. S. Lincoln, 435–508. Thousand Oaks, Calif.: Sage Publishers.

Stein, Janice Gross. 1995. Political learning by doing: Gorbachev as uncommitted thinker and motivated learner. In *International Relations theory and the end of the Cold War*, edited by R. N. Lebow and T. Risse-Kappen, 223–58. New York, N.Y.: Columbia University Press.

Swan, Maureen. 1985. *Gandhi: The South African experience*. Johannesburg, South Africa: Ravan Press.

Test Design Project. 1995. *Performance-based assessment: A methodology, for use in selecting, training and evaluating mediators*. Report on the project directed by Christopher Honeyman. www.convenor.com/madison/method.pdf.

Thompson, L. M. 1960. *The unification of South Africa 1902–1910*. Oxford: Oxford University Press.

Vaughan, Diane. 1986. *Uncoupling: Turning points in intimate relationships*. New York, N.Y.: Oxford University Press.

———. 1992. Theory elaboration: The heuristics of case analysis. In *What is a case? Exploring the foundations of social inquiry*, edited by C. C. Ragin and H. S. Becker, 173–202. Cambridge: Cambridge University Press.

Volkan, Vamik. 1997. *Bloodlines: From ethnic pride to ethnic terrorism*. Boulder, Colo.: Westview Press.

———. 1998. Transgenerational transmissions and chosen traumas. Opening address for the twelfth international congress of the International Association of Group Psychotherapy. London.

———. 1999. The tree model: A comprehensive psychoanalytical approach to unofficial diplomacy and the reduction of ethnic tension. *Mind and Human Interaction* 10: 142–206.

———. 2004. *Blind trust: Large groups and their leaders in times of crisis and terror*. Los Angeles, Calif.: Pitchstone Publishing.

Wallas, Graham. 1926. *The art of thought*. London: Butler & Tanner.

Weiss, Joshua N. 2002. Which way forward?: Mediator sequencing strategies in intractable communal conflicts. Ph.D. diss., George Mason University, Fairfax, Va.

Wertheimer, M. 1945. *Productive thinking*. New York, N.Y.: Harper.

Winnicott, Donald W. 1953. Transitional objects and transitional phenomena: A study of the first not-me possession. *The International Journal of Psycho-Analysis* 34: 7–97.

Wyte, John. 1990. *Interpreting Northern Ireland*. Oxford: Clarendon Press.

Index

acceptance, definition 9
accidental teenage pregnancies *see* teen pregnancies episode
active nonviolence 30, 41, 178
agency-led creativity 11, 13, 14, 139
aikido 119–21, 136, 202
Åland Islands dispute: and identity 82; pedagogic applications 205–6; primary conflict parties 12; solution 11, 14–15
Ally, Haji Ojeer 156, 158
alternative pathways, contributing phenomena **110**
alternative reality: definition 113, 118, 130, 137, 202; grassroots mobilization episode 130; and outcome/process creativity 201; process 119, 197; selected cases 129; transcendence episode 130–1; and value commitment 133, 196
American approaches, Galtung's reflections on typical 114
American labour dispute episode 84, 100; context 48; demonstration of creativity 49, 51; Kuhnian illustration 52; procedure 49–50; rules 50
American peace movement 32, 108
analogizing: contexts 97–8; definition of analysis 97; process 181; *satyagraha* campaign 181–90
analysis–resolution link: Burton's rationale 57; complexity 6; Fisher's methodology 5; impact of expanded awareness of 203
analysis: defining units of 106–7; levels of 106; rationale for the second stage of 104
Andorra 8
Anglo-Boer War 144, 147, 150–1, 179, 182, 188
Arab–Israel conflict *see* Israeli–Palestinian conflict

Arafat, Yasser 59, 101
Awad, Mubarak 24, 30–1, 41–2, 97–8
Azar, Edward 127

Beilin, Yossi 35
belief systems 1
bicommunalism episode *see* Cyprus conflict
big picture 91, 102–3
Botha, Louis 149
Boulding, Elise 88–91, 94–5, 98–100, 107–8, 113, 116, 129–32
Boulding, Kenneth 89, 90
Burton, John 43, 54–8, 62, 68, 85–6, 99, 111–13

Calvert–Henderson Quality-of-Life Indicators 28
Cameroons 8
Camp David I 8
carrying capacities, social factors conducive to generating 209
civil disobedience movements 8; *see also* Palestinian nonviolence; *satyagraha* campaign
civil war in Sierra Leone 53–4, 84, 101
Cohen, Stephen 59
Cold War 71–3, 76, 81, 95, 115, 127
colonial instrumentalism 193, 196, 210
combining known elements in a new way 23, 82, 96, 99, 103, 134, 195
common security policy 8
comparative analysis: emerging themes 96–103; findings 134–7; outcome/process creativity 11–13, 111–15; paradigms 124–33; summary 133–4; system-element framework 115–24, 136
conflict, definition 3
conflict dynamics: in dual function parties' creativity 95; manifestations of 8

conflict paradigms *129*; comparative analysis findings 136–7; in Johnston's episode 129; steps toward breaking 128
conflict parties' creativity: episode summary *25*; versus intermediaries' creativity 42, 86–7; overview 24–6; reflections on 40–2; Volkan's observations 63; *see also* Environmentalists for Full-Employment movement; Palestinian nonviolence; teen pregnancies episode; US–Vietnam War
conflict resolution, concept analysis 3
conflict resolution creativity: comparative analysis 96; five-phase model 10; interrelated elements 1; stimulating 99; useful concepts 11
conscious processes, focus on 4
contingency-based processes 40, 52, 61, 85, 96, 102–3, 123, 134, 195
conventionality and unconventionality 96, 100, 103, 134
creative action, risk-taking as enabling factor for 31–2, 34
creative change: acceptance 27; as bottom-up process 136; conceptualizing the origin of 14; evaluating 3; failure 34; pathways of 109–10; precursors 37; recognition of 11
creative pathways 107, 116–18
creative processes, conceptual approaches 8–9
creativity in conflict resolution: literature review 6; working definition of **2**
creativity: definitions 1–2, 28, 71, 89; Awad's description 30; Boulding's view 89; Burton's view 54; conflict parties *see* conflict parties creativity: dual function parties *see* dual function parties creativity: Falk's argument 32; formative process of children's 65; Galtung on 80–1; Henderson's view 28; intermediaries *see* intermediaries creativity: Johnston's view 26; Kelman's observations 58; origination phase of 27; Osman's description 53; Pundak's view 34–8; relationship between culture and 83–4; Saunders' view 92; six common patterns of 103; Smith's description 47; Törnudd's view 71; unconscious origin 66; Volkan's understanding 62, 65
CSCE (Conference on Security and Cooperation in Europe) 71–3, 108, 123

CSMHI (Center for the Study of Mind and Human Interaction) 62–5, 109
culture, relationship between creativity and 83–4
Cultures of Peace: The Hidden Side of History (Boulding) 90–1
Cyprus conflict (bicommunal approach): 85; alternative realities 130; intermediaries' creativity 66–71; Kuhnian applications 124; origination phase 105; viability 101

data collection 18, 20, 104
deep listening episode *see* US–Vietnam War
definitions: acceptance 9; alternative reality 113, 118, 130, 137, 202; conflict 3; creativity 1–2, 28, 71, 89; evolution 9; identity transformation 165; incipience 9; interdependent origination 202; origination 9; outcome (substantive) creativity 111, 135; process (procedural) creativity 111, 135; *satyagraha* 138; sustenance 9
deniability 35, 37
Diamond, Louise 43, 45, 66–71, 85, 101, 105, 124, 129–32
diplomacy: shuttle 37, 92–4, 95, 97, 102, 117; Track-Two *see* Indonesia–Malaysia–Singapore conflict
directionality 102–3, 119, 134
discoveries in retrospect 96, 101, 103, 134
dispute-handling, local mechanisms for 118
dual function parties' creativity: episode summary 88; overview 88; reflections on 94–5; *see also* family dialogue episode; shuttle diplomacy
Duong Quynh Hoa 33

Ecuador, border dispute with Peru *see* Peru–Ecuador conflict
effectiveness 2, 32, 38, 42, 71, 75, 162, 180, 193
Emery, Fred 56–7
empowerment, resistance through *see* Palestinian nonviolence
Environmentalists for Full-Employment movement (connecting dots in a new way episode) 41; alternative reality 130; context 28; demonstration of creativity 87, 111; enabling factors 30, 100; evolution 99; tools 28–9; value commitment 29

episodes: categorisation 24; summaries 25, 44–5, 88; as unit of analysis 21
Erikson, Eric 165–6, 189–90
Estonian–Russian psychoanalytic dialogue (symbolic activation episode) 85; context 62–3; demonstration of creativity 63–4; enabling factors 64–5; and transitional experience theory 65–6; Volkan's role 62
ethicality 2, 42, 180, 193, 208
etic and emic perspectives 122–3
evolution: definition 9; in Helsinki process 106

Falk, Richard 24, 32–4, 41–2, 101, 107–8
Falkland Islands 8
family dialogue episode (Quaker method): alternative realities 130; combining known elements in a new way 99–100; context 89; creative pathways 117; demonstration of creativity 89–90; dynamic tension 122; Helsinki process comparison 123–4; lessons 92; as process creativity example 113; value commitment 90–1
family dialogues, longitudinal process type 108
Finland 8, 12, 45, 71–2, 75, 85, 111, 120–1, 123, 205
Fisher, R. *et al.* 5
five-phase model (longitudinal nature of creativity): in bicommunalism episode 105; comparative analysis 104, 105–10, 135; concept analysis 104; in Helsinki process 106–7; revised working model **105**, 106
future inquiry, questions for 208–11
future–present approach 37

Galtung, Johan 39, 43, 76–84, 86–7, 98–100, 111, 113–16, 118, 129–32
Gandhi, Mahatma: on attainment of *Moksha* 169; birth and background 141; education 142; experimental settlements 145; identity transformation 165–7, 173; involvement in South African regional politics 143–5, 153; journalism 145; life before mahatmaship 140; marriage and children 142; military service 144; Palestinian inspiration 31, 97; value commitment 168, 172, 175–6; vow of celibacy and voluntary poverty 146; and the Zulu rebellion 145–6, 186; *see also satyagraha* campaign

Gandhi, Manilal 110
Goldschmidt, Arthur 39
grassroots mobilization episode *see* Environmentalists for Full-Employment movement

Habib, Haji 156, 158, 188
Helsinki process 8, 85; versus family dialogue episode 123–4; five-phase model 106–7; intermediaries' creativity 71–6; origination phase 106; system–element framework 123; systemic context 120
Henderson, Hazel 24, 28–30, 41–2, 87, 99–100, 111, 113–14, 129–32
Hertzog, James B.M. 149
heuristic pointers *129*; concept analysis 130; conscious use of 132–3; typology 130–1, 137
Hind Swaraj (Gandhi) 169, 171–3, 177, 191–2
Hirschfeld, Yair 35, 37, 97

Iceland 81
identity transformation: Erikson's definition 165; *satyagraha* campaign 165, 167
impartiality 24, 43, 114, 136, 201
incipience: definition 9; in Helsinki process 106; three major phases 106
independent origination 119, 122, 202
Indian Opinion 145, 153, 158, 181–2, 187–8, 192–4, 196
individuality, inadequacy of conventional focus on 4
Indonesia–Malaysia–Singapore conflict (philosophical creativity episode) 8, 85; Burton's essay 55; context 54–5; demonstration of creativity 58; demonstrations of creativity 56; lessons 57; solution 56–7; workshops 55–6, 57, 58
inner resources episode 43, 46–7
integrative agreements 6, 115
inter-group conflict resolution 7–9, 14–15, 21, 212
interdependent origination, definition 202
interest-based principled negotiation 5, 115
intermediaries' creativity: civil war in Sierra Leone 53–4, 101; conflict parties' creativity versus 42, 86–7; episode summary *44–5*; overview 43; racial conflict in Tajikistan 43, 46–7;

reflections on 84–7; *see also* American labour dispute; Cyprus conflict; Estonian–Russian psychoanalytic dialogue; Helsinki process; Indonesia–Malaysia–Singapore conflict; Israeli–Palestinian problem-solving workshop; Peru–Ecuador border dispute
interpretive framework, elements 21
interview questions 20, 212–15
interviewees: geographic locations 20; organizational affiliations 20; selection criteria 7, 19–20
Intifada 39
isomorphism 81–2, 98, 133, 186
Israeli–Palestinian conflict: key resolution principles 101; shuttle diplomacy 37, 92–4, 95, 97, 102, 117; *see also* Oslo peace process; Palestinian nonviolence
Israeli–Palestinian problem-solving workshop: context 60; contingency-based approach to 61; demonstration of creativity 62; participants 59; PLO's status 59–60; salient features 60–1

Jakobson, Max 72, 74–5
Johnston, Linda 26, 41, 98, 107–8, 129
joint appeals 53
justpeace 2, 164, 180, 194

Kelman, Herbert 40, 43, 58–62, 68, 85, 101–3, 113, 123, 125
Kissinger, Henry 33, 88, 92–5, 102, 117
known elements, combining in a new way 99
Konczacki, Zbigniew A. 154
Kuhn, Thomas 3, 14, 52, 124, 202
Kurile Islands dispute 8, 205–6

lateral thinking 6, 115
Le Duc Tho 33
League of Nations 12, 90, 206, 215
Lederach, John Paul 2
legitimate representation 37, 44, 60–2, 101–3
levels of analysis (system-element link) **116**; applicability 116; concept analysis 115–16; illustrations 117, 118–21, 123–4; importance of distinctions between 115; origination of creativity 118–20; practice implications 122–3
listening, deep *see* US–Vietnam War
local communication channels episode 53–4, 101
Logan Act 33

longitudinal processes: family dialogues 108; *satyagraha* campaign 155–64; teen pregnancies episode 108; typology 107–9, 135, 200–2; US–Vietnam War 107
longitudinal transitions 8

McDonald, John 66
Magnusson, Thor 81
Malaysia, conflict with Indonesia and Singapore *see* Indonesia–Malaysia–Singapore conflict
Marcelia, Gabriel and Downes, Richard 76
methodology 18–24
Métis settlement 8
Mian, Essop 159, 187–8
Middle-East peace process 102–3; *see also* Israeli–Palestinian conflict
mutual recognition 44, 60–1, 74, 101–3

NATO (North Atlantic Treaty Organization) 74, 81
negotiation issues, strategic sequencing of 6
Netanyahu, Benjamin 39
neutral state episode 71–6; *see also* Helsinki process
NIA (Natal Indian Association) 174
NIC (Natal Indian Congress) 143, 153, 155, 162, 174–5
nonviolence *see* Palestinian nonviolence; *satyagraha* campaign
Northern Ireland 8
Norway 36, 39

origination: definition 9; independent 119, 202
origination process: ensuring viability 133; recognizability 101
OSCE (Organization for Security and Cooperation in Europe) 71, 73, 106, 108, 123
Oslo peace process (pushing the envelope episode) 8; agenda 35; analogizing 97; Camp David comparison 37–8; demonstrations of creativity 35–6; deniability principle 35; draft zero 35, 37; environmental congeniality 38; evolution 37; Gaza–Jericho first approach 36; and the Intifada 39; reasons for failure 39–40; risk-taking as enabling factor 42; salient issues 34–5; status upgrade 35–6; temporal sequence 37–8
Osman, Abdullahi Said 43, 53–4, 84

240 *Index*

outcome (substantive) creativity: definition 111, 135; in American approach 114; Burton on the nature of 56; comparative analysis findings 135–6; examples of 111; implementation requirements 113; preferred terms 112; process creativity and 11–13, 75, 111–15, 201

Palestinian nonviolence (resistance through empowerment episode) 41; context 30; features 98; insights 31; inspiration 31; precursors 97; risk-taking as enabling factor 31–2; *see also* Israeli–Palestinian conflict
paradigm-accepting breaking creativity 11, 14–15, 19, 26, 52, 80, 124
paradigm shifts, Kuhn's theory of 202
paradigm: applicability of Kuhnian sense of 124–6, 136; Kuhnian versus conflict *126*
peace business initiatives 8
peace diagram method, Galtung's **78**, 83, 115, 131
peace-making, multi-track 67
Peace Theory: Preconditions of Disarmament (Burton) 58
pedagogic application, integrating key findings for 203–8
Peres, Shimon 35
perestroika 8
Peru–Ecuador conflict (transcendence episode) 8, 86; alternative realities 130–1; context 76–7; demonstration of creativity 80; Galtung's role 77–8; pedagogic application 204–6; Rio Protocol 77; tools 78–9, 83
Pham Van Dong 32–3
PLO (Palestine Liberation Organization) 36–7, 39, 42, 44, 59–61, 101, 103
power asymmetry, adjustment through deep listening *see* US–Vietnam War
preparatory activities 6–8
principled flexibility 35, 38–9, 61, 92, 94, 96, 102–3, 117, 123, 134, 195
principled negotiation, interest-based 5, 115, 166
principles of satyagraha 196
problem-solving workshop episode *see* Israeli–Palestinian problem-solving workshop
process (procedural) creativity: definition 111, 135; in American approach 114; comparative analysis findings 135–6; examples 113; examples of 111–12; implementation requirements 112–13; and outcome creativity 11–13, 75, 111–15, 201
Protracted Social Conflict (PSC) 127
Pundak, Ron 24, 34–8, 40–2, 97, 101, 107–8, 113, 125
pushing the envelope episode *see* Oslo peace process

Quaker method *see* family dialogue episode
questionnaire, for researcher-practitioner interviews 212–15
Quinn, Leung 158

Rabin, Yitzhak 39
racial conflict, Tajikistan 43, 46–7, 84
relational creativity, subtypes 122
reliability, acknowledgment of challenges to 22
resistance through empowerment episode *see* Palestinian nonviolence
Rio Protocol 77
risk-taking, as enabling factor for creative action 31–2, 34
Russia 12, 63, 184–7

Sankoh, Foday 53
satyagraha ('holding on to truth'): definition 138; advent of 146; characteristics 139; principles of 196; significance in conflict and peace research history 138
satyagraha campaign 8; actions 158–63; actors 146–7; analogizing 181–90; and the Anglo-Boer War 144, 147, 150–1, 179, 182, 188; central driving force 156; context 146–52; creativity propositions 164–94; decline 201; effectiveness 162; female participation 145, 162, 164; formal beginning 156; founders 156, 158; Gandhi–Smuts negotiations 160; Gandhi's role 152–3, 158; identity transformation 165, 167; interactions between working propositions 190–4; longitudinal process 155–64; mass pledges 158, 161, 181–2, 187, 189; paradigm shift 176–81; pedagogic applications 210; political environment 149; primary conflict parties 12; primary purpose 12–13; principles 196; procedural creativity 13; Russian influence 184–5, 187, 194; salient shifts 159; and the Searle judgment 161, 164;

and Shankeranand's movement 175; social change patterns 110; and South Africa's 'mineral revolution' 148; stakeholder profiles 152–5; trigger 155–6; value commitment 167–76; *see also* Gandhi, Mahatma
Saunders, Harold 88, 92–5, 102–3, 117, 123
Searle judgment 161, 164
selection criteria 7, 19–20
Sharon, Ariel 39
shuttle diplomacy: Dutch mediators' 97; Kissinger's 37, 92–4, 95, 102, 117
Sierra Leone, civil war in 53–4, 101
Simmons, Beth A. 76
Singapore, conflict with Indonesia and Malaysia *see* Indonesia–Malaysia–Singapore conflict
Smith, John (pseudonym) 43, 47–52, 84, 100, 103, 106–7, 116, 118, 123
Smuts, Jan Christian 149–50, 160
social change, examples of 110
South Africa 107; pre-1914 map **143**
Stephen Cohen 59
Structure of Scientific Revolutions, The (Kuhn) 52
sustenance, definition 9
Swan, Maureen 152
Sweden 8, 12, 205
system-element link *see* levels of analysis

Tajikistan, racial conflict 43, 46–7, 84
teen pregnancies episode: alternative reality 130; conflict paradigm 129; conflict parties' creativity 26–8; longitudinal process type 108
Tehranian, Majid 43, 46–7, 84
Temple Mount 39
Toda Institute for Global Peace and Policy Research 43

Törnudd, Klaus 43, 45, 71–4, 85, 106–7, 111, 113, 116, 120
Track-Two diplomacy *see* Indonesia–Malaysia–Singapore conflict
TRANSCEND 19, 76–7, 80
transitional experience, Winnicott's theory 65–6, 85

unconventional viability 1, 11–14, 52, 202, 208–9
unconventionality: concept analysis 1–2; conventionality and 96, 100, 103, 134; reducing the perception of 110
US–Vietnam War (deep listening episode) 41, 107; favorability of 1968 proposal 33; longitudinal process 107; risk-taking as enabling factor 34; salient issues 32

validity, acknowledgment of challenges to 22
value commitment: Environmentalists for Full-Employment movement 29; family dialogue episode 90–1; nature and sources 98–9; *satyagraha* campaign 167–76; term analysis 98
value judgments, developmental process 5–6
viability, essential core of 2
Vietnam, US war with *see* US–Vietnam War
violence 6, 67, 82–3, 99, 113, 178, 185, 204, 210–11
Volkan, Vamik 43, 62–6, 85, 109, 117–18, 127, 210

Wallas, G. 8
Winnicott, Donald W. 65
worldview 1, 42, 66, 168, 170–1, 195

Zulus 145–6, 150, 178, 186, 190

eBooks – at www.eBookstore.tandf.co.uk

A library at your fingertips!

eBooks are electronic versions of printed books. You can store them on your PC/laptop or browse them online.

They have advantages for anyone needing rapid access to a wide variety of published, copyright information.

eBooks can help your research by enabling you to bookmark chapters, annotate text and use instant searches to find specific words or phrases. Several eBook files would fit on even a small laptop or PDA.

NEW: Save money by eSubscribing: cheap, online access to any eBook for as long as you need it.

Annual subscription packages

We now offer special low-cost bulk subscriptions to packages of eBooks in certain subject areas. These are available to libraries or to individuals.

For more information please contact webmaster.ebooks@tandf.co.uk

We're continually developing the eBook concept, so keep up to date by visiting the website.

www.eBookstore.tandf.co.uk